Skylark Meets Meadowlark

Skylark

Reimagining the Bird in British Romantic and

Meets Meadowlark

Contemporary Native American Literature

THOMAS C. GANNON

University of Nebraska Press
Lincoln and London

Publication of this volume was assisted by a grant from the University of Nebraska–Lincoln Research Council, funded in part by the Charles J. Millard Trust Fund.

Library of Congress Cataloging-in-Publication Data

Gannon, Thomas C.

Skylark meets meadowlark : reimagining the bird in British romantic and contemporary native American literature / Thomas C. Gannon.

p. cm.

Includes bibliographical references and index.

ISBN 978-0-8032-2057-7 (cloth : alk. paper)

1. English poetry—19th century—History and criticism. 2. Birds in literature. 3. American literature—21st century—History and criticism. 4. American literature—Indian authors—History and criticism. 5. Romanticism—Great Britain. I. Title.

PR590.G36 2009 821'.709145—dc22

2009013939

Set in Minion Pro by Kim Essman.
Designed by A. Shahan.

To the various family members, friends, mentors, and colleagues who have tolerated my avian eco-eccentricities these past several years; and to the northern cardinal in Iowa City, who assured me that they would.

A poem should always have birds in it.

MARY OLIVER, "Singapore"

O thin men of Haddam,
Why do you imagine golden birds?
Do you not see how the blackbird
Walks around the feet
Of the women about you?

WALLACE STEVENS, "Thirteen Ways of Looking at a Blackbird"

See! the eagle comes,
See! the eagle comes;
Now at last we see him—look! look! the eagle comes,
Now at last we see him—look! look! the eagle comes;
Now we see him with the people,
Now we see him with the people.

CADDO GHOST DANCE SONG

Contents

Preface

A man and a woman
Are one.
A man and a woman and a blackbird
Are one.
—WALLACE STEVENS, *"Thirteen Ways of Looking at a Blackbird,"* 4.1–4

Walking out of the English-Philosophy Building a few years ago, I took a sharp turn around a cedar and stumbled upon a grackle in an old elm. For several seconds, we stared at each other from a distance of two feet. And for at least one of those seconds, I was struck by how utterly *alien* this two-winged iridescence really was, and how incredible it would be to see such a creature if I were a visitor from another planet, or even just a *Homo sapiens* who had not been habituated to the ubiquitous shapes and sounds of such beings from my first days of consciousness. Then, as I returned to the mundane, I wondered at how little of the actual bird I was still really "seeing," overlaid as my raw perception was with all the cultural accoutrements that had also been donned at a relatively early age, from nursery rhymes of "four and twenty" blackbirds "baked into pies" to critical readings of Wallace Stevens's thirteen different, apparently esoteric (though all thankfully nonculinary), ways of "looking" at such a bird.

Our psychohistorical relationship to birds, at last, has always been a folly of misrecognition, it would appear. I can immediately point to my five-year-old daughter's emotional adoption of a local robin pair as neighbors of domestic felicity, and as co-opted surrogates for a togetherness that she rightfully intuited as having already ended, for her, with her parents' divorce. But that small girl's love for those robins! "How cute," some would say, and yet how pathetic, and ultimately how symptomatic of a long tradition. For she was only doing what Wordsworth, for example, did again and again in his poems, though my daughter did it in far fewer words and with perhaps even more "spontaneous" affection. But her co-optation of that particular, *other* species is only another version of, for example, we Americans viewing a wild bald eagle, almost by necessity, through a culturally colored lens, as an icon of (a bit bedraggled) national pride, as an emblem of rugged individualism, and, perhaps today, as an untoward reminder of our fear and shame regarding the possibility of our own ecological suicide.

And who is to say that the impending ecological Armageddon is not, in large part, the result of our "seeing" the bird, the animal, the very land, as but fit objects for mere poetry, for occasional weekend outings to the country, and, at last, for some botched self-therapy that makes us feel better (though only for a while) about ourselves? The animal, including the avian, Other has long been, no doubt, a major outlet for our own human fixations, from politics to domestic affairs to a pervasive cultural psychomachia that has rendered them but playthings in a pathological exercise of ego compensation and recuperation. One might reasonably call, then, for an earnest re-"seeing" of the bird, both for our own sake and for the sake of these oh-so-*other* species, whose very alterity may still be able to draw us out of our own insular selves and cultures and species. And yet the human benefits of such a change in consciousness should not be its main motive; indeed, once such a re-vision has been achieved, unthinking anthropocentrism will have met its timely end, in an awareness of a posthuman interrelatedness that recognizes the criticality of the rest of the ecosphere.

Now when I see that grackle again, and I hear his rusty-playground-swing "schlEEEnk," I think *that he's saying, "You bastard. Why is that river just three trees down from us so filthy? That's where my redwing cousins raise their babies. You bastard." And then—I realize that I've just been* projecting, *too. But I still wonder. . . .*

I became a birdwatcher at the age of nine, after brief, frenzied forays into collecting rocks, collecting butterflies, collecting. . . . Well, birds were different: I could "collect" birds by simply writing their names down on a piece of paper, a much neater, more concise way of appeasing my obsessive-compulsive nature (and my mother's sanity). Sure, I would eventually collect the bad poems I wrote about birds, the bad pictures I drew of them, and even a few ceramic and framed ornithic knickknacks, but at least bird-watching wouldn't require, at some future point, a room of its own to house some huge, painstakingly labeled physical collection.

But there *were* the books: because I was already a voracious reader, my new hobby had the additional attraction of a great amount of literature on its subject. When the weather or bedtime—or school—kept me inside, I would pore over that great windfall that only a library card could procure. There were introductory how-to books on birding itself, on building bird feeders, on choosing the right equipment and clothing for "Big Days." There were more sophisticated life histories of individual species and even books on the lives of famous ornithologists; indeed, I grew up idolizing the ornithologist Roger Tory Peterson as much as I loved Harmon Killebrew and Johnny Cash. There was even juvenile "naturist" fiction that could bring tears to my eyes with, say, the tragic tale of *Bubo, the Great Horned Owl.* But above all, there were the field guides, those magnificent little collages of graphics and text that seemed to speak best of the magic of birds, or at least of my own kind's ability to categorize them, to capture each species wholly in the brief span of a textual blurb and a picture.

One could even own, or should I say *collect* such books. But as the eldest boy of a single mother on welfare, I couldn't buy such frivolities with food stamps. However, there was Christmas, and I could also save my fifty-cents-a-month allowance; I could even interest my younger brothers in my hobby, thereby "borrowing" *their* allowances to procure the birding essentials that "we" needed. "Our" initial acquisition was that crucial first bird guide, Robbins, Bruun, and Zim's *Birds of North America*, about six dollars for the hard-cover first edition. One Christmas brought me the essential pair of 7x35 binoculars from K-Mart, and the next brought me my second treasure of avian literature: Pearson's monumental *Birds of America.* A sheer tome it was, fit for a coffee table, not the field, with its lengthy life histories and full color-plate illustrations. Originally published in 1917, the book was, I immediately realized, completely archaic. The names of many of the birds were just plain *wrong*, I knew, and the visual depictions were closer to Audubon's crude dead-bird-stretched-out poses than to those of a modern bird guide. But I still fell in love with a text that, in contrast to the more objective tone of my field guide, wrote of each species as if it were almost human, or at least implied that the birds had been placed on this planet for the aesthetic, moral, and economic good of humankind. I found this—at the time—reassuring, although I was troubled even then by the presence of a long, almost apologetic entry on the passenger pigeon, including a pathetic photo of the last surviving member of that doomed species. The book, indeed, was part of a crucial period when naturalists themselves were just making the transition from guns to binoculars, and I prided myself on being beyond that guilty era—much like the unconscious racist, perhaps, who is forever pointing out that slavery and the Indian wars are things of the past. For I myself was still a "ticker," a lister and categorizer, whose ideological *colonization* of these other species was just as swiftly effective and certain.

Then, as a junior high enthusiast of both words and birds, of books and binoculars, I greeted the various references to birds in the poetry of William Wordsworth as an attractive bridge to a corpus composed some two centuries ago and a wide ocean away. In place of the poet's voluble redbreasts and throstles, I heard an American robin; for his loquacious linnets, I had a variety of similar native (and noisy) finches at the imaginative disposal of my mind's ear. And from an aesthetic point of view, Wordsworth's avian sights and sounds often seemed to work as fit accompaniment to his flights of enthusiasm and to his descents into melancholic darkness. Could this be the best of both worlds, my youthful naïveté asked, a collection of great poems and a bird guide, all in one?

But no, "the glory and the freshness" of that "dream" faded in the face of mature circumspection. As a doctoral candidate in English exposed to cultural theories of (human) alterity, colonial discourse theory, and post-structuralist relativism, I found it an obvious step to apply said theories to birds—to consider them as the Other of *species*, victimized by anthropocentric colonization, both physically and ideologically—at last, as uncanny aliens apparently out of the loop of human-as-language-maker discourse. But this was the easy part, really, though my various critiques of such speciesist imperialism make up much of the work at hand. The second (and, I think, necessary) step is to reconnect the loop between human and avian—and other species in general, of course—the more arduous task of this venture's final sections.

This study aims, then, to be much more than another birds-and-literature thematic compendium. Rather than some pale index in which one might find the typical symbolic meanings of the skylark, wren, nightingale, crow, et al., I will instead examine the various metaphorical (or not?) uses of birds in British Romantic and Native American literature via a concerted cultural critique of what such prototypical tropes say about the worldviews in question. I also ask of each representative figure in the dominant Western ideology—as emblematized in his or her avian imagery—whether such-and-such image of the bird is more a psychopathological othering of the avian as surrogate object, or instead a blueprint toward a more ecotherapeutic seeing and hearing of the bird that may well be crucial to realizing what I believe to be the next great cultural paradigm. For, at last, a *reimagining* of other species as vital family members of this communal ecosystem that we call Earth is, I would argue, essential to our own species' continued existence into the next millennium.

The ostensibly disproportionate pairing—in terms of literary reputation—of such canonical Anglo poets as Wordsworth and Keats with contemporary Native American authors such as Linda Hogan and Joy Harjo in this project is intentional, in part, as yet one more arrow directed at the Dead-White-English-Male canon. But my eventual turn to Native writers, and the conjunction of the avian and the "Indian" throughout this work, has another purpose, as a concerted declaration of the longtime cultural conflation of the Native American with the wild and the eagle and the crow. In quite parallel ways, the New World human Native has been othered as some "natured," subhuman, savage, and bestial entity whose preferable status is one of extinction; likewise, the Old and New World eagle and crow have been othered as sheer and mere *animals*, both idolized and reviled, above all, for their asocial, extrahuman status, and who have thus been deemed better off dead, too, unless redeemed by some (at last *savage*) nobility that has been ascertained, finally, by the great gods of Western iconography.

To augment this theme of an Indian-bird connection that will be developed throughout, I recall a journal entry that I received from a white student at the University of South Dakota, whom I'd never told that I was part Indian. She culminated a two-page-long diatribe against the local Native population by calling Indians "feather-fuckers." As angry as I was, I still took the metaphor itself as rather a compliment, as one more verification of the connection between bird, and (the sexual) body, and us (apparently vulpine or corvine) "gut-eaters," to cite another epithet of hers. But a "gut-eater," a Lakota, can look around, can sometimes see and hear things that the blithe Euro-American colonizer cannot see or hear. Indeed, in part as compensation, perhaps, of having felt the pain of growing up hearing my mother called a "squaw," I also grew up *feeling*—as I saw and heard—my own (nonhuman) western South Dakota milieu: the golden eagle above me, the great horned owl beside me, and the burrowing owl on the very ground around me. And I have felt *changed,* felt a kinship that transcended the "us versus them" (and mostly "white versus them") dichotomizing disease of Western civilization.

However, this book is hardly a simplistic "Anglo" versus "Indian" diatribe; as I note several times in the chapters that follow, my very choice of subject matter issues from my longtime perception that the poetry of Blake, Wordsworth, and company displays a greater affinity to American indigenous worldviews than anything else in Western literature. But a cultural difference remains. One of my mentors, upon learning that my mixed-blood-Irish-French-Lakota persona still wanted to write at length about such an Anglo-canonical figure as Wordsworth, made the point that the Sage of Grasmere could only write *about* eagles but never conceive of *being* one; in contrast, that mentor had witnessed Native American dances in which such a possibility seemed very much realized. To anticipate my conclusion, then, my own version of the new myth will have a definite Indian feel. But it cannot be some facile retreat to a traditional worldview that, honestly, scarcely exists any longer. It must be a renascent syncretism and synthesis that both evokes an ancient/authentic relationship to the alter-species Other and yet is also a new and creative and viable *reimagining* of animal alterity—an incorporation, at last, of traditional Native views and Euro-Romantic ecological emphases that are both very much evident, I think, in recent Native American literature. Perhaps this latest Native vision (or rather, *re*-vision) may provide the answer for what Keats and Shelley were looking for but failed to find in their nightingale and skylark—an answer right before our eyes, for instance, in the mundane indigenous blackbirds and meadowlarks of my native U.S. Midwest, and in their literary images as conjured by indigenous writers of the New World. Through such a lens, that shock-of-a-grackle I felt for one moment might be reinvigorated as a more constant source of alien magic.

The grackle episode begs me, at last, to recall my academic defense of a similar extended avian treatise. I stood outside the English-Philosophy Building once again, sweating in the Midwest heat and feeling anxious in the certainty that my learned Ph.D. superiors would find my "listening-to-the-birds" thesis to be utterly ridiculous. But then a cardinal alighted on a low branch just a few feet away from me and began to whistle its two-tone phrase over and over. And I swear that it was looking straight at me, and that I was the one for whom the song, the "message," was intended. "You're doing this for *us*," the bird seemed to be saying, and I felt a new confidence in my endeavors. And I think that, ultimately, I defended my dissertation fairly eloquently because of that avian intervention. This anecdote sounds, no doubt, like a purely superstitious interpretation of a chance event. But I have taught *Black Elk Speaks* several times since then, and when the eagles and hawks and kingbirds *talk* to Black Elk—well, I think I understand. Yes, it is a century and an "end of a dream" later, the waning of a Lakota common-cultural consciousness that "heard the bird" as a veritable discourse of power. But one can have a new dream. No—one *must* have one.

I must acknowledge at last one major lacuna in this work, the ostensibly strange omission (for the most part) of nineteenth- and twentieth-century Euro-American authors. I had actually outlined another several (middle) chapters for the book, which were to treat in detail the British Victorians and U.S. writers from the Romantic era through today, as a more coherent transition to the Native American chapters. But obviously the project is long enough as it is, and length considerations finally obviated against such a plan. I have thus had to limit myself to brief comparative references to, for instance, the poetry of Thomas Hardy, T. S. Eliot, and Wallace Stevens; I do make several sojourns into the writings of Audubon, Whitman, and John Burroughs, but only in terms of their vital relationship to native birds and Native Americans. And though I have already published several articles on Whitman's connection to birds and Indians, a book-length treatment of mainstream American literature and avians must await another day.

This book would not have been possible without an eclectic medley of inspirations, from Nietzsche and Black Elk to Gary Snyder and Linda Hogan. And as much as I take them to task in chapter 1, the leading lights of ecocriticism have obviously been seminal to this work, especially Lawrence Buell and M. Jimmie Killingsworth, both of whom are as magnanimously humble in person as they are magnificently eloquent in their prose. I would also like to thank my several mentors at the University of Iowa: Ed Folsom, for his many insightful suggestions about this work's eventual organization and argumentative focus and for his Zen-like supervision that let me find where, as he intuited, I needed to go; Ruedi Kuenzli, for his assistance in my readings of the British Romantics and his unending faith in my scholarship;

and Linda Bolton, for her great help with the Native American sections and for being the walking emblem of an ethical commitment to the Other, both human and nonhuman. Finally, I express my deepest appreciation to my chief mentor here at the University of Nebraska–Lincoln, Ken Price, for his wonderful oversight of the later stages of this manuscript's development.

Portions of this work, in different versions, appeared in the following:
"Complaints from the Spotted Hawk: Flights and Feathers in Whitman's 1855 Leaves of Grass." *Leaves of Grass: The Sesquicentennial Essays.* Lincoln: University of Nebraska Press, 2007. 141–75.
"An Essay on Eagles." *South Dakota Review* 42.3 (Fall 2004): 142–49.
"Of Avians and Indigenes: Preliminary Notes on the Orientalization of the New World Native and Natured Others." *Viewpoint. Literature Compass*, Summer 2004. http://www.blackwell-synergy.com/doi/full/10.1111/j.1741-4113.2004.00054.x.

Skylark Meets Meadowlark

CHAPTER 1 Birds of a Feather
Avians, Indigenes, Animal Rights, and Ecology

> Pictures of animals & other productions of nature as seen in conservatories, menageries, museums, etc.—would do little for the national mind, nay they would be injurious to it, if the imagination were excluded by the presence of the object, more or less out of a state of nature. If it were not that we learn to talk and think of the lion and the eagle . . . from the impassioned introduction of them so frequently into Holy Scripture and by great poets . . . the spiritual part of our nature . . . would derive no benefit from such intercourse with such subjects.
>
> WILLIAM WORDSWORTH, *Fenwick note to "Suggested by a Picture of the Bird of Paradise," in Poetical Works*

> I'd rather understand how to sing from a crow
> who was never good at singing or much of anything
> but finding gold in the trash of humans.
>
> JOY HARJO, *"The Path to the Milky Way Leads through Los Angeles," in A Map to the Next World*

Like the eagles in his several sonnets on Dunolly Castle, Wordsworth's eagle in this epigraph suffers its own "imprisonment," enchained at last in a dominant discourse of use value that Wordsworth spells out baldly and unapologetically. The first full clause implies that the sheer unadorned reality of an animal itself is pedagogically useless, if not downright dangerous. The second half of the passage is abundantly clear in its import: a picture of an eagle needs the "spiritual" coloring of the Western cultural tradition to render it beneficial; that benefit, moreover, is predominantly a religious and moral one. Harjo's crow, in contrast, is evidently more free, a discordant (and Native) voice that would yet "sing," and even be a better judge of true value than its human neighbors. But even this passage recycles, seriously or not, an anthropocentric aesthetic of sound, in which the crow's caw is sheer cacophony compared to, say, the voice of the meadowlark, and the corvid's general outsider-with-greater-vision status still issues, above all, from Harjo's political perception of her own status as a *human* poet of indigenous otherness and outrage.

And yet, although such literary anthropomorphisms of the bird would appear to be ubiquitous, perhaps even inescapable, Harjo's crow at least, and much avian imagery in contemporary Native American literature, has a far different feel than most comparable imagery from the British and American literary canon, issuing, I claim, from a new poetic world in which the bird itself is more frequently given the right, as it were, to be an autonomous, integral being, and is able, one might even say, to speak back, dialogically, to both human poet and audience. By examining the various imagistic and tropic *uses* (a telling word) of the avian from British Romanticism to recent Native American literature,[1] one might ask if and why and how, in the grand scheme of the past two hundred years of literary history, such a no doubt laudable evolution has occurred. The ultimate questions, then: Is the traditional, seemingly inevitable, othering of the avian symptomatic of a human worldview that is fundamentally inimical to an ecotherapeutic relationship with the rest of the planet? Conversely, is this recent positive change in literary portrayals of the bird concurrent with an evolution of consciousness in which other species are becoming less other? And what of the agency of poetry and imaginative nature writing—past, present, and future—in such a change in interspecies awareness? With such concerns in mind, one might be able to consider the textual eagle and dove, lark and crow, as microcosmic types and symbols of how Western civilization has addressed the nonhuman ecosphere.

ARCHETYPAL AVIANS

> Birds are thoughts and the flight of thought.
>
> C. G. JUNG, *Collected Works*

> The birds were among the *numina* longest to survive. Many qualities touch them with such powerful magic—flight, migration, song, eggs and nests, seasonality—that even the ideologies of transcendence retained them as angels. Bird life is a highly visible, poetic analogy to human life. . . . Yet they are kin to the earthbound, cold-blooded reptiles, egg-layers with scaly legs and toothless mouths.
>
> PAUL SHEPARD, *The Others*

As an interpretation of bird imagery in dreams, Jung's dictum is circular, defining the symbol by retaining the metaphor, that of birds in flight. It is as if one cannot even discuss the avian as trope without the vehicle corrupting the tenor. To this day, poetic fancy, too, is a flight, as it is throughout nineteenth-century British poetry, most notably, perhaps, in the works of Keats, Shelley, and Swinburne. In such poets, too, both Love and Fancy are forever "winged"; as for Love, it must be one of the most lamentable accidents in the English language that "love" and "dove" just happen to rhyme. And as for religion, the dove is also requisite to any Catholic who attempts to picture the *image* of the ethereal Holy Spirit in his or her mind. Between the Christian deity and humankind are the angels, blessed with wings, of course, as if through some strange act of theo-alchemico-bestiality. (Indeed, "angels are really birds," after all [Jung, *cw* 5: §368n].)[2] The eagle, especially, is a vehicle inevitably loaded with human cultural baggage, as Christopher Manes reminds us: "According to medieval commentators, eagles soar higher than any other kind of bird and could gaze upon the sun, undazzled, because they were put on Earth to be a symbol of St. John and his apocalyptic vision, not the other way around. From this hermeneutical perspective, it was inconceivable that eagles should be autonomous, self-willed subjects, flying high for their own purposes without reference to some celestial intention" (19). At last, the sociocultural fact that birds—and the ornithic synecdoches of wings, flight, songs, and nests—have long been crucial projective surrogates for so much that humankind adores and admires and desires, or mourns and fears and feels oh so anxious about, needs little support. But why they have been so is no small matter of interest.

As one editor of a bird poetry anthology has claimed, "After Love and Flowers, as many poems have been written on the theme of Birds as on any single subject" (S. Carr 11). Leonard Lutwack, in *Birds in Literature*, also chimes in: as neighbor species of both "familiarity and transcendence," birds have "a wider range of meaning and symbol in literature than any other animal" (xi).[3] Indeed, not only are poems and belles-lettres essays about birds rampant, but so are natural histories about birds, field guides to the birds, and, yes, even studies *about* literature about birds, like this one. Almost a hundred years ago, W. H. Hudson was already lamenting the situation of those who would still write about such a common, apparently overdone subject. Calling the first chapter of his *Adventures among Birds* an "Apology," he has a hypothetical friend ask, "What, another book about birds?" (2). A more detailed rationale for my own effort is forthcoming, but the very existence of such a plethora of studies begs for initial commentary.

In terms of literary scholarship in particular, many such studies have examined a particular bird image in a particular work, sometimes from a concerted theoretical point of view (often psychoanalytical),[4] but more often not. Some earlier efforts even attempt a proto-structuralist assignation of the bird images in question, in what might very loosely be called an archetypal approach. Such a bent is epitomized in Beryl Rowland's *Birds with Human Souls: A Guide to Bird Symbolism* (1978). The very title is telling in its acknowledgment that these birds of poetry and myth are anthropomorphized versions of the avian and symbols, after all, of a human soul in need of surrogate support. Western humankind's psychic strivings have resulted in a great number of avian tropic conventions, of course: the turtledove as emblem of faithful love (46); the nightingale's nocturnal song as representative of a lover's grief (110); the magpie's "evil reputation" (102)[5]—a negative ascription, by the way, common to most corvids, including the raven's association with prophecy and death (147–48). Rowland can also unthinkingly render such anthropocentrism as the truth itself; for instance, cormorants *are* "sinister, predatory creatures" (30), and the domestic rock pigeon actually has "hard, mean-looking eyes," its gaze "cold, shrewd, and secretive as that of a CIA agent." The old poets' versions of the lovey dove weren't drawn from "looking at nature": "They were thinking of the bird's symbolism," of course (41). But Rowland is projecting something, too, perhaps reflecting some cold war paranoia, into the eyes of *Columba livia*.

For Rowland, the dominant trope is that of birds' flight as representative of spirituality and transcendence, and she invokes the Jungians Joseph L. Henderson and Joseph Campbell to help her find such a connection to be archetypal, that is, "universal" (xiv), an essentialism, as I will argue, that is ultimately untenable. In her defense, Rowland does go out of her way at times to note how the "real bird" is nothing like its usual literary emblematizations, and she even laments the "vanishing" of various species in her introduction. But at last, her "concern is not, of course, with birds as they are in nature but as they exist in the mind" (vii–viii)—in sum, Jung's birds as "thoughts and the flight of thought."[6] Unfortunately, Rowland's relative lack of concern for the "real" bird may be symptomatic of an attitude implicated in the avians' very vanishing.

The most recent full-blown study in this particular room (or aviary) of my own is Leonard Lutwack's *Birds in Literature* (1994), yet another still rather traditional and thematic treatment of bird symbolism. Again, the songs of various passerines are "preeminent symbols[s] of poetic inspiration"; blackbirds and crows (especially if in a tree in winter) seem "to appeal to many poets as an image of forlornness," even death and evil (48, 29, 108–112);[7] sparrows are "lecherous" (and therefore numerous) little fellows (193); and, following Rowland, the human soul is most commonly conceived of as a "winged creature" (119). In the tradition of Jung and Northrop Frye, Lutwack even offers a psycho-anthropological origin for the ubiquity of ornithic tropes in general: these species' "unfailing rhythms of migration, song" and "nesting . . . have supplied poets with easily comprehended symbols of the cycle of life and death" and "of moral and philosophical values" (24, 38). As evidenced by a chapter subhead, "From Fact to Symbol," Lutwack is quite aware that the literary bird is ultimately an imaginary construct, for better or worse.

Lutwack emphasizes the better. More so than Rowland, he presents a definite ecopolitical agenda, a plea for those real birds drowned in the sea of symbols that make up the rest of his book. Indeed, Lutwack's concluding chapter is an eloquent defense of literature's valuable role in "restoring to the animal the significance it once had for humans" (250), and this seminal direction will be dealt with more concertedly in my own concluding chapter. However—and regarding my own "bird and Indian" dual thesis—although Lutwack's treatise refers to various recent literary texts, none are Native American. His sole reference to the indigenous and birds is insulting: the "worship" of "bird-gods" by such "primitive peoples" speaks of a superstitious and "childlike identification with animals" (82–83).[8] My own argument's main gist will include a resignification of such a "childlike identification" as actually more redeeming and ultimately more conducive to psycho- and ecological health than the mentality that could utter such a facile and ultimately speciesist and culturally demeaning statement.

As I've indicated, this tendency to assign bird tropes to various all-too-human categories easily allows for a structuralist approach to the bird, since the avian Other has been, throughout history, a most attractive object for anthropocentric projection, fit bearer, at last, of the Jungian archetype. In his most extended discussion of the archetypal and poetry, Jung defines the archetypal image as a figure (or process) "that constantly recurs in the course of history and appears wherever creative fantasy is freely expressed. . . . In each of these images there is a little piece of human psychology and human fate, a remnant of the joys and sorrows that have been repeated countless times in our ancestral history" (CW 15: §127). And so the skylark sings our joys, the nightingale our sorrows. We have soared, and still soar, as proud children of the sun and sky, with the eagle, but we all have a dark and private shadow side—all ravens, too, if you will.

The stereotypical import of many common bird species and genera can be fit into such an intrapsychic schema. For instance, the more positively regarded birds of prey such as the eagle and falcon—traditionally, birds of patriarchal majesty—are the ego or *I* itself, or the ego in the state of inflation. Ego alienation, conversely, might be figured as the proud, loner birds such as the raven, owl or, again, the lone eagle in flight. The vanity and loquaciousness attributed to the peacock, magpie, jay, and various parrot species fit well Jung's concept of the persona, the public, ultimately false mask of the ego. For many reasons, birds have also been traditionally figured as feminine; the *anima* and mother archetypes are well represented by the maternal bird, passive, nesting, and nurturing, soft and warmly feathered, loving and frail: the dove, the swan, and the more homebody passerines such as the robin and wren. In contrast, the inspirational propensity of such songbirds as the skylark, oriole, and various thrushes for vocal outburst, often in the morning and in the spring, render them fit as emblems for the archetypal process of psychic rebirth. This is related to their common association with the soul, as is bird flight itself, of course, epitomized in such winged paragons as the swallow and the swift and various waterfowl. Thus the Jungian archetypal journey, too, finds a fine symbolic analogue in bird migration, epitomized in the swallow, just as the flight of birds in general commonly connotes human psychic growth and change.

Then we have the archetypal shadow side of darkness and night; if these birds are thoughts, they are dark thoughts indeed. Because of their weird, *un*human setting (i.e., night: the owl, the whip-poor-will) or eerie song (the cuckoo, the owl) or foreboding color (the raven, crow, and blackbird), these birds bear associations of the mysterious, the occult, and evil. The crow and blackbird, in particular, have often been contrasted with the more ethereal songsters as compensatory mundane, earthly foils to the flights and songs of (human) fancy. And then various seabirds—magnificent migrant geese, mocking gulls, Coleridge's albatross, the holy kingfisher, the loon with its otherworldly laugh—all beckon toward that border region between consciousness and the unconscious (land or air versus water) and to the collective unconscious itself as the sea.[9] Finally, the unconscious Self's *coniunctio oppositorum,* or reconciliation of opposites, is sometimes figured as a union of eagle and dove or eagle and vulture.[10] Indeed, like the truest symbols, in the Jungian sense, the avian is a veritable *coniunctio*, a yin yang of male activity and female passivity, of gregariousness and privacy, of day and night, of sky and water, of heavenly voice and mundane squawk. The crow and its ilk, especially, are birds of built-in contraries. In one of his long lists of archetypal binaries, Jung juxtaposes (chthonic) blackness with the (ethereal) bird (CW 13: §462). But the raven and the crow, finally, are creatures of both categories, border figures par excellence.[11]

The schema above is offered as a tentative, "as if" exercise, at best. Such a dualistic approach reduces the real animal and bird to an either/or conceptualization, to the detriment of both other species and their literary representation; as Gerald Vizenor protests, such a "generic animal is structural, a binary beast in a prosaic simile" ("Literary Animals" 140). As cross-culturally conscious scholars such as Frantz Fanon have warned us, such a methodology, relying as it does on a supposedly innate and culturally monolithic "collective unconscious," is fraught with the ideological dangers of essentialism, reductionism, and a tendency to whitewash both cultural differences and the chance permutations of literary history—a universalizing *langue*, as it were, without the local and historical *parole*.[12] Thus we have Jung claiming that birds have "*always* symbolized spirits or thoughts" (CW 13: §321; emphasis added), and we have Rowland and Lutwack speaking of the association between bird flight and spirituality as universal and inevitable, and of particular species as having a certain archetypal or pan-human meaning that just isn't the case. For instance, Harjo's crow is more than a mere minority resignification of an essential avian evil and otherness, an evil universal only to Western civilization; indeed, crows, ravens, and even vultures have commonly had anything but sinister connotations in many Native American cultures.[13] For a dominant white culture to other the crow (in part) for being *black* may be just as culturally biased as to discriminate against humans of the same color. From racism to sexism, now: the Western portrayal of raptors, for instance, as patriarchal majesty and egohood (in Jung, the *I* is implicitly male) is especially indefensible, given the ornithological fact that the female bird of prey is usually larger (and therefore more majestic) than the male. Finally, the greatest problem with the whole archetypal approach is the reductionist (and Romantic Idealist) othering of the avian as an image and object for the workings of the human psyche in some grand marriage of Mind and Nature.[14] As even the sometime Jungian Paul Shepard remonstrates (with Joseph Campbell in mind), the birds and animals of myth are not entirely "about the psychic life of humans" (93).

One can reject a rigid archetypalism and yet still posit the image of the bird as a central trope, or complex of tropes, in what might be called the natural Imaginary. Following Houston Baker's conception of a "blues matrix" as *the* central heuristic metaphor for African American discourse, even "the *All* of American culture" (3, 13), I propose an avian matrix, a crucial subset of many cultures' discursive representations, including Western and Native. How each culture's nest (if you will) of tropes and iconography relates to the real bird, to avian alterity, could be a major focus of any analysis of cultural discourse, and would, I think, be more revelatory of a culture's environmental values system than previous topic studies of birds and literature could have imagined. Extended to animal representation in general, I might dub such an approach *zoöcriticism*; applied to birds specifically, the (admittedly more ungainly) term *ornithicriticism* will have to do for now.

To approach humankind's infatuation with birds from another angle: imagine for a moment Lewis and Clark's, or even Willa Cather's, first audition of the meadowlark's primordial prairie song. Indeed, indigenous bird species in general can be veritably viewed as unconquered Native tribes that have escaped, by and large, the imposed borders of Western colonization, and that serve as seminal reminders of our frontier—and animal—heritage. The calls today of migrating Canada honkers and sandhill cranes *should* evoke from us that jolt of electricity up the spine that speaks of a time before Western rationalism turned us into cogitating primates out of touch with important parts of our primal selves, or bodies. Here I point to the close evolutionary relationship between avians and reptiles, naturalist Loren Eiseley's claim that we can "see the singing reptile in the bird" (*Firmament* 57), and then propose the continued existence of both *within* the human psyche, via physiology, in the older regions of the brain. Certainly, from the Serpent in the Garden to *Jurassic Park*, humankind has had nearly as great a fascination with reptiles as it has had with birds. Perhaps that's why I've always been haunted by an early childhood memory of an artist's rendition of Archaeopteryx, the first species making the crossing from reptile to bird, like some young mutant pterodactyl dressed in a new and crazy evolutionary garb called feathers, making its way tentatively up the side of a tree, an evolutionary ladder incarnate. In *Pilgrim at Tinker Creek*, Annie Dillard offers a more startling equation between the feathered and the scaled: to revive her ability to see a bird with fresh vision, she "reverse[s] its evolution and imagine[s] it as a lizard," a leap facilitated by the bird's "scaled legs and that naked ring around a shiny eye" (106). Here is the intersection of reptilian and avian and the intersection of so much of humankind's own dualities, a mixing of the chthonic and spinal with the aerial and ethereal, of archetypal human fears and fascination.[15] One might argue that both halves of this chthonic/ethereal dual deity may owe much of their psychological resonance to their relation to what brain neurologists have identified as the reptilian brain: primitive, instinctual, and eerily arational.[16] That haunting that I've felt at the image of Archaeopteryx is inevitably accompanied, fittingly, by a shiver of the spine. This shiver may be what Jung champions, however homocentrically, as "the *animal in us*" (CW 10: §32), that long past and yet still present kinship with feather and scale, the unasked for raw emotion erupting at the base of the brain.[17] From this, perhaps, issues even our yearning and need to sing, and a racial memory of flying and wings that has now become the symbolic basis of our very spirituality. Whether these archetypal resonances evoked by the avian are evolutionary and genetic, or learned and transmitted within the social collective, as Fanon has it (188), there still seems to be some uncanny trace of Archaeopteryx within us all.

In partial support of my argument, the scientist and naturalist Paul Shepard's *The Others: How Animals Made Us Human* offers an eccentrically welcome reading of cultural anthropology that convincingly traces the coevolutionary importance of other species in the psychosocial development of humankind, at times gesturing toward an archetypal basis, à la Jung. Because the human psyche, Shepard contends, "is the result of a long series of interactions with other animals," other species have long been "the most powerful metaphoric source of our self-consciousness" (15, 284). Through the aeons, human "categories of the self and society were shaped by the traits of animals observed, the dangerous, competitive, beautiful, tasty, scrounging Others" (24), to the point that, now, "a whole fauna is in us still, tacitly" (119). Not only is Shepard's privileging of instincts acquired in earlier periods of our evolution as still crucial to our species and in need of exercise even today akin to Jung's primitivism, but his psychology seems a very literal, genetic take on Jungian archetypes, for even our very self-identity is really a multiplicity, a "diverse zoology of the self" made up, apparently, of the various species encountered in our evolution, who still return in dreams as the "dispersed elements of the unknown self"—that is, Jung's unconscious Self (Shepard 80, 75).[18] Animals in fairy tales and myths—and even in poems?—reflect a similar vital function, such characters serving as "surrogates in the collective unconscious of humanity" (90). How this surrogation works in British Romanticism and Native American literature is the subject of this study. But next I turn to another, human surrogate closely linked to the avian.

"GENUINE LITTLE SAVAGES"

> My bird is a genuine little savage, doubtless, but I value him as a neighbor. . . . [Nature] is an Indian maiden, dark, subtle, dreaming, with glances now and then that thrill the wild blood in one's veins.
>
> JOHN BURROUGHS, *The Birds of John Burroughs*

> "Mating birds and mating Indians are the same," says a white
> friend as we watch the handsome fancydancers
> in their red, yellow, orange, and blue feathers. "It's the men
> who wear the brightest colors."
>
> SHERMAN ALEXIE, "Powwow Love Songs," in *One Stick Song*

If civilized humankind still bears the birds and beasts within, we also carry within us (as Jung and Shepard would claim) the "natural man," fresh from the cave and the hunt. But just as the raven and wolf have been co-opted and demonized in Western discourse as shadow figures, so have the human primitive and indigenous Native—"genuine savages" all. We have already seen, in Rowland, Lutwack, and Jung, the intimation, at least, that earlier cultures' "superstitious" awe of the avian and the animal positions such people firmly in the same "bestial" realm. For Walt Whitman, Native Americans are veritable animals themselves, and thus the fit prey of Manifest Destiny and biblical rule by fiat: they are "close to nature, and like natural objects such as trees and animals subject to . . . removal in the face of the progressive march westward" (Killingsworth, *Walt Whitman* 87). In Charles Darwin's *The Voyage of the Beagle*, the biologist's ethnological observations of the Natives of South America and Australia make up almost as much of the book as his natural history notes; but then, these creatures are so much "like animals" that they apparently qualify as subjects of natural history themselves (229). Dr. Johnson, epitome of so many prejudices, makes a comparable identification upon meeting an officer from the "wilds of America," who waxes effusively about being "amidst the rude magnificence of Nature, with this Indian woman by [his] side." Johnson later speaks of the man's happiness as a "gross absurdity. It is sad stuff; it is brutish. If a bull could speak, he might well exclaim,—Here am I with this cow and this grass; what being can enjoy greater felicity?" (Boswell 209–10). The satire on the romanticization of the wild is all well and good, but the Native woman seems to have been glibly transformed into a cow in the process.

To invoke Jungian psychology again, images of other species, because of their supposed instinctual arationalism and sheer alien difference, most often represent the unconscious—more specifically, the "dark" side of the unconscious, that is, the shadow.[19] Furthermore, to the Western white ego, the other main generic shadow figure entails another, usually more primitive, human race, whether black or yellow or red.[20] For the Anglo-American, especially, the shadow is often "represented by a Negro or an [American] Indian" (Jung, *CW* 5: §267). If not ostracized as animal, both bird and Native are conversely idealized as spiritual, as abundantly evidenced in the imagery and metaphors of the Western literary canon. The bird is incorrigibly either some etherealized skylark or oriole or some chthonic owl or raven; so, too, the Western imagination can only see the Indian as a heathen savage id, a Jungian shadow figure, or, in typical bipolar fashion, as a nostalgically redemptive Noble Savage.

This is one of the dominant themes of Frantz Fanon, who finds a Western conflation of shadow figures that include "the Wolf, the Devil, the Evil Spirit, the Bad Man, [and] the Savage" (146). The raven and crow, those "winged devils" (to paraphrase Jung again),[21] can easily be added to this abbreviated list of villains, as infernal confreres of the devil, savage, and wolf. In North America in particular the wolf and raven are—or should I say, were?—often partners, in both myth and reality. In her magnificent essay "Deify the Wolf," the Chickasaw writer Linda Hogan also acknowledges "the psychological fact that wolves carry much of the human shadow" (*Dwellings* 71). In describing her animal subject, she notes that the wolves she is watching are accompanied by a group of "gypsy ravens," who "direct the wolves to their prey" to partake in the leftovers; sometimes "a person happens across a coal black raven standing inside the wide arch of those ribs like a soul in a body"

(65). This dark avian spirit of death in Hogan's essay is yet another shadow image, although, as a Native American and champion of eco-awareness, Hogan refuses to vilify either wolf or raven: they are simply there, fulfilling their roles in nature, and the truly fearful things are humankind's untoward projections regarding them. It is fitting, too, that Hogan, as Native American, would defend and resignify these alter-species shadows; like the wolf, raven, and human of Fanon's *Black Skin*, the Native American has long been an unwilling bearer of the Western collective shadow.

This Western shadowing of the American indigenous immediately calls to mind Edward Said's formulation of the discourse of Orientalism (*Orientalism*, e.g., 1–4). It is readily apparent that Said's general ideology of othering inherent in the very concept of Orientalism is equally applicable to the central ideological framing device of the New World, the Euro-American imperialism and colonialism regarding the natives here, both human and nonhuman. The correlative New World version of Said's Foucauldian notion might readily be dubbed *Indianism,* all the more happily, given the Orientalism still ironically implicit in the very origins of the word.[22] The general discourse of othering nonhumans as lower life forms fit for exploitation has already been aptly defined as *speciesism*,[23] and my own contribution to this line of thought is to emphasize how crucial, and yet largely ignored, this lamentable Orientalizing of other species has been to the ecology and biodiversity of the planet.

In one of the first books by a Lakota, *Land of the Spotted Eagle* (1933), Luther Standing Bear's titular homeland is appropriately dubbed that of the Spotted Eagle, not that of his human Oglala band, to reflect, no doubt, "the Lakota belief that man did not occupy a special place in the eyes of Wakan Tanka, the Grandfather of us all," that both humans and birds were *oyate*, or "people." Standing Bear later finds another parallel between Native Americans and other species in terms of the European settlers' attitude toward both: "Only to the white man was nature a 'wilderness' and only to him was the land 'infested' with 'wild' animals and 'savage' people" (22, 38). Such infestations needed to be removed: "I know of no species of plant, bird, or animal that were [*sic*] exterminated until the coming of the white man. . . . The white man considered natural animal life just as he did the natural man life upon this continent, as 'pests.' Plants which the Indian found beneficial were also 'pests.' There is no word in the Lakota vocabulary with the English meaning of this word" (165). Standing Bear's Lakota contemporary, Black Elk, notes another avian-Native similarity, with similar tragic ramifications: "Our tepees were round like the nests of birds," which are set "in circles, for theirs is the same religion as ours. . . . But the Washicus [whites] have put us in these square boxes," and so "the power is not in us any more" (Neihardt 150–51). In U.S. history, the colonizer's treatment of both animal and Native has been one of abuse, even betrayal, according to Hogan; not only have we, both white and nonwhite Americans, "strayed from the *treaties* we once had with the land and with the animals," but "we have created a world for ourselves where all of our actions have dire consequences in a way reminiscent of federal Indian policies" (*Dwellings* 11, 69; emphasis added).

In sum, both feathered beings and feather wearers have long been othered as comparable objects in Western colonial imperialist discourse. Historically, the English language itself offers further lamentable correlatives. Both Others, for example, have been deemed close kin, as tribes fit for reservations; by both poets and ornithologists of the eighteenth and nineteenth centuries, birds were often referred to as the "(feathered) tribes,"[24] and in the early twentieth century bird reserves were also called "reservations" (Pearson 1.xiv). In much of the literature that is my purview, the Native *is* "nature": wild, and in the raw. To refer to the bird as comparably native, as in Burroughs's "genuine little savage," is hardly a great leap, given its intrinsic *animal* relationship to the very land and (above all, for my purposes) the long Western cultural conflation of Indians and birds, epitomized in the eagle feather of popular iconography and in the words of Black Elk himself: "The life of an Indian is just like the wings of the air. . . . The hawk swoops down on its prey; so does the Indian. . . . The coyote is sly; so is the Indian. The eagle is the same. This is why the Indian is always feathered up; he is a relative to the wings of the air" (DeMallie 317).

My readings in subsequent chapters will often be two-pronged takes on the passages in question, in which the othering of both bird and Native are at least implicit. Indeed, as we'll see in so much nineteenth-century Anglo literature, Wordsworth's words in this chapter's opening epigraph, on filtering the lion and the eagle through a moral, "imaginative" framework, could just as well apply to the Native American, who could be dealt with only by a Western imagination that could only see the Indian as either an irredeemable savage or a Romanticized ecosaint. At last, in Western discourse, the animal, the bird, is framed through the literary bars of the zoo; the Indian, through the literary borders of the reservation.[25] The Harjo epigraph on the crow, in contrast, exemplifies the Native reaction that writes back against this very Western imagining, resignifying both Indian and avian. I maintain that Harjo's various images of crows and eagles and redwings have an intrinsic importance in her corpus, not only as living parts of that natural world that she would champion and mythically reinvigorate, but as real and individual Others like her, repressed and belittled afterthoughts in the psyche of Western civilization. However unfortunate the historico-political rationale for this connection between Indian and bird, it at least provides an immediate vital link between human and animal; it may well be through this motif of the othered-as-animal Indian that a closer connection between human and animal, words and birds, can be at last perceived.

The Anishinaabe poet, novelist, and theorist Gerald Vizenor has also attempted a reinvigoration of both Others, but his adoption of Baudrillard's poststructuralist theory of simulation has led him to deconstruct the identity of the Indian itself as, after all, a Western cultural projection; in text after text, in popular representation after popular representation, Vizenor concludes, "This portrait is not an Indian."[26] (I could rightfully conclude many of my own subsequent readings of the avian in literature likewise: "This portrait is not a bird.") As for the Indian and animal, Vizenor recognizes that the stereotypical connection of other species and Native Americans is another "nostalgic" mistranslation, like "Indian" itself; underlying this association, nonetheless, is "the insinuation of a creature presence," through which "nativism, animism, and naturalism" are privileged "over theories of evolution and modernism" ("Literary Animals" 131–32). In this seminal essay (1998), Vizenor continually links Native and animal as possibilities for "native survivance" against a dominant worldview that would assimilate both via inauthentic simulations (122). Crucially, this "native" insurgence can take place in literature, especially (though not exclusively) in the literature of Natives themselves, whose metaphoric animals can, at times, "create a sense of creature presence" and even contain "traces of animal consciousness" (125, 135). In my later chapters part of my task is to argue that, in terms of the avian, Vizenor is right.

Again, the Native Other and the alter-species Other have much in common, as two "birds of a feather," as icons of Nature and the primitive and the wild. One is almost amused, then, to note the totemic aspect of various professional sports team names in the United States, as if the combatants were in need of the spirits of Bear, Lion, Falcon, Eagle, and of Redskin and Brave (wielding a "tomahawk chop"), totemic figures all, of brute force and mindless courage: a further symptom of the conflation of the animal and the indigene ubiquitous in Western ideology. The Native writer is perhaps left little choice but to (re)invoke his or her fraternity with the eagle, crow, loon, et al., and to "sing back" (however dissonantly) as that avian Other, as Harjo does:

> I'd rather understand how to sing from a crow
> who was never good at singing or much of anything
> but finding gold in the trash of humans.

Harjo and her crow are still rummaging together through the trash.

THE TROUBLE WITH ECOCRITICISM; OR, DR. DOOLITTLE IN THE POSTMODERN WILDERNESS

> A long-winded gloss on *ecocritic* might run as follows: "a person who judges the merits and faults of writings that depict the effects of culture upon nature, with a view toward celebrating nature, berating its despoilers, and reversing their harm through political action."
>
> —WILLIAM HOWARTH, "Some Principles of Ecocriticism"

Having found wanting an outdated archetypalism in representing the "natural" Other, I turn now to a more promising tack through which to defend the avian. How exciting it was to discover a recent critical approach that does attempt a merger of literary and naturalist concerns similar to my own. Indeed, because birds *are* part of nature, my general argument could well be said to fall within the scope of what has come to be called ecocriticism, and so a close examination of this school of thought deserves a place here. Although I may seem to be wandering at times from my avian subject, a look at current literary scholarship's relationship to "Nature" in general is very much in order.

However, it is still not entirely clear what ecocriticism *is*. It could simply be writing *about* nature writing, or exploring the themes and uses of nature in literature, or, most commonly, critiquing literature from a purely political stance, as Marxists and feminists have done. However, the vast preponderance of such ecocritical readings has centered on such generalities as the land, the ecosystem, or Nature itself; only sporadically have such endeavors ventured into a concerted discussion of the specific alter-species inhabitants of our hallowed Mother Earth. I would like to resignify ecocriticism's main focus to date, on the environment in general, to the animals that inhabit said environment (and eventually to birds in particular, of course). For after the human Others of class, race, gender, and sexual persuasion have been admitted into the halls of the dizzying edifice known as Critical Theory, the next (perhaps not so obvious because even more occluded) candidate is that of *species*; granted, ecocriticism has already gone far in establishing a thematic link between the female and minority Other and the nonhuman Other, be it the land or other species. Furthermore, theoretically speaking, the more radical ecophilosophical critiques that issue from Arne Naess's deep ecology have at least one thing in common with poststructuralist theory and, indeed, may be said to represent one more manifestation thereof. For the notion of an egalitarian ecocentrism is certainly another decentering or deconstruction, in this case, of the man/nature hierarchic binary.[27] Given poststructuralists' relative antagonism toward Enlightenment humanism, Peter Singer's animal rights attack on speciesism, too, fits right in with poststructuralism's overall decentering (and often rights-extending) agenda.

However, here the ground gives way. Mentioning Naess and Singer in one breath might misleadingly give the impression that there is some monophonic voice in favor of both animal and ecological concerns. However, the theory and politics thereof have produced a Bakhtinian polyphony, or cacophony, of voices, of attitudes. In tracing the various threads of ecological philosophy, Donald Worster has found the past two centuries to be commonly divided into the "arcadian" and the "imperialist" camps, epitomized in Thoreau and Darwin, respectively (e.g., 2, 29–30, 114, 346). But the contemporary debates within even the arcadian school (within which I'd perhaps too boldly place both the deep ecologists and the animal rights spokespeople) are strident indeed. Attending to this conversation, I listened to deep ecologists scorning the vegetarianism of animal rightists for privileging animals over plants; I heard animal rights people scorn deep ecologists for considering worms and rocks as equal to cows and dogs. I heard hunter-gatherer types mourn the advent of agriculture and agro-pacifists mourn the advent (or continuation) of hunting. I heard St. Francis of Assisi called both the patron saint of ecology and a loose screw whose mystical feelings were like those of a mushroom eater. I watched ecocritics thumb their nose at French theory and other ecocritics thumb their nose at ecocritics who thumbed their nose at French theory. I also heard animal rights philosophers complain that the environmentalist and ecology movements were taking attention away from their agenda, as if the animals they've championed didn't require the right to a decent environment in which to survive. And I read ecocritics wax euphoric a whole essay long about the land and landscape and environment, without one word about the fauna inhabiting said environment. (Symptomatically, Lawrence Buell ultimately confesses in his most recent work, *The Future of Environmental Criticism*, that his summary of major ecocritical schools has "relegated a number of significant ethico-political positions to the sidelines, most notably the discourses of animal and other nonhuman rights" [126].) Above all, I perceived the need to fashion my own synthesis of these various antagonisms into a study of animal alterity that more fully acknowledged, say, the black-capped chickadee as an organic part of both ecosystem and ecocriticism.

A key term in much recent ecoscholarship is that of bio- or eco-relatedness, a holistic notion that would make the environment and its creatures the original worldwide web, as it were. Such an idea is, of course, apropos of poststructuralist decentering in general, in this case, the deconstruction of homocentrism by a radical ecocentric egalitarianism that would deprivilege any aspect, including species, of the whole. This radical ecocentrism originated in Arne Naess's 1972 lecture, "The Shallow and the Deep, Long-Range Ecology Movement," in which he divides ecological approaches into two camps, the shallow and the deep. The former, under which Naess would group most mainstream environmentalist agendas, is shallow in its short-sighted quick-fix goals and its ultimate anthropocentrism: at last, the earth's ecosystems must be saved for the greater benefit and salvation of the *human* race, these shallow people claim.[28] This is the philosophy of most environmentalists to this day, whether or not they are conscious of it. (As a current manifestation thereof, witness the sad capitalist co-optation of green discourse in the advertising of U.S. big business.)

Deep ecology, in contrast, has a deeper (that is, more reflective and explicit) philosophy, or "ecosophy," as Naess calls it, based on the concept of "biospherical egalitarianism." Through an understanding of the earth as a relational "total-field" (95), Naess attacks the Western master-slave relationship of man over nature, champions species diversity, and even laments one species' (i.e., humankind's) overpopulation as a threat to that diversity (96).

To reduce such master-slave relationships and loosen "hierarchical chains," Naess also embraces "local autonomy" and "decentralization" (98), a move closely related to what would soon become known as bioregionalism.[29] However, the local seems to require some universal tenets, no matter how tentative any stated agenda of those tenets may be. Naess acknowledges that his is a more "vague" and "global" approach than shallow ecology's "one-sided stress on pollution and resource depletion," and yet the "norms and values" of deep ecology are the result of "remarkable convergencies" of like minds around the planet (apparently, minds that think, and feel, as *deep*ly as he does [98–100]). "Feel" is, in fact, the key term here, for eco-egalitarianism is "not derived" from "logic or induction"; it is instead "intuitively clear" as an ethical truth ("The Shallow" 98, 96).[30] The sympathetic reader may be in total agreement yet still wonder whether Naess's ecosophy has really developed anything new, as a philosophy, beyond the intuitions of Blake or Wordsworth; the less sympathetic reader might simply accuse him of a mushy Romanticism.

Naess's central tenets are reiterated in Devall and Sessions's *Deep Ecology* (1985), which might be deemed a manifesto and summary of the deep ecology movement, as the authors frequently invoke (and quote extensively from) the movement's big guns, particularly Naess, Sessions himself, and the many precursory figures in the minority-mystical tradition, or "perennial philosophy," of which deep ecology sees itself as an integral extension (e.g., Devall and Sessions 18–19, 80–82).[31] Deep ecology's minority precursors include Native American traditions, Eastern religious philosophies, Spinoza, the Romantics and Transcendentalists, Heidegger, the "new physics," and even St. Francis of Assisi; these are contrasted, naturally, with the mainstream Western patriarchal and positivist faith in progress, a "domination of Nature" that is ultimately alienating.[32]

Deep ecology's two main tenets (again, from Naess) of "biocentric equality" and "Self-realization" (Devall and Sessions 66–69) are expanded into Naess and Sessions's eight "basic principles" of deep ecology, the sum of which, bio-egalitarianism and diversity, leads to their most controversial statement, that a "substantial decrease of the human population" would be better both for the planet and for the "quality" of human life (70).[33] (Gary Snyder has suggested a specific goal of "half of the present world population" [*Turtle Island* 92]). Such a quality speaks for a quite personalist-subjectivist perspective, an ideal calling for (a few) more John Muirs and many fewer factory workers.[34] Indeed, for better or worse, the truths of deep ecology rely heavily on their Romantic forebears: a "biocentric perspective" can "satisfy our deepest yearnings," in "joyous" and "sensuous" fashion, via "spontaneous, playful intercourse," especially through "silence and solitude"—in sum (it would appear), through the blessed few's "direct intuitive *experiencing* of Nature" (Devall and Sessions 7–9, 47).

And yet, amazingly, just as we saw in Naess's originary essay, such ultimately individualistic intuitions still result in a "comprehensive . . . philosophical worldview" with a crucial "religious component" and also allow for a political activism whose agendas "naturally" follow from these tenets (Devall and Sessions 65, 76). Problematically, this emphasis on the intuitive and "experiential" sometimes comes across as an anti-intellectual obscurantism, and the philosophy herein is ultimately a quite poetic one: significantly, "ecological consciousness seems most vibrant in the poetic mode" (102).[35] If deep ecology would seek to understand nature without imposing "an ideology upon it" (37) (if such a thing were even possible?), its project must be considered a grand failure, however gracefully the authors find themselves "dancing on the brink of ecological awareness . . . without analyzing and rationalizing": "Dancing has always been part of living for primal peoples. For us, the dance may be a Ghost Dance for all that is lost: condor, bison . . . and passenger pigeon. Or it may be the dance of a new revelation of Being, of modesty and Earth wisdom on the turning point" (207). But at last, this dance is so infused with tinges of Romantic nostalgia and messianism that Devall and Sessions's book, and the movement, is in some ways a failed "Ghost Dance" itself.

In fact, deep ecology's intuitive holism may well be a remnant of the overarching monism that its proponents preach against, a continuation of Christian monotheism, Spinozan rationalism, and Romantic idealism. Its best, and worst, feature is the arational faith in species equality that defies Western logic and rationalism (despite Naess's frequent quotations of Spinoza), a "feeling"-based ethos that reminds sympathetic readers of the philosophy of Romanticism at its most powerful, and unsympathetic readers of a "blood-and-soil" fascism at its most terrifying.[36] I've dealt with deep ecology in some detail because much ecocriticism either accepts much of deep ecology's tenets implicitly or explicitly or makes a concerted effort (especially the constructivist version thereof) to distance itself from such a totalizing worldview. Also, deep ecology's deep attention to *other species* is one that I will invoke often, as an emphasis often neglected in the ecocriticism of the 1990s. And despite my own criticisms, the emphasis on intuition and the poetic is potentially fruitful, perhaps even requisite, for my own later arguments.

The Others of nature and gender coalesce in ecofeminism. Françoise D'Eaubonne's original French manifesto (1974), calling for a "synthesis" of "feminism and ecology," laments the past "fifty centuries" of men abusing both their environment and their countersex, "sowing the earth as they do women" (175, 177). Anglo-American ecofeminism is exemplified well in Annette Kolodny's analysis (1984) of white male American colonialism's "conquest" of nature. This victory was ultimately based on an archetypal metaphor of the earth and landscape as feminine; to this day, American culture has been torn between its originary idolization of the earth as mother and the painful consciousness of its subsequent "rape" of the "feminine" that is the American landscape (171, 174, 176). Vera Norwood epitomizes another crucial ecofeminist angle by wondering whether women nature writers conceive of nature in a more "immanent" fashion, with less striving to "overcome" nature as some masculine "challenge" (344). For other ecofeminists, this concern for the twin Others of gender and nature eventually becomes a trinity of abjection, with the addition of ethnicity; thus the writing of ecocentered Native women such as Paula Gunn Allen and Linda Hogan might well be deemed a Native ecofeminism.[37] Ecofeminism is also crucial to avian alterity in particular: nature-as-female, like nature-as-Native, is often reified as a bird: in the beautiful (and curvaceous) swan, the maternal dove, and the domestic wren and robin. The ecofeminist Susan Griffin develops this relationship between female and avian in a set of parables in which "she" is the "animal": "Now, he must conquer her wildness, he says, he must tame her before she drives him wild, he says" (209). Fleeing from the beast-taming patriarchy, the archetypal "she" returns to nature, and to *birds,* at essay's end, "to play with the berries and the plants and finally to whisper to the birds. And the birds, she said afterward, whispered to her" (212).

The ecofeminist Carolyn Merchant's *Radical Ecology* (1992) calls for a synthesis of various radical ecologies, including deep ecology, ecofeminism, spiritual ecology, and social (i.e., neo-Marxist) ecology.[38] A coalition of such theories and political praxis, she hopes, could fashion a "global ecological revolution" in the next fifty years (14). However, Merchant laments a continuing schism between mainstream ("homocentric") groups and radical ("ecocentric") activists, à la Naess's distinction between "shallow" and "deep" ecologies, but perceives that their interests may be "beginning to merge" (181) as willing foot soldiers in the revolution to a "worldwide socialist order" (235). Only then can the unjust hierarchies of human over nature, (human) rich over poor, and (human) male over female all come to an end. I might first question the present viability of the synthesis itself, a rather big-tent picture with lots of clowns and wild animals still on the margins of the circus, outside the tent. The near exclusion of animal rights activists from this circus is especially problematic. Finally, the phrase "worldwide socialist order" may also beg the continuing relevance of a nineteenth-century Western, very homocentric political philosophy that is nearly as complicit with the Western positivist worldview as its capitalist opponent.

Turning to literary ecocriticism itself, the earliest definition of "ecocriticism" per se is William Rueckert's, in 1978, when he defined it as "the application of ecology and ecological concepts to the study of literature" (107).[39] But this initial conception of ecocriticism is a counterintuitive one: humankind's creative endeavors *are* ecology at work, renewable expenditures of "stored energy" that are "used" again and again by readers (108); the literature classroom is an ecosystem itself, where the poem as "stored energy" is released and "recycled" (110) in some grand cultural imitation of nature (and good ecological praxis). But the particular poets and poems that Rueckert goes on to cite are specifically ecological in content (a shift, apparently, from his general notion of the writer and reader as ecosystem): Whitman's *Song of Myself*, for example, is a "complete ecological vision" (118), and Roethke, Merwin, and Snyder are pretty ecologically sound, too (116–19). The essay ends with the italics, "*Free us from false figures of speech*" (121). Exactly. But one is left wondering if such statements as "Poems are green plants among us" (111) are just the sort of metaphors we need to be freed *from*.

Thus the 1970s ecocritical writings of Rueckert and Meeker (whose contributions to ecocriticism will be addressed in the next section) seem rather hesitant, wayward starts to a school that would receive a clearer direction in the 1990s with Cheryll Glotfelty et al. Glotfelty is as responsible as anyone for the eventual renaissance of ecocriticism; in her introduction to the 1996 anthology *The Ecocriticism Reader* she offers the following: "Ecocriticism is the study of the relationship between literature and the physical environment" (xviii); however, she emphasizes "place" to the apparent exclusion of flora and fauna as crucial aspects of said environment. Later she also distinguishes an ecocriticism per se and its literary and rhetorical aspects: "Ecocriticism takes as its *subject* the interconnections between human culture and the material world, between the human and the nonhuman. Ecological *literary* criticism is that subset of ecocriticism that focuses specifically on the cultural elements of language and literature and their relationship to the environment; it is a critical stance that has one foot in literature and the other on land" (qtd. in Branch 47). One might still wonder what "interconnections" of the first, larger category, lying as they do beyond "language and literature," can viably be dealt with in *discourse*. Moreover, despite the verbiage regarding "interconnections," Glotfelty's explicit disjunction of human and nonhuman may well be what a more fruitful ecocriticism might want to bridge. But at last, the human versus nonhuman schism here remains intact.[40]

The subsequent plethora of such ecocrit definitions soon begins to sound like self-parody. Howarth's fine semi-tongue-in-cheek definition of the ecocritic may well be, in spite of the intentional self-satire, the best *description* of the present state of ecocriticism, for better or worse, especially its overt admission of a political agenda.[41] It correlates well with Lawrence Buell's more solemn definition of ecocriticism as the "study of the relation between literature and environment conducted in a spirit of commitment to environmentalist praxis" (*Environmental Imagination* 430).

But this commitment is problematized when nature and environment as social constructs become the focus. Thus the British brand of 1990s ecocriticism has often put a more social constructivist emphasis on the project. Richard Kerridge is characteristic here, defining ecocriticism as "the new environmentalist cultural criticism," which includes a critique of environmentalism's own "fascist and colonialist forms" (introduction 5, 7). Similarly, the American Michael Branch sees ecocriticism as an exploration of "constructions of environment in literary texts and theoretical discourse," as "an ecologically informed approach to nature and literature . . . which questions the hegemony of anthropocentric constructions of environment" (42). Such questions, as we shall see, often look askance at the "nature" of the environment itself, to the point of rendering environmental activism a rather muted or moot concern.

In sum, these definitions range from a rather transparent approach to the land in literature to a radical deconstruction of the environment. But let me anticipate my conclusion by predicting that all such proposals may fall prey to the very Western poststructuralist critiques in which many of them partake; indeed, a truly efficacious ecocriticism may well require a transcending, first, of the dominant Weltanschauung (e.g., through Native American worldviews) to finally go beyond the Western anthropocentrism that these same scholars perceive to be the original sin. Second, the current landscape-centered bias of ecocriticism, as noted earlier, has fashioned a huge aporia in its subject matter: an ecocritical approach that relegates species alterity to the periphery is an unnecessarily limited and impoverished one, symptomatic of the ideological schism between ecoscholars and animal rights theorists, or, put another way, between an ecosystemic total field and Blake's particular "Little Fly."

Glotfelty attempts to delineate a clear evolution of 1980s and 1990s ecocriticism, and its future direction, parallel to Elaine Showalter's three stages of feminism. Thus ecocriticism's first task has been to critique old, canonical, "bad ecology" texts, especially the ways that nature has been stereotypically depicted. (Notably, these stereotypes include the Indian [xix] and, I would add, the vulture and the crow.) The second task is the championing of (usually more recent) "good ecological" works and nature writing per se. The third task is to develop some theoretical acumen, evidenced so far in deep ecology and ecofeminism and in various rapprochements with poststructuralism (xxii–xxiv).[42]

Although some efforts at such an engagement with critical theory are evident in Glotfelty and Fromm's *The Ecocriticism Reader*, one must look overseas for greater evidence thereof. Compared to that U.S. eco-anthology, *Writing the Environment,* edited by Kerridge and Sammells (1998) is quite British in its greater emphasis on the theoretical and political concerns of neo-Marxism, postcolonialism, and cultural studies. Thus, as the title indicates, contributors are more likely to view the environment in terms of critical theory, as a problematic text inevitably marked by class, race, and gender. Poststructuralist critiques are therefore even more common here, but whereas Kerridge's use of Žižek's Lacanian reading of environmental crises as returns of the "repressed," as eruptions of the "Real," seems inordinately promising, Žižek's claim of an "irreducible gap" between nature and language, of a nature that is "real" beyond "representation," signals a huge theoretical gap that Kerridge fails to bridge satisfactorily (introduction 2–3).

Indeed, that the holism that ecocriticism characteristically invokes falls through the hole of poststructuralism becomes a recurring theme in the dialogue of ecoscholarship. To deem the Earth in the statement "Save the Earth" a constructed false essentialism strikes the tree-hugging right brain as rubbish, but the left brain finds any cognitive rebuttal difficult. Arren E. Gare's *Postmodernism and the Environmental Crisis* assails the twentieth century's main schools of critical theory for, by and large, having created an intellectual climate of political ineffectuality and intellectual nihilism. Against the postmodern hegemony of global capitalism that they have diagnosed so well, "poststructuralists . . . are totally inadequate as guides for political action" (2) because their conception of epistemology as a solipsistic world-as-text leaves them helpless. What can be done in the realm of the Real if (paraphrasing Nietzsche) "we simply find in nature what we project onto it" (50)? Similarly, and scarier yet, "for poststructuralists, [even] the notion of a 'global environmental crisis' can be deconstructed" (99)! And so, in attempting to escape this psychoanalytical prison of a Self forever unable to truly know the Real, can one do more than invoke Jonathan Bate's end-around effort to counter poststructuralism? Just look, says Bate, at the current disaster that is the environment, you nature-as-construct people, and then tell me that "*there is no nature*" (*Romantic* 56).[43] But one still feels like Dr. Johnson kicking a stone to refute Bishop Berkeley, painfully aware that Berkeley's postmodern philosophical descendants would sneeringly deem such a stance to be naïve realism.

The trouble continues with other poststructuralist-grounded ecocritics like Michael Branch, whose essay "Ecocriticism: The Nature of Nature in Literary Theory and Practice" (1994) epitomizes much ecocriticism of a poststructuralist influence. Indeed, he sees nature as one of the oldest "cultural artifacts" and yet would offer his own "biocentric" revision of our constructs of nature, which he calls "ecosophy" (41, 42).[44] Branch's ecosophy goes beyond traditional eco-aware literature by stressing a poststructuralist interconnectedness that he equates with intertextuality; thus ecocriticism and poststructuralism both perform a "deep questioning of standards of objective certitude," especially of anthropocentrism (44, 46), and both emphasize that human "interpretations" aren't "objectively correct" (45). Furthermore, poststructuralism's "decentering" of the "human subject" is, according to Branch, akin to "ecosophy's wish to replace anthropocentrism with an affirmation of the value of ecosystemic wholes" (46).

But therein lies the problem, as Branch's "system" and "whole" (46) self-deflate from the holes with which deconstruction would pierce it. He can blithely assert that "ecosophers locate value in natural wholes" and that ecosophy "is integrative" and "holistic," not "reductive" (44, 49), a continuation, I contend, of the grand Romantic metaphor of Absolute Spirit. But finally, what "values," from a poststructuralist perspective, can allow Branch to speak of "the *spiritual* consequences of nature and the *moral* consequences of its violation" (49; emphases added)?

Like Jonathan Bate, Branch would ultimately avoid the critique of poststructuralism by asking "What about that nature 'out there' . . . ? How are we to know when our tireless manipulation of the signifier 'nature' constitutes a morally unacceptable endangerment of our home planet and the diversity of species it sustains?" Indeed, poststructuralism's "'subversive' suggestion that the world is somehow made of words may also be seen as simply the latest avatar of anthropocentrism—as an attempt to use the ubiquity of language to *keep* humans at the center of our cosmological paradigm" (50). And so Branch admits that ecocriticism "must openly confront . . . both the positive and the negative implications of its remarkable relationship to poststructuralist literary theory" and that this theory's "infinite deferral of meaning is strongly at odds with an ethos of environmental concern." In point of fact, ecocriticism is "more interested in environmentalism's goal of freedom from decimation than in deconstructionism's goal of freedom from meaning" (49–50). Stronger yet: "Few ecocritics would concede that nature ultimately has no determinate meaning, or that the natural system can adequately be described as simply the interminable 'freeplay' of its 'signifiers.' On the contrary, normative concepts such as intrinsic value and the rights of natural objects demonstrate that contemporary ecosophy retains a genuine concern for specific loci of meaning and value" (50). Earnest, even powerful, and yet "value" and "normative" are dangerous (even incredible) words that still smack of deep ecology's propensity for intuitive, and ultimately arationally *imposed* truths.

Branch's attacks on homocentrism, however, remain legitimate: "Anthropocentrism has caused unjust domination and exploitation of other members of the ecosystemic community," and therefore the need for "resistance to the ethical Ptolemaism of a human-centered theory of value" (46)—though, again, one might wonder what *value*, as a human-centered notion, is not "human-centered." Branch would have his cake and eat it, too: his very appeals to poststructuralism, despite his eventual rejection of it, still place him in an intellectual milieu that disallows any transcendence of anthropocentric textuality.

I may be accused of continually slamming ecocriticism from some Bloomian anxiety of influence. But a recurring call in ecocriticism of the 1990s is for the need of this very self-critique; ecocriticism should, first of all, cast a wary glance at even its favorite genre of nature writing and point out the political biases that underlie these works. Moreover, this self-policing should include within its scope the various utterances of environmentalists, ecologists, and ecocritics themselves, especially those relatively unaware of how much they themselves are indeed *constructing* nature. In sum, I would first emphasize the need, and applaud the efforts, to provide ecocriticism with a greater theoretical sophistication through the insights of, especially, poststructuralism and postcolonial theory. But second, a way out of a closed circuit of anthropocentric narcissism is the next order of the day, without begging the (poststructuralist) question by simply kicking a rock or uttering knee-jerk dismissals of Derrida and Bhabha. Somehow, some way, I would like to conclude with an environmental and ethical stance that navigates between high theory and Romantic intuition, aware as I am that this may be a rough-water trip in a *bateau ivre*.

John Gray has expressed the state of affairs most concisely: "Postmodernists tell us that there is no such thing as nature, only the floating world of our own constructions" (54). Several ecocritics, such as Michael Branch, have expressed an approach/avoidance relationship with poststructuralism; other ecocritics have blithely ignored it, and some have gone out of their way to reject it as a dead end for eco-consciousness.[45] William Howarth's "Some Principles of Ecocriticism" (1996), for instance, includes a disdain for and an explicit rebellion against poststructuralism (and new historicism [76–80]) in a manner that is perhaps more representative of ecocritics in general than my emphasis so far might lead one to believe. But can anything be done if one confronts the dilemma of postmodernist skepticism head-on? How can one counter Dana Phillips's reluctant conclusion that, in a postmodern milieu of Baudrillard and Jameson, of simulacra and commodification, "whatever remains of nature . . . is . . . unknown to us" ("Is Nature Necessary?" 217)?

Karl Kroeber's escape from poststructuralism in *Ecological Literary Criticism* (1994) is straightforward, via an emphatic acceptance of materialism and a frontal assault on constructivism. As with Jonathan Bate's work, many of Kroeber's ideas are best addressed in the chapters on British Romanticism to follow, but his extreme (for a humanities scholar) embrace of hard science in support of a "new biological, materialistic understanding of humanity's place" in nature (2) is noteworthy. For starters, Kroeber "accepts as entirely real a natural environment existent outside of one's personal psyche" (19). The casual reader might well ask why one would even need to affirm such a notion of commonsense philosophy; that Kroeber feels the need to do so not only affirms the influence of critical theories that question this very assertion, but highlights the central dilemma in which ecocritics have found themselves. In defense of his materialist credo, Kroeber's attacks on the Yale school and new historicism are scathing; in general, these schools are part of a cold war theoretical mentality, both "power-obsessed" and based, moreover, on "obsolete" nineteenth-century conceptions of biology and physics (17, 40, 20). The skepticism of the "there-is-no-nature" view not only "obscures the complex dynamics of culture-nature interaction" by privileging the former, but is "dangerously constrictive and socially threatening" to an endangered natural world, and the "culture" that survives in it (17, 152). Kroeber even defends (recent) science against Carolyn Merchant's often blanket condemnation of the scientific worldview as a disastrous "monolith" (35).

But his contrary insistence on the "pluralistic nature" of science entails at least one dogmatic tenet, for Kroeber's own "ecologically oriented literary criticism" assumes, as we have seen, that an "ecological view of the world . . . must be fundamentally materialistic" (35, 1, 9). Humans are "natural creatures," after all, and their literary works are unique natural or material artifacts (104, 25). Less syncretic than Lawrence Buell will be, this scholar has no time for alternative eco-views: true ecology requires this Darwinian or materialist foundation, including a "biologically materialistic understanding of mind" (23, 142). Central here is his use of Edelman's neural Darwinism, which ultimately blurs the boundaries of an autonomous self. Not only is the "conscious brain . . . inseparable—does not in a significant sense *exist* apart—from the environment with which it interacts" (one is reminded of Wordsworth's "divine marriage"), but the brain—indeed, all organs, and perhaps even the individual cell—is "like a species" (7, 145, 146). Thus a biosphere of process, flux, and interdependence—an almost democratic cellularism, even atomism—deconstructs the notion of a discrete human individuality, offering a biological underpinning for what Buell will call the "relinquishment" of the self.

Kroeber's approach to literature is ecological in a sense reminiscent of Rueckert: the text itself is an eco-entity both holistic yet individual (1), part of a literary and cultural ecosystem of open-endedness and diversity (96). In practice, rather than dogmatically applying any critical method, it is far preferable to treat "each work of art" as a "unique contribution to the success of human life conceived as composed of many cultures each multifariously constituted. Ecological criticism . . . would reestablish on every level the significance of diversity" (140–41). This radical pluralism is one of the most leveling and de-centering of ecocritical tacks to date, as difficult as it is to imagine such democracy at work. Every poem is a new, unknown species, rebelling against humans' will to categorization and meaning: "Ecological criticism . . . endeavors to sustain the poem's resistance to the imposition of any definitive interpretation and thereby through criticism to renew its vital, hence changing, meaningfulness" (47). Even more so than in Rueckert, it is as if humankind's creative artifacts have a biological existence, and Kroeber's defense of such biota sounds like an animal rights theorist defending his or her species of choice against the onslaughts of anthropocentrism.

Kroeber's elevation of the British Romantics follows from these poets' "proto-ecological views," their belief that "humankind *belonged* in . . . the world of natural processes" (5). But here Kroeber's bias becomes rather overwrought, as he tends to make proto-*scientists* out of these same poets. Their bent was "toward a biological materialistic understanding of the human mind," and their works "anticipate . . . attitudes and conceptions that only in our century have been given . . . a solid scientific basis" (8, 19). Hardest to swallow is Kroeber's claim that, "at their best[?]," the British Romantics characteristically denied transcendence and idealism for immanence and naturalism (52); in sum, the "English romantics . . . were not religious believers" (98). If by "religion" Kroeber had meant orthodox Christianity, one might readily agree,[46] but no, he means to make Darwinian materialists out of the lot of them and must view Coleridge's turn to German metaphysics as a sidetrack, not as symptomatic (as I see it) of an ongoing need for spiritual meaning so evident in Romanticism in general. This scholar's notion of the best in Wordsworth is predictable, then: the immanence of "Tintern Abbey" makes it a superior poem to the metaphysical mumblings of the "Intimations" ode, and thus much of Wordsworth's later corpus (and

Coleridge's full-blown adoption of German Idealism) are betrayals of a truer (materialist) Romanticism (e.g., 47–52).

As we have seen, Kroeber calls for an open-ended approach to the text that cultivates its diversity. Unfortunately, his scientistic ideology is hardly conducive to the democratizing critical ideal that he preaches, denying as it does, for instance, the relevance of Merchant's "spiritual ecologies" and deep ecology's "perennial philosophies," including Native American attitudes that necessarily predate any "superior" Western notion of Darwinian evolution (27). His near deification of the Romantics as the original ecologists also seems too facile, and his almost rabid evolutionary materialism is troublingly strident, as if he is aware that its application to the Romantics doesn't quite fit, or is at best a necessarily extremist response to two centuries of Romantic readings of the Romantics. Finally, Kroeber evinces the hubris of many a scientist (and Darwinian) in maintaining the centrality of humans' "higher consciousness" (146): "We are better adapted to natural existence on this globe than any other species." (Watching the evening news, I am speechless.) Moreover, it may be that "humankind is not alienated by its attainment of self-consciousness" (151). (I am dumbfounded, and alone.) Unfortunately, such an almost logical positivist spin on evolutionary progress puts more faith in humankind's left-brain abilities and accomplishments than this maladapted and alienated reader can fully appreciate.

In an attack on poststructuralism similar to Howarth's, Gare's, and Kroeber's, Lawrence Buell, perhaps the most notable contemporary spokesperson of academic ecocriticism, also laments the "philosophical antireferentialism" that "underrepresents the claims of the environment on humanity by banishing it from the realms of discourse except as something absent," warning that "not mimesis [i.e., naturalist realism] but antireferentialism [the poststructuralist denial of referentiality] looks like the police" (*Environmental Imagination* 102). With Buell, as with Kroeber, the "Real" of nature returns in earnest, as he wonders unabashedly "whether the discrediting of realism" undertaken by modernism and postmodernism "has gone too far" (87). Buell's *The Environmental Imagination* (1995) is, in the eyes of many, the most important statement of ecocriticism to date.[47] Buell's main task is to examine texts that allow one "to imagine a more 'ecocentric' way of being" (1), an ethical commitment that leads to an acknowledged privileging of "environmentally oriented" texts (7), that is, prose nonfiction nature writing. To "arrive at a more ecocentric state of thinking than western culture now sustains," he would perform a three-step agenda, first analyzing the "pathology" of current Western literature and culture's relationship to the environment (similar to Glotfelty's first stage), then taking "stock of the resources within" this very tradition (thus his extended treatment of Thoreau), and finally considering "alternative models, be they antique, exotic, or utopian"; these last include Eastern philosophy, feminist neopaganism, and "Native American culture" (21–22). But this scholar's main route is the second, "Anglo-traditional" route, through Thoreau, Aldo Leopold, and Barry Lopez, whose works, he claims, can nonetheless serve as radical "agent[s] of change" (40). Indeed, Buell acknowledges a rather white canonical conservatism: "a more radical critic," he admits, would be more likely to consider "the prospect of a complete, ground-up reconstruction of western values," via Taoism, Native American thought, and so on, but he doubts that any of the latter could "become paradigmatic," most likely serving instead as constituents of a "new eclecticism" (22).

Buell's revelatory analysis of the Western "pathology" is also a call to reeducate scholars and readers, whose educational backgrounds have been fashioned by the current critical emphasis on representation, indicative of a "disjunction between text and world," and "fiction and nonfiction," ultimately symptomatic of the "cloistral, urbanized" milieu of academia (5). Given this untoward split between word and world, Buell asks, "must literature always lead us away from the physical world, never back to it?" (11). In response to what he perceives to be an academic marginalization of nature writing,[48] and as the literary genre least guilty of ignoring the physical world, Buell champions a "literary naturism" (e.g., 11, 431), the "imaginative" nature writing epitomized in *Walden* that he distinguishes from more straightforward naturalist or natural history writing. Such naturist writings' "extrospective character" allows for "an affirmation of environment over self, over appropriative homocentric desire," and has the "capacity . . . to model ecocentric thinking" (80, 104, 143).

In his new nonfiction aesthetics, Buell tries to avoid a simple relapse to realism as a mirror on the world through his notion of "dual accountability," an acknowledgment of both real "matter" and of (imaginative) "discursive mentation" (92). In this way, both a viable ecocritical vision and the exemplary works of such a vision involve a "symbiosis of object-responsiveness and imaginative shaping" (99). Transcending the either/or of "objective-world" replication and "linguistic" textualism (13), such a dual lens, Buell insists, "is far more productive than" a Foucauldian constructivism and best serves a "counterculture . . . in resistance to the intractable homocentrism in terms of which one's psychological and social worlds are always to some degree mapped" (113–14). Like Cheryll Glotfelty, Buell would stand with "one foot in literature and the other on land." Problematic, however, is Buell's main binary of "extro-" versus "intro-," his very "dual accountability," which seems stuck in, while obfuscating, the traditional Western dialogue of subject-object dualism; in other words, "both 'subjective' and 'objective' modes of knowing" (278), it seems to me, *are* subjective, as epistemologically filtered "knowings," after all, and Buell never really frees himself from this dilemma.[49]

To prop up such a countercultural privileging of naturist literature, Buell fruitfully appeals to critical theory via Bakhtinian heteroglossia. Against a monologic view of mimetic nature writing, he stresses "American naturism's ideological multivalence" and deems such works in general to be capable of even greater "polyphonic" discursiveness than Bakhtin's own favorite genre, the novel. Thus the writings of Thoreau, Dillard, and Lopez partake of an often "variegated" and diverse rhetoric, sometimes "fragmenting into multigeneric collage," for instance, in *Walden*'s "stylistic breaks" and "discursive chunks" (36, 397).

Buell then attempts to undermine the traditional Western self through a lengthy treatment of "relinquishment" (144). This involves, first, the relinquishment of Western civilization's materialism, as in the "voluntary simplicity" of Thoreau and Leopold (145). (Thus, in Thoreau's "experience of place," "ecocentrism replaces egocentrism" [154–55].) But more crucially, there is the relinquishment of self, or "individual autonomy itself." This second is more radical, for one thing, because it "implies the dissolution of plot and calls into question the authority of the superintending consciousness"; it is an abandonment of "literature's most basic foci" of plot, character, and "narrative consciousness" (144–45). Buell spends a good deal of time examining various modern Anglo-American poets who have attempted a similar "relinquishment" (most notably, Ammons, Roethke, and Snyder [158–67]), but such a tack has been more successful in "environmental nonfiction," of course (168). Yet even here, self-relinquishment has inevitably been only momentary, a "suspension" rather than "*eradication*" of egohood (178). No one has yet approached Buell's own ideal, so brilliantly expressed, of "imagining human selves as unstable constellations of matter occupying one among innumerable niches in an interactive biota" (167).

Descriptions of landscape or place allow the naturist to perform another "readjustment of the familiar" (263), or a defamiliarization: at last, a "seeing things new, seeing new things, [and] expanding the notion of community so that it becomes situated within the ecological community" (266). Seeing the bird *anew*, too, can no doubt be part and parcel of this enterprise. But here Buell adopts, characteristically, a careful postmodernist circumspection. Place, especially, is always a construct, and the idealization, common among ecoscholars, of "the sense of place" runs "almost as great a risk of cultural narcissism as when we accept the myth of place-free, objective inquiry" (253). One may now turn again to the "imagination" of the book's title and reread it in a way that the more naïve ecocritic might consider rather sinister. Certainly Buell's, and ecocriticism's, greatest contribution to literary studies is the reminder that, in the midst of all our theory, "there is an actual nonhuman world out there" (*Future* 110). And yet Buell's emphasis on this imagination is nearly as concertedly constructivist as the poststructuralist or new historicist theory from which he takes some pains to distance himself. His title *means*, ultimately, that "Nature" is, once again, a construct. If the various naturist literary devices of defamiliarization and so on have been successful in imparting a "new-fashioned delight in the materiality of natural *things*" and in creating a new "environmental bonding" (*Environmental Imagination* 98), it is through their role in discourse, their depending "heavily on metaphor, myth, and even fantasy to put readers in touch with place" (266). And so such writings play the game of the dominant discourse (as part of discursivity itself), and yet somehow (polyphonically) tease one out of that discourse whose very *nature* it still seems to be to separate human and animal, "man" and "nature."

Moving to our contemporary social concern with environmental catastrophe, Buell sees the environmental aesthetics he has championed as instrumental in any future solutions or amelioration (3). But it seems to boil down to another "imaginative" metaphor, that of apocalypse, the "single most powerful master metaphor that the contemporary environmental imagination has at its disposal" (285). Silko's *Almanac* and Carson's *Silent Spring* get lots of play here—indeed, "Carson invented doomsday by environmental genocide" (295)—but our circumspect scholar can only conceive of such "totalizing" concepts such as "biotic community and ecosystem" not as the truths of faith that deep ecology and Michael Branch would have them, but as imaginative propaganda, as it were, "readily adaptable to apocalyptic ends" (302). Then there is the curiously muted phraseology of the following: "Carson goes so far as to suggest[!] that life without birds and trees is not worth living" (304). Carson's position here seems to be presented as an extremism hard to fathom without the supplement of Buell's notion of imaginative discourse, with the implication that much of humankind might happily go on living without such scenic accessories. I hope to eventually argue (with a bit more enthusiasm) that a life without birds is a bare life indeed.

Buell also embraces the cause of ecofeminism, praising the "gynocentric paradigm" over the "androcentric" one (25, 23) and countering the general "misapprehension that women have avoided the field of environmental writing" (26) with concerted studies of such long-neglected American women writers as Susan Cooper, Celia Thaxter, and Mary Austin. Our Thoreauvian scholar will even admit that these three authors "managed to cultivate a nonegoistic, ecocentric sensibility toward which Thoreau had to grope his way laboriously" (177). (There is some hint of gender essentialism here, however, as if such writers were more innately, more naturally attuned to nature.) Buell also refers approvingly to the recent work of Kolodny, Merchant, and Susan Griffin, though he has mixed feelings about the contemporary "reemergence of feminist neopaganism" (216). And again, Native American spirituality receives limited approval throughout.

The Environmental Imagination may be the most eloquent formulation of ecocriticism to date, a learned synthesis of mainstream (Glotfeltyan) literary ecocriticism, some remnants of deep ecology, a serving of high theory, but perhaps not much that might encourage one to go out and save the California Condor. Buell's more concerted treatments of the "animal Other" are explored in the next section, but I must remonstrate again that my relationship to the ecocriticism that climaxes in Buell is a problematic one. As I intimated in several places earlier, ecocriticism has most often entailed a discussion of place (often the author's); much like the chasm between environmentalists per se and animal rights spokespeople, there seems to be some implicit assumption that the "eco-" in ecocriticism concerns an environment as land and landscape, usually including an *erasure* of the fauna (and, to a lesser extent, the flora) of ecocriticism's own hallowed ecosphere. As an ecocritic who would concentrate on the animal and avian of our biosphere, as the logical extension of the democratization of the Other that has marked the past thirty years of humanities and cultural studies, I have rebelled already in positing a new school of zoöcriticism as response and reaction to a current ecocriticism that would flourish almost solely upon the flowers, weeds, and soil of its critical terrain.

To step back and view ecocriticism itself in its best light: we have seen that, even in its early manifestations, it hasn't been just some blithe reprivileging of nature writing. The issues under debate within this school are as politically based as its poststructuralist and new historicist predecessors; nor is it (in general) some blithe retreat from the sociopolitical (though, of course, the emphases and omissions of individual scholars are necessarily open to critique). As evident from the earlier discussion, what "Nature" is—as a quite human, and especially Western, construct—remains in great question in a debate fraught with various poststructuralist and cultural studies maneuvers, including the attribution of sexist, colonialist, and (above all) speciesist motives to even the most laudable (proto-)environmentalist writers. (Thus the tendency to deify a Thoreau or Muir is often a muted one.) Finally, how *not* to be speciesist, anthropomorphic, and homocentric is the most difficult question of all; especially given the inevitable symbiosis of ecocriticism and poststructuralism, the very possibility of transcending the species via some viable posthuman awareness that withstands the onslaught of poststructuralism itself is likewise tenuous at best. Current cultural and literary ecology, then, seems to be on a precarious perch—let's say, a perch beside a nest in a cottonwood tree. On the one side, our fledgling's fatal drop to that hard asphalt below means the death of nature, an admission of constructivist solipsism and defeat; on the other side is a flight into a clearing, into a multicolored fog or mist or rainbow? But there's the problem: we can't quite make out that fog yet, and hope it's not a retreat to some foggy mysticism, nor are we sure whether we have the wings or the will to leave the nest. In fact, would transcending the human by such a flight be too much a hubris deflation that one best not venture there? Or is the postmodern dilemma in some ways a rather smugly conservative fear of just such a venture?

The gist of the previous paragraph has been, in some ways, my own ideal of what ecocriticism's basic questions and possible responses are, or should be (if one adds the fogward venture and leap from the nest). Plenty of ecocritics *have* assumed that their job is to write about the value of nature writing or to critique literature via the (often homocentric) politics of environmentalism. And, yes, some may even resort to quaint and awkward tropic identifications with some aspect of nature, as I just did with my bird's nest analogy; others, from a more critical stance, would question the efficacy of an author who imagines himself as a bear (i.e., Momaday). As I turn now to specific theories regarding other species, I would immediately claim that to even seriously consider such an imagining signals a progress from a humanistic insularity to what might be called the posthuman.

IMAGINING THE POSTHUMAN; OR, CAN THE ECO-OTHER SPEAK?

> If, however, we and the gnat could understand each other we should learn that even the gnat swims through the air with the same pathos, and feels within itself the flying center of the world.
>
> FRIEDRICH NIETZSCHE, "On Truth and Falsity in Their Extramoral Sense"

> How do you know but ev'ry Bird that cuts the airy way,
> Is an immense world of delight, clos'd by your senses five?
>
> WILLIAM BLAKE, *The Marriage of Heaven and Hell,* in *Poetry and Prose*

Assuming Blake's utterance as an intuitive truth, and with the bird especially in mind, I have long adopted a course of reading in search of some confirmation of such a belief.[50] But like some recent ecocritics with a background in colonial discourse theory, I wondered (half-cynically), how can these poets and scholars actually speak for the Other, in this case, the nonhuman Other, without implicitly propping up their own imperialist (including anthropocentric) agendas? And like some recent ecocritics acquainted with poststructuralism, I wondered (half-despairingly), can the Real of nature even be represented in discourse, without the seemingly inevitable bevy of human constructions and projections that accompany any such linguistic enterprise?[51] In the end I was torn between my naturalist avocation and my academic training, an experiential holistic impulse to embrace the animal Other opposed by an intellectual bent to tear down all such *grands récits* and to question all surrogate god candidates for Transcendental Signifier, including "Nature."

Thus the ecoscholarship I have called to question has really been a Rorschach test of my own foibles and self-contradictions, especially my intuitive desire for a mystical holism that is continually shattered by a propensity, just as strong, to murder to dissect. And no doubt an apology is in order, too, for the ironic and homocentric hubris involved in claiming some new spot of ground (i.e., zoöcriticism) in the name of those who cannot speak, much like Spivak speaking (or not) for the subaltern or a well-to-do white feminist speaking for the poor black or Indian unwed mother. I also realize that the critical theory advocates of the human colonized of class, sex, and race may very much resent my general cross-species analogy between such groups and the animal Other, just as some socially conscious scholars have questioned the use of "genocide" and "holocaust" in some animal rightists' discussions of the human-enforced extinction of animals.[52] But to read the treatment of other species vis-à-vis current theory, as a colonization and an othering, may at least be an effective strategic step in breaking down the barriers between species.

"A viable environmental ethics must confront 'the silence of nature'—the fact that in our culture only humans have status as speaking subjects" (Manes 26). My guiding rationale for reading the texts of the following chapters as, quite often, acts of discursive colonization has been an attempt to extend Edward Said's call for "articulating those voices dominated, displaced, or silenced by the textuality of texts" ("World" 1222). Said has in mind the human colonized, of course, but the avian voices of the naturalist's museums of textuality are even more dominated, displaced, and silenced. However, any attempt to incorporate the nonhuman Other into something close to human alterity theory becomes immediately problematic if one broaches the ubiquitous postcolonial theme of the Other's potential, or need, for *resistance*, for speaking back. Obviously (assuming for now that discourse = human language), a discursive counternarrative of resistance on the part of birds themselves is a ridiculous notion, unless one invokes some nightmare from Alfred Hitchcock, although the notion of a transspecies, transsemiotic discursivity remains an intriguing thought and a potentiality that is addressed in the final chapters. We return, then, to environmentalists or ecocritics who, again, must provide a surrogate defense, like Third World academics attempting to speak for the subaltern. Karla Armbruster offers a precedent, at least, in noting that "humans who speak for" the nonhuman Other are similar to feminist critics and others, in that they are at least "part of a larger group," in this case, nature itself (220). As I have suggested, after the decentering of (human) race, class, and gender, ecocriticism's decentering of the human per se as the sole viable site of subjectivity is the next logical step in a general theory of alterity.

And so, as will be very evident in my eventual treatment of the poets, such a critique must be applicable to even those quite sympathetic toward their subject matter, who (like me) would speak *for* the animal Other. Thus Armbruster's analysis of television nature documentaries underlines how problematic it is to speak for nature, and specifically animals.[53] Such problems include a "monolithic" focus on one species that misrepresents and downplays the larger ecological context and the schism between human and nature created by displaying animals and landscapes sans humans: this "distancing" actually allows human viewers to detach themselves from any real concern for the documentary's subject matter (221) and to remain ultimately alienated from the natural world. (The people who do occasionally show up in such programs are usually "savages," of course, or criminal poachers, thus still allowing the viewer an us-them splitting and a denial of responsibility [229–30, 225].) Some programs, moreover, stress the human lesson to be learned or the human use to be enjoyed from the animals or their life histories, exemplifying an "obsessive focus on what humans can gain from nature" (227). Most apropos of my project, Armbruster also finds many of the anthropomorphic fancies in which such documentaries indulge (e.g., an animal going out on a date) to be ethically criminal, a "colonizing move of turning what was *other* into the *same*" (230–31; emphases added). Whether the medium be cinematic or literary discourse (as my subsequent chapters amply demonstrate), speaking for the animal Other is a problematic enterprise.

One is tempted to turn to writers relatively unaffected by the "linguistic idealism" (as Gare calls it [109]) of humanities academia, to those who have a more obvious philosophical and political concern for the rights of animals themselves. Such a consideration is all the more important given ecocriticism's relative disregard of this eco region of study. The current animal rights movement received its first great impetus with Peter Singer's *Animal Liberation* (1975), which popularized the concept of speciesism as "a prejudice or attitude of bias toward the interests of members of one's own species and against those of members of other species"; it is analogous, moreover, to racism and sexism and thus another shameful example of human "tyranny" and injustice, "prejudice and discrimination" (7, vii, x). However, Singer's call for an end to their "oppression and exploitation" (viii) is based on thoroughly utilitarian reasons (i.e., happiness equals the absence of pain). Because we can easily infer that "animals can feel pain" (17), such practices as animal experimentation and factory farming must end, because beings who "are similar" in their capacity to feel "have a similar right to life" (21). But although his first chapter is titled "All Animals Are Equal," Singer *won't* claim (in contrast to, say, Naess or Sessions) that "all lives are of equal worth" (23); a pig, he is *almost* sure, can suffer much more than an ant and thus deserves greater consideration. In sum, his argument is entirely based on "minimizing suffering alone" (24), allowing for a hierarchy of sensitivity to pain arrived at solely by inference.

Singer's main subjects, animal experimentation and factory farms,[54] are chosen because of the sheer number of animals and the sheer quantity of suffering involved; the "most practical and effective step" in combating these practices, and speciesism in general, is vegetarianism and a "boycott of the produce of agribusiness cruelty" (173, 246). But to buttress such a proposal, Singer must counter the possibility that plants may "suffer," too; however, he finds "no reliable evidence" for this possibility (262). To the objection that humankind is genetically omnivorous, he poisons the well by claiming that any such argument is just an excuse to eat meat (172)! Singer also has little time for people like St. Francis who would see life and divinity in everything, "not only sentient creatures." In an ad hominem attack, he can only equate this man's ecstatic visions with those of someone high on drugs (215). Tellingly, he also argues that a "stone does not have interests because it cannot suffer" (9), establishing a clear tension between his brand of animal rights and the more all-embracing philosophy of deep ecology, for whom St. Francis is a patron saint.

Singer's later chapters on the history and continuing domination of the speciesist worldview are convincing, as he traces its Western origins in Greek and Old Testament thought, in Christianity's privileging of humankind as uniquely blessed with an "immortal soul" (208), through Renaissance humanism and Descartes' view of animals as "unconscious automata" (10, 218), and to nineteenth-century Darwinism, which would place "Man" at the apex of evolution (224).[55] Even today, Singer wrote (in 1975), fairy tales, children's books, and television condition us to be speciesist, and current animal welfare societies have been, by and large, co-opted by big business and scientific researchers (236–39). One of Singer's most seminal points is that speciesism involves language itself—witness "humane," "animal," "beast," and "pest" (xiii, 248, 260)—that the evolution of language itself been complicit in and instrumental in fostering an ideology of speciesism.

But a few more quibbles with Mr. Singer. After arguing that humans have exaggerated other animals' "savagery" (e.g., the wolf), he goes on to defend wolves with quite *speciesist* values: they are really "highly social" beings, "faithful" to their "spouse," "loyal," fair, and merciful (248). Maybe this is how some men want their wife to be, but it's hardly an acceptably standard set of guidelines for other species. His own privileging of humans includes the huge assumption that humans have free will (and thus can make moral decisions), whereas other animals can't; maybe other animals' pain is a valid inference, but the assumption of their complete lack of choice (or better yet, humans' free will itself) is a great leap, and very speciesist. Singer even ponders the possibility of eliminating "carnivorous species" but immediately rejects it (252). Yet even to bring up such a question reveals a relative ignorance of ecological interrelationships.

As for Singer's contention that his appeal "to [human] reason" throughout the book is "more universal" than any appeal to (human) emotion (270), one might argue with this on several grounds. First, "reason over emotion" is at last a claim that humans are *above* other species (we are rational; animals can merely emote and feel pain). Second, he has already pointed out how fallacious (and emotionally biased) the entire project of speciesism has been, and yet it has been a "success" as a dominant worldview; ergo, "man" is not such a rational animal either. Third, Singer's entire utilitarian, pleasure-and-pain argument is based on inference, one of the weakest, most tenuous exercises of human reason, anyway. Fourth, as hinted at earlier, Singer has little time for any environmental issue that doesn't involve a vast amount of pain for a great number of animals (the Benthamite influence). He even blames the media for giving too much attention to "threats to endangered species" (239)—not enough pain to too few individuals, one assumes. And he speaks of the environment as a different issue altogether that the media has privileged above the rights of animals (245–46). The last few pages of *Animal Liberation* do attempt a rapprochement with the environmental movement of the day (272–73), but Singer's general emphasis is too one-sided to win a great regard from those who would deem a whooping crane as worthy as a hog or an outcrop of igneous rocks as worthy as a university professor.

A response to and continuation of Singer's controversial stance, Tom

Regan's *The Case for Animal Rights* (1983) may well be the most elaborate and traditionally philosophical defense of animal rights to date. The book's more than four hundred pages are a compendium of close critiques of every position on the subject that Regan can imagine, from Aristotle, Descartes, and Kant to John Rawls and Singer. Descartes' notion of animals as machines is rebutted with a "cumulative" set of evidence and inferences that animals do possess consciousness (25–30). However, the author limits this ability (usually) to "mammalian animals," as beings "most . . . like us" (33). Regan then argues at length that mammals, at least, have their own desires, intentions, concepts, and beliefs. It follows, then, that these species have autonomous self-interests like ours that deserve respect; indeed, "we have more than ample reason to deny that human and animal welfare differ in kind" (119). He then distinguishes legal from moral rights (the former socially acquired, the latter "universal"), and allows "higher" animals the latter, the "moral right of *moral patients* to respectful treatment" (267, 279), including the "right not to be harmed" (329). This includes, à la Singer, the right not to be eaten, the right not to be owned as property (though qualified), the right not to be hunted, and the right not to be used for scientific research (e.g., 330–31, 347–49, 353–59, 363–98).

A problem arises with this last right: What about experimentation on nonmammalians (e.g., frogs and birds) that he hasn't really included under the "consciousness" rubric? Regan's best answer is that it is "possible[!]" that they may be conscious, so he's against it; moreover, it may lead to an insouciance regarding harming *mammals* (366–68). In the end, the animal rights views of both Singer and Regan are very mammalocentric, privileging those species most closely related to the authors' own species.[56] Aside from the poultry industry, birds get rare mention by either author; the avian remains a problem or border creature once again, a little more advanced than a reptile, maybe, but not quite as good as a mammal.

Endangered species also get short shrift. One animal individual has the same rights as any other; species are nothing special, and concerns for rare species may actually be a distraction to animal rights in general (359–61). Having little idea of the importance of species diversity, Regan also has little time for the "holistic or systems approach" of deep ecologists and environmentalists in general; the "rights view rejects" the notion of a "biotic community," although it may still turn out that animal rights activists and environmentalists may some day "be in harmony" (396). (Not as long as the main spokespeople for animal rights adhere to a rather dated, legalistic notion of individual rights and are blind to eco-interdependence, I would think.)

It would appear that Regan's concern for the harm to the individual isn't that far from Singer's utilitarianism.[57] Although his book is arranged as a dense series of logical syllogisms and rebuttals, the author comes to the same general conclusions as the less weighty Singer does, at least in terms of praxis: he is against animal farming and for vegetarianism, and he has a relative unconcern for endangered species and the environment itself. Moreover, Singer's reliance on inference is also Regan's method; indeed, rather than claiming a completely logical approach, Regan admits that an argument's appeal to our common sense and its "conformity with our intuitions" (148) are crucial components of any ethical conclusion. But apparently Regan's intuitions can't go beyond the mammalian order. Moreover, his constant use of the term "moral patients" for other mammals also seems an ill-chosen, paternalistic phrase. Finally, humans do have more intrinsic worth, after all, given their greater "opportunities for satisfaction" (324); thus does a still quite anthropocentric qualitative hedonism remain the rule of the day for the main spokespeople of animal rights.

Much more complex in its animal rights arguments is *The Lives of Animals*. J. M. Coetzee's 1997–98 Tanner Lectures at Princeton is actually a metafictional novella, that is, the novelist Coetzee's lecture about a fictionalized novelist (Elizabeth Costello) giving two lectures on animal rights. Elizabeth is a "feeler," not a thinker, and thus Coetzee's(?) argument for animal rights differs profoundly from those of Singer and Regan. In addition to the problem of such a character arguing against Western rationalism largely through that very tradition (she admits she's not very good at it [22, 26]), she herself is "old," "tired" (18), and just not very good with people; she often responds to her opponents' objections with an exasperated (and apparently sincere) "I don't know" (e.g., 45). As a result, she hardly comes off as the self-assured hero of the story, and even her most eloquent statements are difficult to read as Coetzee's own views—as he intended it, no doubt.

The novella's tension centers on her hosts' sheer incomprehension at Elizabeth's vegetarianism and her arguments for her choice, especially her comparison of animal cruelty to the Holocaust (19–22). Most fascinating are her diatribes against reason, which she sees as just one, very specialized human faculty that has been elevated to godhood as a universal principle (23–26).

Her recounting of Köhler's experiments on apes is an amazing example of how humans have projected their own emphasis on instrumentalist problem solving on other species whose "thought" processes are likely far different (27–30). Elizabeth's claim that she can "think" her "way into the life of a bat" and feel its "*joy*" is less satisfactory *from a rationalist's point of view,*[58] but the poet in her (and Coetzee?) has come out: animals experience a joy and "embodiedness" that humans have repressed in their journey to rationalism (33). But people today can still *feel* such things: "There are no bounds to the sympathetic imagination" (35).

Day one of the novella ends with this strange confession: Elizabeth refuses to eat meat, "to save" her "soul" (43), a quite problematic admission, to be sure. (That is, is this some metaphysical soul that makes humans superior to other animals?) The second day of Elizabeth's visit concludes with a debate in which her opponent makes three points: (1) the animal rights movement is a specifically "recent" and "Western crusade," the values of which aren't accepted by many other cultures; (2) animals have no legal or even ethical right not to be killed, in part because they have no comprehension of death; (3) animal lovers are themselves motivated by "abstract" ideals and usually have little experience living with actual animals (60–64). To the first, Elizabeth replies that kindness toward animals is also "natural" to children and many earlier cultures (61). As for rights, this is a totally homocentric concept, as is the notion that other animals are "imbeciles" and unconscious enough to qualify as experimental subjects (62). Those who believe that animals have no notion of death have never "held in [their] hands an animal fighting for its life" (65), an experiential, concrete appeal that apparently serves to counter her opposition's last argument, too.

After this final debate, her son drives her to the airport. As she tries to explain to him that animal abuse is a "crime of stupefying proportions," she begins to cry, and he consoles her: "There, there. It will soon be over" (69). We are left wondering, given the fictional framing, whether he means that such cruelty will soon come to an end (and is humoring her?), or, more likely, and more pathetically, whether her impending death will end her own suffering and outrage.

In spite of Elizabeth's eloquent reasons against reason, the question remains regarding the efficacy of our species' ability to "think . . . into the life of a bat." Thus her opponents' best argument still stands: "There is no position outside of reason where you can stand and lecture about reason and pass judgment on reason" (48). What about a critique via emotion and poetry, then? When asked whether lectures on poetry (and presumably the poetic art itself) can "close down the slaughterhouses," Elizabeth can only answer "No" (58).

Others answer, at least tentatively, yes, including Lutwack and Vizenor and as I do in this chapter's conclusion. Buell, too, allows that literature can effect a change for the better in eco-awareness, in part through cross-species empathy. For my purposes, Buell's most important myth of the environmental imaginary entails what he calls "nature's personhood," the "ascription of something like[!] human subjectiveness to the nonhuman world" (*Environmental Imagination* 180, 143). To hearken back to this section's initial epigraph of Nietzsche's gnat's point of view, Buell likewise asks, "What happens when we reread Euro-American literature with biota rather than homo sapiens as our central concern?" (22). Through naturist writing, at least, a change of consciousness might occur: "If like Thoreau one imagines animals as neighbors; if like Muir or traditional Native Americans one imagines life-forms as plant people, sun youths, or grandmother spiders, then the killing of flies becomes as objectionable as the killing of humans" (303). While Gary Snyder and Barry Lopez represent, in some ways, a reaffirmation of a mother nature, including animal nature, whose "personification still tugs at the western sensibility" (214–15), this move has, of course, its high-canonical antecedents. *Moby-Dick*, for one, may be the best nineteenth-century American example of "making a nonhuman creature a plausible major character" (4), and Thoreau's pond is an "evocation of a nonhuman entity as a major presence, superior to any human being in the text," an "extraordinary event in the premodern American literary canon" (209).

But Buell anticipates my own suspicions that something went awry between Romanticism's esteem for Nature and the late twentieth-century revival of that good Mother. The "kinship between human and nonhuman" had "withered" in the late nineteenth century, and "modernism announced its death" (180). And so, besides Melville and Thoreau, Buell must go back to British Romanticism as the most laudable naturist forebears, touching on Thomson's *Seasons*, Coleridge's *Rime*, and William Blake's "The Fly" (184–85). Buell also tackles the problem of anthropomorphism in these poets, noting, in their defense, their real concern for such overpersonification, evident in Wordsworth's "Preface" and in Ruskin's very conception of the "pathetic fallacy" (188). Besides, nineteenth-century naturalists themselves were frequently guilty of blatant anthropomorphism, leading at last to the rage for animal fiction at the turn of the century. But this literary fad was not entirely a bad thing, according to Buell, for "the practice of representing reality from the animal's perspective tended" to reduce the gap between human and nonhuman (195–96).

But the best contemporary naturist works go much further, doing their best to take the human out of the equation, in their (sometime) "refusal to imagine nature existing for human benefit or yielding a moral for human consumption" (205). The apparently eternal "myth of kinship" between human and nonhuman has experienced a revival, then, in part through the science of ecology (200) and in part through the genre of writing for which Buell has proselytized throughout his book. In fact, such a feeling of transspecies interconnection may even serve some archetypal need. The return of Mother Nature via James Lovelock's "Gaia" and the "upsurgence" of feminist neopaganism are "contemporary signs that the idea of an earth-humanity continuum of more than a material sort may be unsuppressible, that people cannot do without the idea of a 'living earth,' and that humanity is perhaps better off accepting it" (217).[59]

Indeed, in the face of scientific and poststructuralist scorn for such notions, "the myth of human-nonhuman kinship has thrived, not withered, in the face of epistemological doubt about where humans stand in relation to the world" (203). True or not, such faith, such an act of imagination, is the best means for arriving at an environmental consciousness and activism: "Nothing dramatizes biotic egalitarianism so poignantly as the myth of the personhood of nonhuman beings" (304). But then Buell reinforces a homocentric attitude when he claims that such a consciousness will at last help humans treat each other better (though the sentence itself is wonderful in its rhetoric): "Who is more likely to treat *other people* like machines, a person who has trained herself to feel that plants and animals are fellow beings or a person who looks at them as convenient resources?" (217; emphasis added). Buell concludes that the pathetic fallacy, myth or no, may be a pretty good thing from the standpoint of ethics and praxis, whatever its philosophical limitations as myth and imaginative construction: "To ban the pathetic fallacy—were such a thing possible—would be worse than to permit its unavoidable excesses" (218).

Buell's animal discussions touch specifically on birds at one point. As part of his argument that "literature functions as science's less systematic but more versatile component" (94), he asserts that the writer (and reader) of naturist writings should be well-versed enough in natural science to know a hawk from, to misquote Shakespeare, an owl: "If environmental nonfiction shows itself ignorant of the known facts of nature, it does so at [its] peril." Such a background is even a great aid in reading fiction and poetry, according to Buell; for example, a knowledge of the habits and song of the hermit thrush is important in an understanding of Whitman's "lilacs" poem. To the question, "Must we study Roger Torrey *[sic]* Peterson's bird books in order to study literature?" Buell replies, yes, "that would be a very good thing indeed," though he acknowledges that he doesn't "believe that the poet's or essayist's highest calling has ever been to teach ornithology" (97).[60]

Seminal as much of *The Environmental Imagination* is, Buell's relative canonical conservatism may rely too much on a notion of polyphony that grants Western naturist texts greater disruptive power than they actually possess, or ignores the intrinsic polyphony of *all* textuality, pro-nature or not. (But no doubt some version of polysemic "insurgence" on the part of the textual bird, as it were, will likely be part of my own angle regarding ornithic imagery and tropes.) His privileging of "imagination" seems too great a concession to his ideological opposition. This reader, at least, comes away from Buell's text unconvinced that nature, place, and especially other species have been adequately redeemed from their textual or constructivist underpinnings that Buell so frequently acknowledges; thus recent ecological and animal rights movements are, for better or worse, revivals of a myth, revisions of an ideology that either flows from some history-of-ideas evolution or issues from some archetypal, very human need. Either way, Buell's move to the Real or "extrospective" seems insufficient, yet one more example of the theoretical move to embrace the natural or animal Other that falls upon the thorns of its complicity within the dominant critical methodology. And so the following call to action returns praxis to the thoroughly discursive realm, however "mind-haunting": "The question is whether it [environmental apocalypticism] will rise to the occasion. As ecocatastrophe becomes an increasingly greater possibility, so will the occasions for environmental apocalyptic expression and the likelihood that it will suffuse essay, fiction, film, sculpture, painting, theater, and dance in unprecedentedly powerful, mind-haunting ways. Can our imaginations of apocalypse actually forestall it, as our fears of nuclear holocaust so far have?" (308).

But the sheer dazzling comprehensiveness of Buell's argument for his naturist genre theory cannot be taken lightly. Above all, his supporting correlatives of self-"relinquishment" and "nature's personhood" are welcome weapons against the Western self of egoism and homocentrism that has repressed for centuries the vital relationships between humankind and nature, between *Homo sapiens* and the other species inhabiting the planet. But Buell's nature, after all, is posited as a construct in quotation marks, ultimately an incomplete relinquishment, it would appear, of the intellectual goings-on in Paris and at Yale, milieus as "cloistral" and "urbanized" (to recall epithets from Buell's own critique of academia) as one can *imagine.*

One of the earliest ventures (if not the first) into a biological reading of literature, Joseph Meeker's *The Comedy of Survival,*[61] anticipates much of the ecocritical reevaluations of the canon that culminate in Buell, yet evidences a maverick streak that will lead us back to Paul Shepard. Like Shepard's, Meeker's theory is based largely on humankind's relationship to other species, emphasizing the animal (and our animal nature), both "playful" and "wild," qualities crucial to the ecohealth of our species, our planet, and our literature. The book's central thesis is that the tragic genre (and related worldview) is *bad,* that is, ecologically unhealthy. Literary comedy, because it is more conducive to our species' "survival and well-being" (7), is good, as is its behavioral correlative, play. (Play, furthermore, is more "universal" to animal behavior in general [9–11, 15].)[62] Comedy is adaptive, working toward a "recovery" of social and natural "equilibrium" (16). Tragedy is Western literature and culture gone awry, from the Greeks on, representative of a homocentric domination of nature, an exaggerated emphasis on the egocentric individual, and a polarized metaphysics and morality that has led only to environmental ruin (e.g., 14, 23–24, 30, 36).[63] But the tragic worldview is on the wane, according to Meeker, and good riddance; the comedic has been on the rise since the Renaissance, apparently (31, 37), as is evident in *Hamlet,* in which the title character plays a comic game in a tragic literary universe, a game of wit, adaptation, and survival in a dangerous world of either/or moral absolutes (31–32, 37–47). Biologically speaking, Hamlet's delay exemplifies the "redirection of aggression" common to many animal species, following an innate directive, as Meeker would have it, not to kill their own (40–42). (Apparently, good, playful animals don't have Oedipal complexes or bipolar disorders.)

The superiority of the comic view is developed in Meeker's dichotomy between the "pastoral" and the "picaresque." The former is an illusory "escape," the latter, realistic adaptation. Pastoralism is a nostalgic retreat to the Garden of Eden and agrarianism (51) and, like tragedy, leads to pathos, even self-pity, as the pastoralist realizes that his or her escape is an illusion and ends in "final despair" (71). (But is this always true, or even the rule, in the pastoral literary genre in general?) For the picaresque hero, on the other hand, nature, and human society, is "not a garden, but a wilderness": it is an amoral landscape with no polarized praise or blame possible, an "infinite game" with no possibility of winning but myriad in its possibilities for adaptation, role-playing, and sheer animal cunning (59). Thus Meeker expresses the comic-picaresque theme of *Catch-22* as follows: "Adapt to circumstances and take evasive action" (61). The message for humankind today is clear: we should be picaresque heroes, living life as "infinite play, with no hope of winning much, but [with] endless enthusiasm for keeping the play alive" (73).

Meeker even speculates on the emergence of a "new story" for Western culture, toward which recent findings in evolutionary psychology and ethology have made crucial contributions in closing the gap between human and nonhuman cognition and instinct (75–77, 85–87). And toward which Meeker offers his (hardly original) notion of play as the instinct perhaps most universal to (at least) birds and mammals, including humans. An obvious critique here, though: the need for adaptive play seems to be *most* required in the amoral landscape of the (post)modern era, but to find the ethical response to such a time in the "timeless" instincts of animal behavior seems, finally, a strangely backward move in this context. One would think that this coming to the fore of more adaptive literature would have led to a general improvement in ecohealth, when obviously the opposite has been the case.

In Meeker's final chapter, we are all called to "cosmic" play once more. Even the simple play of phatic conversation may be therapeutic enough; it's like the play of birds' songs, after all, which say, "I'm here; where are you?[!]" (108). (I might swear, in my more enthusiastically empathetic moments, that a red-eyed vireo does say this, but not cardinals, or Western Meadowlarks, or most other songsters.) Seriously, whether all or any bird songs can be so translated is indicative of the main problem that I have with Meeker's book. While he refers or defers to the science of ethology at several points, his examples of animal behavior are inevitably idealized, as if all nonhuman species are instinctively wise players in the Divine Comedy of the cosmos.

Indeed, Meeker can criticize pastoralism as an ideology of false perfection, and yet his own deployment of play and instinct is, at times, an idealization that is itself pretty hard to take.[64] But it is still important to note that this first work, perhaps, of ecocriticism deals with other species in a much more earnest manner than most later ecocritical pronouncements.

Meeker's scorn for the pastoral and privileging of the wild points to his affinity with that champion of hunter-gatherers, Paul Shepard, a friend whom he quotes often. For both authors, humankind's agricultural stage was an evolutionary period to be lamented, and Meeker also finds it sad that "no pastoral poet ever gets nostalgic thinking about Paleolithic hunters" (57). But at least Paul Shepard does. Shepard might best be labeled an evolutionary primitivist, in the sense that he believes that humankind's primate and hunter-gatherer heritage has determined much of our current psychology and culture. In the coevolutionary journey, the animal Others have played a pervasive role in this evolution, not only as fellow "counterplayers" in the ancient "game" of hunter and hunted (81–82), but also in the development of our very language and cognition and our music, dance, and ritual. For starters, it has always been a very *visceral* (including gastronomical) interspecies relationship: "Our species . . . emerged in watching the Others, participating in their world by eating and being eaten by them" (11). But animals have also fashioned our mental development, and the child today still learns to name and classify primarily through animals, those "prototypes of categories" (48); such animal categorization, indeed, was "the beginning of language itself" (54). (A bold claim, no doubt, but supported by the centrality of children's animal games in their development of signs and metaphors.)[65]

Human constructs of sociality also evolved from our primate observations of other species' interactions; later, animals then became co-opted metaphors for rationalizing human social hierarchies. Furthermore, humankind's psychosocial rites of passage find their mirror in the physical metamorphoses of animals (yes, Shepard refers us to Kafka here); the hibernating bear and the tadpole and frog, for example, are at last "bearers of our souls across boundaries and borders" (117–26). Also significant, but more deplorable in Shepard's general hunter-gatherer view of things, are the ubiquitous figures of the cow and dog; domesticated animals of the later agricultural (or pastoral) period of humankind's evolution are a devolution of sorts (243–50), and the modern practice of keeping pets is sheer slavery (267), the pets themselves "ecological wrecks" (250). The domestication of horses, moreover, was the greatest (d)evolutionary tragedy in history, allowing for aeons of rapid human conquest and imperialism (250–58). In the historical period, and in contrast to humankind's early polytheistic embracing of the "many," Christianity and monotheism in general have also done us a disservice in casting animals out of theology; the Christian myths of Eden and the Ark (and its modern counterpart, the zoo) are really acts of estrangement from our natural and animal natures,[66] to the detriment, obviously, of the animal Other and our own psychic health. "The loss of numen or spirit . . . in animals" is "the great modern defeat" (328), and this includes our "loss of sensitivity to birds" (198).[67] As a current cultural example, one need only point to the devolution of the eagle from a Native spirit mediating earth and sky to a two-dimensional iconic signifier of U.S. nationalism as a sad reflection of this "great modern defeat."[68] A good part of this defeat is the anthropocentrism inherent in both traditional Christian cosmology and the dernier cri of postmodernist theory: "My experience tells me that neither the creationists nor the postmodern critics are right, one thinking that the world was made for us and the other that it is made by us. A better vision of the animals is that we are one among them" (11–12).

Finally, Shepard accepts, grudgingly, the animal rights concerns of Regan et al. for the plight of domesticated animals raised for food. But the public's misguided concern for *wild* animals is based on a false privileging of the individual animal, whose lamentable death is really our own individual fear of death(?), and an ignorant disregard for the ecosystem (304–15): in sum, it's "bad ecology" (313).[69] "Wild animals," Shepard concludes, "do not have rights" (308), because "rights," as a term, is a human social and legal construct, after all: "Human political rights are meaningless as interspecial relationships" (320). Besides—and here Shepard grabs for the obvious rebuttal—"what about the predator's right to a meal?" (309). (Shepard also anticipates my objection in noting that Regan and his ilk inevitably end up extending greater rights to dogs than to locusts, as species more similar to or having greater value to humans [310].) Death is natural to the ecocycle of life, and vegetarianism is really a "state of beatific mastication" that humankind has evolved beyond "six million years ago" in becoming omnivores (315). In short, Shepard views the animal rights movement as "disastrous" in "articulating the relationship of our species to others" (304).

Thus does Shepard propose a rather speculative view of evolutionary science against what must be considered the animal rights mainstream. At its worst, the book does read at times as if it had been written by a triumvirate of Robert Bly, Joseph Campbell, and some eccentric anthropologist-biologist, all three half-dressed in bear furs, dancing around a fire, bloody spears in their slightly unsteady, book-weary hands. But one may yet accept a great deal of Shepard's specifics without his yearning for the Pleistocene and his worship of the hunt.[70] At its best, *The Others* provides a fascinating theory (and welcome emphasis) on the roles of the animal Others in the cultural artifacts of humankind, a new book in which to read the often seemingly trite and stock animal metaphors that pervade our literature, and life. Combined with Gerald Vizenor's distinction between animal metaphors and similes, Shepard's theories may offer one viable means of transcending the species.

I end with a theorist of Native American blood as a final attempt to fly with something more than the downward wings of poststructuralist skepticism. Vizenor's essay on animal tropes in literature, "Literary Animals," makes several keen distinctions that may provide a feasible way out of a blanket condemnation of all such tropes as merely anthropomorphic constructs, and therefore necessarily co-opting and othering. But like much of Vizenor's nonfiction prose, the essay is a tough read for those accustomed to sequential argumentation. Instead of a straight line of transitionally linked paragraphs, "Literary Animals" is rather like a series of circles that return again and again to such refrains as "animal [or 'creature'] presence," "native survivance," and "natural reason," the meaning of each becoming clearer with each return, as if the essay itself were a chimney swift making a multitude of swerving flights around the same building. (Indeed, the essay is very like the disjointed, polyphonic naturist writing that Buell loves.) Most crucially, the ideals of "natural reason" and "native survivance" in Native literatures are repeatedly juxtaposed with the literature and worldview of Western "dominance," the former mode a "union of nature and language, not a separation" (121), the latter, a monotheistic, speciesist, causality-based bad translation of such a union, resulting in a "separation" of human reason and animal nature (125, 134).[71] Hence the West's literary animals are usually anthropomorphic "simulations, the mere poses of nature" (131).

Certainly, all "nature is a trope," Vizenor acknowledges, but language itself can create "one of the real environments" for the kind of "authored animals" that he has in mind (126, 133). Some literary animals, for instance, are inordinately "memorable . . . with their own manners, consciousness, and points of view" (127).[72] Although these can be found even in the literature of dominance—(e.g., Jack London's Buck), Vizenor associates them more naturally with Native American literature. Here both authors and their animal creations are thus "creature presence[s]" and "resistance[s] in the literature of survivance," fraught with a "native sense of presence" that is especially evident in the novels of Momaday, Silko, and Louise Erdrich. Momaday's bear, in particular, becomes a "presence and transcendence at the same time"; indeed, Momaday turns into "a bear in his own stories" (127–28, 132, 139, 136, 137).[73]

Finally, Vizenor presents his own versions of metaphor and simile as another way of contrasting Native and dominant modes of animal representation.[74] Native metaphoric animals, those "traces" of "survivance," are tropes "closer to nature and animal consciousness than a literal simile" and create that union of animal nature and human language in which the "authors are animals, the readers are animals, [and] the animals are [often] humans" (141–42). In contrast, (Western) "simile animals" are straightforward anthropomorphic projections, merely "caricatures in literature" (133), symptomatic of "speciesism and comparable to manifest manners and the monotheistic separation of animals and humans" (136).[75] Thus the Native or animal metaphor is a joining, a *transspecies crossing*; the simile, on the other hand, is a "disseverance" of humankind from its natural (and indigenous) "horizon" (142).

The obvious problem with Vizenor's reading is how to ascertain the truly metaphorical and the mere simile literary animal without appealing to some new canon of Native American authors who are truly able to become bears, coyotes, or eagles in their narratives and poetry. Vizenor at least intimates that Western authors could succeed at cross-species metaphor, and the Native succumb to othering simile. One might then extend Vizenor's apparati to Anglo-American literature and ask whether Robinson Jeffers's "Hurt Hawk" is a more successful union of language and animal than Tennyson's "The Eagle." Do D. H. Lawrence's "Snake" and Eberhart's "The Groundhog" somehow interject a trace of animal consciousness that transcends the homocentric concerns of their authors?[76] By allowing such questions, Vizenor's "postindian" ruminations might thereby prove seminal in a new theory of representation of the posthuman, of transspecies intersubjectivity.

Despite the many connections made between the various eco and animal texts encountered, any aspiration to a full integration of these works has long fallen by the wayside. As I indicated earlier, cacophony is the rule of the day. Indeed, the scholar of an ecological or animal rights bent must perforce act like SueEllen Campbell's scavenging metaphor of a magpie, lining one's bulky, almost inchoate nest from an eclectic scrap heap of gaudy trinkets and hidden gems (13). One might play at least with labels and dub several of the figures in question "paleo-hunters" (Shepard, Meeker, Aldo Leopold, and many deep ecologists). Some, adapting Worster's terminology, are earnest "pastoral Arcadians" (e.g., a good deal of recent environmentalism issuing from Gilbert White and Thoreau). Those who most vehemently proclaim a species egalitarianism I might call "radical-egals" (e.g., Naess, Devall and Sessions, and Gary Snyder). There is also a school of (utilitarian, for the most part) animal rights philosophers who might be dubbed "utilivegans" (i.e., Singer and Regan). Last but hardly least, and most problematic and provocative, are those I would diagnose as victims of "careful constructivitis"—and here, I plead *mea culpa*—those suffering from the current intellectual deconstructivism of the age, who must place all matters of nature under the heady banners of relativist textual-linguisticism, psychologism, and social constructivism, who try to wallow their way, like tadpoles, out of (or rather don't, and relish?) their own intellectual-miasmal mud.

My own stance certainly embraces many of the ideas presented here, including biospheric relatedness, eco-egalitarianism, and the denial or transcendence of the Western deification of the human self or individual. This last rejection, to repeat one of my refrains, is an extension of the critically reputable poststructuralist decentering of the entire Western agenda, and yet, as conceptualized by more radical ecoscholars—and, as I will eventually claim, implicit in Native American worldviews—it is also a decentering of the entire philosophical Weltanschauung that has resulted in the poststructuralist dilemma that we in the humanities currently face. In terms of my ecological subject matter, I also willingly embrace the genre reprivileging of Buell and company and, going further than some, would deem bird guides just as worthy of study (in a cultural studies sense) as the poems of Wordsworth or Hopkins. Moreover, recent nonmainstream Native American writing will serve as the climax of this study, in the hope that the Native American worldview(s) may well provide me with the best, uh, moccasins with which to take one last Johnsonian kick at the ideational stone of Bishop Berkeley's now ascendant progeny.

But I also sense, as I indicated earlier, that Buell sees a Native American approach per se, in spite of his various appreciative readings thereof, as perhaps a retreat and dead end.[77] He considers recent New Age impulses to recuperate that view, and, say, the Wiccan view, and most feeling-based deep ecology views as mere symptoms of the imaginary that is his subject than as viable contributions to a truly new synthesis (however syncretic) of the archaic and the Romantic and the Native and the woman and the animal. My own take on the contemporary cultural climate is that such a grassroots synthesis is indeed taking place. A new, greater concern for the plight, the very lives, of the dolphin, whale, and wolf is certainly evident in the collective consciousness. (I'm even tempted to read the equally popular fascination with extraterrestrial contact and computer intelligence as symptomatic of the same general movement toward the cross-species Other.)[78] Though one might easily deconstruct or psychoanalyze the infatuation of the masses with such books as *Your Dog and His Dreams*, one can't deny, following Buell himself, the renaissance of such interspecies concerns in the Zeitgeist. The ecocritic Glen A. Love expresses this renaissance more generally, more environmentally: "Why does nature writing, literature of place, regional writing, poetry of nature, flourish now—even as it is ignored or denigrated by most contemporary criticism?" (237). But much of this recent poetry of nature, for instance, more specifically expresses a new infatuation and obsession with animals, to the point that, at last, there must be a place in the so-called humanities for the serendipitously intuitive notion of interspeciality or transspecies intersubjectivity, a reaching out, a "bridging" of the "species gap," as Linda Hogan puts it.[79] One also discerns in such works the collateral need to defend animals in their own right, as victims of speciesism, however anthropomorphically loaded the term "right" is.

This new consciousness I speak of is most evident in recent ecofeminist texts (most specifically in Native women writers). Linda Hogan and the other editors of *Intimate Nature* (1998), noting the connection of female and animal in Jung's concept of the anima, assert that both Others "have existed together in the interior world of the soul," and "like animals," women "have . . . often been cherished at the same time" that they "have been hated." But there is hope for the future in this very connection, because women's "respect for feeling and empathy" and their "intimate bonds of connection" with both other species and their "own bodies" offer a way out of the patriarchal human/animal binary. Through such an intimate connection with nature, one may "know the animal other as worthy, alive, and even as a beloved peer" (Hogan, Metzger, and Peterson xi, xiii, xiv). The willing embrace here of an essentialist equation of the female with greater intuitive empathy would trouble even many feminists, but the essays in *Intimate Nature* are the proof, offering a far greater (however emotional) "bridge" to other animals than do the often abstract ruminations of Kroeber or Meeker. Appropriate to this goal of intimacy with nature, the genres of preference in ecofeminism are personal, creative, even poetic essays and poems. To have begun this chapter with Wordsworth and Harjo, then, was not merely for rhetorical effect; perhaps that unique language form that is poetry, as some scholars have suggested, has particular merits (and comparable special dangers, no doubt) in allowing the eco-Other to speak.

A DEFENSE OF POETRY

> The poetry of earth is never dead.
>
> —JOHN KEATS, "On the Grasshopper and Cricket," in *Complete Poems*

> Environmentality worthy of the name means letting the goldfinch be, not petrifying it into the kind of "golden" bird the Yeatsian speaker imagines as his immortal body in "Sailing to Byzantium."
>
> —LAWRENCE BUELL, *The Future of Environmental Criticism*

As coda to this chapter, I must address in more detail my choice of the poetry genre as this book's main literary subject, given ecocriticism's dominant propensity, to date, to champion prose nature writing. For one thing, the nonfiction naturist writing privileged by Buell and others, as Dana Phillips has pointed out, is itself, as linguistic discourse, representationally problematic in a way that Buell fails fully to acknowledge. If the pictures in a bird guide can be easily criticized for their problematic mimesis, the *writing* of, say, Thoreau or Dillard is even more tenuously connected to reality: "It is still more difficult to turn words into birds" (*Truth* 177). All words are tropes in their very origin, as Nietzsche demonstrated ("On Truth" 90–93); poetry is simply more metaphorical, usually, than other uses of human language.

Furthermore, the genre of poetry has the advantage, perhaps, of allowing for the greater possibility of actual ecospeak(ing), if you will. Angus Fletcher thus contends that, even more than prose nonfiction, "poetry takes environmental concerns to a higher level" because of its "close[r] personal" engagement with "environmental matters" (3). In a move similar to Rueckert's original ecocritical definition of literature as ecosystem, Fletcher identifies a certain kind of poetry "*as environmental form*," what he calls the "*environment-poem*" (6, 9).[80] For Fletcher, it was Whitman who "invented a new kind of poem, which we must call the *environment-poem*. His poems are not *about* the environment, whether natural or social. They *are* environments" (103). I would twist this dictum a bit to say that, yes, in certain special cases, this poem is not *about* a bird, but *is* a bird (as it were), as opposed to most bird poetry, which is more obviously a group of words merely about birds. The former instance, obviously, is where the avian can best be said to speak.

However, the distinction between imaginative naturist nonfiction and poetry per se involves a false binary; the dualism is rather a continuum within which some prose examples are no doubt better environment-poems than most attempts at formal verse. An ecopoetics, then, can pretty well ignore matters of literary form, concentrating instead on the images and tropes of discourse, whatever their ostensible genre. M. Jimmie Killingsworth states the goal of his own "project in ecopoetics" well: it is "to understand the myths and metaphors by which human beings identify their own purposes with the creatures and processes of nature" ("Voluptuous" 14). I would optimistically extend this definition via a consideration of the possibility that, ideally, homocentric "purposes" might be (nearly) erased in the best ecowriting and remain open to the eventuality that, in such discourse, a veritable acknowledgment of species alterity can occur *without* the projective and identification mechanisms usually at work in humankind's propensity to other the natural world by colonizing it as the same.

One might also turn to a recent ecocritical tack by Hubert Zapf in this regard, and his emphasis on literature's defamiliarizing aesthetic qualities over any high regard for mimesis. Indeed, as "an ecological force-field within culture," literature's ecoforce really lies in its "aestheticising transgression of immediate referentiality" (88). In the wake of Rueckert and Kroeber, one is less surprised to learn that the "aesthetic transformation" that literature occasions results from "procedures in many ways analogous to ecological principles" (93). Such principles apparently include biological, or rather, cultural diversity, for literature confronts cultural ideologies "with a holistic-pluralistic approach that focuses specifically on that which is marginalized, neglected or repressed by these systemic realities. . . . In this way, literature activates and semiotically empowers the culturally repressed" as "an *imaginative counter-discourse*" (93). The phrase "culturally repressed" is no doubt welcome to the feminist, the Marxist, the critic of color, but Zapf has most in mind the dominant culture's repression of its very biology, of human *life* itself, and its fundamental kinship with other life forms; at last, literature "is a form of textuality that relates cultural history to its vital interconnections with natural history," that is, "with the biophilic memory of the human species" (99).

This is a wonderful claim indeed, but unfortunately, Zapf's failure to define "literature" renders his whole argument problematic; however, one can safely intuit here something close to a Russian Formalist definition, that "literature" is a special self-referential language that highlights its difference from everyday discourse via defamiliarizing "devices," a definition that easily includes poetry and creative (naturist) nonfiction but probably doesn't include straightforward nature writing of an expository sort. But I cast this quibble immediately aside, finding in Zapf's formulation of literature as biophilia a means of inscribing one of the central criteria of zoö- or ornithicriticism. Two general versions of such an approach can now be tentatively identified, distinguished by their results: (1) an ecopoetic analysis of discursive representations of other species, critiquing how the text in question reinforces (to whatever degree) homocentrism via its imagery and tropes, and (2) an ecopoetic analysis that lauds instead how the text in question achieves (to whatever degree) a veritable eco- or biocentrism, "letting the goldfinch be," in Buell's words. "To whatever degree" is key here, of course, because either extreme is problematic; even the most anthropocentric portrayal of other animals is, one might claim, better than a work with no other species at all (as in certain urbane drawing-room fiction). On the other hand, to escape homocentrism entirely, *within human language*, is (probably?) also a patent absurdity.

Maybe we can't escape the untoward anthropocentric metaphors endemic to discourse, but at least we can be aware of them: "Perhaps the most we can ask is that ecopoetics seek a heightened consciousness, a reconsideration of verbal practices that involve categorizing, naming, or identifying with natural objects" (Killingsworth, *Walt Whitman* 16). Maybe the crime of language and representation and self-interest must just be acknowledged, without abandoning pragmatic activism. In a pro–animal rights study that worries about (and at times embraces) poststructuralism as much as I do, Steve Baker willingly admits that "the animal rights movement itself claims a proprietary [i.e., self-serving] interest in the animal" and deals as much in anthropomorphic metaphor as any other ideology. These are "not matters for shame or signs of hypocrisy, however; they will only discredit animal rights in the minds of critics who consider that a rather narrow sense of philosophical consistency matters more than the sense of social justice which motivates supporters of that cause" (232).

My own "narrow sense of philosophical consistency" may not be a good thing. Right now the crows are speaking outside my window, and I feel an absence, a gap, because I am unable to answer them. I can only hope that this study will serve as a (poor and tentative) response to this other species, and language, that I hear—an acknowledgment of, a beckoning to, a vision, or rather, "hearing" of the posthuman.

I think I can still hear such voices in the Romantics, despite my many subsequent diatribes against such a reading or hearing in this work. Indeed, what drew me to these writers originally, I'm sure now, was the (however problematic) link between the Lakota worldview and the various gestures of animal empathy evident in Wordsworth, Clare, and company. Perusing Arthur Symons's tribute to and defense of symbolisme, a movement that was perhaps the dying gasp of European Romanticism and the ultimate aesthetic retreat from material reality, I occasioned upon his praise of Huysmans for showing "how inert matter, the art of stones, the growth of plants, the unconscious life of beasts, may be brought under the same law of the soul, may obtain, through symbol, a spiritual existence. . . . What is Symbolism if not an establishing of the links which hold the world together, the affirmation of an eternal, minute, intricate, almost invisible life, which runs through the whole universe?" (145). What is ecological consciousness, I would ask, but the *reverse* (and truer) translation of this, a demonstrating of how the (idealized and homocentric) laws of the human soul are actually those of stones, and of plants, and of the unconscious life of that beast of a crow speaking outside my window?

CHAPTER 2 Wandering Voices

The Avian Other from Cowper to Wordsworth

For the discerning intellect of Man,
When wedded to this goodly universe
In love and holy passion, shall find these [images of nature]
A simple produce of the common day.
—I, long before the blissful hour arrives,
Would chant, in lonely peace, the spousal verse
Of this great consummation.

WILLIAM WORDSWORTH, *Prospectus to The Excursion, in Poetical Works*

Wordsworth's Prospectus is a self-proclaimed "spousal verse" to the divine marriage of the "intellect of Man" and "this goodly universe," or "Nature." Recent literary ecologists have no doubt rightly grasped the crucial importance of such key Romantic pronouncements to their own agenda, which includes both a revisionary naturalist reading of such canonical works and a self-legitimization of their critical tack via these very texts. But despite, say, Jonathan Bate's and Karl Kroeber's hagiographic elevation of Wordsworth and company as proto-environmentalists, the circumspect reader might well point to the poet's bald assertion just previous to this passage, that his "main region" remains firmly grounded in the "Mind of Man" (40–41),[1] and then analyze both "Mind" and "Man" as problematic terms that have historically tended to militate against the very ecological vision of Wordsworth's "goodly universe" that Bate and Kroeber would champion. Thus "Mind" has long served as a Cartesian or Kantian abstraction, a selfhood independent of the (racial and gendered) body's situatedness in a specific environment, or place. That Wordsworth's "I" in this passage is an ego in isolation, "in lonely peace," is thus symptomatic.[2] The privileged position of this idealized bridegroom, rational "Man"—or human, let us say, to put aside the man/woman binary for the moment—sets up our own species over other animals, the primal act of anthropocentrism that is a major theme, too, among ecocritics. For these reasons, many ecological scholars have put forth such terms as "biocentrism" and "ecocentrism" with which to counter the dominant anthrohegemony.

Wordsworth's call for a future, nearly millennialist marriage of mind and nature, furthermore, is already imbued with a notion of ameliorative progress, of psychosocial evolution; no doubt, the primitivism in Wordsworth is rampant enough, but one can easily guess that the "growth" of this particular "poet's mind" moves on a more advanced plane than the playful hopping birds whose "thoughts" he "cannot measure," or even the puerilized psyche of his "dear Sister" in "Tintern Abbey." In sum, Wordsworth's "Mind of Man" is still that of patriarchal Western civilization, whatever the poet's atavistic tendencies; to this Western male logos, women, children, and the "primitive" serve as but recuperative "spousal" Others for the vulnerable, and often melancholy, mind that is the poet, alienated as that self is from the body and, in the end, from nature, that feminized bride who may have no need of Wordsworth's ravishments. Indeed, another motif ubiquitous in the theoretical works dealt with in my first chapter concerns how the body, the female, and the Native American have been conflated with nature and the animal in this act of othering, this construction of a metonymic series of Hegelian slaves that prop up the colonizing subject as master.[3] The ubiquitous figure of the Romantic solitaire, too, often involves an alienation from or return to nature, and the "border" theme that permeates current discussions of the nineteenth-century British relationship with the non-British Other concerns in large part the border between civilization and the wild. At last, all such otherings might be said to concern a space of liminality from which alienated and repressed natural alterity might speak, or, more usually, one can assume, *not* speak. Viewed in this way, the Romantics' would-be marriage of the "Mind of Man" with "Nature" becomes a troublesome betrothal indeed.

In general, British Romanticism can be viewed as an ideology of the Self and the Same that is ultimately dependent on attempts to assimilate, to colonize various aspects of the Other and the repressed—that is, women, "savages," children, the "mad,"[4] and the landscape itself—all border figures of marginality toward which the Romantic-Poet-as-Self was inordinately, at times, it seems, desperately, attracted. The animal or avian Other falls all too easily subject to this same psychomachia; it is no surprise, then, that I would immediately read the various nightingales, skylarks, swallows, swans, robins, and wrens in Wordsworth, Shelley, Keats, and Clare as recuperative emblems for, above all, very human strivings and needs, as ultimately failed attempts to recuperate the Romantic self or "I" through an avian Other.

However, my general attitude will necessarily be a "mixed-feelings" critique of, but appreciation for, Romantic naturism in general, sans the recent knee-jerk impulse to present them as the non-plus-ultra progenitors of contemporary eco-consciousness. But I did grow up reading Wordsworth, Keats, and Shelley *as* nature poets—before Hartman, de Man, and Harold Bloom could deconstruct my enthusiasm—and I deemed the characteristic Romantic "pantheism" epitomized in Wordsworth's "one life" (*Prelude* 2.430) as the closest thing in Western literature to Native American notions of an immanent natural "theology."[5] Thus my intended progression from British Romanticism to recent Native American literature is not a wild sweep of the pendulum from an attitude of complete and reprehensible othering to some utterly splendid opposite ideal: it is instead a matter of degree.

However one ultimately evaluates its portrayals of avian alterity, British poetry has always been a textual grove frequented by the "feather'd tribes," from "The Cuckoo-Song" and Chaucer's *Parlement of Foulys* to the twentieth-century poems of Ted Hughes and Charles Tomlinson. Perhaps England's special geography and climate, with a relative lack of large mammals and reptiles, led its human inhabitants to invest their avian neighbors with even greater emotional significance than is usual for a national literature and national character.[6] But certainly much of the avian's ubiquity in English literature can be attributed to the archetypal reasons spelled out in chapter 1; the frequent appearance of such trans-European species as the nightingale, cuckoo, and swallow is due in no small part, as W. H. Hudson reminds us, to the "convention[s] of the continental poets, ancient and modern" (188).

Again, the English robin and blackbird weren't suddenly hatched from the fertile brains of Charlotte Smith and William Wordsworth, as numerous studies on the birds in Chaucer, Spenser, and Shakespeare demonstrate.[7] But not until the late eighteenth-century Age of Sensibility does the animal or avian Other—and the human indigenous Other, for that matter—become a common subject and concern of, let's say, *sensibility*.[8] Without the time, space, or inclination to defend this assertion in great detail, I would only point to the baldly aggressive appropriation, indeed imperialism, of nature in Alexander Pope's "Windsor Forest" (published in 1713) as an epitome of the previous neoclassical modus operandi vis-à-vis the "natured Other":

to describe trees as "future navies" (222), to describe the hunting of birds (including larks) with near glee (111–34), and to offer such a biodevastating "sylvan war" as a socially acceptable displacement for human warfare (148, 369–72)—this is miles from typical Romantic gestures in this regard, however earnestly one might psychoanalyze the motives of the latter. Robert Bly also discusses Pope as a model of the Enlightenment's "general disdaining of nature" and notes, significantly, that women and Native Americans are similarly naturized in this period as "lower links" in the dominant hierarchy. Indeed, critiquing the "poor Indian" passage in *An Essay on Man*, the primitivist mystic in Bly is almost jubilantly ironic: "The main evidence of inferiority that Pope mentions in the Indian is that he sees the divine in clouds and wind" (*News* 11, 15). But Bly, a latter-day Romantic himself, can only write such a sentence in the wake of an Anglo tradition of poets such as Wordsworth and Shelley musing about a "divinity" in those very "clouds and wind." The ground springs of this tradition are clearly evident in various precursors of the literary revolution of 1798, notably in the writings of Cowper, Burns, and Blake.

AVIAN RIGHTS AND WRITES

> Nature inanimate employs sweet sounds,
> But animated Nature sweeter still,
> To soothe and satisfy the human ear.
> Ten thousand warblers cheer the day, and one
> The live-long night: nor these alone, whose notes
> Nice finger'd art must emulate in vain,
> But cawing rooks, and kites that swim sublime
> In still repeated circles, screaming loud,
> The jay, the pie, and ev'n the boding owl
> That hails the rising moon, have charms for me.
> —WILLIAM COWPER, *The Task*

Just as the publication of *Lyrical Ballads* was not the great epistemic break that previous generations of literary scholars have made it out to be, nor was the just previous Age of Sensibility the radical improvement in an appreciation of animal alterity that my subsequent examples may lead one to believe. And yet the Romantic privileging of the alter-species Other begins in earnest at this same time, evident, for example, in William Cowper's frequent outrage at cruelties to animals and his obvious love for his own animal "neighbors," including the least esteemed of the "feather'd tribes." Indeed, among the eighteenth-century poets of sensibility, Cowper demonstrates "the most articulate expression of a concern for the rights of animals" (McKusick 23). His "character sketches" in *The Task* (1785) of the dog joyfully cavorting in the snow (5.45–51), of his hare neighbor who has at least one human "friend" (that is, the poet himself [3.334–51]), and even his sympathetic first-person self-comparison to a hunted, "stricken deer" (3.108–11) all attest to an empathy that could never conceive of trees as "future navies." (Indeed, these trees are, instead, "fallen avenues" fit for mourning, victims of a "fate unmerited" [1.338–39].) With pride, Cowper tells us that such avian neighbors as the "stock-dove" like *him*, too, and tolerate his "near approach" (6.307, 309).

Moreover, as Wordsworth will similarly claim in *The Prelude*,[9] this poet deems the love for the natural Other as the foundation for authentic human relationships:

> The heart is hard in nature, and unfit
> For human fellowship, as being void
> Of sympathy, and therefore dead alike
> To love and friendship both, that is not pleas'd
> With sight of animals enjoying life. (6.321–25)

The contrary attitude is reprehensible to Cowper, and his several protests against animal cruelty are heated: "Witness," for example, the "spaniel dying . . . Under dissection"; "Witness the patient ox . . . Driv'n to the slaughter"; and witness the poor horse, with "His murd'rer on his back . . . With bleeding sides and flanks that heave for life," who arrives at last at his destination and dies (6.417–21, 428–30). Domesticated animals are not the only victims in need of defense, for hunting, too, is practically genocidal; if his fellow humans continue to "persecute, annihilate the tribes / That draw the sportsman over hill and dale," the "game-fowl" may never "hatch her eggs again" (3.309–10, 312).

Cowper's poetic treatment of birds allows him, for one, to combat the tyranny of sight, in recognizing that "There is in souls a sympathy with sounds" (6.1) and to praise "Nor rural sights alone, but rural sounds" (1.181), especially those "Ten thousand warblers [that] cheer the day" (1.200).[10] The inimical effect of urban sprawl on such songsters is also noted, as Cowper apostrophizes the city thus: "Your [dissonant] songs confound / Our more harmonious notes: the thrush departs / Scar'd, and th'offended nightingale is mute" (1.766–68). The country is Cowper's welcome retreat, where the absence of white noise, if you will, allows him to more fully contemplate a lone robin singing in the winter and to describe its behavior with some marvelous aural detail:

> No noise is here, or none that hinders thought.
> The redbreast warbles still, but is content
> With slender notes, and more than half suppress'd:
> Pleas'd with his solitude, and flitting light
> From spray to spray, where'er he rests he shakes
> From many a twig the pendant drops of ice,
> That tinkle in the wither'd leaves below. (6.76–82)

Bird notes and breaking ice create a slight shimmer of sound in this setting of "No noise," and the Western psyche addicted to specularity shudders as if before a Zen koan.[11]

But Cowper's finely tuned warblers aren't the only birds that catch his ear and evoke appreciation. If he has little tolerance for the botanical abject,[12] he can at least appreciate "weeds" with wings, those *other* avian Others: the "cawing rooks, and kites . . . screaming loud, / The jay, the pie, and ev'n the boding owl," all "have charms for" this poet (1.203–06). Significantly, three of the five in this hall of fame of cacophony are corvids: the rook (close kin to the crow), the Eurasian jay, and the common magpie. (Another, the red kite, is the scavenger who fills his "maw" with "offal," of *Hamlet* fame.) Cowper's gesture here will become a resonating motif in Wordsworth and John Clare, a reprivileging of the humble, even despised, among the animal and avian kingdom.

Such a reprivileging and democratization has its human parallel in the lower and rural human classes, no doubt, who also get their due in the work of Cowper, Wordsworth, and Clare. Cowper even extends his ken beyond the sea and addresses human racial alterity. If his civilized British fellows "persecute, annihilate the tribes" of woods and fields, they also are guilty of persecuting other *tribes*. Thus he laments the "gentle savage" brought from his "native bow'rs" to England because of imperialist "curiosity" or "vain glory"; all that their English captors can really show off is the "superior skill [with which] we can abuse / The gifts of Providence, and squander life" (1.633–38). Cowper's retreat to a rural life among his friends the hare, stock dove, and robin issues, in part, from this same disdain for the false trappings of human civilization; these other species don't "squander life," presumably, and they might well peer out from a London cage and look askance at the artificially attired human lookers-on.

But as for the "gentle savage," "this portrait is not an Indian," as Gerald Vizenor says, but is rather an idyllic, Rousseauian foil against what Cowper perceives to be the vices of British imperialism and luxury. Nor, really, are Cowper's birds and other animals paragons of eighteenth-century virtuous friendship who really thought of Cowper as a true and good neighbor with their last dying thoughts. Indeed, the poet's own deistic rationalism (and ultimately, his anthropocentrism) won't allow it: humans are still "Distinguish'd much by reason . . . From creatures that exist *but for our sake*" (6.601, 603; emphasis added). Although Cowper occasionally spins off the occasional happy line on nature that reminds us of Wordsworth, such as "there lives and works / A soul in all things, and that soul is God" (6.184–85), the tone is much more smugly *theistic*: "God" is still the keyword here, not "Nature."

Less patently theistic in his approach to nature is Robert Burns: "While other poets may have been finding divine analogies in nature, Burns found, characteristically, human ones" (Gaull 265). As with Cowper, the animal affections of Burns are legion, from "lowly" mice, lice, and wounded hares to dead or dying mares and dead pet ewes,[13] despite the homocentric moral tags that often conclude such animal poems. (And, as in Cowper, the "humbler" species get their due, if not privilege.)[14] His birds are, in general, less tragic than his many dying mammals, however. Rather than doomed creatures on which he can project his melancholy, and thereby relieve it, they are more often emblems of unself-conscious life and joy, painful teases to a poetic psyche thus reinforced in its awareness of its own melancholia and alienation. Just as Wordsworth will grieve for "what man has made of man" in self-consciousness's divestiture of authentic connection with the rest of the ecosystem, so Burns's characteristic complaint concerns how "man's dominion / Has broken Nature's holy union" ("To a Mouse" 2.1–2).

The love-crossed speaker in "The Banks o' Doon" is characteristic of this pained consciousness, exclaiming, "How can ye chant, ye little birds, / And

I sae weary fu' o' care!" (3–4). Poetic license and hyperbole granted, the accusatory tone still strikes this reader as odd, even an affront, as other species going about their everyday business of breeding and phatic conversation are subsequently inculcated in the speaker's possible cardiac arrest, as it were: "Thou'll break my heart, thou warbling bird" (5). To see this as more than just a maudlin or silly figure of speech may be an extremist position, but I still resent how these little, warbling avians, bonny birds all, to be sure, are yet othered and used as excuses for the speaker's own insipid sadness. These same untoward, however cute, accusations are also evident in "Sweet Afton," in which the "stock dove," "whistling blackbirds," and "green-crested lapwing" (2.1–3) are all chided to pipe down and not wake up the speaker's darling Mary.[15]

My remonstrance against such poetic othering of the avian may seem but a petty sort of nit-picking, but if one posits a close connection between such rhetorical acts of othering and the actual praxis of treating the nonhuman as a virtual nonentity only of use value to the human, then my protest is more to the point. There is a definite exploitation going on, according to Steve Baker, in this "perpetuation of the cultural stereotype of the animal" at even a "symbolic or representational level" (23–24), including, I would add, representations thereof in belles-lettres. Baker continues, "It *may* be that the practice [of animal othering and abuse] somehow accounts for the rhetoric," and yet and also "it *may* be that the rhetoric sustains and substantiates and consolidates the practice, leading us to continue to hold animals in contempt" (90). If the various ornithic inanities in British poetry are in one sense mere reflections of a dominant cultural anthropocentrism, they are also complicit in contributing to the ongoing repression and oppression of other species. Baker writes, "It is not clear to me that the animal rights movement will be able to bring about any fundamental change in popular attitudes until it is prepared to acknowledge and to take more seriously the symbolic and representational functions of the animal in the culture at large" (211). His emphasis on popular art makes his argument perhaps all the more obvious, but my own current ruminations on highbrow art are equally valid efforts, I believe, in the study of alter-species abjection.

Burns's "Composed in Spring" also juxtaposes a "rejoicing Nature" with a narrator made miserable by love. Nature's revelry includes the voices of the "mavis" (mistle thrush), "lintwhite" (linnet), and "lark" (1.1, 2.4, 6.1) and a panoply of waterfowl:

The wanton coot the water skims,
Amang the reeds the ducklings cry,
The stately swan majestic swims,
And ev'ry thing is blest but I. (4.1–4)

(If "stately" is a neoclassical cliché redolent of class privilege, "wanton" is certainly one of the happier adjectives ever applied to the coot.)[16] The singing passerines and the waterfowl species of near domestic familiarity again represent a biosphere of spontaneous bliss, making the speaker yearn for the dreariness of winter—in a textbook case of the pathetic fallacy—when "nature all is sad like me!" (7.4). But just as it is an obvious projection that wintering nature is sad, so is it a projection that Burns's birds are usually manic optimists who can't keep their mouths shut about it. Such happiness and sadness in nature both are creations of humankind's psycholinguistic dualism, symptoms of a basic human bipolar disorder, as it were.

"Composed in Spring" does contain one dissonant bird, in its "Chorus," where we learn the cause of the speaker's sorrow, a scornful woman with eyes "jet-black, an' it's like a hawk / An it winna let a body be" (3–4). Here the "hawk-" or "eagle-eye" necessary to the soaring raptor becomes a sinister surveillance, especially given its association here with the color black. Archetypally speaking, in the Western "Mind of Man," birds of happiness and light coexist with their shadow opposites, avians of dirge and darkness. Indeed, the former seem to evoke their opposite via some enantiodromic psychic mechanism: beneath the singing skylark lurks the crow.

In the context of visual iconography, Steve Baker has also noted that, "in the post-Cartesian West with its continuing appetite for the dualistic and the oppositional, animals seem to figure . . . overwhelmingly negatively in our imaginative and our visual rhetoric" (116). All such "negative and demeaning and objectifying constructions of animality" can be largely attributed to "the dualistic thinking expressed in binary oppositions"; "when animals figure . . . in binary oppositions, *they invariably represent the negative term in the opposition*: 'the Other, the Beast, the Brute'" (83). Baker's support from popular cultural representations is compelling, but he pays less attention to instances in which both sides of the binary are animal; avian imagery, as I have argued, is especially conducive to signifying both poles of the binary.

Amid all his songsters of painful bliss, Burns writes another avian poem in a far different tone, a meditative plaint worthy of his more famous "To a Mouse." In "On scaring some Waterfowl in Loch Turit," the poet immediately addresses the fleeing ducks or geese as "fellow creatures" and asks, "why / At my presence thus you fly?" (3–4). The answer, the ballistic behavior of others of his own kind, leads the poet to shame and outrage:

> Conscious, blushing for our race,
> Soon, too soon, your fears I trace.
> Man, your proud, usurping foe,
> Would be lord of all below:
> Plumes himself in freedom's pride,
> Tyrant stern to all beside. (13–18)

One can imagine similar words from a feminist damning patriarchy or a postcolonial scholar damning imperialism, but here Burns's empathy for another's "fears," his sincere sorrow at another's mortal vulnerability, feels like a veritable transcendence of the border of species. Burns goes on to admit that the eagle kills these same birds, but out of "Strong necessity"; a human kills "for his pleasure" (22, 26). The poem ends by entreating these birds to fly away if and when humans come again:

> . . . if Man's superior might
> Dare invade your *native right*,
> . . . .
> And the foe you cannot brave,
> Scorn at least to be his slave. (33–34, 39–40; emphasis added)

Substitute "Man" with, say, British slave traders or the U.S. Cavalry, and "native right" places us firmly in the human sociopolitical realm, amid the historical wrongs against the African and Native American. But Burns, poet of the downtrodden common man, also sees such wrongs committed in the natural realm, by one abusive species toward another, the latter a victim as truly *native* as the rest.

After two poets so obviously alive to external nature and its alter-species inhabitants, I turn to William Blake with some trepidation, for such a mystical introversion seems most amenable to a Jungian intrapsychic approach. In fact, the view that Blake is *not* much interested in real nature has become almost a critical truism.[17] I am nonetheless encouraged by recent ecocritical reexaminations of such dense literary forests of deep symbolism; as Lawrence Buell reminds us, Thoreau's oft-interpreted pond *is* also a real pond, after all (*Environmental Imagination* 277). There is also a lot of real nature in Blake, including a rather amazing sympathy for avians, whether in cages or in flight.[18] Indeed, in a survey of British poetry from Collins to T. S. Eliot, Josephine Miles finds the "highest incidence" of "anthropomorphic nature imagery" in the author of *The Four Zoas*. Such anthropomorphism, in Blake's case, even Buell would deem a "pietistic sentimentalism," at the same time, however, praising "The Fly" for its imagining "a complete interchangeability between animal and human" (*Environmental Imagination* 185–86). I would argue that the question "Am I not / A fly like thee?" (5–6) can be read as more than sentimental pietism, as the very intuitive act of *cross-species* identity and "interchangeability" that Buell can only imagine as an "imagining." The pietism is, admittedly, still the great flaw in this poem, for its very homocentrism; the introjection of some metaphysical and fateful "blind hand" (11) leading to the speaker's acceptance of death is a theological view to which very few flies are probably inclined to subscribe.

But there is something else at work in Blake that critiques both the species divide and the bipolar disorder referred to earlier, a textual landscape in which the intermingling of the "I" and the Fly and the lamb and the Tyger and the bird make up a sort of mythopoeic menagerie that at last deflates the tyranny of the human "I." The lyric "Spring" ("Sound the Flute!"), for instance, is ostensibly a simple song of seasonal rebirth via birdsong, à la Wordsworth's "Written in March":

> Birds delight
> Day and Night.
> Nightingale
> In the dale
> Lark in Sky
> Merrily
> Merrily Merrily to welcome in the Year (3–9)

The poem ends with the childlike exuberance typical of many of the poems of *Songs of Innocence*, via an interaction with another species that, indeed, seems downright silly, as the narrator asks the "Little Lamb" to "Come and Lick" his neck, to let him pull on his wool; finally, "Let me kiss / Your soft face. / Merrily Merrily we welcome in the Year" (19, 21, 25–27). I have already spoken of the Romantic association of animals and children, in many ways a positive reprivileging of the othering of both, evidenced in the dictums of the psychologist Bruno Bettelheim: "A child is convinced that the animal understands and feels with him[!]" (qtd. in S. Baker 123). Steve Baker is right in noting Bettelheim's utter (rationalist) incomprehension of "the child who intuitively, which is to say *wrongly*, holds open the possibility of an identification with the animal and the inanimate. This prejudice constructs the animal as absolutely *other*, and by association those who identify with the animal themselves come to be seen as other" (124). And so such verses in Blake have been deemed either (negatively) childish or (positively) childlike, but neither view admits the child or the animal into the pantheon of Western right thinking.

However, this juvenile wooly-mindedness must also be read in the context of Blake's more well-known lamb poem and the contrapuntal trochees of "The Tyger." What kind of consciousness, Blake seems to be asking, allows one to forget and deny the possibility of "making love" (*so to speak*) to a newborn of another species, or the possibility that larks and nightingales are sentient beings who might take a modicum of pleasure in the warming and lengthening of the day? Or can imagine a double-edged deity dividing nature into meek Christian lambs and infernal tygers, meadows and dark forests, the domesticated and playful versus the exotic, savage, shadowy, and libidinal? Only a dualistic religion and worldview could ask, "Did he who made the Lamb make thee?"

It is the same bipolar mind, I surmise, that distinguishes between human and animal, and it is the same (both biblical and Cartesian) worldview that errs in conceiving a divide between mind and body. For "Man has no Body distinct from his Soul," as Blake argues in one of his "heretical contraries" in *The Marriage of Heaven and Hell* (34);[19] there is no "Soul" distinct from the body, to recast Blake for the modern temperament. False dualistic ideologies, and language itself, originated in the very physicality of nature, Blake intimates in the same work, because "sensible objects," including the "properties of woods, rivers, mountains, lakes"—and birds and animals, as we saw in Paul Shepard—allowed the "ancient Poets" to (re)"animate" them via (animistic) poetic tropes; these were then co-opted by the priesthood into institutionalized religions, idealisms at a pale second remove from the real fauna and flora and earth (37). One is reminded of another Blake lyric,

"The Garden of Love," often read as a poem about psychic (and ecclesiastical) repression. But that "Chapel" of repressive religion has, significantly, taken the place of the "green," or nature itself, and the Garden of Love—the human psyche?—is now full of "tomb-stones where flowers should be" (3–4, 10). But the trope of a psyche fettered by false rules is also an earth no longer "green" or flowering, as if human psychological health is paralleled, or even, to a great degree, determined by the relative healthiness of humans' relationship with the rest of the ecosystem.[20] Here, the result for both psyche and nature is a deathlike pall.

But I don't mean to read Blake as some blithe return to innocence and facile monism, to the skylark and the child. His was a psyche and corpus that would encompass both tyger and lamb, through an antinomic mode in which "Opposition is true Friendship" because "Without Contraries is no progression" (*Marriage* 41, 34). At work here instead, no doubt, is a dialectic of psychic evolution that lies beyond both Innocence and Experience, but I would still argue that Blake's ideal of psychic health (as hermetic as it may be) is closer to the innocence of the child and animal than the experiential nay-sayings of jaded adult egohood.

This "beyond" also includes a millennialist expansion of human consciousness, beyond even the bounds of species, perhaps, through a new perception of the physical world itself: "If the doors of perception were cleansed every thing would appear to man as it is, infinite. / For man has closed himself up, till he sees all things thro' narrow chinks of his cavern" (39). Cowper and others have tried to counteract the tyranny of the dominant sense of sight; Blake would apparently remove entirely the sensory complex or gestalt that gives the ego its sense of individuality in isolation, Wordsworth's almost overbearing "Mind of Man." Beyond this "abyss of the five senses" Blake frames the following question: "How do you know but ev'ry Bird that cuts the airy way, / Is an immense world of delight, clos'd by your senses five?" (35). At last, through a cleansing of the "doors of perception," perhaps an authentic cross-species empathy is possible. This brief reinterpretation of the psychology of Blake's *Marriage* also returns us full circle to the apparent mundanity of such lines as "Birds delight / Day and Night," allowing a reading of greater sophistication and (*interspecies*) understanding. One can now better envision how a possible leap beyond the "abyss of the five senses" is at work here, too, a small peek into other "immense worlds of delight."

"VERY PROPER SPIES"

> With regard to the *œdicnemus*, or stone curlew, I intend to write very soon to my friend near Chichester, in whose neighbourhood these birds abound. . . . This gentleman . . . will be a very proper spy upon the motions of these birds; and . . . I shall expect that he will be very exact in his dates.
>
> The language of birds is very ancient, and, like other ancient modes of speech, very elliptical: little is said, but much is meant and understood.
>
> GILBERT WHITE, *The Natural History of Selborne*

Blake's "airy" birds of "delight" are noticeably generic, usually either the bare signifier "bird(s)" or the common poeticized genera of lark, eagle, and so on, types rather than particular species presented with any great concern for observational realism. But, to return to Miles's survey of "anthropomorphic nature imagery," the second-place poet is none other than Charles Darwin's grandfather, Erasmus Darwin, whom Buell contrasts with the "sentimental" Blake as a writer in the throes of the opposite extreme: the drive to scientific classification, or taxonomy. Darwin's literary efforts are "pedantic poems that set Linnaeus to music" (Buell, *Environmental Imagination* 185–86).[21] Buell's own proposed naturist genre is more of a middle ground, of "heart" and "head," of imagination and observation, but the fact that the "meddling intellect" of natural science did find its way into English poetry is a fascinating event in itself.

Indeed, while Erasmus Darwin's poetic efforts are easily derided, his intentions evince a laudable drive to marry literature and natural science in a way that is utterly foreign to the notion of serious literature later inculcated by Matthew Arnold and F. R. Leavis, until the recent reprivileging of naturist literature led by Buell himself. Darwin's *The Loves of Plants* (1789), the second volume of his *Botanic Garden*, consists of four cantos on botanical lust, in heroic couplets, with copious scientific footnotes almost as weighty, wordwise, as the verse. His stated purpose is "to inlist Imagination under the banner of Science" and "to cultivate the knowledge of Botany" via the "Sexual System" of Linnaeus (i). But this lesson in sexual science smacks of a certain kinkiness, with "Confederate Males," "Feminine Males," "Clandestine Marriage," "imperfect males," and "eunuchs" (v, 7, 65). There is secrecy, rapture, virginity, polygamy, "promiscuous marriage" (183), "Satanic love" (100), and lots of anthropomorphic fondness, sighing, and virtue. But above all, a certain wantonness characterizes the love lives of the plant kingdom.[22]

However anthropomorphic the poetry, Darwin's goals aren't completely eccentric, and he defends his verse's "prosaic" nature against what he perceives to be a hostile audience in the introductory "Proem" and the prose interludes that divide the cantos. He admits that "Science is best delivered in Prose, as its mode of reasoning is from stricter analogies than metaphors or similes" (51); his poetry, then, is a supplement, as it were, for both instruction and pleasure, and he later defends his (many egregious) "similes . . . Homeric" as but agreeable ornamentation (92). (Unfortunately, such ornamentation demands a rare taste for both botany and the worst of euphuistic Augustan poetry.) But Darwin's defense also includes the desire to combat the rampant mythologizing of other species in Ovid's *Metamorphoses*, and—a nice turn of phrase, this—to "restore some of them [i.e., plants] to their original animality" (x). Of course, this "animality" is a very anthropomorphized one, as it includes "the beauty of their persons, their graceful attitudes," and "the brilliancy of their dress" (xi), thus rendering such (stem-and-petal) beings more welcome in the drawing rooms of high society, perhaps.

Darwin's defensiveness regarding his untoward grafting of science and poetry notwithstanding, there was a growing audience for such literary excursions into "natural history,"[23] and that interest wasn't confined to concupiscent chrysanthemums; in fact, the history of this merger has as much to do with birds as it does with plants. The newfound public infatuation with natural science circa 1800, in both England and the United States, spawned a general interest in amateur nature study and collecting,[24] but the science of preference in this popularization was ornithology. Marilyn Gaull attributes this preference to the unique "social" and symbolic status that birds had acquired through the centuries:[25] soon "ornithology became the most popular scientific discipline," supplemented by a good many "handbooks and periodicals" for its new tag-along hobbyist public (369). If the birds in question were the local avian natives, interest redoubled; indeed, "anything about birds or accompanied by verse or with the word British in the title would . . . find an appreciative audience" in this period (340).

Birds and a British locale are both major foci in Gilbert White's *The Natural History of Selborne* (1789). (The book is also "accompanied by verse," with quotations from such luminaries as Virgil, Shakespeare, Milton, and

Thomson.) Popularity aside, White's journal on the flora and fauna of his own "very narrow compass" of ground (122), Selborne and its environs, set the early standard for "aesthetic" English nature writing.[26] Published as two sets of letters, to a famous naturalist (Pennant) and to an amateur naturalist like White (Barrington), *The Natural History* justifies White's faith that long-term amateur field notes on specific regions could ultimately be more fruitful than the more comprehensive, and thus more hastily generalized, tomes by professional naturalists. The author's self-perceived role as a "very proper spy" on the doings of local birds is thus that of one who "takes his observations from the subject itself" rather than "from the writings of others" (57, 109).[27]

A good spy, White is the first to distinguish the three different British species of "willow-wrens" (wood warblers [46, 272–73]); he tentatively identifies a major European migratory flyway, via Gibraltar (82, 132); and he rightly concludes that cuckoos are not birds of prey, boldly contradicting Linnaeus's ruminations on the subject (126, 190). His studies of the "life and conversation of . . . birds" (80) include a keen interest in their flight, nidification, and song;[28] his various descriptions of bird calls are as helpful as many a later bird guide, and he even attempts to ascertain in what musical key owls hoot (134–35).

White's wonderfully detailed observations are (usually) of live birds, in motion in their native habitats, aware as he is of the importance of field identification versus knowledge acquired via books or guns: "A good ornithologist should be able to distinguish birds by their air as well as by their colours and shape;[29] on the ground as well as on the wind, and in the bush as well as in the hand" (213). Yet, like many a later bird-loving writer, his descriptions combine a naturalist's curiosity and a poet's wonder, as in his infatuation with the European nightjar:[30] "There is no bird, I believe, whose manners I have studied more than that of the *caprimulgus* (the goat-sucker), as it is a wonderful and curious creature: but I have always found that though sometimes it may chatter as it flies, as I know it does, yet in general it utters its jarring note sitting on a bough; and I have for many an half hour watched it as it sat with its under mandible quivering, and particularly this summer" (60–61).

White's various efforts at a naturalist's objectivity are characteristically tempered by an empathy that gives a personal, nearly loving touch to his essays into animal alterity. The book's first crucial anecdote, for instance, involves a raven pair whose nest at the top of a huge oak has become an institution. This "Raven-tree" has long been impervious to boys' many attempts at nest robbing, until it is finally chopped down: "At last, when it gave way, the bird was flung from her nest; and, though her parental affection deserved a better fate, was whipped down by the twigs, which brought her dead to the ground" (11).

White's personal touch is nowhere more evident in his various descriptions of his longtime pet tortoise, Timothy.[31] This lugubrious reptile is quaintly anthropomorphized into some slow human cousin; even this "most abject reptile and torpid of beings distinguishes the hand that feeds it, and is touched with the feelings of gratitude!" (140). After this appreciative but "strange being" becomes his "property," White must still wonder at its yen for hibernation, the fact that it "appears to relish it[s longevity] so little as to squander more than two-thirds of its existence in joyless stupor" (233). (Perhaps Timothy's brief glance at White's letter 41, a lengthy list of the plants found around Selborne, led to this inveterate somnolence.)[32]

As for White's personal relationships with birds, his favorite species seems to be the barn swallow, again for pretty much thoroughly anthropocentric reasons. Swallows in general "are a most inoffensive, harmless, entertaining, social, and useful tribe of birds" who "amuse us with their migrations, songs, and marvellous agility"; the natural fact that swallows reduce the insect population is not only the food chain at work, but a "friendly interposition" on the swallows' part, apparently, to make life more comfortable for us humans (145–46). Social, graceful, and "domestic" (and let us not forget its immense entertainment value as an aerial clown), the barn swallow is a true friend to humankind, and to Gilbert White, whose letter 18 is a paean to this avian neighbor, with detailed descriptions of its flight, voice, and nest building. Not only is it a "delicate songster" and a "bold flyer," but its summer activities offer "a most instructive [and utterly bourgeois] pattern of unwearied industry and affection" (158). But characteristically, White ends this monograph with a return to "straight" observation and the following unusual breeding instances: "A certain swallow built for two years together on the handles of a pair of garden-shears, that were stuck up against the boards in an out-house, and therefore must have her nest spoiled whenever the implement was wanted[!]: and, what is stranger still, another bird of the same species built its nest on the wings and body of an owl that happened by accident to hang dead and dry from the rafter of the barn." But the human imposes itself again, as the owl, "with the [swallow's] nest on its wings, and with eggs in the nest," is taken away—we don't learn by whom—as "a curiosity worthy the most elegant private museum in Great Britain" (159–60).

So there is in White this strange mixture of a genuine love for birds and an unthinking adherence to the prejudices of his day, both social and scientific. His greatest ornithological misstep is his obstinate belief that (at least some) of these same swallows *hibernate,* possibly underwater, rather than migrate, and he fills many pages talking himself into this conclusion (e.g., 31, 131, 138, 153–54, 156, 198–99, 234).[33] White also suffers from the blindness of his time regarding hunting. Though he laments the disappearance of the black grouse and the wood pigeon from his region, he can yet speak of deer as "temptation[s]" to humankind's hunting instinct (22, 103–4, 23); as both "a sportsman and . . . naturalist" (20), he is hardly reluctant himself to procure specimens of the "brute creation," including songbirds, with his gun to further the interests of natural science.[34] Like his naturalist descendent, Aldo Leopold, writing a century and a half later and an ocean away, White's ecological consciousness is combined with a love for blood sport, the justifications of which jibe incongruously with his other naturist ruminations.[35]

A certain provincial country clergy smugness also allows occasional ethnocentric slurs on the barbarity of the Spanish (41) and the Irish; the latter are superstitious "wild natives" with "their sordid way of life" (99). Gypsies, moreover, are othered as "sturdy savages" who "infest" England with their "harsh gibberish" (179). (This immediately calls to mind Luther Standing Bear's critique of white colonialists in America who deemed the natives, both animal and human, as but infestations and "pests.") Our good country curate also displays a relative unconcern that his village "abound[s] with poor" (17), who are, after all, too "superstitious" and the "worst œconomists" besides (184, 182). In fact, White's book is one of those rare volumes in which other species come off better, in general, than the humans therein.[36] As for other "economies," White comes close to the yet unborn science of ecology in his various discerning comments on the interrelationship of species;[37] noting a particular interspecies symbiotic relationship, he concludes that nature is the "great economist" (27). But it is finally the "œconomy of Providence" (50), the Creator's fashioning of the Great Chain of Being, that is at work here.

White's overall genial and humble persona and style save him from making the reader wince too often, and his genuine interest in other species' "life and conversation" remains the dominant tone,[38] reflecting an attitude closer to the enthusiasms of Cowper than the "scientific-treatise" style of Erasmus Darwin. White argues that "every kingdom, every province, should have its own monographer" (125). Selborne and its "winged nation" (37) were lucky indeed to have had him as their own "very proper spy."

White's *Natural History*, as I intimated earlier, has been crucial to the development of literature that combines imagination and naturalistic observation, be it essays or poetry. Not only would White's "lively anecdotal" style and "vernacular language" soon "prove essential to [the poetry of] John Clare" (McKusick 27), but his book also "laid the foundations for the natural history essay in England and America" (Worster 5). The eventual popularity of this latter genre, through John Burroughs and W. H. Hudson to Rachel Carson, is also "an essential legacy of" what would become a "Selborne cult," which made Selborne the site of pilgrimages by Charles Darwin, James Russell Lowell, and Burroughs (Worster 16, 23, 14–15).[39] Indeed, according to Frank Stewart, *The Natural History of Selborne* is "the most beloved and influential British nature book of all time," the first "self-consciously *literary* natural history" that would later steer both Charles Darwin and Thoreau in a similar direction (20, 24, 27).

Donald Worster's history of ecology cites White as a central figure in a central dichotomy. As alluded to in chapter 1, Worster perceives two discordant views of nature from the eighteenth century to the present: the "arcadian" (or pastoral or Edenic), epitomized in White and, later, Thoreau, and an "imperialist" view that would both categorize and dominate nature, evidenced in the work of Linnaeus and other scientists of the day and culminating in Charles Darwin (Worster 2, 29–30, 114, 346).[40] According to Worster, the Linnaean classification system, static, hierarchic, and anthropocentric, both originated in and served as a prop for the Christian belief that nature was a great chain of being designed for humankind's use, and that animals were but lower links in the chain or small cogs in the great deist machine (31–43). Nature had become more than ever an object of use value: "The study of ecology was for them [the British Linnaeans] a means to the vigorous conquest of the living world" (51).[41]

But Worster's imperialist-arcadian binary deconstructs itself, as hard science and Edenic arcadianism both partook of the supplement of religion. If the Linnaean imperialist view may have been even worse than Christianity in rendering nature a spiritless object (29), Linnaeus's popularity was yet fostered by a Christian deistic concern "to find the hand of God in nature" (33), a nature created as a vertical hierarchy culminating in humankind (34–46). Likewise, White's faith in an organically ecological Providence, given the increasingly dark, urban backdrop of the Industrial Revolution, ultimately relied on the same theistic underpinning, allowing Selborne to serve as a seminal "mystical" thread that led to Thoreau's "Romantic ecology," continued in the writings of Burroughs and Hudson, and flourishes to this day (Worster 7–8, 14–17, x, 58, 61–62).[42]

Gaull's prime example of the new great interest in birds is not White's *Natural History*, but the work of one Thomas Bewick (340). One of the first popular works of British ornithology, Bewick's *History of British Birds* found a place in the libraries of both William Wordsworth and John James Audubon, spurring a pilgrim's visit from the latter (Shaver and Shaver 22; Audubon 829; Marqusee 5).[43] In the preface to the sixth edition, Bewick insists that observed facts, not superstition or tradition, are the basis for his bird descriptions and life histories. Yet tradition lives on, for if the book leads others to an interest in "Natural History," all the better: such a study is the surest foundation for "Religion and Morality" (19, 17). In fact, if natural history is a direct route to God's designs, why, then, "a good naturalist cannot be a bad man" (177).[44]

The book's layout consists of a reproduced woodcut of each species, followed by a textual exposition of at least the bird's physical appearance, geographical range, and (often declining) numbers; many entries also include information on nesting habits, diet, and song, plus human-interest anecdotal tidbits. (The modern bird guide hasn't advanced much beyond this basic formula but for a greater concision in layout.) A rude attempt at taxonomic organization and an inclusion of Linnaeus's and Buffon's Latin and French names for bird species reinforce the scientific tone embraced in Bewick's various prefaces, and he presumably enhances his authority by frequent references to and quotations from Gilbert White's *Natural History* and White's ornithologist correspondent, Thomas Pennant. But there is still much unscientific silliness. While denying White's hypothesis that swallows hibernate underwater, Bewick still believes that wintering birds "fall into a torpid state" (33). And ravens, believe it or not, can live for over a century (45–46).

Some of Bewick's anthropomorphisms are precious to the point of tears: hawks and owls are armed for "destruction and rapine," and even the robin-size shrike's "appetite for blood" ranks it among "the boldest and the most sanguinary of the rapacious tribe"; those "crafty" magpies, moreover, are "addicted" to "stealing and hoarding"; and a flock of jays sounds just like a "distant meeting of disorderly drunken persons" (30, 78, 90, 93).[45] All that this really tells us is that Bewick's England likely had lots of *human* violence, thievery, and drunkenness. The "homebody" English robin, in contrast, is feminized, with its "expressive" eyes, "aspect mild," and dainty eating habits (129–30).[46] The poor, lugubrious grey heron is "a silent and patient creature" with "a melancholy deportment" (193); more likely, it is the human witness who can't imagine another creature being that patient (waiting for its food to swim by) without becoming a great deal sad.

As for the skylark, although Bewick includes footnotes regarding the *taste* of and preferred cooking method for many species, he finds it "not a little reproachful[!] to humanity" that these songsters are still being slain by the thousands for food (124n); indeed, "the prodigious numbers that are frequently caught are truly astonishing" (124, 123). But then he nonchalantly continues, "Notwithstanding the great havoc made among these birds, they are [still] extremely numerous. The winter is deemed the best season for taking them, as they are then very fat" (124)!

Our naturalist also blithely considers the amenability of various native songbirds to captivity: "In a state of confinement they [European goldfinches] are much attached to their keepers"—no doubt—"and will learn a variety of little tricks" (117).[47] But then, all of Bewick's birds could be said to have learned to do tricks in the cage that is *The History of British Birds (and Cookbook)*: how to look both live and yet-so-dead in a woodcut reproduction, how to be a mirror for British society's both destructive and protective tendencies, and maybe how to be incredibly "silent and patient" while all this silly verbiage is going on. One longs to return to poetry as quickly as possible, but tomes such as these, for better or worse, were the British Romantic poets' scientific guides to the avian when they sought such aid.

WOMEN AND CHILDREN AND BIRDS

> Women, children, and animals are the obscure matter upon which Civilization erects itself.
>
> URSULA LE GUIN (qtd. in S. Baker, *Picturing the Beast*)

One final link from Cowper and Gilbert White to William Wordsworth remains: Charlotte Smith, both poet and amateur naturalist.[48] Her love of poetry, birds, and plants—and children, apparently—led to such books as *Conversations Introducing Poetry, Chiefly on Subjects of Natural History for the Use of Children and Young Persons* and the posthumous *The History of Birds*, intended for a similar youthful audience. The apropos yet ironic situation of the Other-that-is-woman writing about the Other-that-is-nature is a complex one, as Barbara T. Gates's study of Victorian women writers has demonstrated, but Smith certainly anticipates the many women in Gates's reappreciation who, perforce or by choice, adopted the role of popularizer of natural history, especially for children (Gates 37).[49] Once again, nature is thereby conflated with the human abject, as here, women and children are allowed a special relationship with other species but are at the same time juvenilized and feminized for such an easy, porous cross-species intersubjectivity.

Smith's adult poetry has a similar naturalist edge, aimed in part at demonstrating a sense of collegiality, even equality, with the male nature writers of the day, including Erasmus Darwin and Gilbert White. Indeed, only an admirer of *The Loves of Plants* could write a poem entitled "To the goddess of botany" and, in a footnote to another poem, proclaim Darwin one "whose imagination so happily applies every object of Natural History to the purposes of poetry" (66n). White's *Natural History* is another favorite in Smith's copious naturalist footnotes to her poems, but she dares to contradict this oracle of ornithology in a note to her "Ode to the missel thrush": to White's claim that the mistle thrush stops singing "before Midsummer," she comments, "It is certainly an error," as she can hear the bird "now," on "the 8th of July" (200), thus countering the prophet of close observation with evidence from her own experiential "spot of ground." But Smith's observing eye, too, is filtered through Linnaeus and Buffon, as her taxonomical footnotes continue to demonstrate. The barn swallow, as he "slumbers in his dome of clay," is footnoted thus: "swallow. *Hirundo rustica*" ("The moth" 9, 185n).[50] In its scorn for pigeon breeders and enthusiasts, another note further asserts her earnest desire to be deemed a serious student of birds: such "Fanciers are to Ornithologists, what Flower Fanciers are to Botanists" (260n).[51] Smith obviously prided herself as belonging to the second of both contrasting pairs.

Various poems from even her first collection, *Elegiac Sonnets*, evidence this concern for scientific accuracy in her avian poetics. Three of these poems concern nightingales, and the first, "To a Nightingale," is quite a stock treatment of the "Poor melancholy bird" (1), though the bird's feminization throughout climaxes in a couplet that a feminist scholar aware of Smith's lifelong struggles with men and money might well dwell upon: "Ah! songstress sad! that such my lot might be, / To sigh, and sing at liberty—like thee!" (13–14). Smith's melancholia will be considered again, but the two other nightingale sonnets, "On the departure of the nightingale" and "The return of the nightingale," are as notable for their emphasis on the question of the bird's migratory comings and goings as for their trite sentiments. The former bids the bird a fond autumn farewell, "Whether on Spring thy wandering flights await, / Or whether silent in our groves you dwell" (5–6), broaching explicitly the era's ornithological controversy regarding which species of birds fled Britain for warmer winter abodes. Thus she footnotes the first line quoted above: "Alludes to the *supposed* migration of the Nightingale" (17n; emphasis added). The nightingale in the latter poem is bid "welcome to our shades again" (10), and the allusion to the "warm wing of the western gale" (1) that brings the nightingale back *may* be more indicative of a migratory journey than a mere return from the deeper "groves" a few miles out of town, but one cannot conclude that Smith is now sure that the nightingale is indeed a bird of passage.[52] Her ruminations on the subject continue in one of her late *Fables*, "The swallow," in which she would "know from what wide wilderness / You came across the sea" (24–25). The poet continues her apostrophe, "Were you in Asia?" (36),[53] but the antepenultimate stanza again considers the possibility that swallows winter underwater instead, and Smith duly footnotes the stanza with a reference to White's belief that they there "remain torpid till the ensuing spring" (276n). That the insectivore nature of the nightingale and swallow renders migration practically requisite for both may seem obvious to the modern student of birds, but the ongoing controversy makes a fascinating footnote itself in the history of British literature.

Smith devotes some poetic verbiage (and ornithological angst) to another favorite of Gilbert White, the European nightjar. One of her many early sonnets to moroseness describes, quite marvelously and hauntingly, "The shrieking night-jar sail[ing] on heavy wing" ("Composed during a walk on the Downs" 8).[54] And yes, there is a footnote. This is the "night-jar or night-hawk," Smith writes, but she is hesitant about the identification: "As I have never seen it dead, I know not to what species it belongs" (41n). (She apparently wasn't in the habit of toting her gun along on nature walks, as was presumably White's wont, or she could have seen plenty of them in such a state.) In a later reference to the "night-jar" in *Beachy Head* (514), her new certainty calls for a lengthy note on the species, reassuring the reader that "this bird" was indeed the one "intended to be described in the Forty-second sonnet" (239n), that is, the poem just discussed. Once again, Smith's dilemma is difficult for the modern birder to comprehend, as the nightjar is the only member of the "goatsucker tribe" found in England.[55]

Via Bartram's *Travels*, Smith does know of one American goatsucker, the common nighthawk, and if her nightingales sing sad songs in a female mindscape, this bird sings, or rather, buzzes, in a quite "native" one. The nighthawk of "Supposed to have been written in America" is "Ill-omen'd" (1) because, as Smith's note tells us (following Bartram), "the Indians . . . believe that the cry . . . portends some evil." Moreover, this is sheer "superstition," we are assured (54n). But the sonnet so footnoted involves her own loss of "Reason," as her "enfeebled spirit" itself succumbs to moribund fear and "Pale Superstition" (13, 14, 10). On one level, her othering of the Native as superstitiously primitive and her own self-deprecation as an "irrational" female reflect a complicity in the main Western male song-and-dance. But one might also say that, through her implicit identification with the superstitious "Indian" and even the nighthawk's anthropomorphized melancholy, the Others of bird and Native and woman simultaneously form a sort of disruptive triumvirate that, polyphonically, looks askance at the rule of "Reason" itself.

In Smith's prosodic evolution from the strict Shakespearean sonnet to a more perambulatory blank verse, *The Emigrants* stands out as her first success in sounding a proto-Wordsworthian note of ruralism and naturism. No longer constrained to rush her naturalistic descriptions into tagged-on anthropocentric couplets, the poet now has the space in which to describe avians in more earnest, a freedom that will climax in *Beachy Head* (where she will pen several Wordsworthian passages, such as the one beginning "An early worshipper at Nature's shrine, / I loved her rudest scenes" [346–47]). But one must guess that the almost misanthropic social protest of *The Emigrants* is, in large part, behind the Burnsian plaintive contrasts of human "dominion" against "Nature's union." Here, too, nature is responsible for "Nothing but good: Yet Man, misguided Man, / Mars the fair work," making the poet "sigh for some lone Cottage" (1.32–33, 43). In such a place, "unspoil'd by Man," she can "delight" in the "sighing winds, / That, on their fragrant pinions, waft the notes / Of birds rejoicing in the trangled *[sic]* copse" (1.56, 267–69). (That the winds are "winged" is a common trope, but for their "pinions" to send the birds' songs flying, as it were, is almost too tortured a metaphor.)

As in Burns, the "delight" must turn to melancholia. By book 2, the narrator is a sad solitary amid the rebirth of April, a poor excuse for sentience compared to the fecund "mossy labours of the Thrush" (2.29). Her suffering has been so great that her "soul / "Feels not the joy reviving Nature brings" (2.39–40). If Smith's autobiographical travails allowed her perhaps even greater reason than Burns for despondency, her alienation from other species results in a similar shame for her species. The immediate cause for Burns is his countrymen's passion for hunting; in Smith, it is the war in Europe that makes the "heart shudder," makes the "Man, who thinks, / Blush for his species." Smith's concern for the European battleground characteristically extends to its avians and flora:

> *There* the trumpet's voice
> Drowns the soft warbling of the woodland choir;
> And violets, lurking in their turfy beds
> Beneath the flow'ring thorn, are stain'd with blood. (2.67–71)

No wonder that her "soul is pain'd / By the variety of woes that Man / For Man creates" (2.412–14). (Surely the Wordsworth who will wonder "what man has made of man" has read this.) Smith's most eloquent protest in the poem is directed against human despotism and war, but one could also interpret the lines as a concurrent complaint against humankind's attitude toward other species, if one reads "hind" as both poor human rustic and poor hunted animal:

> Restrain that rage for power, that bids a Man,
> Himself a worm, desire unbounded rule
> O'er beings like himself: Teach the hard hearts
> Of rulers, that the poorest hind, who dies
> For their unrighteous quarrels, in thy [God's] sight,
> Is equal to the imperious Lord, that leads
> His disciplin'd destroyers to the field. (2.424–30)

But the poet is addressing the Deity, and He is the same *deistic* gentleman we witnessed in Cowper, whom, at poem's end, Smith expects to resolve all strife with a final "reign of Reason, Liberty, and Peace!" (2.444). This is also the "great Power" at the poem's beginning, "Who . . . knows / If but a Sea-Mew falls" (1.26–28). But the death of the gull here seems but the least trivial movement of one mechanical cog or spring in the Great Timepiece of the Universe, and these grandiose appeals, or retreats, to patriarchal Enlightenment Reason (and to a *male* godhead) feel forced, especially when uttered by a woman poet and by a watcher and lover of real, live birds. All things considered, Smith perhaps had no choice but to fall back upon the mechanistic formulae of her age: she so deeply wanted the natural science of the Father, but she also got his God.

Perhaps Smith achieves her greatest escape from all this in *Beachy Head*, where, once again on the shore, she gives more attention to the seabirds, the "terns, and gulls, and tarrocks [kittiwakes]" as they "seek their food" (23). Like such border creatures of water, land, and air, the poet is also a "guiltless exile" (288) whose life has been torn between England and France, whose naturalist aspirations have been forced into the heavy trousers of a patriarchal science and metaphysics. One might say that Smith had to behave like the feinting mother bird in the following descriptive passage:

> And often, from her nest, among the swamps,
> . . . .
> They scare the plover, that with plaintive cries
> Flutters, as sorely wounded, down the wind. (203, 205–206)

Aside from the observational realism of this passage,[56] it is as if Smith is also mourning the compromising moves that she must make in order to be considered a viable thread in the literary and social fabric of the day. No doubt the poet also feels truly outraged by bird trapping, but perhaps she, too, has felt hunted and trapped, and "victim" of both England and the Continent, like the wheatears in *Beachy Head*, those "timid migrants" who are sacrifices to a boy's "wired trap" (463, 461).[57] At last, when bird and woman are conjoined, the exegesis becomes all the more problematically multivalent.

Unfortunately, a lot of Smith's bird poems are self-acknowledgedly blatant *Fables*. Characteristic is "The jay in masquerade," which is interesting enough for the sheer number of bird species mentioned in the verse tale.

But that dandy of a jay is a mere Aesopian signifier for human vanity. The introductory note to these fables is the fascinating part. By way of apology for adopting such a quaint genre, she says, "If the mind momentarily acquiesces in the *absurdity* of animals having the passions and faculties of man, every thing else may be granted" (251; emphasis added). The apology is only necessary because so many have unconsciously acquiesced (to this day) that such a belief is absurd, but Smith's great consciousness of the problem reflects a psyche that has heard an individual mistle thrush singing on the "8th of July." Perhaps this awareness partially explains Stuart Curran's belief that Smith's is "an alternate Romanticism that seeks not to transcend or to absorb nature," as the canonical male Romantics do, "but to contemplate and honor its irreducible alterity" (xxviii). I can't say that I agree with such a baldly dichotomous assertion; indeed, Smith's anxiety of influence, complicated as it is with male father figures, led much more to an adoption of typical Augustan animal tropes than to anything like their opposite. But Curran may have in mind a passage such as the following:

> . . . the master travelling,
> Scares the rooks rising slow on whispering wings,
> While o'er his head, before the summer sun
> Lights up the blue expanse, heard more than seen,
> The lark sings matins; and above the clouds
> Floating, embathes his spotted breast in dew. (*Beachy Head* 473–78)

The lark's apparent religiosity is certainly ludicrous, an "absurdity," but the visual and aural image of "rooks rising slow on whispering wings" does evoke an alterity of sorts, a vision of another species "unto itself." The line's meter, with the jarring initial trochee, then spondee, can be heard, first, as imitative of a flock of corvids suddenly taking flight; then it assumes a quieter and more measured iambic "flapping," to the alliterative "wing beats," of course, of the *wh* and the *w* sounds. Given Charlotte Smith's "fathers," one can perhaps hardly ask for more. And given Wordsworth's high praise for a marginalized figure that he knew was "not likely to be . . . remembered" in the English pantheon of poets (qtd. in Curran xix), one might also finally acknowledge Smith as a mother to another, better remembered poet who loved the birds.

WILLIAM WORDSWORTH: WORDS AND BIRDS

The little birds are piping yet
  Among the bushes and trees;
There's a cuckoo, and one or two thrushes,
And a far-off wind that rushes,
And a sound of water that gushes,
And the cuckoo's sovereign cry
Fills all the hollow of the sky.

—WILLIAM WORDSWORTH, "Evening Voluntaries" VIII

Friends shall I have at dawn, blackbird and thrush
To rouse me, and a hundred Warblers more;
And if those Eagles to their ancient Hold
Return, Helvellyn's Eagles, with the Pair
From my own door I shall be free to claim
Acquaintance, as they sweep from cloud to cloud.
The Owl that gives the name to owlet-crag
Have I heard whooping, and he soon will be
A chosen one of my regards.

—WILLIAM WORDSWORTH, *Home at Grasmere*

As indicated in my semiautobiographical preface, my adolescent enthusiasm for both words and birds led me early to the poetry of Wordsworth, as a corpus that seemed to best combine literature and nature. However, the earnest nature lover and amateur ornithologist in me would soon come away from Wordsworth with a sense of disappointment. My later reading about the poet seemed to corroborate this impression, as the post–new criticism rediscovery of the Romantics in the mid-twentieth century led to the following critical commonplace: Wordsworth's major contribution was a *psychological* one, and, in his central "marriage of mind and nature," the emphasis was really on "mind," or imagination.[58] Wordsworth allows for such a reading in his preface to the *Lyrical Ballads*: yes, his "principle object . . . was to choose incidents and situations from common life," but such subject matter required "a certain colouring of the imagination" (PW 2:386). Thomas Love Peacock was perhaps the first to highlight Wordsworth's "mind over nature," claiming not only that the Lake Poets were ignorant of nature, but that Wordsworth could not even "describe a scene under his own eyes without" ruining it with some supernatural coloring, some "fantastical parturition of the moods of his own mind" (*Four Ages* 513).

To the contemporary reader, however, such a critique seems to apply much better to Coleridge or Shelley, and the more usual critique has been that Wordsworth's nature wasn't "colored" enough. Thus F. W. Bateson could write that, for a so-called nature poet, Wordsworth's nature was "curiously uncreative and dead" (56), and Anthony Easthope's recent Lacanian-inflected study of Wordsworth can bluntly begin, "Wordsworth is not interested in nature" (1).[59] At bottom, nature was, for Wordsworth, but "a mirror in which his subconscious mind could reflect itself" (Bateson 56), a Lacanian mirrored Other appropriated by the Lacanian self in its quest for a stable identity (Easthope 45–52).[60] The extent to which Wordsworth's birds are but endlessly metonymic mirrors of intrapsychic machinations will no doubt be a major focus here, but I would like to at least begin with the working hypothesis that his cuckoos and skylarks may be more than feathered glosses of psychological projection.

And yet a cursory glance at the relative lack of specificity among Wordsworth's many bird references seems to support Bateson's bald assertion. Using the five-volume Oxford edition of Wordsworth's poetry and Cooper's venerable *Concordance* as starting points, I performed a content analysis of Wordsworth's avian allusions.[61] One immediate finding of my obsessive-compulsiveness is that a striking percentage of such references are to generic birds or generic songbirds, a nomenclatural casualness rather disconcerting to the lover of birds. Thus, though he owned a copy of Bewick's *History of British Birds* (Shaver and Shaver 22),[62] Wordsworth nonetheless demonstrated no great interest in the identification of particular species, and many of the specific genus and species names that he does employ were apparently derived either from his travel reading or (more usually) from the communal knowledge that every child acquires, much as the child growing up in the United States today learns how to point to a robin, sparrow, and crow, but not much else. Wordsworth's literary antecedents were also a factor; his diatribe in the preface against "gaudiness and inane phraseology" (PW 2.386) notwithstanding, he commonly subsumed even his more particularized birds (e.g., the nightingale and the eagle) under the conventional tropes of traditional English poetic practice (as in "Philomel" and the "Bird of Jove"), with often conventional results. My main point here, that Wordsworth was no Audubon, may border on the self-evident, but it wasn't so clear, for instance, to the Victorian scholar whose own list of the birds in Wordsworth was aimed, he said, at "the Wordsworthian naturalist" (Tutin, *Wordsworth Dictionary* 206).[63]

However, the Sage of Grasmere did spend years working through several editions of his own "nature guide." If such a genre is "relatively minor" in the literary scheme of things, it was Wordsworth who "raised [it] to an art form" (Gaull 317). The *Guide to the Lakes* is Wordsworth's prose paean to the Lake District and his most explicit plea for its preservation. Intended as a tourist's guidebook to the region, it was, surprisingly perhaps, Wordsworth's "best known and most frequently republished" work until his death (McKusick 54). The *Guide* begins with a general description of the local terrain: the lakes, islands, valleys and, especially, the "sublime" mountains. Indeed, the portrait is ultimately one of stasis and relatively devoid of bird or beast, as if Bateson were dead on: it is more a prose poem to "rocks, and stones, and trees" than to skylarks and cuckoos. In his introduction to a reissue of the 1822 *Guide*, Jonathan Wordsworth agrees that "[a]s a poet Wordsworth is seldom descriptive," going on to praise his namesake's more expansive natural descriptions in the prose that follows.[64] But despite a half-page description of waterfowl that was added to the 1835 edition of the *Guide* (36–37),[65] the person interested in what birds might be seen in the Lake District could well come away from this book with the notion that there are *very few* of them. Granted that the *Guide*'s very intent, its emphasis on the more permanent features of topography and terrain, perhaps justifies the relative exclusion of such a transient and migratory subtopic, but Wordsworth's very choice of genre remains symptomatic, for even his poetry may be said to ultimately privilege the monolithic and ("permanent") "One" over the abundant and prolific "many."[66]

However, the *Guide*'s very real environmentalist protests must be acknowledged. Unhappy that entrepreneurs and tourists had recently discovered the Lakes, Wordsworth feels it necessary, in the *Guide*'s third section, to lay down strictures regarding the future development of the region, ways that will least disturb the area's "peace" and "rusticity" (67). He laments that much has already been "defaced" by the "introduction of discordant objects," both human architecture and imported flora, from the "craving" for profit and "prospect" (68, 71, 73). Against this untoward "application of machinery," he still wishes to "preserve [what is left of] the native beauty of this delightful district," even if it has to become "a sort of national property" (99, 98, 101).

The book's final sections are more specific recommendations for the tourist, during which we learn that eagles were "formerly" seen at a certain spot (151); another place is one of the few left in England where red deer can be found (155). Spring may be the best time to visit, when one can hear the "Linnets and Thrushes" who are safer at this time of year from birds of prey (the "Destroyer" [105]). In a similar manner, Wordsworth hopes that his home district can still elude the fatal grasp of another "Destroyer."

However, what strikes one again and again in Wordsworth's use of birds is his *using* of birds. But this segue into Wordsworth's poetry per se must come with a few disclaimers. Wordsworth's natural empathy usually steers him clear of the baldly aggressive appropriation of nature we saw in Pope's "Windsor-Forest"; the later poet's appropriation of nature includes a humanizing projection that disallows for such a heartless objectification, however problematic his own "heartfelt" *subject*ification is. I must also admit that my initial denigration of Wordsworth's ornithological knowledge is, in good part, a rhetorical overstatement. The assumption that Wordsworth's birds consist mostly of "a cuckoo, and one or two thrushes" falls under the weight of my content survey, in which I've tentatively identified sixty specific bird species or genuses that fly, sing, mother, and mourn through some two hundred poems of Wordsworth's corpus.[67] (Compare this to Chaucer, fifty-one species, and Milton, thirty-two species [Harrison 135].) Wordsworth's sometimes marvelously *real* observations of bird behavior will be dealt with in a later section. Indeed, the standard line that Wordsworth is *not* really a poet of nature may be in need of an overhaul, if one believes Jonathan Bate: "I trust the intuition that locates Wordsworth firmly in nature and I reject the counter-intuitive readings which have been so influential in the academy over the past thirty years" (*Romantic* 10). But first, on to such a counterintuitive reading, through a visit to the Mother.

I must emphasize immediately, however, that the following sections are offered as an "as if," to be read dialogically, either as a deconstruction of mainstream ecological takes on literary Romanticism or as even a tongue-in-cheek symptom of the postmodernist solipsistic constructivism that ecocriticism must finally combat, or come to terms with, in some way more satisfying than the attempts that I surveyed in the first chapter.

OTHERING THE MOTHER: THE BIRD AS RECUPERATIVE OTHER

Behold the Parent Hen amid her Brood,
Though fledged and feather'd, and well pleased to part
And straggle from her presence, still a Brood,
And she herself from the maternal bond
Still undischarged; yet doth she little more
Than move with them in tenderness and love,
A centre of the circle which they make;
. . . .
She scratches, ransacks up the earth for food
Which they partake at pleasure. Early died
My honour'd Mother.
—WORDSWORTH, *The Prelude*

This, one of the remarkably few references to his mother in Wordsworth's corpus, might initially strike the reader as a painful non sequitur,[68] but the transition from avian mother (be it hen or wren or swan) or avian familial pair to a *human* mother or pair of lovers is no uncommon leap for the poet. Moreover, this is but one particular schema through which Wordsworth appropriates the bird as a metonymic Other for his own purposes of ego recuperation. I would immediately direct this Other to a specific psychogenic origin, that of Lacan's "real Other," the mother (Wilden 264), or, as Kristeva puts it, "Freudian theory detects everywhere the same *impossible mourning for the maternal object*" (*Black Sun* 9). If one might then assume the Freudian or Lacanian notion of maternal lack and the ego's necessary propensity to anxiously and unsuccessfully fill such an original lack via an endless series of metonymic displacements, the oft-repeated notion that nature serves as a displacement for this poet's mother becomes all the more attractive. (Indeed, orphaned at a relatively early age, Wordsworth may have felt the primal loss more than others. But this biographical specificity need not be emphasized in the psychoanalytic readings that follow.) Richard McGhee, for instance, referring to the lines from *The Prelude* just quoted, claims that "Wordsworth has in this passage come as close as he can to the source of his originating anxiety" of maternal separation, and that the stumbling end to this seminal passage, the poet's admission that his "drift" has hardly "been obvious" (5.290–91), is an "interruption . . . akin to those scenes of division, of woundings in sacred places where the mind turns round upon itself." McGhee concludes that associating a bird with the mother is a common Wordsworthian conflation, though this critic's fixation on the details of Wordsworth's biography seems rather too much here: "There is more security in the natural world of the barnyard than there was in his childhood" (91, 90), and therefore the hen and brood receive the displaced brunt of this passage's energy.

Neo-Freudian critics lose no time in finding this maternal theme ubiquitously displaced on Wordsworth's natural environment in general, as in Peter Sachs's assertion that the poet's "consoling" images are often "derived . . . from a scarcely transformed sexual impulse toward the mother earth" (33). McGhee likewise identifies Wordsworth's "Nature as Mother" very early on in his study (4), and according to J. P. Ward, Wordsworth's "longing necessarily finds harbor . . . in such safeties as Nature and Imagination" (191). While Wordsworth's nature most immediately evokes images of mountains and lakes and flowers, the poet's birds play no small role as substitute objects in this metonymic *glissement*, this "incessant sliding of the signified under the signifier" (Lacan, "Agency" 743). In sum, I would argue that through this Lacanian displacement, Wordsworth's birds are synecdoches of nature, and both are stand-ins for the (now occulted or repressed) Mother or Real Other, and that Wordsworth's appropriation of the specifically avian Other is also a Lacanian gesture, the drive to recuperate a sense of integral self that finally is wanting, insufficient.[69] Expanding the Lacanian fraction of "S/s" (signifier over signified), one might express the formula as follows:

> *signifier chain: [etc.] ←→ other human females/mothers ←→ nature ←→ birds ←→ mother hens ←→ [etc.]*
> *occulted signified:* MOTHER ("Real Other")

The chain can be extended on the left to Wordsworth's use of "innocents" in general (e.g., rural folk, children, the developmentally disabled, the elderly solitaires) and on the right to various other bird species to be dealt with in subsequent sections.

Given the psychosexual nature of the occulted signified, much has also been made of Wordsworth's apparently excessive guilt before nature in *The Prelude*, often explained as a specifically Oedipal guilt. In contrast to his pious words for his mother and the hen, the poet elsewhere seems to dwell upon his transgressions against the Mother, notably in the nest-robbing incident, in which the young Wordsworth is a "plunderer" of ravens' nests on the crags, where the "Mother Bird had built her lodge" (1.336–339). One is even tempted to see the line "Oh! when I have hung / Above the raven's nest" (1.341–42) as an erotic position, and thus as support for Easthope's discernment of "strongly incestuous undertones" in the poet's nest robbing (67).[70] "Fears of guilt," too, erupt into the poet's "conscious mind" (McGhee 87) when the trapped woodcock of book 1, "Which was the captive of another's toils / Became my prey" (*Prelude* 1.327–28),[71] as if the youngster were ransacking the entire landscape for one Lacanian object displacement after another, as a "consoling substitute" or a "consolation prize" for his original traumatic loss (Sachs 4, 5).

That Wordsworth's birds often "express erotic desires" is a recurrent theme in McGhee's study (22), but he points to one type of bird as the avian epitome of Wordsworth's maternal fixation. In another guilt-charged passage in *The Prelude*, the youth's stolen boat goes "heaving through the water, like a Swan" (1.404). McGhee notes the "heaving" eroticism here (87) and comments elsewhere that the swan has been "long a favorite erotic symbol for" Wordsworth (252). I would also point to a rather strange sonnet in Wordsworth's corpus—"I heard (alas! 'twas only in a dream)"—as a further example, an etherealized wet dream, as it were, in which the poet dreams of "a fair Swan [that] on drowsy billows heaved" (7). After several lines of trite piety that seem but incomplete sublimation, he exclaims, "Mount[!], tuneful Bird. . . . She soared—and I awoke" (13–14). At last, the swan's ostensible signification within a rather strained Christian-Platonic idealism serves only as an insufficient cover for an image of bestial eroticism.

Common for Wordsworth, too, is to present swans, especially in pairs or in families, as analogues, consolations, or inspirations for humans, also often in pairs or families. A prime example is the lengthy swan family passage in *An Evening Walk*,[72] a family complete with virile male, a "female with a meeker charm," and the "brown little ones" who are "by all a mother's joys caress'd" (209, 210, 241). The remarkably realistic aspects of this description will be addressed later, but their avian felicity, their happy domesticity is offered, above all, as a contrasting prelude and foil to the poor "wretch" of a husbandless human mother who follows (242), who dies with her children at her breast. (The interpolation of this human tragedy anticipates many a poem in which Wordsworth will champion the plight of poor mothers.)

Opposed to this broken human family, too, is the mock-heroic image of the strutting rooster in this poem, that "monarch" of the barnyard, whose vain, "cocky" egoism and machismo may well evoke a chuckle from the reader: "Spur clad his nervous feet, and firm his tread, / A crest of purple tops the warrior's head" (130–32). McGhee points out that, in *An Evening Walk*, "the animal being . . . benefits most from his impassioned description, whether in the lighthearted passage on the stalking 'monarch' . . . or in the . . . picture of the family of swans with which the destitute family is contrasted." As for this Lord of the Hens, "obviously the poet is sympathetic with the erotic power of this stately creature. Just as obvious is his enchantment with the regal grace of the male swan who leads his family in domestic contentment over the lakes' dimpling deeps" (42). Thus both male swan and domestic fowl reassure Wordsworth's masculinity,[73] perhaps even his notion of the traditional patriarchal family unity. In Lacanian terms, Wordsworth's identification here with the Father, or the Law, is evident, as a talisman against the various lost and mourning women of his poetry who recur again and again as metonymic reminders of his primal loss, and whom he must as insistently "conquer" again and again via various patriarchal or mirror-stage-monist consolations.

Another significant swan passage is found in *Home at Grasmere*, in which Wordsworth's use of the swans as inspirational analogues for human behavior is even more explicit. The "lonely pair / Of milk-white Swans" (238–39) are appropriated as mirrors of the human dyad—"we a solitary pair like them" (255)—who are returning to Grasmere, hopeful of the same felicity.[74] (Earlier in the poem, William and Dorothy have been driven to the valley by the wind, "like two Birds" [161].) But now the swan pair is "missing" (238), having not returned for the spring, and can only be described as a presence in absence, like the Derridean trace, rendering the swans' past-tense appropriation all the more tenuous and pathetic. The birds are "more dear" because their "state so much resembled" that of William and Dorothy, and so the poet earnestly desires them back:

> Shall we behold them, consecrated friends,
> Faithful Companions, yet another year
> Surviving, *they for us, and we for them*,
> And neither pair be broken? (248, 252, 261–64; emphasis added)

The "they for us" is pure appropriation, the "we for them," pure fantasy.[75] "Thus do we soothe ourselves" (290), the poet admits, one passage on universal love later, and such an assuagement no doubt also characterizes the swans' role here. But the poet's immediate reaction is one of betrayal: "They should not have departed" (256). Then Wordsworth becomes quite consciously ashamed of such presumption, when he realizes that they may have been victims of the hunting "Dalesmen" with "the deadly tube" (266). He even apologizes: "Recall, my song, the ungenerous thought; forgive . . . the conjecture harsh . . . Inflicted upon confidence so pure" (269–70, 272). And at last, these swans, and the other nonhuman species at Grasmere, have no need of our species' positive regard:

> They who are dwellers in this holy place
> Must needs themselves be hallowed. They require
> No benediction from the Stranger's lips,
> For they are blessed already. (277–80)

Quoting this very passage, Karl Kroeber insists that Wordsworth is thus "not tempted to distort perceptual reality . . . but, instead, is enabled to project visions, memories . . . upon perceptual realities as fulfillments of their actualness" ("'Home at Grasmere'" 140). However, how such "actualness" can remain undistorted after such a list of blessed projections is difficult to imagine.

Such passages have indeed led to several ecocritics' great esteem for this particular work. Kroeber, for instance, lauds the poem as an epitome of "a special originality and relevance in Wordsworth's prosaic celebrations of serene egoism amidst remote mountain valleys" (132). Indeed, according to Kroeber, the poem's superimposition of interspecies relationships—part of a general "rhetoric of repetition"—are indicative of a grand "nurturing ecosystemic wholeness" (*Ecological* 54–55). The double pairing of swans and humans can be read positively as an ecotherapeutic interrelational overlapping, a cross-species merger, as can the vale's waterfowl, those "Birds that haunt the flood" (Wordsworth, *Home* 193), whose "impulsive" flocking behavior represents a unity-in-multiplicity that the poet so earnestly desires:

> I cannot take possession of the sky,
> Mount with a thoughtless impulse, and wheel there,

> One of a mighty multitude whose way
> Is a perpetual harmony and dance
> Magnificent. (199–203)

Grasmere's "spiraling birds," according to Kroeber, are "the most compelling image of [the vale's] living unity" ("'Home at Grasmere'" 134). Indeed, the flight, in a "large round," in "progress intricate," proceeds in accord with recent findings about the remarkable mass coordination of flocking behavior, "as if one spirit swayed / Their indefatigable flight" (Wordsworth, *Home* 211, 214, 215–16). Moreover, the local spot of ground that is Grasmere can be read as the ecologist's bliss of bioregionalism: "this individual Spot" is deemed by the poet a "Centre," a "Whole without dependence or defect," a "Unity entire" (145, 148, 149, 151). This bioregionalism includes a component of alter-species egalitarianism, as McKusick would have it: Wordsworth's "sense of family solidarity extends beyond humankind" to "all living things that dwell in the entire regional ecosystem" (72–73).

But a more circumspect reading of Wordsworth's acts of othering and appropriation in *Home at Grasmere* remains viable, and Kroeber's vision of Grasmere as an ecological "blissful Eden," as Wordsworth dubs it (105), might itself be subject to a Freudian undermining. The waterfowl of the famous passage above are yet again objects of manic contagion: "They show their pleasure, and shall I do less?" (197). The innocuous statement "'Tis themselves" (224) can be taken as Wordsworth protesting too much, once again, in claiming them *not* to be vessels of his own projection. The reference early after his arrival to Grasmere's birds can be easily read as one of appropriation, even ownership: "Have we not . . . thickets full of songsters . . . ?" (126, 129). Later in the poem comes another extended avian paean, beginning "Friends shall I have at dawn, blackbird and thrush," a passage embracing "a hundred Warblers," "Helvellyn's Eagles," and "The Owl that gives the name to owlet-crag," who is to be "A chosen one of my regards" (515–16, 518, 521, 523). Thus, in his return home to Grasmere, an attempt to return to a presymbolic, undifferentiated union with the Mother, one might say, it is as if the poet frantically tries to surround himself with as many substitute objects as possible. For McGhee, Wordsworth's Grasmere is a veritable womb, a "place of regression" (48); the poet's Freudianization of nature here reflects "his general tendency to retreat to the warm luxury of maternal security" and serves as "an extension of his satisfaction of erotic desire in the company of his Emma, the 'Eve' of his return to paradise" (49).

In support of my Lacanian chain of displacements, I would first note McGhee's insistence that "Emma" (Dorothy) provided the poet with "a new object of love, a 'real object' to displace the image of his mother in his fantasy" (111), and then point out that Dorothy is commonly associated with birds. In *Home at Grasmere*, for instance, Dorothy's "Voice was like a hidden bird that sang" (91). In *The Prelude*, animals, including the "birds in bower," are "Children of her Love" (11.27–28), and any bird that could have "known her, would have lov'd" her, for "she was Nature's inmate" (216, 214). (As we shall see, it is she who eventually teaches "the little birds to build their nests / And warble in" the "chambers" of Wordsworth's soul [13.228–29]). Thus are two metonymically related signifiers of the maternal signified brought together, as if to reinforce the maternal absence by an overdetermined presence.

The nesting habits of birds in Wordsworth's poetry provide an abundant subset of this relationship between birds and mothers. The titular thrush of "'Hark, 'tis the Thrush, undaunted, undeprest,'" who, as one can by now expect, charms the speaker's "cares to rest" (8), also provides the poet with an example of "Love and nest" (4), which helps him "renew the life of their [his and his wife's] partnership in love" (McGhee 285). But several other nest poems are less ostensibly analogic; they appear rather as outlets for the poet to dwell on motherhood at large, without having to deal with the occulted signified. Thus in "A Wren's Nest," the emotional climax is the speaker's exhortation "Rest, Mother-bird!": that is, rest up for migration and think back on "thy late home" (65, 68). A fond tribute to maternity, at last, but for the fact, perhaps, that yet another mother will soon be making herself *absent*. More indicative of Wordsworth's own youthful plight, if one follows McGhee, are those places in his corpus where the sanctity of the nest has been violated, as in the "poor bird—her plundered nest / Hovering around with dolorous moan!" (*Peter Bell* 649–50). Similar in tone is his description of the lover's heart as "more desolate, more dreary cold / Than a forsaken bird's-nest filled with snow" ("'Why art thou silent!'" 11–12). If this feeling of loss or desertion is indeed symptomatic of Wordsworth's intrapsychic preoccupations, the poet is still relatively safe in viewing the process of loss at a distance.

A final bird nest poem deserves particular mention because of its strange mix of "delight" at the sight of a "sheltered bed, / The Sparrow's dwelling" ("The Sparrow's Nest" 4, 6–7) and Dorothy's less than delightful reaction to it: "She looked at it and seemed to fear it; / Dreading, tho' wishing, to be near it" (11–12). Why is she so afraid of a bed? A related question regards the human pairs I've been discussing, at times Wordsworth and his wife, at times his sister and him: Why are these two pairings, in general, less clearly distinguished than a social worker would like? If the nesting pair is a displacement for the human pair, as McGhee would have it, Dorothy may well be expressing a fear of (and yet a wishing for) incest. More to the point, may the poet be displacing his own desire and fear of the taboo upon his "sister Emmeline" (9)? One even wonders finally if the common substitutions of "Emmeline" and "Emma" for Dorothy were made for reasons beyond mere euphony and a conventional respect for anonymity. All such questions commonly revolve around a poet and his maternal nest.

WORDSWORTH'S MANIC AND MELANCHOLIC ORNITHOLOGY

> But most the Bard is true to inborn right,
> *Lark of the dawn*, and *Philomel of night*,
> *Exults* in freedom, can with rapture vouch
> For the dear blessings of a *lowly* couch.
>
> WILLIAM WORDSWORTH, "Liberty" (emphases added)

I now venture from the original trauma of maternal separation to the medley of psychological mechanisms through which that trauma is managed. Whether the British in general "were melancholic by nature as well as habit" (Gaull 217) is a speculative venture into ethnic typology and essentialism that need not be pursued; Wordsworth's own psychobiography, however, is fairer game. The poet admits, from an early age, to "Having two natures in me, joy the one / The other melancholy" (*Prelude* 10.868–69). To analyze such a psychic schism, I follow Lacan's idea of an originary maternal lack through its necessary consequences, a psychic melancholy or endless, "impossible mourning," and a compensatory manic state, through which the ego futilely attempts to transcend melancholy via a wishful, recuperative return to prelingual *jouissance*, or bliss. In other words, Wordsworth's two main procedures for filling this lack are to *mourn* the lack in a secondhand fashion by displacing his loss upon other substitute objects (mourning mothers, lugubrious nightingales, etc.), and to *deny* the lack via a recuperative manic enthusiasm (e.g., soaring skylarks) or a myth of monistic union (the "One" of nature, etc.). The second attempt I deem prelingual because, in Lacan's view, it is an impulse of the "dialectic of return" to the mirror stage ("Agency" 751), that "vision of harmony by a being in discord" (Wilden 174). But this harmony is ultimately ironic and illusory, especially when attempted in the medium of language itself. Finally, I would claim immediately that the relative preponderance of, say, skylarks over nightingales in Wordsworth's corpus indicates a preference for this latter "manic" strategy.[76]

Regarding the impulse toward harmony, Sachs, too, notes "how often a mourner is forced back to this primitive form of narcissism" (10), as a recurrence of the "primary desire . . . for a state preceding or abolishing genuine individuation" (16). In a similar way, Easthope attempts to demystify Wordsworth's mystical experiences in general via the Freudian concept of derealization, that is, "the effect of seeing the perceived as fantasy," which "leads to an overpowering vision of subject/object unity" (43). This last is the defining characteristic of the mirror stage, too, and one is tempted to see the Lacanian and Freudian mechanisms as versions of the same regressive "vision of harmony." Such a vision is alluded to, I think, in Wordsworth's well-known note to the "Intimations" ode: "I was often unable to think of external things as having external existence, and I communed with all I saw as something not apart from, but inherent in, my own immaterial nature." Here we have the self/Other unity of the mirror. And now for the return to the Law and the split self: "Many times while going to school have I grasped at a wall or tree to recall myself from this abyss of idealism to the reality" (*PW* 4.463).

Yet, having come (back) to the Father and the Law, the ego "must suffer guilt and exhibit the symptoms of endless mourning. Melancholia is a continuing symptom of mourning" (McGhee 105).[77] Like many recent scholars, McGhee doesn't consistently distinguish melancholia from mourning in the firm fashion that Freud did; the former involves the "unconscious loss of a love-object, in contradistinction to mourning, in which there is nothing unconscious about the loss" (Freud 166). As we have seen, *the* unconscious loss, for Lacan, is clearly the repressed signified or Mother, or (expressed dialogically) the Imaginary unity of the child-mother dyad. So Wordsworth's "mourning [or melancholy] is a recuperative mourning for what could never be in the first place . . . the full subject" (Easthope 86).[78]

To return to Wordsworth's birds, they often serve him as othered emblems of this ongoing oscillation between melancholy and mania, mourning and compensatory denial. (Indeed, Wordsworth's poetry is a stunning example of my notion put forward in previous discussions of Burns and Blake, regarding that bipolar disorder seemingly endemic to the Western psyche.) But first, a few introductory words on melancholy's smiling twin are in order. Freud notes melancholia's "remarkable . . . tendency . . . to turn into mania accompanied by a completely opposite symptomatology" (174), the latter symptoms being similar to outbursts of psychic relief in general, "characterized by high spirits" and the "discharge of joyful emotion" (175). Kristeva speaks more positively of this "so-called manic phase of exaltation" (*Black Sun* 9), but also notes its recuperative role as a denial of melancholy: "With manic persons . . . denial . . . walks on stage and becomes the tool that builds a shield against loss" via "variegated arrays of substitutive erotic objects" (50). I have already suggested the almost omnipresence of such a metonymic shield in the poetry of Wordsworth.

Two other general characteristics of mania are especially relevant to Wordsworth. First, given the poet's use of nature, often in its "April Morning" manifestation, Sachs's Frazerian emphasis on vegetation myths, on gods dying and reborn is worthy of note, as these "images of resurrection" are, at last, indicative of "the movement from grief to consolation" (2) and will lead us directly to Wordsworth's manic linnets, thrushes, and skylarks. Second, one must not forget the recuperative nature of the creative act itself, not only as a ritual in Sachs's sense, but in Kristeva's privileging of "poetic form" as the "sole 'container' seemingly able to secure an uncertain but adequate hold over the Thing" (*Black Sun* 14), which I take to be her version of the Lacanian Real. Through "aesthetic exultance," then, the successful poem is "at least a survival, a resurrection" (50–51), and Kristeva even wonders whether poetry might thus "bear witness to a (for the time being) conquered depression" (65). Whether or not Wordsworth's own words are entirely adequate in dealing with the *real* avian is another question. For now, we are concerned with how his birds are appropriated into the melancholic-manic mechanisms of self-and-Other.

"THEN SING, YE BIRDS": WORDSWORTH'S BIRDS AS MANIC RECUPERATION

The birds around me hopped and played,
Their thoughts I cannot measure:—

But the least motion which they made,
It seemed a thrill of pleasure.

— WILLIAM WORDSWORTH, "Lines written in Early Spring"

Wordsworth's oft-anthologized "Lines written in Early Spring" might first be taken as an obvious manic appropriation of nature, but a mania severely qualified by the first stanza's transition from "pleasant" to "sad thoughts" (3–4) and by the final stanza's "mourning" of humankind's postlapsarian status: the split self of the Law in contrast to nature's Imaginary holism. But nature in this poem is the *poet's* Imaginary, as the very first line merges the raw data of nature into "a thousand blended notes" (1), a synaesthetic unity of derealization. The birds stanza just quoted, especially, is a further attempt at a reunification of the split self, as the avians' (really the poet's) "thoughts," the Symbolic, are quite indistinguishable from their sensory bliss, the Imaginary. Of course, this is all pathetic fallacy—more specifically, a projection of unitary exultance by a self conscious of its divided status and frantic in its attempt at metonymic consolation.

Kroeber finds in this poem's hopping birds and happy twigs an expression of Wordsworth's "naturalistic" belief that nature is "inherently delightful" and delighting. That this faith is expressed with great "tentativeness," as an hypothesis, with such words as "seem'd," is actually a plus for this hard-minded critic (*Ecological* 43–46).[79] Kroeber's reading is itself an enticing delight, and I half-believe it, as I also concur with his assertion that Wordsworth's pathetic fallacies actually do, at times, "bestow on natural landscape the power of 'speaking' without encrustations of personifying conventions" (127). But my other half looks back at the narrator's own "sad thoughts" and wonders whether the rather manic twitches of the poem's other life forms aren't necessarily compensatory gestures. If, as Ward puts it, the "rills and the birds" of Wordsworth's nature "have sudden movements and starts," that fitful movement is at last "not of nature but human" (30). Relevant here, too, is McGhee's comment on Wordsworth's wont to identify "his passions with various kinds of animals" (107). The birds' "thrill of pleasure," then, is ultimately Wordsworth's, and his rediscovery of this projected pleasure outside himself gives it, perhaps, a surer ontological status than is possible within the painful dualism of his own psyche.

Wordsworth's "Ode: Intimations of Immortality" is a clinical case of the attempt to think oneself out of an inveterate mourning, a version of the recuperative "Abundant recompense" of "Tintern Abbey" (88) that, here especially, comes across as ultimately unconvincing. Bateson tentatively agrees: "It is possible he was consoling himself here . . . by making as much as possible of his newly-acquired" natural moralism (142). In this consolation, the birds provide a small but crucial accompaniment to the lambs, shepherd boys, and "immortal sea" (9.35).[80] But the fact that they are "birds," and not sparrows or linnets, I would claim, further foregrounds their ultimate role as empty markers of metonymy.

What is especially notable in the "Ode" is the poet's apparent *consciousness* of his "split Self"; indeed, the Neoplatonic myth of origin and the following stanzas on a child's maturation might be seen as metaphoric expressions of the individual's development from psychic union to multiplicity. On the birds' first appearance in "joyous song" (3.1), the poet is already a melancholy observer, alienated from the scene: "To me alone there came a thought of grief" (3.4). There is an immediate recovery—"And I again am strong" (3.6)—but that newfound strength is momentary and at last illusory, as he will proceed through strophe after strophe to cull the sour grapes of the "philosophic mind" (10.19). To reinforce his manic recuperation, the birds return toward the poem's end as "images of resurrection": "Then sing, ye Birds, sing, sing a joyous song!" (10.1). However, the poet's entreaties are strained at this point, to which the awkward and forced spondee in the line's middle seems to attest. Likewise, it is hard to fully believe his earlier exclamation, "The fulness of your bliss, I feel—I feel it all" (4.6); one is even tempted to conclude that Wordsworth himself intended the strained protesting too much of such lines, and that there is much more ambiguity and tension in Wordsworth than the new critics usually gave him credit for.

In Wordsworth's use of birds in manic recuperation, one immediately notices two species that serve time and again in such a process: the European linnet and the song thrush (or "throstle").[81] Moreover, these two birds often appear in tandem, sometimes even as grammatical coordinates in the same line or stanza:[82]

> . . . *the linnet and the thrush*,
> Vied with this waterfall, and made a song . . .
> ("Poems on the Naming of Places" I 26–27)

> *A linnet* warbled from those lofty elms,
> *A thrush* sang loud . . . ("The Ruined Cottage" 531–32)

> Come, hear *the woodland linnet*,[83]
> How sweet his music! . . .
>
> . . . .
>
> And hark! how blithe *the throstle* sings!
> He, too, is no mean preacher! ("The Tables Turned" 10–11, 13–14)

The linnet and thrush of "The Tables Turned" may be the most famous examples of these particular species in English poetry. The ecocritic *hears* these birds in a very positive fashion: "This poem turns the tables," above all, because it "proposes a new role for humankind among the speaking presences of the natural world. The place of poetry . . . is thus inherently dialogical; the poet must seek to engage those inhuman voices in conversation, at some risk to his own sense of identity" (McKusick 60–61). But the word "preacher" posits a very definite *human* (and didactic) message in what sounds to the uninitiated very like a meaningless mishmash of whistles, trills, and warbles. Their songs' theme, ultimately, is the "Spontaneous wisdom" ("The Tables Turned" 19) of a unified self, contrasted with Matthew's "books" (1), which can only lead to melancholy, and with the "meddling," dissecting "intellect" (26), the Lacanian prison of thought and language that is, by definition, a melancholic psyche itself already dissected. It is this same split psyche, I would argue, that must find an ameliorative bliss in a projected world of musician linnets and preacher thrushes.

Another bird, the blue tit, or "Blue-cap,"[84] dances his manic way through "The Kitten and the Falling Leaves" (64). As is often the case, the poet here employs a metonymic aggregate galore in his attempt at recuperation through the following signifier chain: *kitten → blue-cap → daughter*. Via Wordsworth's by now familiar use of animals and people "closest" to animals (children, etc.) as substitute objects, the poem begins by describing the kitten cavorting with the leaves, turns metonymically to the tit, who is a "giddy Sprite" (63) and the "Lithest, gaudiest Harlequin! / Prettiest Tumbler ever seen!" (72–73), and ends, for that precious human touch, with his daughter Dora, whose instinctive "transports" (108) establish her kinship to the poem's other species at "play." Through such projective embodiments of an inner need and lack, the poet claims some surcease from sorrow:

> And I will have my careless season
> Spite of melancholy reason. . . .

. . . .
Now and then I may possess
Hours of perfect gladsomeness. (111–12, 115–16)

However, the lame self-promise and personification of the poem's last line—"To gambol with Life's falling Leaf"—rather ruins an otherwise charming ditty, as if some inkling of guilt over his using of the kitten, bird, and child sabotaged his poetic instinct. The flight toward a purely manic poetry once again entails an untoward descent, a fall.

Elsewhere Wordsworth still attempts to climb, via the skylark:

Leave to the nightingale her shady wood,
A privacy of glorious light is thine;
Whence thou dost pour upon the world a flood
Of harmony, with instinct more divine.
("To a Skylark" ["Ethereal minstrel!"] 7–10)

The Romantics' employment of the skylark as an emblem of the inspired poet's flights of imagination has often been noted. Anna Sue Parrill, in fact, generalizes this motif to songbirds in general: "The songbird was for the English Romantic poets an important metaphor representing their concept of the poet and his imagination. In particular, the English Romantic poets found the nightingale and the skylark to embody characteristics of the poet as the Romantics defined him . . . such as the act of singing, the act of soaring to great heights, isolation, invisibility, and profound impact upon the listener" (44).[85] The importance of the nightingale and cuckoo as Romantic songsters will be addressed in their appropriate place; it is the lark of "joy and spontaneity" (46) who, above all, serves as fit object for a poetic projection of the manic state, the poet's ongoing attempt to escape the melancholic "Philomel of Night" via this recuperative "Lark of the Dawn." Indeed, given its inevitably recuperative guise as "the buoyant Lark," the "happiest bird," and "Gay lark of hope" (A Morning Exercise" 23, 30; *Descriptive Sketches* 632), it's no surprise that the skylark is, with the robin, the most common bird in Wordsworth's poetry.[86]

Wordsworth's most frequently anthologized skylark poem, "To a Skylark ('Ethereal minstrel!')," explicitly contrasts the lark's daylight effusions with the nightingale and "her shady wood" (7), and both the skylark's musical "flood" of "harmony" and the physical heights to which its "wings aspire" (9, 10, 3) attest to the poet's desire for an Other that is very like his poetic persona at its most manic: a singer of words inspired by feelings that take him above the sublunary banalities of ordinary folk.[87] Our bird is also apparently on a noble theological mission here, evident in such words as "Ethereal," "pilgrim," "glorious light," and "divine" (1, 8, 10). Then the concluding couplet: "Type of the wise who soar, but never roam; / True to the kindred points of Heaven and Home!" (11–12). "Type" is especially revelatory: the small brown-mottled bird is hardly the real point. Rather, Wordsworth is projecting his own issues: his need to "soar" via inspired poetry and yet avoid the fate of Chatterton by maintaining that modicum of down-to-earth level-headedness that more ethereal Romantics subsequently ridiculed him for, and his need, perhaps, to juggle the roles of (again) inspired poet of special sensibility and good, devoted British family man, one firmly attached to the "dear blessings of a lowly couch." In the Fenwick note to the poem, Wordsworth himself provides the best evidence that the skylark is, at bottom, a substitute object: "Rydal Mount 1825. (Where there are no skylarks, but the poet is everywhere. *pencil addition*)" (PW 2.518). Indeed, replace "skylarks" with "birds" in this quotation, and we have a summary of much of chapters 2 and 3 of this book.

The earlier "To a Skylark" ("Up with me!") has a similar movement from high-flying avian to human-moral conclusion. This "Drunken Lark" (20) is again the manic minion of song in flight, embodiment of the "madness" and "joy divine" (12) of Romantic poesy. But the speaker's psyche is split between an (incomplete) identification with the manic bird and a melancholy observer who mourns the incompleteness of the identification, a tension we've already seen in the "Intimations" ode. Thus the poet's initial exhortation—"Up with me! up with me into the clouds!" (1)—is as ironic as the great ode's "The fulness of your bliss, I feel—I feel it all." As for the final compensation of a Christian afterlife, let the reader judge the plodding coda: "I, with my fate contented, will plod on, / And hope for higher raptures, when life's day is done" (30–31).

"I heard the sky-lark warbling in the sky," Wordsworth writes in "Resolution and Independence" (5.1), a sure sign now that the heights of mania must be near. And yes, the poet acknowledges himself as much a "happy Child of earth" (5.3) as the poem's birds and bounding hare, but this is yet another poem of mixed-mindedness, in which an enunciating melancholy is found frequently observing enunciated mania. Notable, too, is Wordsworth's expressed awareness of the pendulum-like bipolar oscillation of the two moods, of, as N. Meihuizen calls it, "the cyclicality of melancholy" (61):

> But, as it sometimes chanceth, from the might
> Of joy in minds that can no further go,
> As high as we have mounted in delight
> In our dejection do we sink as low. (4.1–4)

This passage's fine relevance to human psychology in general is qualified when, later, he posits a singular linear progression from delight to dejection that is peculiar to poets, indicative of those concerns in "To the Skylark" in which he seeks a balance between the "kindred points of Heaven and Home": "We Poets in our youth begin in gladness; / But thereof comes in the end despondency and madness" (7.6–7). Characteristically, the poem is resolved by the poet's chance encounter with a surrogate Other, the Leech-gatherer, whose fortitude reassures Wordsworth that he need not necessarily fear going the way of Chatterton. Wordsworth's subsequent, and long, poetic output is certainly proof of that.

"GRAVE CREATURES": THE PLEASURES OF MELANCHOLY

> Grave Creature!—whether, while the moon shines bright
> On thy wings opened wide for smoothest flight,
> Thou art discovered in a roofless tower,
> . . . .
> Or spied where thou sitt'st moping in thy mew
> At the dim center of a churchyard yew;
> . . . .
> Thou giv'st, for pastime's sake, by shriek or shout,
> A puzzling notice of thy whereabout.
> —WILLIAM WORDSWORTH, "Evening Voluntaries" VII

From Wordsworth's birds as manic heights we must now "sink low," toward those of a more melancholy feather. The birds that Wordsworth chooses to evoke melancholy are by and large those of the standard literary tropes of nocturnal sadness and mortal foreboding: thus there are many owls, nightingales, and ravens, with an occasional rook and magpie. Even the cormorant appears, in "heavy flight, / Portending ruin" (Ecclesiastical Sonnet I.iii ["Trepidation of the Druids"] 4–5).[88] But the most surprising bird of melancholy in Wordsworth's corpus is certainly the strange North American bird in *The Excursion*, the "melancholy Muccawiss" of the "plaintive cry" (3.947, 949). The identity of this mystery bird is clarified in a manuscript variant of these lines, in which the bird is dubbed instead the "Whip-poor-will" (PW 5.107n). Interestingly, this bird is paired, or rather juxtaposed, with "the merry Mocking-bird" (*Excursion* 3.946), creating a New World version of the Old World's contrasting tropes of skylark and nightingale, a version derived entirely from Wordsworth's, or "Matthew's," books.

More than even the nightingale, perhaps, the owl is Wordsworth's favorite bird of darkness: in "Evening Voluntaries" VII, it is the "Owlet" of the "unexpected scream," "the imaginative Bird," and the "headless Owl!" (8, 12, 27), and yet this poem also includes the incongruous pun of an epithet, "Grave Creature!" (14). In *The Waggoner*, "yon screeching owl" is feared (3.98), his screech "worse than any funeral bell" (3.113). But in this poem, too, he is also a "Wanton" and a "jolly bird" (3.118, 120), a trickster playing games with humankind, according to the wagoner Benjamin. My argument for Wordsworth's owls as birds of melancholy seems to be breaking down immediately.

Wordsworth's rendering of the owl's call in the traditional syllabics of "halloo" and "tu-whit—tu-whoo" identify it as the tawny owl, whose wavering call is certainly open to an interpretation (and projection) of either foreboding sadness or carnivalesque derision. By sometimes combining these two anthropomorphic readings of the bird in the same poem, indeed in the same passage, the poet seems to have invested his object with traces of both mania and melancholia. A tortured hypothesis, no doubt, but one that derives support from several similar references to the raven. At times Wordsworth's raven is the expected "solitary raven" of the death-tolling "iron knell!" (*The Excursion* 4.1178, 1181). At other times, however, this bird, too, wears the Janus-faced guise just referred to, as when "Blithe ravens croak of death" ("A Morning Exercise" 7) and when the raven of *Home at Grasmere* "croaks and fills the upper air / With a strange sound of genial harmony" (581–82).

This sad-glad tension is nowhere more evident than in two versions of the same line from *An Evening Walk*. First, the early Quarto version: "The tremulous sob of the complaining owl" (443). Melancholic enough, that.

But now the authorized revision: "The sportive outcry of the mocking owl" (375). Apparently, even poem revision can be consolatory. It is as if Wordsworth's melancholy owls and ravens are infected by the poet's impulse to denial and recuperation. The manic-melancholic polarity is evidently a slippery one, indeed, one of those binary pairs that Wordsworth speaks of in his first "Essay upon Epitaphs," which are present "both in the natural and the moral world" and whose "qualities pass insensibly into their contraries, and things revolve upon each other" (*PW* 5.447).

The owls who "hoot" and "curr" in "The Idiot Boy" (104) are the raw material for the most stunning example of this transformation, in which the title character not only misapprehends these night birds' calls as the rooster's crowing for the morning (in one of the more hilarious cases of avian misidentification in literature), but confuses his heavenly bodies: "The cocks did crow to-whoo, to-whoo / And the sun did shine so cold!" (450–51). According to Ward, these lines "are remarkably prophetic of Lacan's example, '*Le chien fait miaou, le chat fait oua-oua* [the dog goes meow, the cat goes arf-arf],' which for Lacan illustrates the creative perceptions very young children impose upon their environments by" binary reversal (118; bracketed translation mine). This is a fine clarification of the childlike mind of the Idiot Boy, but I have suggested that such enantiodromic reaction formations are at work elsewhere in Wordsworth's poetry, too.

One can't leave the subject of Wordsworth's owls without mentioning the Boy of Winander, who "Blew mimic hootings" to them so "That they might answer him" (*Prelude* 5.398–99), and without immediately noting here a similar manic corruption of the owl as stock melancholy figure. They answer the boy "with quivering peals, / And long halloos, and screams, and echoes loud / Redoubled and redoubled": so far, as expected, until the "concourse wild" becomes one "Of mirth and jocund din!" (5.401–4). This jocularity seem out of place with the general tone, as if, again, some manic impulse had invaded these lines. Still, the owls' responses do fulfill their recuperative role, if the boy's calls are indeed attempts "to recruit the Other as witness to the boy's existence and identity" (Easthope 44). But then the subsequent "silence" creates a "shock of mild surprise" (5.406–7), as if he realizes that the owls are but arbitrary psychic signifiers and yet also independent beings in the Real who could care less about soothing his ontological angst by mirroring his existence. As he listens to this "nothing," his surroundings induce in him (or rather, he induces in himself, through them) a trance of recuperative derealization. Finally, Wordsworth kills the boy off, so to speak, to mourn the death of his illusory integral self through the death of a fictionalized alter-ego, and also as a means of denying, perhaps, that such anxious uncertainties could ever have occurred to the future Sage of Grasmere.[89]

Parrill admits that, despite the English Romantics' attempts to bring a more observational realism to literature, they still "take liberties with their birds"; as an egregious example, the nightingale is usually associated with the night, "even though the bird also sings during the day" (45). But such an association was already centuries old, as evidenced in the bird's very name. Indeed, the nightingale's long-standing existence as a literary trope renders it perhaps the most literary of Wordsworth's own birds. Not only does the name "Philomel" survive in Wordsworth's poetry, as in the "dire grief" of "the voice of Philomel" ("A Morning Exercise" 20), but the nightingale is also the only specific species to which Wordsworth gives the rather old-fashioned designation of "songstress," and a "shy songstress" at that ("On the Power of Sound" 11.6).[90]

I'm convinced at this point that Wordsworth was much more reluctant to wear his melancholy on his sleeve than Shelley or Keats were. He more characteristically goes at it secondhand, through compensatory reversal; thus are the skylark, linnet, thrush, and redbreast, day singers all, more common in Wordsworth than the nightingale is. But the trope was there, and Wordsworth made use of it, although one can hardly say that he ever completely embraced the trope when he did use it. In the early *Descriptive Sketches*, he does dub the nightingale "Evening's solemn bird," who "melodious weeps," and the "solemn songstress" (136, 751). But in a much later poem, "To Enterprise," the "sweet Bird" that "Pours forth in shady groves" has only been "misnamed the melancholy" (145–46), presumably by those elder stilted versifiers whom he condemns in the Preface.[91] Wordsworth seems constitutionally unable to wallow in pure nightingale sadness; his instinct is for the day (and birds that offer a denial of the night), or at worst a night-in-day that is yet a consoling compromise and containment.

Another poem directed at the bird of melancholy ("'O Nightingale! thou surely art'") reveals Wordsworth's reluctance to cash in this stock trope for its full market value:

O Nightingale! thou surely art
A creature of a "fiery heart":—
These notes of thine—they pierce and pierce;
Tumultuous harmony and fierce! (1–4)

Yes, her song is "Of shades, and dews, and silent night" (8), but the bird's initial description has such a strained violence that a self-pitying melancholic poet could hardly feel comfortable identifying with it. Indeed, as if realizing some inner resistance, Wordsworth quickly searches his linear database of metonymic signifiers and grasps at a more soothing surrogate, the stock dove, whose contrasting "homely tale" (12) is praised in the second half of the poem. This second bird "cooed—and cooed; / And somewhat pensively he wooed" (15–16). Much more to the poet's liking, this, the pensiveness only "somewhat" sad, and the cooing and cooing probably putting him half to sleep. Yes, this is "the song—the song for me!" (20), the poet concludes. It appears, finally, that Wordsworth doesn't like his birds *too* melancholic, preferring the safer, "semi-mourners," such as the dove and the cuckoo:

O blithe New-comer! I have heard,
I hear thee and rejoice.
O Cuckoo! shall I call thee Bird,
Or but a wandering Voice? ("To the Cuckoo" 1–4)

"Shall I call thee Bird?" Wordsworth asks. My main refrain of an answer in this chapter has been *no,* not really. Wordsworth literally agrees: it is "No bird, but an invisible thing, / A voice, a mystery" (15–16). The blithe bird of this poem is, after all, another manic recuperation—in ways, we shall see, that are peculiar to the cuckoo[92]—but this is not always the case. Elsewhere the insomniac poet is taunted at dawn by the "first cuckoo's melancholy cry" ("To Sleep" ["A flock of sheep"] 8); as a longed-for *avis in absentia,* this bird is only rarely invested with the unadulterated bliss of the skylark. Yet, if the bird cannot be conveniently classified as thoroughly manic or melancholic, it *can* be characterized as something that, again, is not even a bird, but a mere "wandering Voice," a solitary, invisible, errant, two-syllable-piping *absence* that makes the cuckoo Wordsworth's weirdest Other. There are many birds in Wordsworth positively valued for their loner status, and a variety of species in his poems are, of course, more heard than seen, notably the "shy songstress" of a nightingale and the reclusive wren, or "hermitess" ("The Contrast" 39). But the cuckoo is the bird most explicitly designated as a physical, or at least a visual, lack—an invisible presence-in-absence. Moreover, this "Voice beguiled" or "*wandering* Voice," this "erratic voice" ("The Cuckoo-Clock" 16, 33; "To the Cuckoo" ["Not the whole warbling"] 14) is a quite mobile and "floating" signifier that allows the poet freer rein (and reign) in his projections of the signified.

Scholars have long noted Wordsworth's propensity for distinctive aural imagery. In early Wordsworthian scholarship, Walter Pater pointed out his "innate sensibility to natural sights and sounds" and, citing "the cuckoo and its echo" specifically, concluded that "he is more finely scrupulous still in the noting of sounds" ("Wordsworth" [1889] 97–98).[93] What are the *poetic* results, finally, of this sensory emphasis? Parrill's metaphysical answer falls into Wordsworth's game: regarding the first "To the Cuckoo," Parrill claims for Wordsworth a "feeling that the cuckoo is an emissary from a spiritual realm" (50).[94] Here the critic seems to be more naïve than our poet in not recognizing the cuckoo, within the context of the poem, as an out-and-out *metaphor*. The question remains: why present the cuckoo in such a fashion? McGhee provides a more satisfying answer: "Wordsworth's ego longs for the sublime, to dehumanize scenes of nature" and "to abstract aesthetic patterns of sound from their natural sources" (227). This abstraction of pure sound for purposes of ego recuperation seems convincing, but in need of amplification.

Critics have struck the nail more firmly on the head when they are able to move, first, from Wordsworth's *human* othering to that of his birds, which leads us to "The Solitary Reaper." Here the girl's song is compared approvingly to those of the nightingale (9–12) and the "thrilling" song of the "Cuckoo-bird" (13–16). As Meihuizen sees it, the girl's Gaelic song is as "meaningless" and "impersonal" as the bird songs, a fact that allows Wordsworth to "search for some meaning in the sounds," to imagine his own "meaning of the content" (52). According to Easthope, one of Wordsworth's crucial strategies for derealizing the Other is to render that Other *in*comprehensible, literally or otherwise, (1) by making "the figure a speaking subject" but refusing to "listen to what he or she says" (the Leech-gatherer comes to mind here), (2) by making such Others "themselves self-absorbed" (various silent solitaires), or (3) by having them "speak a foreign language," as with the singer in this poem (48). Easthope mentions animal othering only in passing (52), but it's an easy step to extend this process to the (literally incomprehensible) language of other species, especially the voluble outpourings of birds, which strike a chord in our emotional beings or in the Kristevan semiotic because, at last, they are outside of the Lacanian Law of language. But despite this book's concluding hypothesis, this emotional reverberation doesn't necessarily make our linguistic responses to such an experience any more valid or any less appropriational. The cuckoo of *The Excursion* who shouts "faint tidings of some gladder place" (2.348) is echoing (a good word for this bird) the poet's own need for "tidings" and his desire for some place "gladder" than where his current split self resides. But that place is only prior to the self—thus various gestures toward "mirror-union"—or *after* the self—thus various eerie gestures toward the grave.

In "The Cuckoo at Laverna," Wordsworth is in Italy, and he feels less homesick for having "heard the Nightingale and Thrush / Blending as in a common English grove / Their love-songs" (22–24). But he misses that other "English" bird, the "invisible" one of the "vagrant Voice," who is usually off somewhere else, "Wandering in solitude" (6, 27, 98). Finally hearing one, he is delighted, and then fills the middle of the poem with meditations on the true religious life, brought to mind by the neighboring monastery. As he finally says goodbye to the bird, it is now reincarnated as the "Voice of the Desert" (103). Thus "wandering" alone in the "Desert" like an ancient prophet, the bare bird is bound up with the religious clutter of the poem's middle, and any authentic delight the poet has felt upon actually hearing the bird falls by the wayside in the properly religious conclusion of the cuckoo—or some dove-like Holy Spirit?—folding his "pinions up in blest repose" (112).[95] My attitude toward all this is now only too clear: I can hardly agree with John Rudy's recent reading of the cuckoo as "a symbol of the power of reconciliation contained in immediate religious experience," through which one becomes "free of the dualisms of Self and Other by which most of us live" (270, 275). Rudy himself others the cuckoo for his own theological argument, and his proffering of the self-Other dualism is merely a neat trick of co-opting the language of a theory that denies the possibility of freedom from said dualism. There is no purpose in further arguing about different value systems here. But where Rudy says "transcendence," the Lacanian says *méconnaissance*. Where Rudy claims a visionary moment in which "there is no longer a separately existing self to relate to a world viewed as other" (277), the Lacanian perceives only a retreat to the mirror stage.

I must finally note two non-cuckoo poems whose bird songs resemble the cuckoo's in their magico-invisible presence-in-absence. "The Green Linnet" (greenfinch) shares with his cousin, the (more usual) European Linnet, a loquacity that Wordsworth immediately associates with manic recuperation, the bird here "far above the rest / In joy of voice and pinion!" (11–12). But he also has an otherworldliness, as the "Presiding spirit" (14) of the new spring, and as, above all, "A Life, a Presence like the Air" (21) that serves as a vast, inviting gap for "oceanic" identification. Even when the bird is seen, Wordsworth allows the sun and foliage and motion of wings to make the bird a derealized vision seen through eyes half-closed:

> There! where the flutter of his wings
> Upon his back and body flings
> Shadows and sunny glimmerings,
> That cover him all over. (29–32)

"The Reverie of Poor Susan" involves this same derealization, now projected through a third person who feels as out of place in London as Wordsworth perhaps felt in Italy. The "Thrush that sings loud" (2) is a vision of home for her, like the poet's Italian cuckoo, and its banal Wood Street whistling suddenly becomes a sweet filling of loss, "a note of enchantment" that evokes in her "a vision of trees" (5–6) and the whole marvelous pastoralized environment of her home. The vision's cinematic fade at poem's end is effectively pathetic, in a way that many of Wordsworth's first-person recuperative gestures are not. This may be because his first-person persona seems unable to bear such a fading of the vision; it needs instead to have the last, consoling word of some positive philosophical "recompense." But through a third person, Wordsworth is more willing to admit the futility of the recuperative enterprise, distanced as he is by expressing its failure (and his own) in an Other. The cuckoo of his persona poems, on the other hand, serves his need for recuperation remarkably well, as a vacuous echo of a signifier whose sound can never fade.

HOMEY, HUMBLE, AND ALMOST HUMAN: "O PIOUS BIRD!"

> Blithe as the lark on sun-gilt wings
> High poised—or as the wren that sings

In shady places to proclaim
Her modest gratitude.

—WILLIAM WORDSWORTH, "Elegiac Stanzas" ("Lulled by the sound")

In this passage, one might have expected the lark to be juxtaposed with a more melancholy bird, but there is only a small, brown wren, "modest" in its neither manic nor melancholic insignificance. But in an important sense, such humble and homey birds like the wren and the redbreast are more crucial to Wordsworth's corpus than his skylarks and nightingales. The skylark might be viewed as one major outlet of Wordsworth's "egotistical sublime," and yet Keats's famous epithet hardly fits Wordsworth's own perception of himself, or of his idea of how he wanted others to see him. In other words, his Jungian persona or Freudian ego-ideal was of a much less high-manic order, a less lofty down-to-earthness already hinted at by his soaring skylark that yet kept its eye on its home below. If Wordsworth's birds are ultimately projective substitute objects of the poet's psychic economy, his wrens and doves and robins are significant as birds that reaffirm that mirror, his notion of who he thought he was, of who he wanted to be, or of who he wanted people to think he was.

This may explain Meihuizen's emphasis on the sheer mundanity of Wordsworth's birds, which "are more firmly rooted in the earth" than those of Shelley and Yeats, "suggesting, overtly, nothing beyond themselves, apart from human song, and their own particular imaginative landscapes" (58).[96] I hope to have shown, however, that Wordsworth's birds are, more usually, nothing *but* "beyond themselves," and that they are, if anything, recuperative Others in the poet's own "imaginative landscape." Easthope offers a better reading of Wordsworth's affinity for birds that resemble his own ego-ideal, again through the concept of derealization: "If the distinction between perception and fantasy can be blurred, if the Other can be stripped of its alterity, if the object can appear to reflect the subject as 'something not apart from, but inherent in' itself," then the self-Other split is temporarily blurred (44), and the wren and dove have done their obfuscatory jobs.

The dove could have been dealt with in my earlier "Mother" section,[97] but its appearance as a humble creature of love and fidelity may also be seen as a flattering mirror for Wordsworth's moralistic ego-ideal. We have already witnessed Wordsworth's privileging of the stock dove over the nightingale in the poem ostensibly addressed to the latter. The true song for Wordsworth's preferred poetic persona is only "somewhat pensive," not wallowingly melancholic or stridently manic. Parrill, as we have seen, emphasizes the skylark and the nightingale as prototypical symbols for Romantic composition. But perhaps the line "Over his own sweet voice the Stock-dove broods" ("Resolution and Independence" 1.5) better represents Wordsworth's own, more tranquil notion of poetic composition.

Wordsworth's wrens include the memorable "single wren" that he hears on horseback in book 2 of *The Prelude*, who sings "So sweetly 'mid the gloom" of an old church. Although single and reclusive like the nightingale, it knows how to find a recuperative equanimity in the gloomiest of situations, as does our poet. Besides being a good churchgoer, apparently, the wren's humble, solitary singing in retreat makes the bird a fit object for Wordsworth's identification:

> So sweetly 'mid the gloom the invisible Bird
> Sang to itself, that there I could have made
> My dwelling-place, and liv'd for ever there
> To hear such music. (2.132–135)

The wren, too, is a wee, humble Lake District bird, no fine caged singer of some London salon, and is thus preferred as such in "The Contrast: The Parrot and the Wren." The parrot (actually a rosella parakeet) is a "dazzling belle" (2), a "feathered Thing most delicate / In figure and in voice" (15–16), an "exiled" exotic who "trills her song with tutored powers" (17, 19), and "a sportive bird / By social glee inspired" (25–26). It is as if the poet is describing some extroverted literary lion from the Augustan Age, hardly Wordsworth's cup of tea. Much more to his liking is the "self-contented Wren," "Nature's DARKLING of this mossy shed" (30, 46). The bird's association here with a "mossy" darkness lends it some of the accoutrements of the nightingale, but its "self-content" saves it from any traditional throes of melancholy. I suggest that the wren is thus in some ways Wordsworth's version, displacement even, of the nightingale, allowing him at once to embrace isolation and poetry (song) and yet deny the unmitigated despair of the traditional emblem.

In the opening lines of "The Redbreast chasing the Butterfly"—"Art thou the bird whom Man loves best / The pious bird with the scarlet breast, / Our little English Robin . . . ?" (1–3)—Wordsworth has already humanized the

European robin in several ways: via human love, moral piety, and patriotic pride.[98] Whether it is called robin or redbreast, its presence is ever conducive to some universal (human) feeling of brotherhood, as the "bird that by some name or other / All men who know thee call their brother" (9–10). Like the dove and wren, the redbreast is another bird close to the poet's own heart: a fair-to-middling singer, a family friend in fair weather or foul, and a bird, of course, of the best moral character. Thus in "The Redbreast chasing the Butterfly," he is both the "cheerer . . . of our in-door sadness" and a "pious Bird!" (30, 38).

There is a problem here, however: the bird is hungry, and, despite some heavy-handed othering by the poet, it insists on a diet different from Wordsworth's, that is, the butterfly. (Of course, that the butterfly has been implicitly appropriated as some beautiful soul in flight is an integral part of the problem.) And so the poet unrealistically asks, "Can this be the bird, to man so good" (20), who would yet eat another of nature's beauties? (Yes, the naturalist wants to shout: of *course*.) Yet the poet concludes by still insisting that this "pious Bird! whom man loves best" should "Love him [the butterfly], or leave him alone!" (38–39). The species colonization is so blatant in this poem that one wants to tell Mr. Wordsworth to just let the poor bird eat.

The robin is a further human consolation in that it stays the winter in England; this fact and its friendliness result in the scenario presented in "The Redbreast," in which the bird actually frequents the inside of human houses, for warmth apparently. Indeed, the robin is welcomed as "a looked-for guest, / Confiding in his ruddy breast" (5–6); the human inhabitants "smile upon the Bird" (27), and soon "the whole house is Robin's cage" (68).[99] Ranging at will, this particular bird develops a special liking for Dorothy, a symbiosis further clarified in a Fenwick note: "My Sister being then confined to her room by sickness . . . had one [robin] that without being caged, took up its abode with her, and at night used to perch upon a nail from which a picture had hung[!]. It used to sing and fan her face with its wings in a manner that was very touching" (PW 2.485–86). Dorothy's own close relationship to birds will be presented later, but the scene here stands as a precious portrait of the Wordsworths' personal avian domesticity.

In Wordsworth's sonnet about a robin, "In the Woods of Rydal," the bird has the "sylvan confidence" (8), apparently, to pluck a morsel from the poet's lips,[100] and Wordsworth puts his best Sage of Grasmere persona forward: "I, whose head is grey, / Am not unworthy of thy fellowship," so "peck or perch, fond Flutterer! nor forbear / To trust a Poet in still musings bound" (5–6, 13–14). That the bird's familiarity flatters the poet immensely is obvious, but the Fenwick note to the poem is even more interesting. We learn not only that the robin frequents the indoors, but that its visits are often a doctor's house call of sorts: "Under my own roof I have witnessed affecting instances of the creature's friendly visits to the chambers of sick persons [such as Dorothy in the previous poem]. . . . These attachments to a particular person, when marked and continued, used to be reckoned ominous; but the superstition is passing away" (PW 3.433). But the superstition that redbreasts have some humane impulse to befriend the human sick still seemed very much alive.

If my treatment of Wordsworth seems to have veered from mania and melancholy as obvious concerns, I must reemphasize the dominant role of displacement and denial in his individual approach to "eternal mourning." In sum, the poet's inscription of the redbreast et al. as Others very similar to himself is one of his major strategies for healing the melancholy inherent in the split self. Wordsworth's robins, specifically, are often appropriated as children of the household almost, or at least as family pets; the inevitable projective othering performed by the "master" upon the "dumb animal" needs no elaboration. The bird's relative tameness renders almost human what is most likely an adaptive opportunism. If every avian species had somehow *learned* that there was safety and warmth (and nails to perch on) in William Wordsworth's house, the poet would soon have been barring his doors and windows.[101]

The poem beginning "I know an aged Man constrained to dwell" gives us a welcome third-person perspective on Wordsworth's use of the robin, the tale of the friendship between this bird and one of Wordsworth's old beggars. When he lived by himself on alms, the old man would feed his friend, who "pecked the crumbs upon his knee" (11). But their "Dear intercourse" is ended when the old man is confined in a "house of public charity" (13, 2). There, the bird's memory becomes his all: "One living Stay was left, and in that one / Some recompense for all that he had lost" (27–28). And so the conclusion:

O that the good old Man had power to prove,
By message sent through air or visible token,
That still he loves the Bird, and still must love;
That friendship lasts though fellowship is broken! (29–32)

It's hard to disillusion such pathos, but the "message" is rendered all the more lugubrious if one thinks for a moment: how would the robin *understand* the message? When language approaches the Real, a chasm is encountered over which no communication is possible. This was written four years before the poet's death, and most of his "living Stays," too, were lost, and a man undeniably needs some "recompense." For the old beggar, it was the bird; for Wordsworth, it was the poem.

I move now from an old man and his robin to a few other old men and their sparrows, birds that, like the robin, are relatively "homey, humble, and almost" tame. (Indeed, this status is reflected in their traditional symbolism as poor, bare "mankind" itself, as a "humble, earth-bound" Everyman [Rowland 159].) However, Wordsworth's sparrows, as a body, follow no special, characteristic pattern of othering.[102] This is due, in part, to the fact that the word "sparrow" has a semantic vagueness that continues to this day, evident in its application to any generic small, brown bird.[103] At times, as with the poet's songbirds in toto, their vivacity is projectively interpreted as an instinctual happiness. Thus Margaret's family would have been "happier far / Could they have lived as do the little birds / that peck along the hedges" ("The Ruined Cottage" 157–59). In one other blatant instance, however, the sparrows' very commonness betrays Wordsworth into calling them "vulgar coppice birds" ("Poems on the Naming of Places" VI 16), the same great sin that birders sometimes still commit in cursing the many house sparrows that seem only to deter our pursuit of more colorful and novel species.

However, in two of Wordsworth's better known solitaire poems, a common motif does occur. An old man is appropriated by the poet, and sparrows play a role in the staging of that appropriative act. The first example is "Animal Tranquillity and Decay," in which the old solitaire himself serves as a recuperative projection of the self in union. His entire mien is "one expression" (3); he "moves / With thought" (6–7), in a unity of mind and body reminiscent of the birds of "Lines written in Early Spring." Like some Zen master suddenly appearing on an English road, "All effort seems forgotten" (9); he is a being "by nature led / To peace so perfect that the young"—and the poet—"envy" him greatly (12–14). His achievement, the title tells us, is thus an "Animal Tranquillity": he is more pure animal, or nature, than split human, a conflation similar to the Leech-gatherer's comparison to a "huge stone" or "Motionless . . . cloud" ("Resolution and Independence" 9.1, 11.5).[104]

No wonder, then, that here the "little hedgerow birds, / That peck along the road, regard him not" (1–2), any more than they'd regard with any interest a mute stump or rock. The sparrows themselves are appropriated into the poem to work on two different levels. First, they are added surrogate witnesses to the poet's own perception that the old fellow has achieved "Animal Tranquillity"; second, because they, too, are fill-ins for an animalistic unified self, they serve as metonymic *reinforcements* of the poem's title and raison-d'être. So the poem's opening isn't the mere empty filler of a scene setting, but rather an accompanying *filling-in* of the poem's main recuperative impetus.

The second poem is "The Old Cumberland Beggar," in which we have another "solitary Man" (24), here appropriated as a more than useless "record" of *others'* human charity (89), as a "silent monitor" (123) or walking superego of sorts. As with the old beggar who befriends the robin, feeding the birds is also one of this fellow's few pleasures:

> . . . the crumbs in little showers
> Fell on the ground; and the small mountain birds,
> Not venturing yet to peck their destined meal,
> Approached within the length of half his staff. (18–21)

In support of his anti-poorhouse polemics, Wordsworth begs for the poor man's right to be among the birds, to partake of their "Animal Tranquillity": "Let him . . . have around him . . . The pleasant melody of woodland birds" (183–85). For after all, be they decrepit old humans or worthlessly innumerable little brown birds, "'Tis Nature's law / That none, the meanest of created things," is useless (73–74). Let the old beggar be one with his metonymic synonyms, the sparrows, and Nature-as-One, as a recuperative "record" of Wordsworth's drive toward a unified self:

> And let him, *where* and *when* he will, sit down
> Beneath the trees, or on a grassy bank
> Of highway side, and with the little birds
> Share his chance-gathered meal; and, finally,
> As in the eye of Nature he has lived,
> So in the eye of Nature let him die! (192–97)

HOMEY, HUMBLE, AND ALMOST HUMAN: THE "OTHER" WOMAN

> The swallows come to the sitting-room window as if wishing to build but I am afraid they will not have the courage for it, but I believe they will build at my room window. They twitter and make a bustle and a little chearful song hanging against the panes of glass, with their soft white bellies close to the glass, and their forked fish like tails. They swim round and round and again they come.—It was a sweet evening.
>
> DOROTHY WORDSWORTH, *Journals*

"Homey and humble" can apply to a woman as well as a bird. Dorothy Wordsworth's *Journals* have been traditionally read as an interesting supplement to and influence on the work of her brother, who is indeed a major presence therein, busily at work at, for instance, "Michael," *The Prelude*, and the "Intimations" ode (e.g., 44–47, 50, 74, 106, 137). Thus William's poem on "The Redbreast chasing the Butterfly" was preceded by Dorothy's journal note: "I saw a robin chacing a scarlet Butterfly this morning" (112).[105] Perhaps William's most explicit tribute to Dorothy occurs in *The Prelude*, as he recounts a period in his life "When Nature, destined to remain so long / Foremost in my affections, had fallen back / Into a second place" (13.230–32). He attributes his recovery to Dorothy's intervention; yes, his soul had been hardened (13.221), but his sister softens it, as he explains in a passage that, fittingly, contains some of his most touching ornithic imagery:

> But thou didst plant its [his soul's] crevices with flowers,
> Hang it with shrubs that twinkle in the breeze,
> And teach the little birds to build their nests
> And warble in its chambers. (13.226–29)

Dorothy's own poetic descriptions of nature (and proto-ecological concerns) have also been championed, as in the "daffodils" passage (109) and in her description of the lone leaf atop a tree, which "danced round and round like a rag blown by the wind" (9).[106] Intertextually speaking, however, it becomes inordinately tempting to read Dorothy's relationship with her brother as a pathetic one, in which the "Dear Sister!" appears as an objectified homebody as othered as William's "cute little" robins and wrens. The sheer domesticity of Dorothy's life dominates the text of her journals, especially her chores: ironing and hanging out the laundry, baking bread and pies, reading to William, and copying his poems.[107] Even the task of journal keeping itself was taken up for her brother's "Pleasure" (15–16). Is it little wonder, then, that she often complained of headaches?[108]

Dorothy did play whist (48–49) and enjoyed an occasional rum and water (e.g., 110), but her greatest escape was the outdoors itself: many entries simply begin "Walked. . . ." As a self-proclaimed "real lover of Nature" (159), she mentions many types of birds, describing some in close detail, as in the following bird-guide-like delineation of the chaffinch: "We [she and her brother] stopped a long time in going to watch a little bird with a salmon coloured breast—a white cross or T upon its wings, and a brownish back with faint stripes" (71). Her favorite bird is the same as Gilbert White's: the barn swallow.[109] When the swallow's nest beneath her window falls down, Dorothy is as heartbroken as the pair who had built it, whose "love" for each other she describes in the warmest terms (137–42; see section epigraph). Dorothy bids adieu to another neighboring swallow pair observed that same summer with a similar fondness: "The Swallows I must leave them the well the garden the Roses, all. Dear creatures!! they sang last night after I was in bed—seemed to be singing to one another, just before they settled to rest for the night. Well, I must go. Farewell.——" (146). Indeed, of the brother-sister human pair, Dorothy is the greater sentimentalist. Her weeping upon Coleridge's leaving is deemed by her brother "nervous blubbering" (57); when William leaves on a trip, she gazes at an apple he has left and exclaims, "O the Darling!" (97; referring to her brother, not the apple). In contrast, William usually comes across as rather a stuffed shirt, but there are occasional glimpses of the two side by side, "deep in Silence and Love" (130), much as Dorothy had imagined her swallow pair to be.

YET ANOTHER ALMOST-HUMAN: THE OTHER RACE

> Oh! many a time have I, a five years' Child,
> A naked Boy . . .
> . . . .
> Made one long bathing of a summer's day,
> Bask'd in the sun . . .
> . . . .
> . . . [or] stood alone
> Beneath the sky, as if I had been born
> On Indian Plains, and from my Mother's hut

Had run abroad in wantonness, to sport,
A naked Savage, in the thunder shower.
—WILLIAM WORDSWORTH, *The Prelude*

At this point in *The Prelude*, Wordsworth, as Walt Whitman would do later, turns "Indian," running "naked" as a young boy, in "wantonness," through the "Nature" that would be his dominant theme.[110] But even more blatantly than in Whitman, Wordsworth's adoption of a Native American persona is inculcated in a Western discourse that conflates the human Native with nature and its nonhuman species, and with a youthful, and primitive or "Savage," naïveté. As in Charlotte Smith, the Native worldview is apparently a primarily emotional response to one's environment; so, too, is Wordsworth's initial exposure to the wonders of geometry in *The Prelude* characterized as an "Indian awe and wonder" (6.142), a metaphor connoting a primitive's amazement at the intellectual doings of an advanced (Western) civilization.[111]

But in Wordsworth's corpus one immediately notices that he more commonly references the alter-race of the New World via surrogates, especially by way of the ubiquitous oppressed women who inhabit his corpus. As McGhee puts it, "At the heart of the Wordsworthian darkness is *an abandoned woman*" (38; emphasis added). If "Nature" is the primary signifier of Wordsworth's atavistic impulses, his various women (including Dorothy), as I have noted, serve as a secondary subject—or rather object, and abject—for his othering tendencies. Indeed, it is noteworthy that many of Wordsworth's other-race references are feminized, here, via association with abandoned women, just as his avians commonly are. "The Complaint of a Forsaken Indian Woman," for example, involves a Native American woman who, having fallen ill, must give up her child and, following the cultural practice spelled out by Wordsworth in the prose introduction to the poem, remain behind the tribe's peregrinations, to die alone. On the one hand, aside from the particular plot line inspired by the poet's travelogue readings, most of the lines, and pathos, of the poem could apply generically to any of the poet's abandoned women of English descent. On the other hand, the exotic setting and character are not only part of a general Romantic propensity, but they allow Wordsworth, perhaps, to project and displace the shocking *British* treatment of poor women. In other words, as comfortable(?) as Wordsworth was in critiquing the social oppression of women in his own country, it was easier yet—and thus I read the poem as a metonymic displacement—to write about the travails of an other across the sea. In sum, the New World Native can be added to the many surrogate-object metonymies in Wordsworth's poetry, of which avians make up such a large subset.

A British forlorn woman is found in "Ruth," but her sufferings are highlighted by an American setting. The gist of the poem involves her jilting by a husband who has been to North America, who has worn the "splendid feathers" of the Cherokee (21)—an image combining avian and indigene—and whose tales of the Natives are an integral part of his wooing her. He asks her to return to America with him, but leaves her, finally, in the lurch. For he's a scoundrel, because he has spent too much time among the "vagrant bands / Of Indians in the West" (119–20)! The influence of the American wilderness has sparked a "kindred impulse" of wildness in the man (130), and no doubt the eerie American medley of whip-poor-wills and mockingbirds played a seminal role in making him turn Native.

As noted, Wordsworth's "Complaint" of the poor Native American woman originated in his travelogue reading. David Ehrenfeld has emphasized, above all, the influence of Bartram's *Travels* on the poetry of both Wordsworth and Coleridge; indeed, Bartram's "description of . . . the Seminole Indians inspired some of the finest poetry of Wordsworth and Coleridge, including 'Kubla Khan'"; however, even Bartram's original reading of the Seminoles was but a naïve "utopia" (12–13), an ideology of othering the New World as an ideal Eden and savage wilderness. Ehrenfeld goes on to claim, "One might be tempted to argue that Romanticism originated in the contact zones of America, North Africa, and the South Seas" (138), a fruitful idea supported by M. L. Pratt's studies of the colonization of the Americas and by similar readings of (Asian) Indian postcolonial arguments regarding the importance of Britain's colonization of India in its ideological defense of its own nationalism and literature. But important as this colonial discourse line of thought is, my main intent has been to demonstrate that Wordsworth's own main contact zone was his immediate environment, notably the avians thereof.

As supplement to my assertion that Wordsworth's empathy was *not* one that truly engaged the Native of the New World, I would momentarily broach this work's later Native American chapters by noting with some shock Matthew Teorey's recent thesis that Wordsworth and contemporary Native writer Leslie Silko express quite similar ecofeminist agendas. Both "advocate in their writing the development of a dialogue with the natural world" (46); "both listen to nature's needs, its 'voice,'" and both insist that humans' "relationship . . . with the natural world be one of respectful, spiritual reciprocity and nurturing physical interconnectivity" (31). However, "spiritual" is a loaded term that carries very different connotations in the disparate cultures inhabited by a nineteenth-century British Romantic and a twentieth-century Laguna Pueblo. That is, besides defining "ecofeminism" rather too broadly, Teorey's argument, like many such scholarly analogues, suffers from an untoward conflation of quite different worldviews.

Before leaving Wordsworth's recuperative othering of birds, I would refer to one more abandoned woman, "The Sailor's Mother." Her son now dead at sea, the woman grasps at the pathetic compensation of carrying around his pet, "a little singing-Bird," in a cage (18), concluding "I bear it with me, Sir;—he took so much delight in it" (36). Thus she performs her mourning, replacing her lost son with a substitute object closely associated with him. Thus does this poem seem an encapsulation of Wordsworth's general avian strategy. He has suffered a loss, the trauma (if we are to believe Lacan) of maternal separation. Furthermore, a major category of recuperative displacements contains the birds I have traced through these pages. It is as if the poet is dragging his birds around to show to people, reassuring them at the same time that he is doing fine: "Look at my pretty birds. (Loss? What loss?)." Each bird poem is a cage, and as the reader peers through the cage at the colorful feathers, the poet crosses his fingers, hoping that the reader doesn't notice that only the flimsiest wire is barely holding together this recuperative container of a self, ultimately, in the throes of lack.

CHAPTER 3 Blithe Spirit and Immortal Bird

The Avian Other from Wordsworth to Clare

Hail to thee, blithe Spirit!
  Bird thou never wert.
—PERCY BYSSHE SHELLEY, "To a Skylark"

Thou wast not born for death, immortal Bird!
—JOHN KEATS, "Ode to a Nightingale"

Oh, what can ail thee, knight at arms,
  Alone and palely loitering?
The sedge has wither'd from the lake,
    And no birds sing.
—JOHN KEATS, "La Belle Dame sans Merci"

Obviously, my view of Wordsworth's birds has come a long way since I naïvely perceived him as some versifying naturalist. One wonders if much progress has been made here, from my opening critique of Wordsworth's othering of the eagle for its moral use value, and the damning argument that Western culture's anthropocentric language, the Lacanian Symbolic, is the determinant grid that necessarily colors (indeed creates) all intercourse with objects from nature. Yet the ecologically minded birder in me still wants to find some saving grace, a way out of the prison of Lacan's Symbolic, the logical extreme of which renders impossible any depiction of real birds in Wordsworth, or indeed, in any production of language. As Easthope asserts, poetry "cannot be itself an experience of Nature but, at best, the *representation* of an experience of Nature in poetic form" (1); and "Wordsworth's poetry is concerned not with 'real things' but with . . . the representation of a psychological effect" (17).[1] How can such a psycholinguistic reductionism be reconciled with any viable naturalist or ecological concern in Wordsworth? In other words, how can these considerations be saved from Lacan's structural grammar of the unconscious, without retreating back to a naïve equivalence of perceptual concepts with external things-in-themselves? Such a salvation seems all the more necessary in the wake of a second generation of British Romantic poets for whom the bird becomes even less real and a more supernal entity best fit for introspective psychomachia.

THE OTHER-IN-LANGUAGE VERSUS THE OTHER-IN-THE-REAL: IS THERE A REAL BIRD OUT THERE?

> It is the world of words which creates the world of things.
>
> JACQUES LACAN, *The Language of the Self*

Several critics have addressed the general question of object representation in Romantic poetry, and from a variety of angles. Drummond Bone, for instance, implies that, as a group, the Romantics were pretty much failures in presenting the individual, the specific, the "real object." *The Prelude*, for instance, "is surprisingly empty of" particulars; the poem "is held in idealist suspension, somewhere between the materially specific and the Universal All" (5). Ultimately, these poets' "action of thought can be conceived of as an *attack on the freedom of the object*. . . . Do we never want simply to go and touch the rock?" (10; emphasis added). This rock-collecting expedition is a noble gesture, but one that falls before the Lacanian insistence that the "attack" of thought is inevitably victorious in its assault and fatal to the object. Moreover, even our tactile perception of the rock is conditioned against our will by the very structure of language.

In his call for a new ecopoetry, Robert Bly contends that "ecology contains in it a secret, over and above its scientific and its political meaning. The renewed attention to the panther and the tree [referring to images of Rilke] in our culture is something to rejoice over" (*News* 254). In sum, it's about time that the poet (re)discovers "the object [that] is not a symbol" (255), the object, in other words, that has not been appropriated by the poet's conscious or unconscious mental baggage. A wonderful sentiment, but the poems Bly gives as examples are often obvious projections of neo-Romantic mysticism (like Bly's own poetry), revisions of Wordsworth's pantheistic unity of the "one life." An argument claiming a monistic *universe* put forth by a psyche heavily invested in a need for a monistic *psyche* is immediately suspect, however appealing. How utterly presumptuous is a concern for a single small sparrow only because it is a part of some Great Whole created by a recuperative homocentric holism.

I'm still left, then, with no readily apparent way across the epistemological chasm of that domain beyond signification, the Lacanian Real. Indeed, if such a realm is beyond words, in a very real sense I've been asking the wrong question, or posing a question that has no reason to be asked or hope to be answered. One is tempted to say, *of course* there is a real bird out there that still comes through in Wordsworth's poems, aside from all your othering nonsense; your self-conscious mental paralysis is a mere glass-bead game. Listen to that cardinal outside your window! I listen, but am only too aware that the bird's very image in my mind is as much a product of book illustrations and cultural praise as it is sheer observation, and that the song is filtered through the many verbal descriptions I've read of the sound, colored even by my own past whistled imitations of the sound. More satisfying to my skeptical nature is an existential leap of faith that would bridge my epistemological nihilism and psychological determinism with my perceived need for an ecological Real. How much recuperation is involved in my gesture I leave to harder-hearted theorists.

With these problems acknowledged, I would still like to pursue the possibilities of Wordsworth's authentic engagements with real birds, first by pointing to those passages in his corpus that reveal a truly observational eye and ear for the avian object. If, in the opinion of psychological critics, "we have not yet entirely recovered from the earlier critical stress on Wordsworth's statement [in *The Preface* (PW 2.390)] that 'I have at all times endeavored to look steadily at my subject'" (Abrams, "Structure" 202), an ecocritic may well reply that, in the past half-century of Wordsworth criticism, we've recovered from it *all too well*, given Wordsworth's very consciousness of such an attempt at naturalistic verisimilitude, as stated in the "Essay, Supplementary to the Preface." Here the poet complains that, with very few exceptions—including, by the way, the lark-murdering "Windsor-Forest"—the poetry between Milton and Thomson "does not contain a single new image of external nature; and scarcely presents a familiar one from which it can be inferred that the eye of the Poet has been steadily fixed upon his object." In such poetry, apparently, "the visible universe was of . . . little consequence to the poet" because "there was little accurate attention paid to" the "phenomena of nature" (PW 2.419–20).

As inverse testimony to Wordsworth's fixing his eye upon nature, one must note the critical ridicule his reputation has endured for letting said eye become too affixed. Indeed, if Crabbe has been the English nature poet most vilified for his inordinate attention to trite details, often of "the most gross and obvious and revolting part[s] of nature" (Hazlitt, *Spirit* 348), Wordsworth is a close second in such an immediate critical backlash, from Coleridge on. The coauthor of the *Lyrical Ballads* condemned the "downright simpleness" that was evidenced by Wordsworth's "preference of mean, degrading, or at best trivial associations and characters" (Coleridge 198); these included, one might guess, the poet's sparrows, wrens, redbreasts, and other "mean" and "trivial" alter-species. Wordsworth's inordinately manic and melancholic avians must also be part of that "intensity of feeling disproportionate to . . . the objects described" (397), and such trivial creatures no doubt resulted in "thoughts and images too great for the subject" (398). Indeed, in contrast to those who find Wordsworth's nature a sparse or barren field, Coleridge complains of his former friend's "laborious minuteness and fidelity in the representation of objects" (391).

Hazlitt is also condescending toward the "meanness" of Wordsworth's "subject," but he also anticipates later, more sympathetic glosses on the poet's naturalistic prosaicisms. If the poet must present "the commonest events and objects," it is a "test to prove that nature is always interesting from its inherent truth and beauty." Hazlitt even sounds occasionally like a deep ecologist professing a biocentric egalitarianism: in choosing the "commonest" of nature, Wordsworth's "Muse . . . is a levelling one," based "on a principle of equality." In the end, "even the lichens on the rock have a life and being in his thoughts" (*Spirit* 270–71, 273)![2] Indeed, among the "excellencies" that Coleridge concedes in Wordsworth's verse is "the perfect truth of nature in his images and descriptions" (402, 407). It is as if the critic must have his cake and eat it, too, complaining of Wordsworth's details, yet praising their fidelity.[3] Whether Parrill has bought into Wordsworth's own statements (or those of his acolytes) of intent about observation or is really reacting to the poems themselves, she also emphasizes the Romantics' general drive toward realistic description: "The Romantic poets . . . give the impression of being interested in real, rather than conventional, birds, and some of their poems reveal careful and accurate observation of birds and their behavior. Wordsworth, for instance, mentions a large number and variety of birds, and usually places them accurately in their natural habitats" (44–45).[4]

An Evening Walk, for instance, is notable in beckoning forward to the poet's later work in several ways: in his recognition of an evolution of his consciousness of nature and, above all, in his descriptions of real places (e.g., Derwent, Rydal, Grasmere) with both sympathy and a fine eye for naturalistic details. The lengthy description of the swan family in *An Evening Walk*, Wordsworth tells us in a Fenwick note, "was taken from the daily opportunities I had of observing their habits . . . in a state of nature" (PW 1.319). His observations are tellingly evident in such images as the "swan [that] stirs the reeds, his neck and bill / Wetting, that drip upon the water still" (305–6), and the swan mother who, in the poem's choicest image, allows her cygnets to "mount her back" (217), "a fact of which" the poet had "been an eyewitness" (PW 1.24n):

> She calls them near, and with affection sweet
> Alternately relieves their weary feet;
> Alternately they mount her back, and rest
> Close by her mantling wings' embraces prest. (215–18)

This maternal gesture is both a tribute to Wordsworth's powers of close observation and also an early indication of the poet's eventual conflation of nature and mother. But aside from the humanistic intrusion of "affection sweet," the passage is a fascinating portrayal of another species' modus vivendi.

Wordsworth also apparently spent a good deal of time observing birds in flight. An extended description of various birds in flight in *The Excursion*, though quite open to Lacanian critique, still characterizes each species fairly well with a single adjective or two; the pity is that they are all "subject" to the "forbearance" of a human with a gun:

> With admiration he would lift his eyes
> To the wide-ruling eagle, and his hand
> Was loath to assault the majesty he loved:
> Else had the strongest fastnesses proved weak
> To guard the royal brood. The sailing glead [kite],
> The wheeling swallow, and the darting snipe,
> The sportive sea-gull dancing with the waves,
> And cautious water-fowl, from distant climes,
> Fixed at their seat, the centre of the Mere,
> Were subject to young Oswald's steady aim,
> And lived by his forbearance. (7.747–57)

In *The Excursion*, too, is the marvelous simile of a boat breaking out of the reeds into more navigable water as "smoothly as a hawk / That, disentangled from the shady boughs / Of some thick wood, her place of covert, cleaves / With correspondent wings the abyss of the air" (9.491–94). Anyone who has seen a large bird of prey's ponderous yet powerful takeoff can only marvel at the aptness of this description. Wordsworth has also noticed the apparent great awkwardness of a heron taking wing, as the bird "Shoots upward, darting his long neck before" its ostensibly ungainly bulk of wings and body (*An Evening Walk* 308).[5]

In *An Evening Walk*, Wordsworth adopts an onomatopoeic Scottish word (as he explains in a note) to describe the sound of swallows breaking the wind in flight: "The *sugh* of swallow flocks that twittering sweep" (317; emphasis added). He also employs the swallow in "Vaudracour and Julia" to describe Julia's anxious wait for her lover: "busy at her casement as the swallow / Fluttering its pinions, almost within reach, / About the pendent nest" (82–84). This realistic depiction of a swallow's careful, roundabout way of entering its nest was either a common sight for Wordsworth or perhaps a single observation thereof that became a sort of spot in time for him, as he uses a similar image in *Descriptive Sketches*, comparing a mountaineer's human concerns to "a swift [that] by tender cares oppress'd / Peeps often ere she dart into her nest" (572–73). (The later version of *Descriptive Sketches* changes the "swift" to the more appropriate "swallow" [482].) The propensity of the barn swallow for building its "pendent" mud nest under the eaves of houses no doubt furnished Wordsworth (as we know it did his sister) with ample opportunity for such an observation.

In my treatment of Wordsworth's cuckoos, I have already made much of his powers of aural acuity, and many of his more realistic bird passages are keyed toward their songs or calls. I would first point to "Resolution and Independence," in which a "Jay makes answer as the Magpie chatters" (1.6). There is no unusual sonic verisimilitude here, although "chattering" is a credibly realistic description of a magpie's percussive racket, and *jay* is onomatopoeic in its very origin. My point here is that the jay and magpie are hardly great vocalists (by human aesthetical standards, at least), and Wordsworth's stooping to notice two such cacophonous species is worthy of note as a new realistic gesture of sorts (though a reprivileging already evident in Cowper, as we've seen). Also, amid Wordsworth's many poeticizations of the golden eagle as a "regal monarch" of a bird, he does display at one point a good ear for one of its actual calls, which he describes as "hungry barkings" ("On the Power of Sound" 13.9).[6] As for another soaring bird of prey, the shrill call and circling flight pattern of the "silver'd kite" are both evoked in the taut image of a "whistling circle" (*An Evening Walk* 89–90)—a fine concision, that.

I would finally touch on one more cacophonous bird (already encountered in Charlotte Smith): the nightjar, which, like its U.S. relative, the nighthawk, produces an unbirdlike sound that one might deem hardly fit for poesy. But Wordsworth embraces its dissonance in more than one poem. The "busy dor-hawk" of "Evening Voluntaries" I flies after a moth while sputtering its "burring note" (22–23), and *The Waggoner* includes a "buzzing dor-hawk [that], round and round, is wheeling" (1.3), catching insects on the wing. An earlier variant of this latter poem replaces "dor-hawk" with "Night-hawk" (both nicknames for the nightjar), who sings "his frog-like tune / On restless pinion wheeling" (PW 2.177n). My point is that such an ear-rending menagerie of croaking, barking, and chattering birds stands in realistic contrast to his more melodious, and more frequently anthologized, "songsters" of "heavenly lays." It is only a small step, then, to Wallace Stevens, whose often Wordsworthian phrasings seem punctuated by the sounds of one clucking grackle after another.

In addition to his realistic observations of birds in flight or song, Wordsworth also reveals an eye for a few other quite specific, almost idiosyncratic bird behaviors. Witness again the blue tit we saw in "The Kitten and the Falling Leaves." If one knows that members of the tit family are some of the few birds to characteristically climb or stand on a tree trunk with their head pointed down to the ground, then Wordsworth's description becomes delicious:

> Where is he, that giddy Sprite,
> Blue-cap, with his colours bright,
> Who was blest as bird could be,
> Feeding in the apple-tree;
> Made such wanton spoil and rout,
> Turning blossoms inside out;
> Hung—head pointing towards the ground. (63–69)

The bird's ravaging of the blossoms is another apt touch of realism, an image repeated in "The Triad," where the maiden is "as a bird is free / That rifles blossoms on a tree, / Turning them inside out with arch audacity" (125–27).[7] Whether or not this simile sparks any life into an otherwise mundane poem, the phrase "arch audacity" applies well to members of the titmouse family, if I may be so anthropomorphic.

I conclude with another strong simile, from *The Excursion*, in which the Sage compares his struggles to those of "a bird that breaks / Through a strong net, and mounts upon the wind, / Though with her plumes impaired" (9.171–73). Another awkward takeoff, but this ascent has as its main impediment a human net. One is reminded of another "poor bird" in Wordsworth, one "entangled in a snare / Whose heart still flutters, though his wings forbear / To stir in useless struggle" (Ecclesiastical Sonnet II.xlv ["Laud"] 4–6). This theme of traumatic human intervention in the lives of avians is strong in Wordsworth, as we shall see.

ECO-EAGLES AND THE POET *ENGAGÉ*

> Wordsworth was truly ahead of his time, and radically innovative in . . . his defense of the poor, the homeless, and all the wild creatures who dwell beyond the pale.
>
> JAMES C. MCKUSICK, *Green Writing*

Perhaps surprising for a man who would begrudge the robin his breakfast of a butterfly or two, Wordsworth still makes many gestures that evidence a true ecological concern for birds as beings intrinsically worthy of autonomy and respect. One thinks immediately of the poem from *Lyrical Ballads* in which one Sir William plans a "Pleasure-house" (6) by Rydal Lake, but his ill-conceived plans result in an unfinished ruin that, like the "Ruined Cottage," returns to a "state of nature," a warning at last for others with a similar hubris to let the other native species be:

> . . . think again; and, taught
> By old Sir William and his quarry, leave
> Thy fragments to the bramble and the rose;
> There let the vernal slow-worm sun himself,
> *And let the redbreast hop from stone to stone.*
> ("Inscriptions" VII 31–35; emphasis added)

The final "let be" appeal for the robin finds a parallel in the swan episode of *An Evening Walk*, discussed earlier. Immediately after describing the cygnets' ride on their mother's back, Wordsworth expresses an earnest plea for the swans' survival: "Long may ye roam these hermit waves" in a setting "untrodden" by humankind (219, 221)—unless the human is a nature poet in search of alter-species analogues, one might add. But one feels that Wordsworth intends more than their mere continued existence as metonymic reminders of some ideal human family. Now what would prevent them from roaming "long"? As we have seen in his *Guide to the Lakes*, Wordsworth was aware of the problems of greater human incursions into the Lake District, and even his poetry mentions the brute reality of the human gun, the "deadly tube" of *Home at Grasmere* that is a danger to his other favorite swan pair (266). Waterfowl, moreover, are not the only birds in danger from such a weapon; the birds that *The Excursion*'s Oswald forbore shooting ranged from the swallow to the eagle.

The eagle receives what may be Wordsworth's most prolonged and eloquent animal rights defense: in the three thematically related poems on the eagles at Dunolly Castle, the poet's authentic outrage at the plight of another species truly comes to the fore. That Wordsworth has left several prose notes regarding the eagles of his poems further highlights his outrage. A note to yet another eagle poem ("Return," of the *River Duddon* sequence) informs us that the golden eagle had been virtually extinguished from the Lake District in the poet's own day: "The EAGLE requires a large domain for its support: but several pairs, not many years ago, were constantly resident in this country [the Lake District]. . . . The bird frequently returns, but is always destroyed" (PW 3.508). As for the eagle of Dunolly Castle itself: "I saw the other day one of these noble creatures cooped up among the ruins, and was incited to give vent to my feelings" (3.529), which he does three times, in "The Dunolly Eagle," "On Revisiting Dunolly Castle," and "Eagles."

"The Dunolly Eagle" introduces us to the "Poor Bird!" of the "castle-dungeon," who is, metaphorically at least, "Kennelled and chained" (12, 4, 7). (Apparently the bird had wandered into the castle's depths and now cannot find his way out, so at least Wordsworth has no immediate human villains to vent upon.) For my argument, this poem is the weakest of the three, for when the eagle retreats even further into the dungeon during a storm, Wordsworth uses this incident to reflect on the relationship of human masters and slaves: "even so / Doth man of brother man a creature make / That clings to slavery for its own sad sake" (12–14).

In the second poem, the poet returns to find the "captive Bird . . . gone"

(1), either fled or dead, but he finds inscribed on a floor of the castle's tower a primitive "art mosaic" of an eagle (6): "An Eagle with stretched wings, but beamless eye— / An Eagle that could neither wail nor soar. / Effigy of the Vanished" (7–9). This poem, too, ends rather weakly, with the poet's insinuating self-praise for his own "memorial rhymes" (13), but at least the carved effigy engages the eagle, in a quite poignant fashion; if the phrase "Effigy of the Vanished" is a trope in danger of vacuously floating into human affairs, it at least evokes ideas of other-species extinction. Interestingly, the signified itself is no longer there. The poet is left to regard a man-made signifier of the bird, Wordsworth's reverie ultimately pointing to the pathetic inequality of signifier and signified. And yet his sonnet itself becomes at last a signifier of a signified, which is a signifier of another signified, now "Vanished."

Before one asks, but where is this authentic outrage?, I turn quickly to "Eagles," the third poem about this "Bird of Jove embarred / Like a lone criminal" (2–3). The castle that is the bird's prison is a "Dishonoured Rock and Ruin!" (1). Here, there is no (at least ostensible) infestation of human politics or aesthetic effigy. The bulk of the poem deserves full quotation:

> Vexed is he, and screams loud. The last I saw
> Was on the wing; stooping, he struck with awe
> Man, bird, and beast; then, with a consort paired,
> From a bold headland, their loved aery's guard,
> Flew high above the Atlantic waves, to draw
> Light from the fountain of the setting sun.
> Such was this Prisoner once; and when his plumes
> The sea-blast ruffles as the storm comes on,
> Then, for a moment, he, in spirit, resumes
> His rank 'mong freeborn creatures that live free,
> His power, his beauty, and his majesty. (4–14)

I hope that this magnificent passage was worth the wait. The ornithologist might quibble that the female "consort" is actually larger and more majestic than "he" (cf. Dorothy?), and so the feminist, too, would have a field day here. (No doubt the new historicist would read the entire poem as a metaphor of human discourses of power.) But the lover of words and birds can only welcome such a grand subject presented so powerfully in language, relatively devoid (though the "Bird of Jove" rankles), of recuperative othering.

A POET "FOREVER GREEN"?

The language of *The Prelude* is fleetingly red but ever green.

—JONATHAN BATE, *Romantic Ecology*

I have already referred more than once to Jonathan Bate's study of Wordsworth, the first major text of British ecocriticism. Written firmly against the grain of the poststructuralist and new historicist critical milieu, *Romantic Ecology* (1991) is Bate's self-proclaimed "preliminary sketch towards a literary ecocriticism" (11), through which the critic would remake Wordsworth as the first English poet with a truly modern ecological conscience.[8] In doing so, Bate must subvert the hegemony of the Yale school and new historicism in recent Wordsworthian criticism to "politicize" literary studies "in a new way" and to render Wordsworth once more, and all the more, "timely" (4). His counterargument: Wordsworth *was* a nature poet, a fact missed or utterly downplayed and obfuscated by the deconstructionists, psychoanalytic critics, and the rest (10). As support, Bate reprivileges several lesser read works from Wordsworth's corpus, especially *The Excursion* (62–71), "Poems on the Naming of Places" (90–101), and the prose "tourist manual" that we've already encountered, *Guide to the Lakes* (41–48). Not only is the *Guide to the Lakes* an "exemplar of the Romantic ecology," with its protests against "influx and innovation" and "picturesque 'improvement'" of the Lake District (45, 47), but Bate claims for the "Poems on the Naming of Places" a preeminent position in what he "would like to describe as an ecological tradition of English place-poetry" (90–91).

Wordsworth's approach to nature, in fact, included a nascent ecological consciousness that had a seminal influence in England, both on later literary figures (e.g., Clare, Ruskin, and Morris) and on subsequent (eco)political activism. Not only was Wordsworth the first to achieve a "truly ecological poetry" (103), but his influence also played a role in the development of English socialism, which subsequently, via Ruskin and Morris, has always been more "green" than "red."[9] Moreover, to consider the Sage of Grasmere in terms of political environmentalism, as Ruskin and Morris supposedly did, "might just be the most useful way of approaching Wordsworth in the 1990s and the early twenty-first century" (4). The poet not only "went before us in some of the steps we are now taking in our thinking about the environment" (5), but later organized clamors for nature preserves and the like are inextricably "bound up with Romanticism and the Lake District."

The seeds of the British national-park movement originally sprouted, apparently, very near Dove Cottage or Grasmere, and "all who walk in the [British] National Parks are legatees of Wordsworth" (48–49).

However, the person who wrote the Lacanian sections of the previous chapter finds it impossible to swallow Bate's entire spiel without a draught or two of Keats's "vintage." Bate seems all too content to ignore the ready critiques of poststructuralist high theory of such a leap to the Real of nature sans consideration of the sociolinguistic constructs that severely color (or perhaps even disallow) such a leap. The peaceful nooks of the "Naming of Places" poems are, I think, as othered by Wordsworth's need to name and appropriate as anything else in his corpus. The alert reader is certainly aware that even most of the poems that I enlisted in support of Wordsworth's observational skills and ecological outrage are inflected in various degrees with his drive toward psychic recuperation. As Freud's delineation of the various ego defense mechanisms suggests, one can say the right things for the wrong reasons.

In asking us to reconsider whether the "economy of human society is more important than . . . the economy of nature" (9), Bate's ecocritical angle is also open to attack from that part of the political left more concerned with human class than species and planet. Having at least implicitly directed his barbs at another faction, the neo-Marxist bent of British cultural studies, Bate is well aware that this group (especially) would view his reading as a conservative, even reactionary act of retrenchment in literary studies. Thus he goes out of his way in claiming that he is *not* ignoring human social issues, even quoting approvingly the letter of a factory worker offering two shillings to the National Trust's nature reserve drive because he "once saw Derwentwater" and could "never forget it" (53–54).[10] In another symptomatic passage, Bate summarizes Hazlitt's critique of Wordsworth in words that might be applied to Bate's own "green" politics: "The problem with this view of nature is that it depends on individual feeling [and] on the leisure to enjoy sunsets and spring days" (53). In the end, the nineteenth-century proto-environmentalists whom Bate champions were hardly peasants or factory workers, making Bate an easy target for a Marxist backlash. If the reader feels reassured that Bate's conservationist interests "need not be the dupe of conservative politics" (114), he or she still may look askance at such statements as the following: "Whatever our class, nature can do something for us" (56). Not only is the "us" versus "nature" mentality disturbingly present, but Bate's continual ideological jousting with British Marxism smacks of a defensiveness that leaves the class-sensitive reader uncomfortable.

But his larger claim that, at present, ecological concerns override those of class can hardly be denied. Responding to the new historicist Alan Liu's restatement of the current view that nature for Wordsworth is but an anthropomorphized and ideological construct—and responding ultimately to all who would take the nature out of Wordsworth and out of literary studies in general—Bate offers the following eloquent retort: "It is profoundly unhelpful to say '*There is no nature*' at a time when our most urgent need is to address and redress the consequences of human civilization's insatiable desire to consume the products of the earth. We are confronted for the first time in history with the possibility of there being no part of the earth left untouched by man. . . . When there have been a few more accidents at nuclear power stations, when there are no more rain forests, and when every wilderness has been ravaged for its mineral resources, then let us say '*There is no nature*'" (56).

Bate's environmentalist appeals continue: "'Still glides the Stream, and shall for ever glide,' wrote Wordsworth . . . but now it is not only water that glides inexorably into the sea off Wordsworth's coast" (61). Bate may move from past to present rather too glibly, but his point is nonetheless telling. More rhetorically impressive yet is a similar pathos in his book's closing sentences: "Of course Wordsworth's poem about the boy of Winander addresses itself to the workings of the mind and the power of imagination. But let us not forget that it is also about a boy alone by a lake at dusk blowing mimic hootings to unseen owls. Which are there to answer him" (115). Another bird species might have served Bate even better. The owls are still there, but the "mournful shriek" and "thick unwieldy flight" of the great bustard who once inhabited Wordsworth's Salisbury Plain ("Guilt and Sorrow" 12.7, 9) is no longer found in England, victim of its poor abilities to *flee*, no doubt.[11] In Wordsworth's own lifetime, as we have seen, the golden eagle, too, was rapidly becoming a thing of the past in the Lake District. Now these "absences" are givens that one must assume to be true, and therefore lament, unless one is committed to the most extreme solipsism. So one can wallow in the ethical paralysis occasioned by the devastating critique of postmodernism, by the almost algebraic mechanisms of Lacanian lack and Law, but no matter how much our true psychic motivation is bound up in a psycholinguistic process of the Other that conditions, even determines our very perception of the external world, we can still make the epistemological leap of faith that the Real Other may not be just our absent or introjected mother, but mother nature, and we can at least act *as if* the preservation of that nature were a pure, authentic gesture.

To return to Wordsworth's poetry itself one last time, perhaps the most explicit expression of his alter-species impulses can be found in the poem "Liberty." Here Wordsworth's ultimate concern is once again a very *human* liberty, a protest against whatever would "cramp the wingèd mind" (136)—including, I would add, reductionist psychoanalytic explanations of that mind. I realize only too well that my attempts to flee such explanations are inordinately recuperative in themselves, and that this final section on Wordsworth is perhaps nothing more than testimony to a human impulse to project its need of self-integrity upon the environment. I would only offer, in defiance, my spine-tingling intuition that the following passage on animal freedom, or animal rights, if you will, stands out as the most authentically impassioned section of Wordsworth's hymn to "Liberty":

Who can divine what impulses from God
Reach the caged lark, within a town-abode,
From his poor inch or two of daisied sod?
O yield him back his privilege!—No sea
Swells like the bosom of a man set free;
A wilderness is rich with liberty.
Roll on, ye spouting whales, who die or keep
Your independence in the fathomless Deep!
Spread, tiny nautilus, the living sail;
Dive, at thy choice, or brave the freshing gale!
If unreproved the ambitious eagle mount
Sunward to seek the daylight in its fount,
Bays, gulfs, and ocean's Indian width, shall be,
Till the world perishes, a field for thee! (27–40)

That this world may well "perish" is Bate's main contention, of course. A few lines later there is a caged bird, "a brilliant fondling of the cage," who, "Though fed with dainties from" a "snow-white hand," still "gladly would escape" (62, 64, 66). Driven like a ghost ship by this thought, I returned the other day to a local John James Audubon exhibit, a very sepulcher of painted birds and stuffed birds and live caged birds. At the cage of European goldfinches, I shouted, "O yield them back their privilege!" And it's no great shame to admit that I've been asked *not* to come back. But how can the American goldfinch be protected by federal law and proclaimed the state bird of several U.S. states while its closest kin is legally shipped around this same country, behind bars?

Wordsworth's literary relationship with nature and animals and birds can be seen as a crossroads of the Western Romantic consciousness regarding animal alterity, which alternately might be viewed as a great beginning in eco-consciousness or a fertile yet doomed dead end. Geoffrey Hartman, not surprisingly, seems to find the latter: Wordsworth "alone stood between us and the death of nature to imagination. . . . He was at a turning point in history which would see either a real marriage of the mind of man with nature or their apocalyptic severance" (*Wordsworth's Poetry* xiv). From "Tintern Abbey" to the River Duddon, there is in Wordsworth "a remarkable conviction [and fear] that man and nature are growing irremediably apart, and that the gap between them . . . already verges on apocalypse" (337). To the psychological-soon-to-be-deconstructionist-critic that Hartman was, Wordsworth's attempt—in the throes of the narcissism and solipsism of the Imagination—never had a chance for success, and Hartman's conclusion is a pathetic one, in which the poet of lakes and robins is ultimately more alienated than any other British Romantic: "Wordsworth . . . can turn to no one in his desire to save nature for the human imagination. He is the most isolated figure among the great English poets" (338). True or not (such psychobiographical statements are really inarguable), the apocalypse to which Hartman points might explain why the next generation of British Romantic poets rarely achieved (or even attempted) the marriage of realism and idealism that characterizes much of Wordsworth's ornithic poetry, as the Real retreated before the high Romantic Symbol, and the poetical milieu might be said, metaphorically, to be more and more a place where no birds sing.

AVIAN BLESSINGS, AVIAN CURSE: S. T. COLERIDGE

> No sound is dissonant which tells of Life.
>
> SAMUEL TAYLOR COLERIDGE, "This Lime-Tree Bower My Prison"

Despite Wordsworth's busy literary aviary, Keats's "plain brown" nightingale and Percy Shelley's skylark remain the prototypical Romantic birds;

indeed, both avian poems, for better or worse, "elevate the songbird to an almost mythic status" (Foss 19). One might wonder whether this mythic elevation was, in general, a falling off from (what I yet insist to be) Wordsworth's various positive efforts at naturalistic realism and eco-empathy, and hypothesize that the British Romantic bird became more and more a disembodied voice, an etherealized spirit, and, ultimately, a use-value emblem for the poetic *I* itself. But as if to frame this distancing from the avian that seems readily evident in Byron, Shelley, and Keats, this chapter continues with a poet nearly as Wordsworthian as Wordsworth himself in his (initial) regard for the avian, Samuel Taylor Coleridge, and ends with a writer who may be the prime exception to this perceived poetic lapse from the real bird: John Clare.

Before venturing on to the second generation of British Romanticism, another first-generation Romantic deserves some mention for avian efforts of note, that is, Wordsworth's *Lyrical Ballads* confrere. Not only is Coleridge's albatross "perhaps the best-known bird symbol in literature" (Halpern 9), but the relationship between Wordsworth and Coleridge and birds can be seen as central to the two poets' early coevolution. Add Dorothy to this triumvirate, and one imagines a late 1790s trio busy writing, and walking, and watching and listening to birds, with Coleridge and Dorothy perhaps more interested in the birds than even William, given Hazlitt's testimony: "I got into a metaphysical argument with Wordsworth, while Coleridge was explaining the different notes of the nightingale to his sister, in which we neither of us succeeded in making ourselves perfectly clear and intelligible" ("My First Acquaintance" 119). In fact, as shall be seen, some scholars have argued that avians are even more central to Coleridge's corpus than to William Wordsworth's.

And yet Wordsworth's concern for the fate of his Grasmere swan pair may have occasioned his suggestion to Coleridge regarding the central incident of *The Rime of the Ancient Mariner*.[12] Why not kill one of the South Sea birds that William had encountered in his reading of Shelvock's *Voyages:* that "largest sort of sea-fowl," the albatross (Fenwick note, PW 1.361)? A cross-fertilization of ornithic imagery and themes between the two poets seems to have been the order of the day. From a larger thematic view, the problematic relationship between animal alterity and human consciousness, and the latter's alienation from the animal and natural, are no doubt crucial to the poetic concerns of both. Applewhite has noted that all three of Coleridge's "greatest" poems "portray aspects of a curse" (93). I would argue that the various manifestations of said curse all involve an alienation from the animal, a self-awareness of being cast out of Eden and the Ark, if you will. Thus are Coleridge's many pious benedictions of other species compensatory and recuperative gestures toward either a psychological or ecological holism, depending on one's critical bent.

I have argued throughout that, from Cowper and Erasmus Darwin on, one main Romantic gesture has been to get back on that Ark, to rejoin the family via a reprivileging of the animal, both without and within. We have already seen that this seminal age of both a new biology and a new Sensibility and Imagination led to an at least intermittent replacement of the "up-down universe" of the Christian-Medieval Great Chain of Being by a "horizontal one of [more equal] relationships between man and nature" (Gaull 354–55). Kurt Fosso has contended, moreover, that Wordsworth and Coleridge were major movers in this axis shift.[13] Unfortunately, the various appeals by Wordsworth and Coleridge to "new forms of social cohesion and identity" via "mysterious human-animal linkages"—how intriguing, this—are in large part, in Fosso's new historicist view, a reaction to the "turbulent" political environment of a "diseased socio-political world" (3–4). Animals become, in these poets' verse, the "makers or markers of community and communitarian feeling" (5). "Makers" is a mere metaphor here; "markers" is telling, as other species remain signifiers and tools for humankind's greater social cohesion. I may finally agree with Fosso on these poets' ultimate homocentrism, but to present this particular sociopolitical reading as positive praise of the pair's naturist yearnings will not do.

However, one is still impressed by the recent championing of Coleridge's own naturism,[14] including his infatuation with birds, evident in both his poetry and life. Jeanne Halpern's study of Coleridge's bird imagery, his use of which "began with his first poem," finds the poet's employment of birds to be distinguished by great realism. Because Coleridge was "a careful observer of nature" who "often walked with pencil in hand," Halpern is not surprised to find that thirty-one of the forty-two species mentioned in Coleridge's verse are native English species (9).[15] Such observations of birds in the wild helped his poetry: "The accuracy of his [avian] knowledge both sharpened and enriched his poetic use of bird imagery" (12). This "accuracy" Halpern cannot emphasize enough, and extends to Coleridge's knowledge of bird calls: "Among the beauties of Coleridge's bird characterizations are his sounds: rooks creak, partridges whir, swallows twitter, gulls scream, drakes quack, and tawny owls say tu-whit—tu-who, exactly as they should[!], according to [the British bird guide of] Peterson" (21).

The relative realism of Coleridge's bird poetry will be examined later. However, the general impression that this reader comes away with from Coleridge's corpus is that he much more often falls back on the common, trope-ridden eagles, owls, skylarks, and nightingales (à la Blake) than the more novel variety of species encountered in Wordsworth's pages. Simultaneous to her championing of Coleridge's great realism, Halpern also remarks on how often the poet employs certain birds as (what I have called) shadow birds. Thus raptors are "his symbols of evil"; the vulture represents "destruction," and the "calls of the scritch owl and the tawny owl are Coleridge's most reliable harbingers of evil and sin" (14). This is hardly in accord with Halpern's main argument regarding the poet's realism and organicism: "Coleridge's use of birds illustrates his poetic principles put into practice. While other poets such as Wordsworth, Browning, and Hardy often use birds suggestively, decoratively, and descriptively, Coleridge uses them organically. They are precise, scientifically accurate, material manifestations of ideas operating within the poems" (17). How using an owl as a symbol of "evil and sin" is scientifically accurate or poetically "organic" in a way transcending the traditional tropic use of avians is beyond this student of literature and birds. The best one might say is that Halpern overstates her case in championing the ornithology of a preferred poet, just as I have probably done with Wordsworth.

The organicism that several critics have emphasized in Coleridge's nature imagery is itself a double-edged sword. Certainly it has positive ecological ramifications. If Naturphilosophie, the unified theory of German Romanticism that "everything [is] potentially alive," found fertile ground in Coleridge (Gaull 358), then his "holistic conception of poetic form" stemmed from his knowledge of the "scientific controversies of his era," especially the "eighteenth-century scientific concept of the organism," that he found in Darwin's *Botanic Garden* and elsewhere (McKusick 28, 37).[16] But this critical attention to Coleridge's "organic" theory also points to other problems with the poet's, or philosopher's, *theory*. In fact, Coleridge's general idealist emphasis that culminated in the *Biographia Literaria* eventually led, I think, to a relative denigration of naturalist specifics, that is, a repression of the *real* bird.

Halpern's own tribute to Coleridgean ornithology includes the significant admission that "half of his bird poems" were written quite early, from 1795 to 1798 (19). The human-interest element here is poignant; as with Gilbert White and Wordsworth, Coleridge complained (at an earlier age than the others, it appears) of a significant hearing loss. That, by 1799, he "seldom heard 'sweet bird songs' any longer" was, Halpern claims, a precipitating factor in the decline of bird imagery in his poetry. Not only were later images of birds "largely generalized," but "none of the poems that he wrote during the last five years of his life contain bird images" (19, 20). However, to attribute all this to a hearing loss seems ultimately unsatisfactory; this particular sensory deprivation may well be considered, above all, symptomatic of a psychological isolation or alienation that culminated in the poet's idealist philosophy, the near solipsism of his "absolute self, the great eternal I AM" of his *Biographia* (298).[17] One is hardly surprised, then, that a late poem, "Work without Hope" (1825), repeats Burns's complaint that "ev'ry thing is blest but I": while "All Nature seems at work" and the "birds are on the wing" (1–2), "I, the while, [am] the sole unbusy thing" (5). This "all nature but me is happy" lament is no doubt a common Romantic formula. But it takes on new significance, even poignancy, from the poet of self-isolating "curses" and the philosopher of the "I AM." It is as if Coleridge is himself the Ancient Mariner (before the latter's rejuvenation), having "slain" the birds in his poetry and found himself "alone, all, all alone" (*Rime* 232).

Indeed, against Coleridge's recent critical revival as ecohero, characterizations of him by his contemporaries stand in marked contrast, epitomized in Peacock's satire of Romantic obscurantism in *Nightmare Abbey*. Portrayed as Mr. Flotsky, Coleridge is the ne plus ultra of the poet who has retreated from the phenomenal world: "I live in a world of ghosts," Flotsky proclaims with pride (69). Stuck in the "transcendental darkness" of "Kantian metaphysics" (8), he has forgotten that "there are any such things as sunshine and music"—and birds—"in the world" (32).[18] Such criticism no doubt flies in the face of the modern notion of Romanticism's, especially the Lake Poets', close alliance to naturism, but a glance at the middle chapters of the *Biographia Literaria* furnishes ample support for such a characterization. His preference for the "spiritual" metaphysics of Boehme and Kant over the mechanistic materialism of Locke and Hume (228–33); his preference for Schelling over Fichte (233–36) because the latter's "theory degenerated into a crude egoismus, a boastful and hyperstoic hostility to Nature, as lifeless, godless, and altogether unholy" (233–34); and his Schelling-influenced vitalistic union of spirit and nature all may be read as positive segues to recent positions put forth by deep ecology. But Coleridge's own marriage of mind and matter, his claim that "object and subject . . . are identical, each involving and supposing each other" (297), intriguing as it is, ends in the "subject" and the *ideal*: for in the end, "idealism" is "the truest and most binding realism" (294), and it is the Imagination that is "essentially vital, even as all objects (as objects) are essentially *fixed and dead*" (313; emphasis added). Thus Wordsworth's give-and-take psychology of half-creating and half-receiving becomes, in Coleridge's "Dejection: An Ode," a one-way street: "we receive but what we give, / And in our life alone does nature live" (4.1–2). This is the hubris of the Mariner, as we shall see.

As for the poetry, however, Coleridge's seminal early efforts of the 1790s often display an attitude toward nature that we might now consider quite Wordsworthian. His abundant recompense for being laid up in "This Lime-Tree Bower My Prison," for example, is the faith that he is still *in* nature, whether he can enjoy a bird walk or not: although "not a swallow twitters," he is still certain "That Nature ne'er deserts the wise and pure; / No plot so narrow, be but Nature there" (57, 60–61). At this point in his corpus, one can accept the apparent moralism of "wise and pure" as akin to Wordsworth's "wise" linnets and thrushes and to the "wise passiveness" that "watches and receives."

This moral Coleridge seems most interested in imparting to or finding innately in the very young. Thus the climax of "Frost at Midnight" bids his "Dear Babe" (44) to accept all seasons, emblematized in the winter robin, as coequal manifestations of nature:

> Therefore all seasons shall be sweet to thee,
> Whether the summer clothe the general earth
> With greenness, or the redbreast sit and sing
> Betwixt the tufts of snow on the bare branch
> Of mossy apple-tree. (65–69)

Another species, the titular bird of "The Nightingale," is made more dear, again, by the poet's "dear babe," who is quite taken by the bird's song: "How he would place his hand beside his ear . . . And bid us listen! And I deem it wise / To make him nature's play-mate" (91, 94, 96–97).[19] What is deemed "wise" here, however, is equivocal. More obviously, one can conjecture that making the boy "nature's playmate" involves Coleridge inculcating him into the joys of amateur nature study, *explaining* to him the different calls of the nightingale as he once did with Dorothy. But one can also read "wise" as what the child has already, an innate propensity for joy in the language of other species, a joy that the father seems to have been less and less able to feel, whether from his hearing loss or his growing allegiance to the Churches of England and Kant.

Indeed, if the *Rime* must be considered one of Coleridge's still youthful efforts, the homiletic piety of the poem's moral strikes a new chord of disjunction and alienation, as if one should best encounter warm and bare Mother Earth through the white-gloved Law of the Father. It may well be true that "He prayeth well who loveth well / Both man and bird and beast" (612–613); moreover, to love "All things both great and small" (615) is a democracy of beings rarely encountered before in Christian literature. But the act of prayer itself and the reason wherefore—"For the dear God who loveth us, / He made and loveth all" (616–17)—still pertain to an anthropomorphic (and male) deity who at some point *created* humans and albatrosses and water snakes, with no doubt an implicit privileging of the human.

Another of Coleridge's positive ecothemes also has theistic underpinnings, however metaphorical the intent: the blessing of other species, including birds. Most famous, of course, is the Mariner's eventual blessing of the sea snakes in the *Rime*, issuing from his epiphany that such "slimy" creatures (125), like the more ethereal albatross and skylark of the poem, are themselves "happy living things" (282) worthy of respect. (This dualistic motif in Coleridge between spirit bird and chthonic serpent will be dealt with later.) Elsewhere, the tribute to nature at large quoted earlier in "This Lime-Tree Bower My Prison" is followed by a finale that blesses one individual avian of that nature, the rook.[20] That the bird is black and hardly a "sweet songster" exemplifies a Romantic motif familiar to us already in Cowper, Burns, and Wordsworth, and in Coleridge's own sea snakes: the reprivileging of the humble, the abject, the nonbeautiful:

> My gentle-hearted Charles! when the last rook
> Beat its straight path along the dusky air
> Homewards, I blest it! deeming, its black wing
> (Now a dim speck, now vanishing in light)

Had crossed the mighty orb's dilated glory,
While thou stood'st gazing; or when all was still,
Flew creeking o'er thy head, and had a charm
For thee, my gentle-hearted Charles, to whom
No sound is dissonant which tells of Life. (68–76)

"Creeking" is a deliciously apt onomatopoeia, and the final line might serve as a motto for egalitarian vitalism, with a happy added emphasis on the aural dimension.[21] One must note, however, that this appreciation of the corvid is filtered through another human, Charles, the ultimate raison-d'être for this entire paean. As if to corroborate Fosso, the emphasis here is once again on human community.

Coleridge's earlier bird poems often emphasize their sounds, as if presciently making up for a later loss and absence. For instance, one of his very early poems, "Songs of the Pixies" (1793), sets its scene with an initial contrast between "the wren of softest note" and "the blackbird [who] strains his throat" (1.5, 7) for no apparent reason but to show off that the poet knows the ornithological difference. But it is the skylark that, understandably, is most amenable to Coleridge's ear. "Reflections on Having Left a Place of Retirement" (1796) includes the "reflection" that the poet has been

. . . Oft with patient ear
Long-listening to the viewless sky-lark's note
(Viewless, or haply for a moment seen
Gleaming on sunny wings). (18–21)

The skylark's frequent invisibility allows for such a response to the bird's "note" alone, as we have seen in Wordsworth and will see in Shelley; for Coleridge, the skylark's song becomes one of his most common emblems of a rejuvenating nature and a natural icon on which Coleridge can project his spiritual yearnings. The compensatory "Sweet influences" of nature felt in "Fears in Solitude" (1798) issue in large part "from the singing lark (that sings unseen / The minstrelsy that solitude loves best)" (21, 18–19). But the shallowly disguised third-person "he" who feels such things also ultimately *uses* the lark as a vacuous vehicle for metaphysical inanity. For, feeling such natural influences, he

> . . . found
> Religious meanings in the forms of nature!
> And so, his senses gradually wrapt
> In a half sleep, he dreams of better worlds,
> And dreaming hears thee still, O singing lark;
> That singest like an angel in the clouds! (23–28)

This tenuous discovery of "Religious meanings" is exactly Coleridge's modus operandi. Here it is occasioned by a half-absent bird who is compared to an even emptier signifier, an angel. (If, as I suggested in chapter 1, angels are really metaphorical epiphenomena of real birds, the tenor-vehicle reversal here is patently absurd.) The value of the lark's singing invisibility will culminate in Shelley's "To a Skylark," but Keats's "Ode to a Nightingale" is also abundantly anticipated here in the willingness to see the real bird with eyes half closed, as it were, to stake out a Romantic self in isolation, an "eternal I AM," that would pretend to have no need of actual skylarks and nightingales.

A final skylark usage must be noted as crucial to the psychomachia that is the *Rime*. Part of the Mariner's return to psychological and ecohealth, and coming soon after the blessing of the water snakes, is his newfound ear for nature's sounds, epitomized again in the lark:

> Sometimes a-dropping from the sky
> I heard the sky-lark sing;
> Sometimes all little birds that are,
> How they seemed to fill the sea and air
> With their sweet jargoning! (358–62)

The skylark's song "establishes the mariner's reentry into the positive circle of nature," according to Halpern (14–15). McKusick interprets the avian images here wonderfully, as border or *coniunctio* creatures that marry opposites: the lark, significantly, "enters the poem as an ecotonal boundary of 'sea and air'" (49). (To quibble: it is, grammatically, "all" the "little birds" who make up this marriage of "sea and air." But this still supports the critic's main point.) However, McKusick then reads the lark's subsequent comparisons to human musical "instruments" and to an "angel's song" (363, 365) as ecologically redemptive. For in this passage, "all created beings, and even inanimate objects, are accorded some form of linguistic expression. The voice of the Lavrock [lark] exemplifies a radical environmental usage, suggesting that the animate creation has its own language" (50). While agreeing with this last clause (and that the fine word choice "jargoning" is apt support for it), I would read the passage less glowingly, just as I have already looked askance at comparing a skylark to an angel in the discussion just previous. The lark's "own language," rather than having been conjoined in a community of equal linguistic signifiers, as McKusick would have it, has instead been translated into the human-all-too-human with, again, a homocentric theistic undercurrent (angel) that especially militates against an authentic rapport with other species.

One can't leave the *Rime* for long in discussing Coleridge and nature and birds. The poet has also received praise for his various overt protests against animal cruelty, and of course, the albatross, whose slaying may be deemed the prototypical act of animal murder, is central here. The donkey of "To a Young Ass," though never overtly blessed, is another abused animal whose defense the young Coleridge is eager to undertake: "Poor little Foal of an oppressed Race! / I love the languid Patience of thy face" (1–2). One isn't entirely impressed, eco-consciously, by the phrase "languid Patience," with the connotations of a "race" marked, perhaps, by sheer benumbedness. But Coleridge's most crucial gesture in the poem is one of equal rights for other species: "I hail thee Brother" (26), he exclaims, and would happily take the donkey away, in "Peace and mild Equality to dwell" (28). Such hailings and blessings of other species in Coleridge's corpus certainly grant much validity to the recent scholarly emphases on the poet's contributions to Anglo-American eco-consciousness.

The albatross, of course, is Coleridge's greatest lesson regarding the failure to appreciate and bless the avian other. But in line with Buell's complaint regarding literary scholars' "tendency to relegate" nature in literature "to the status of symbols or reflectors" (*Environmental Imagination* 260), this particular bird has become such a critic-encrusted symbol that it is more and more difficult to see the crime as it is: the sheer murder of another, feathered, species.[22] Coleridge hardly helps matters by first hailing the bird "As if it had been a Christian soul" (65), but the plot itself remains: "With my cross-bow / I shot the albatross" (81–82). The Mariner's act is a "hellish thing": "For all averred, I had killed the bird / That made the breeze to blow" (91, 93–94). Superstition aside, the bird's association with the wind connotes vitality and life; the ego-in-isolation that would other such a being, then, is a living death. This same ego, soon "all, all alone," thus views other species as abject *others*: "Yea, slimy things did crawl with legs / Upon the slimy sea" (232, 125–26).

But again, Coleridge muddies this particular ocean with explicit Christian symbolism: "Instead of the cross, the Albatross / About my neck was hung" (141–142). Rendered now as some generic cross to bear, the slain albatross is thus open to all sorts of intrapsychic interpretations, many of them quite valid. Applewhite's Jungian reading certainly rings true in general: the Mariner's ship is ego consciousness, and the sea and its creatures represent the unconscious "depths"; more specifically, "the skeleton ship symbolizes consciousness in an attitude that finds nature in its essence somehow alien." The Mariner himself is a Western rationalist "too little sensitive . . . to nature and the unconscious," cursed at last by a "psychic sterility," until his eventual psychic rebirth and regeneration (112, 115–16, 99, 110). Unfortunately, the Jungian concepts of the ego and the (unconscious) Self are latter-day products of the very German Idealism that led to a Mariner "all, all alone," and that still allow for a reading in which all images are "symbols within" a psyche on the road to individuation.[23] The actual killing of a real bird is at a distant remove in such readings, and the ego alienation (from nature or the unconscious, *as if synonymous*) of which such critics speak is exemplified, at last, in their own self-absorbed hermeneutic vistas.

Worse yet is the scholar who would meet Coleridge's theological bent on its own terms. G. Wilson Knight, for instance, asserts that the albatross "seems to suggest some redeeming Christ-like force in creation that guides humanity from primitive and fearful origins" (159). Not only is the "primitive" to be feared and in need of redemption, but our bird is now some white dove as Holy Spirit, or rather, "that in nature[?] which helps man beyond[?!] nature, an aspect of the divine purpose" (160). How quickly does this Christian moral critic rid the bird of any actual, natural being. And how predictably dualistic to contrast the albatross with the denizens of the ocean depths: the "slimy things," in Knight's cosmology, stand for "an alien, salty, and reptilian force" (160). As in *Christabel,* this "contrast of bird-life and the reptilian" evokes an archetypal "fearful fascination" (163) for a scholar ridden by the Manichaean inner torture of good versus evil. To come to Coleridge's defense, the point of the *Rime* is the transcendence of such a dualism, the acknowledgment that holy birds and infernal reptiles are on an equal plane, the realization that all life is but that: life, blessèd and holy.

Recent critics have made some overtures in reprivileging the albatross as a real bird and the crossbow shot as a literal crime against the natural Other. But even some ecologically minded scholars cannot get the concept of "symbol" out of their heads. Halpern does rehearse Lowes's idea that this particular bird is the sooty albatross, derived from Coleridge's reading of Captain Cook's *Voyage to the Pacific Ocean*; moreover, the poet's description of the bird "is scientifically accurate" in portraying the bird "as having long, narrow, pointed wings, capable of flying fast over long distances, soaring for weeks, and feeding on scraps from ships" (12). But then Halpern almost becomes a reincarnation of G. Wilson Knight: "The bird represents not only a positive force of nature, but also innocence, spiritual unity in nature and human society and poetic imagination" (14). (Is that all?) Better is McKusick, for whom the albatross is an "innocent emissary from the unspoiled natural realm," although "innocent" is still, as in Halpern, an ascription with great moralistic overtones. Less stuck in the symbolic, McKusick instead translates Coleridge perhaps overmuch in terms of recent environmental ethics. Yes, the Mariner's terrible retribution occurs "as if[?] the destruction of a single creature had disrupted the whole economy of nature" (45), and very likely the Mariner's ultimate lesson is to have "learned that the deliberate destruction of any wild creature may bring unforeseen consequences." All sound ecology, this, with the possible exception of the "as if." But that the poem at last "exemplifies the environmental advocacy that is integral to Coleridge's ecological vision" (48) may be going too far. One still hears, by poem's end, so many echoes of "Christian soul" and the "dear [Creator] God" that such an eco-advocacy of the rights of other species becomes somewhat beside the point.

The greatest debate regarding Coleridge's purported naturalist realism involves "The Nightingale," in which he both laudably stands the traditional trope of the melancholic nightingale on its head, and yet unduly leaps to the manic side of the spectrum in finding the bird to be an emblem of joy and love. In a poem from a few years later, "Answer to a Child's Question" (1802), Coleridge is even more blatant: "Do you ask what the birds say? The sparrow, the dove, / The linnet and thrush say, 'I love and I love!'" (1–2); the lark, too, "is so brimful of gladness and love . . . That he sings, and he sings; and for ever sings he— / 'I love my Love, and my Love loves me!'" (7, 9–10).[24]

The realistic bent of "The Nightingale" (1798) explodes the convention of the bird's melancholia:

> 'Most musical, most melancholy' bird!
> A melancholy bird? Oh! idle thought!
> In nature there is nothing melancholy.
> But some night-wandering man . . .
> . . . .
> First named these notes a melancholy strain.
> And many a poet echoes the conceit. (13–16, 22–23)

Coleridge counters this age-old misreading via a realistic description of several nightingales in vocal interaction, as

> They answer and provoke each other's song,
> With skirmish and capricious passagings,
> And murmurs musical and swift jug jug,
> And one low piping sound more sweet than all. (58–61)

"Capricious" and "musical" are completely subjective judgments, but the onomatopoeic "jug jug" (however commonplace) and that "one low piping sound" are evidence of a poet who has certainly listened closely to the actual song.[25] The poem is also graced by an amazing, almost haunting visual image, of the birds' "bright, bright eyes, their eyes both bright and full, / Glistening" (67–68). The repetition of "bright" and "eyes" asks the reader to pause and really try to see another species, even meet its gaze, and the passage seems, in its sheer contextual incongruity, a veritable irruption of avian alterity.[26]

The debate regarding the poem's relative realism versus its own othering of the nightingale includes much hyperbole in favor of the former. Kroeber heaps praise on the "naturalistic accuracy" of the poem (*Ecological* 73–75),[27] and Fosso is no doubt right in praising Coleridge's skepticism regarding all this "melancholy" business, and the poet's consciousness that this is at last humankind's propensity for "narcissistic" distortion at work (6). But Coleridge's own poeticized avian becomes, in the hand of Fosso and others, a veritable transcendence of human projection. This nightingale "remains intriguingly beyond the culturally constraining powers of human categorization and understanding" and offers "a curious resistance to its own anthropomorphic reductions" (8); the birds' warblings are "'delicious' for their difference, resistance, and mystery" (9). (I argued earlier that the strongest element of "resistance" in the poem is rather the interjection of the visual image of the birds peering back at the reader, as it were.) For Frank Doggett, admittedly a critic of the "old school," such realism and "difference" is cause for transcendental celebration: "The nightingale is a voice of nature, rather than a symbol of poetry, and its song is an intimation of . . . primal reality" (551). But nature here is at last but an ideational generalization that *can only* be symbolized, perhaps, and the phrase "primal reality" rather facilely assumes some noumenal set of things-in-themselves that, again, as the critic admits, are only "intimated." The nightingale fades once more into symbol.

Jean-Pierre Mileur has attempted one of the more elaborate recent analyses of "The Nightingale." He first gives Coleridge's projection-rejection a fair shake, stressing the poet's awareness of "the degree to which our responses . . . are projections of states of mind thoroughly conditioned . . . by literary and textual models." "The Nightingale," then, expresses "a new determination to avoid projection" via a "detextualization of nature," as Coleridge "experiments with the possibility of reversing the effects of figuration . . . to experience nature in an unmediated form" (46, 48). But the key word here is "reversal," fully evident in Coleridge's resignification of the bird: "'Tis the merry Nightingale," after all, whose "fast thick warble" is a veritable "love-chant" (43, 45, 48); here his "attempt to set aside mediation," as Mileur puts it, "runs into trouble immediately," with the replacement of traditional melancholia for "love" (49). Similar to my critique of Coleridge's vehicular angels and human music as returns to a thoroughly human discursive realm of thoroughly human metaphor, Mileur finds this poem to be another example of figurational failure. Indeed, the more the poet tries to avoid othering the bird via human projections, "the more recourse he must take to figurative language," and—wonderful, this—the effort is finally so "intrusive" and "forced" that "there is even some question of whether the bird is not less real than before" (49)!

Here I would nod in agreement, but Mileur goes on to put a positive spin on this whole dialectic. Coleridge's "attempt to dispense with mediation brings us face to face not with the nightingale but with the indispensability of projection or displacement if meaning is to be achieved" (50). This awareness is apparently Coleridge's, too, as his "I AM" is now the "mature consciousness [that] inevitably distorts nature and mediates all experience in the image of its own desire"—and *knows* it, and regrets this knowledge (51). Much as Easthope's and J. P. Ward's recent readings of Wordsworth have presented him as a great precursor of poststructuralist indeterminacy, so Mileur discovers his own theoretical inclinations in his very subject matter, transforming the yea-sayer of idealist absolutes into a naysayer of constructivist doubt.[28]

But all these nightingales of love seem to have taken us far from my general impression of the cursèdness of Coleridge's opus, a body of poems in which the manic joy of both skylark and nightingale are at last undermined and overridden by an atmosphere of nightmare. As briefly alluded to already, Coleridge has no compunctions about using the avian, in particular the owl, to further this characteristic melancholic gothicism. In the *Rime*, for example, as the pilot and hermit approach the now ghastly ship, their fear is objectified by an extended metaphor that ends in twin figures of eeriness, the owl and wolf: "And the owlet whoops to the wolf below, / That eats the she-wolf's young" (536–37). Employed intermittently throughout Coleridge's poems as an emblem of melancholia (can't owls sing "love-chaunts," too?), even atheism,[29] the owl's most prominent role is in *Christabel*. Two key passages are relevant here. At the poem's very beginning, the gothic atmosphere is established by "the owls [who] have awakened the crowing cock; / Tu—whit!——Tu—whoo!" (2–3). Later, after Geraldine's infamous embrace of Christabel, these "night-birds" are "jubilant anew . . . tu—whoo! tu—whoo!" (307–9). The tension between the realistic and the symbolic code, and the victory of the latter, is reflected in various critical commentaries. Halpern, for one, is quick to point out that the owls' hooting is presented realistically: "The sound is precisely that quoted by W. H. Hudson for the tawny owl" (17). But the incongruous deference here to a late Victorian belle-lettrist nature writer is misleading, for *tu-whit, tu-whoo* has been the standard English transliteration of the tawny owl's call at least since Shakespeare, and is as much, if not more, a *literary* group of syllables than one immediately and empirically derived from an original hearing of the bird. As I indicated earlier, Halpern's gloss that Coleridge's raptors are "symbols of evil" renders such attention to Coleridge's purported realism rather moot, especially as the poem's initial owls' hoots also establish the eerie "pattern of the poem," in that their waking of the rooster "immediately produces an atmosphere that is unnatural and suggests a sinister quality in the owl" (17–18).[30] Halpern's reading of the second owl passage is even more *sinister*: the "owl chorus celebrates[!] Geraldine's powerful witchery" (18).

The owls in *Christabel* actually play a more important role than is immediately apparent, if I might read them as close signifying kin to the poem's other animal incarnation of evil, the snake, and thus as similar foils to the poem's bird of meekness and goodness, the dove. (And so the owls' "celebratory" association with the serpentine Geraldine in the second passage is all the more appropriate.) To rehearse the crucial plot elements involved, the bard relates his dream of a dove and a "bright green snake" as an omen against Christabel's father's intended journey: "For in my sleep I saw that dove, / That gentle bird . . . Fluttering, and uttering fearful moan," then "lo! I saw a bright green snake / Coiled around its wings and neck" (531–32, 535, 549–50). Later in the poem, the dream's prophecy is fulfilled when Geraldine's eyes become snake-like: "A snake's small eye blinks dull and shy, / And the lady's eyes they shrunk in her head" (583–84). But the "coiling," the "union" of bird and snake in the dream also suggests a symbiotic or enantiodromic relationship between the two that goes beyond some simple good-evil dichotomy,[31] beyond the facile reading that the dove has simply been corrupted by the serpent. Soon after, Christabel herself "Shuddered aloud, with a hissing sound" (591), as if our pure little dove (for obviously, Christabel is the dove of the dream) had acquired the qualities of a serpent. Halpern perceives here "an exchange of symbolic qualities"; replacing snake with owl now, "both birds [owl and dove] and both women can be viewed as two sides of nature, neither entirely separate or consistently distinguishable" (19).

This is a welcome exception to my general notion expressed in several places in this work that avians as symbols are revelatory of a bipolar (Western) psyche that must oppose manic songbirds with melancholic owls, eagles, and vultures, and orioles with blackbirds. Maybe the curse that is *Christabel* is this very bifurcation of dove and maiden versus snake and owl, and the strange "marriage" of Geraldine and Christabel, of snake and dove, is a move toward ridding the human psyche of this schismatic curse, a disease that projects its schizoid nature on the natural world. But if Coleridge can occasionally glimpse at the higher truth that albatross and sea snakes, and doves and serpents, are equal members of the biosphere, some of his later commentators could not. In part 2 of *Christabel*, "we get perhaps the most . . . nightmarish use of the recurring serpent-image in our literature: both in [the bard] Bracy's dream of Christabel as a 'sweet bird' . . . with a 'bright green snake' coiled round it and Christabel's tranced hissing later, mesmerized by 'shrunken' serpent eyes. The poem expresses fear of some nameless obscenity" (Knight 159). The true obscenity is reading *Christabel* in such a dualistic fashion. But one must offer the caveat that any reading of this poem is suspect, given its unfinished nature and the enigmatic nature of the plot that is extant. (I regard the current coda as published to be an incredibly weak tag-on of an afterthought, as if repressing the real story that could not be spoken.) Perhaps Coleridge never (truly) finished the poem because he, too, feared "some nameless obscenity"; some smug moralistic ending, à la the *Rime*, would have been just that. One would like to think that the poet had inklings of a *coniunctio oppositorum* of dove and snake/owl transcending the bipolar malaise that can only relieve melancholic nightingales via the mania of love or endlessly rehearse the metaphysical dichotomy of dove and serpent, feathers and scales, flight and fundament. But one is left with the Mariner, unreformed at the last, spouting smug bromides on bio-egalitarianism, while his heart is a two-part tortured organ, a snake crushing a dove.

EGO AND EAGLE: LORD BYRON

> Nature must come to him to sit for her picture—he [Byron] does not go to her.
>
> WILLIAM HAZLITT, *The Spirit of the Age*

If my final metaphorical impression of Coleridge and birds was a bit hard to bear, the dominant avian metaphor for Lord Byron is more straightforward. Byron is a self-proclaimed eagle, with both the positive and negative symbolism traditionally surrounding that bird: proud and alone and defiant; fierce and amorally cruel. There is no Wordsworthian humility here in identifying with a wren or a robin or a titmouse. Byron's is an ego and egoism whose ornithic analogue must inhabit high clouds or high mountains.[32] Acknowledging the danger of identifying author and poetic personae, one can't help but read *Manfred*, for instance, as Byron's persona per se.[33] Count Manfred, the Faustian melancholic loner steeped in necromancy, can be seen as a second-generation Mariner, in the throes of ego alienation. "Why are ye beautiful," he asks mother Earth early in the play, since "I cannot love thee"—in toto, anyway. Instead, he can only identify with a passing eagle, that "winged and cloud-cleaving minister, / Whose happy flight is highest into heaven" (1.2.9, 7, 30–31). *Manfred* is replete with self- (or persona) comparisons to birds of prey, wolves, and even a lion,[34] as the titular character sets himself up as a combination of Faustian angst-monger and Nietzschean superman. To the chamois hunter who preaches patience, Manfred distinguishes between human types as if they were different species, and his own species is, again, of a loftier sort: "that word [patience] was made / For brutes of burthen, not for birds of prey . . . I am not of thine order" (2.1.34–36, 38).

Ornithologically speaking, Byron's order is that of *Falconiformes*, which includes hawks, eagles, and falcons, and this identification continues in *Childe Harold's Pilgrimage*. In the Greek mountains, Harold can hardly contain his admiration for a setting so conducive to large, lone "beasts" in the wild: "Here roams the wolf, the eagle whets his beak, / Birds, beasts of prey, and wilder men appear" (2.42.7–8). Childe Harold, aka Byron, would be one of those "wilder men," and by analogy, one of those birds of prey, of clouds, and mountains, and even the night. Thus the avian of this setting also gets its due. After yet another story in the *Pilgrimage* of incredible human cruelty and stupidity, Harold invokes another wild setting, as welcome dark retreat: "Then let the winds howl on! their harmony / Shall henceforth be my music, and the night / The sound shall temper with the owlets' cry" (4.106.1–3). Notwithstanding such gothic posturing, the diurnal birds of prey remain Byron's favored avian imagery.

Among humankind, in contrast to a mountaintop habitat, Harold is a less than happy, indeed a caged falcon: within "Man's dwellings," our loner hero "Droop'd as a wild-born falcon with clipt wing":

As eagerly the barr'd-up bird will beat
His breast and beak against his wiry dome
Till the blood tinge his plumage, so the heat
Of his impeded soul would through his bosom eat. (3.15.1, 3, 6–9)

A stirring image of an enslaved raptor, no doubt. But all this verbal noise about flight and freedom is really in no way akin to the eagle's "happy flight" initially viewed in *Manfred*. (In sum, "this portrait is not an eagle.") Manfred and Harold alone, in their native habitat, as they would have it, are *not* happy, but are instead alienated egos as little at home in nature as a business traveler speeding through Yellowstone. This aquiline or lupine persona is the end result of one who has "thought / Too long and darkly" (*Childe* 3.7.1–2). Manfred's final vow and curse is not only a denial of human sociality but of life and nature itself: "Away! I'll die as I have lived—alone" (*Manfred* 3.4.90); even Manfred's earlier Charlotte Smith–like condemnation of humankind's hubris-driven "degradation" of nature is best applied to Manfred himself:

> How beautiful is all the visible world!
> . . . .
> But we, who name ourselves its sovereigns, we
> . . . make
> A conflict of its elements, and breathe
> The breath of degradation and of pride. (1.2.37, 39, 41–43)

(Childe Harold will later complain, "Our life is a false nature; 'tis not in / The harmony of things" [*Childe* 4.126.1–2]. Again, the lines are most descriptive of Childe Harold.) If there is any redeeming ecolesson in Manfred's final fate, it is that of a diseased animal who, by instinct, leaves the communal group to go off and die by itself—the proper end, then, for Wordsworth's melancholic egoist in "Lines Left upon a Seat of a Yew-tree," for Coleridge's (preredemption) Mariner, for Byron's Manfred.[35] Perhaps the greatest flaw of *Childe Harold's Pilgrimage* is that the narrator lived, and emoted, too long. But *Childe Harold*'s very length is still instructive, for the four-book evolution reveals a narrator more and more estranged from his own species. Significantly, the many admittedly powerful descriptions of nature are more common in book 3 and climax in book 4. But, granting such gestures toward the natural realm, I would protest immediately, in line with my reading of *Manfred*, that much of this positive privileging of the wild is really more a misanthropic retreat than an eco-advance *toward* nature and its kind.

Childe Harold's preface includes an emphasis on the "correctness of the descriptions" (179), but by this Byron means the (human) local color and culture of each country, not the natural environment per se. Whenever the lone Childe Harold does run off "To sit on rocks, to muse o'er flood and fell, / To slowly trace the forest's shady scene" (2.25.1–2), the "scene" is inevitably out of focus. One is pleased to learn that, yes, "Dear nature is the kindest mother still. . . . Oh! she is fairest in her features wild, / Where nothing polish'd dares pollute her path" (2.37.1, 5–6). But even when his nature is obviously and observationally alive and teeming,[36] Harold stresses its *solitude*: Rousseau's blessed haunts are

> A populous solitude[?] of bees and birds
> . . . .
> Who worship him with notes more sweet than words,
> And innocently open their glad wings,
> Fearless and full of life. (3.102.1, 3–5)

The tension of the oxymoronic "populous solitude" is revealing: if the insects and birds are actually as abundant as it appears, then the "solitude" (and gladness) is pure projection on the part of Rousseau/Harold/Byron, or worse yet, an assumption that one human being alone equals an entire ecosystem of solitude.

The motivation for this rush to "nature's solitude" is all too evident, however. If being by ourselves, full of the "feeling infinite" of the great outdoors, is actually "where we are *least* alone" (3.90.1–2), it is but the opposite (and in Byron, reactionary) pole to being "midst the [human] crowd": "This is to be alone; this, this is solitude!" (2.26.1, 9). Byron/Manfred is conscious enough of possible charges of misanthropy to defend himself explicitly on this count, including a recourse to an immersion into some grand pantheistic scheme of things:

> To fly from, need not be to hate, mankind. . . .
> . . . .
> Is it not better, then, to be alone,
> And love Earth only for its earthly sake?
> . . . .
> I live not in myself, but I become
> Portion of that around me; and to me
> High mountains are a feeling, but the hum
> Of human cities torture: I can see
> Nothing to loathe in nature. (3.69.1, 71.1–2, 72.1–5)

The last line is reminiscent of Coleridge's line, "In nature there is nothing melancholy." But certainly, for Byron, the regal birds of the high mountains (i.e., eagles) are even less melancholy and loathsome, more exhilarating, than the proletarian sparrows and thrushes chirping and whistling among the "hum of human cities." And "regal" here is no mere metaphor: Childe Harold's nobleman creator did have the leisure and money to travel among the "high mountains" of Switzerland, after all. (Might not moneyed leisure itself be a predominant cause of malaise, melancholy, and misanthropy?)

The "Nature" coda of book 4 is also, in part, a continuation of Byron's defense against his escapist motives. The famous rumination beginning "There is a pleasure in the pathless woods, / There is a rapture on the lonely shore" concludes unconvincingly (and with a debt to Richard Lovelace), "I love not Man the less, but Nature more" (4.178.1–2, 5). "Woods," "shore," "mountains," "bees," and "birds": the Byron neophyte might well hope that he describes *human* society and character in better detail. (Of course he eventually would, in *Don Juan*.) Another oft-quoted nature passage, "Roll on, thou deep and dark blue Ocean—roll!," also ends in misanthropy, pitting the sea against humankind, who "marks the earth with ruin," finally, and willingly, throwing "Man" beneath the waves: "the vile strength he [Man] wields / For earth's destruction thou [Ocean] dost all despise"; therefore you "dashest him again to earth:—there let him lay" (4.179.1, 3; 180.3–4, 9).

Above this imagined cataclysm of drowned bodies flies Byron, presumably, an eagle in ego isolation, for whom (as Hazlitt says of Childe Harold) the rest of the "universe is changed into a stately mausoleum" (*Spirit* 257). Hazlitt's general faint praise of Byron includes several telling observations of his relationship to nature that seem today even more damning: "Even nature only serves as a foil to set off his style" (254)—and his ego. For finally, "Nature must come to him to sit for her picture—*he does not go to her*" (253; emphasis added). Instead, he soars above her, as high as a bird of prey, but without the latter's true "eagle eye." The Byronic eagle is a myopic bird, with a vision far from loving "Earth only for its earthly sake," as Manfred would have it. This eagle is blinded instead by its own imagined snow-capped heights.

SPRITE OR BIRD? SHELLEY

> Teach me half the gladness
>
> That thy brain must know.
>
> PERCY BYSSHE SHELLEY, "To a Skylark"

In Percy Shelley's most notable eagle image, in *The Revolt of Islam*, one might perceive a critique of what I have taken the Byronic eagle to ultimately signify: an isolated egohood that finds its parallel in an isolating dominant and oppressive Western ideology. Shelley's eagle and snake of this poem represent a Blakean inversion of good and evil, through which the high and ethereal eagle is the lamentable tyranny and might of the status quo,[37] and the serpent the chthonic spark of revolutionary insurrection. At the height of conflict, the avian and reptile seem almost joined in a *hierosgamos:* "An Eagle and a Serpent wreathed in fight" with "Feather and scale inextricably blended" (1.8.4, 1.9.3).[38] Sundered, the snake is finally defeated, "lifeless, stark and rent," and falls into the ocean, while the eagle continues in Pyrrhic victory, "Heavily borne away on the exhausted blast" (1.14.5, 9). In the poem's specific sociopolitical import, the allegory involves the ultimate failure of the French Revolution, but Shelley's championing of the serpent has greater ramifications, as an analogue to Blake's "Hell" and Shelley's own shadowy Demogorgon figure in *Prometheus Unbound.* Aside from resignifying the traditional positive iconography of the eagle, Shelley is also attacking the Urizen or Jupiter (of *Prometheus Unbound*) worldview that includes a reification of the rest of nature and the othering of alter-species.

That Shelley's revolutionary attitudes incorporated such an ecoview is best revealed in *Prometheus Unbound.* Because the drama is so commonly read as a political or psychological allegory,[39] it is easy to forget that Nature is an actual speaking character therein—"I am the Earth, / Thy mother" (1.152–53)—and that the insurrection against Jupiter is also a physicomaterial one: "The sound is of whirlwind underground, / Earthquake, and fire, and mountains cloven" (1.231–32), a natural cataclysm that resonates beyond all metaphor today, in a world of global warming and exponentially increasing natural disasters. Shelley's envisioned utopia, usually discussed as a human or social one, includes a new eco-reverence for all life on the planet, much like that of the reborn Mariner.[40] Against the various previous disgusting animal images in the drama, there is a "new dawn," marvelously climaxing in the image of a pair of kingfishers:

> . . . and when the dawn
> Came, wouldst thou think that toads, and snakes, and efts,
> Could e'er be beautiful? . . .
> . . . .
> All things had put their evil nature off;
> I cannot tell my joy, when o'er a lake,

Upon a drooping bough with nightshade twined,
I saw two azure halcyons clinging downward
And thinning one bright bunch of amber berries,[41]
With quick long beaks, and in the deep there lay
Those lovely forms imaged as in a sky. (3.4.73–75, 77–83)

The several amphibians and reptiles call to mind both the Mariner's sea snakes and Shelley's own subversive serpent of *The Revolt of Islam*. But here these traditionally chthonic creatures merge with and marry the sky, via the mediation of the winged "halcyons" (kingfishers), both sky-colored and sky-dwelling, but also "clinging downward," as if to join the depths and heights of a "cosmic" ecosystem.

Several other poems in Shelley's corpus reflect a similar nascent eco-consciousness. In stark opposition to the utopian millennialism of *Prometheus Unbound*, the biblical-like Plague of *The Revolt of Islam* (10.14.1) is a veritable ecodisaster that sounds rather like Rachel Carson's *Silent Spring* set to verse:

The fish were poisoned in the streams; the birds
In the green woods perished; the insect race
Was withered up. . . .
. . . .
The deeps were foodless, and the winds no more
Creaked with the weight of birds. (10.15.1–3, 18.4–5)

I will eventually argue, against the grain, that such death-of-nature passages, epitomized in Keats's famous refrain, "And no birds sing," point ironically to the very death of nature and birds in their poetry, via oversymbolization. But these poets' occasional prophetic intimations of a real and imminent natural apocalypse cannot be denied.

In accord with the animal rights thread evident throughout these chapters on Romanticism, Shelley strikes another eco-conscious note in "The Woodman and the Nightingale," involving "A woodman, whose rough heart was [so] out of tune" that he "Hated to hear . . . One nightingale," whose singing imbued "love / In every soul but one" (1, 3–4, 38–39), that is, the woodman, whose alienation from nature allows him to pursue his occupation of tree killer. The poem is a fragment, without any plot resolution, but the finale, like Shelley's scenarios of ecological disaster, still resonates today:

> The world is full of Woodmen who expel
> Love's gentle Dryads from the haunt of life,
> And vex the nightingales in every dell. (68–70)

Any discussion of Percy Shelley's status as a harbinger of eco-consciousness must acknowledge Karl Kroeber's belief that, among the British Romantics, Shelley most notably anticipated current scientific, especially biological, theory (e.g., *Ecological* 111, 125). *Prometheus Unbound*, for Kroeber, is "a vision of natural life reborn" (130).[42] The drama's concluding act, in which "heaven and earth [are] united now" (4.273) in the eco-utopian vision discussed earlier, does include an awareness of the new geology and even evolution: now that "bare [are] the secrets of the earth's deep heart" (4.279), extinct species come back into view, as "The anatomies of unknown wingèd things" (4.303). Whether one envisions fossilized flying reptiles or ancient birds, one is reminded that British poetry would never be the same after the discoveries of Lyell and company, whether it be in the form of an optimistic awe and wonder at the workings of evolution (as in some of Tennyson) or an anxious and haunted sense that the homocentric worldview had lost much of its theological underpinnings.[43]

But a dualistic metaphysics is alive and well in Percy Shelley, nowhere more evident than in his schismatic othering of the avian. If he is capable of the imaginative gall to portray a malevolent (and bedraggled) eagle, he is still disturbingly comfortable with the traditional malevolence of owls and vultures, ravens and crows. If the gut-eating vulture ("Heaven's wingèd hound") of *Prometheus Unbound* (1.34) is but a fateful minister of (in)justice, other such birds are just as theriomorphically useful in Shelley's scathing attacks on politicians, clergy, and literary reviewers. "To Sidmouth and Castlereagh" characterizes two repressive government ministers in a series of inimical feathered signifiers as "Two empty ravens" (1.2), "two gibbering night-birds" (2.1), "two vultures" (4.1), and "Two crows" (4.4)—as if one offal-eating avian weren't sufficient. The priests in "Ginevra," apparently practicing a strange form of extreme unction, leave Ginevra's dead body "like ravens from a corpse whereon / A vulture has just feasted to the bone" (193–94). The reviewers whom Shelley blames for Keats's death are "herded wolves," "obscene ravens," "vultures," and "carrion kites" (*Adonais* 28.1–3, 38.2). To repeat a by now formulaic reaction of mine, the true obscenity is a cultural worldview so afraid of death (and the physical and the animal) that the natural ministers of a natural process are othered as sinister agents of perfidy.

Among these ostracized avians in Shelley is one of the most mysterious birds in British literature: the "night-raven." Shelley names it in one of his earliest poems, "Omens" (1807), as one who, along with the "owlet," "sings / Tidings of approaching death" (1, 3–4). In "Victoria," these same "night-ravens were yelling" in a gothic storm setting, as they "bodingly presaged destruction and woe" (4–5). Because the common raven is not noted as a primarily nocturnal bird, the name is especially peculiar (and all the more ominous, no doubt); divested as it is of species specificity, it becomes an inordinately slippery (and compound) signifier, of darkness and "ravening." Lockwood glosses "Night Raven" as a "literary word used at all periods of the language"; however, "the name was little understood and vaguely identified with various birds in some way active at night" (108). That these various nocturnal birds coalesced into "raven" is significant: the darkness of night thereby becomes a doubled *blackness*.

Shelley's vilified vulture and the kingfisher that he nearly deifies in *Prometheus Unbound* come together in a remarkable poem of avian and intrapsychic binaries, which follows the typical Romantic progression of hope to despair. In "Lines" ("Far far away, O ye"), the hope is already long gone, returning only in brief glimmers, as "Halcyons of Memory," who are told to "Seek some far calmer nest" than the "abandoned breast" of this particular British poet persona (1.2–4). Such nostalgic flashbacks are but a "false spring" to his "heart's winter" (1.5–6). Instead, the poetic psyche's true birds are the "Vultures" of his "Future's towers" (2.1–2), who are asked in the second, concluding stanza to let his "Dying joys . . . serve your beaks for prey / Many a day" (2.4–6). The poem's contrasting ornithic images are, again, built out of a cultural system of representation that must divide, must oscillate between the manic-ethereal and the depressive-infernal. The final preference here for the vultures is hardly a matter for praise: their association is with a psyche filled with self-pity and self-loathing, who invokes them to act as Prometheus's "wingèd hounds" in his own psychic torment and death.

If not vilified, the avian can still be othered, as we have seen, via feminization, often conjoined with victimization. The "imprisoned" lady addressed in *Epipsychidion* is so idealized that one might not blink twice at such stock epithets as "Poor captive bird!" and "adored nightingale!" (5, 10). But the brief lyric "To Mary" ("O Mary dear") returns us to the problematics noted in the relationship between William and Dorothy Wordsworth, in which the woman in the real interpersonal dyad seems by default to share both a female and avian othering. Mary's most noteworthy attribute, apparently, is her "sweet voice, like a bird / Singing love to its lone mate / In the ivy bower disconsolate" (3–5), a one-note song of pure emotionalism. The "adored nightingale" is also symptomatic of the feminization of that particular bird. Indeed, when reading British poetry, one sometimes wonders where the *male* nightingales are, to continue the species.

The nightingale also takes us to another major avian theme, that of birdsong, culminating in Shelley with "To a Skylark." Many of the other significant bird music passages in Shelley also involve the nightingale at times, with the same invisibility and ethereality more usually associated with the lark:

. . . soon her strain
The nightingale began; now loud,
Climbing in circles the windless sky,
Now dying music; suddenly
'Tis scattered in a thousand notes;
And now to the hushed ear it floats
Like field-smells known in infancy,
Then, failing, soothes the air again. (*Rosalind and Helen* 1104–11)

In point of fact, the singing in high flight and the diffusion of "scattered" notes sound much more like a lark than a nightingale. The most engaging image, of "field-smells known in infancy," is a simile: what is most real to the poet, finally, is his own Proustian medley of memories, as distant and vague as they are, whose objective correlative is a derealized medley of flight and sound just as distant and vague.

And so to the skylark:

Hail to thee, blithe Spirit!
Bird thou never wert,
That from Heaven, or near it,
Pourest thy full heart
In profuse strains of unpremeditated art. ("To a Skylark" 1–5)

"Bird thou never wert," indeed. Immediately, the skylark is rather a paragon of unconscious happiness and love, closer to God—and above all, closer to the Romantic ideal of the inspired poet—than the mundane versifier below. But before considering the versifier's efforts, I would pause here to argue that part of the slippery referentiality of the skylark may stem in part from its very etymology. The traditional English word for this species is the plain and simple "lark": "skylark" entered the language in 1555 via a translation from the German (Lockwood 141) and was thus already a consciously poetic appellation. Moreover, the lark received its highfalutin "heavens'-gate" symbolic resonance, in part, by way of a venerable linguistic confusion of the Latin, the belief that *alauda* (lark) came from *laus* or *laudare* ([to] praise), when in actuality the word stemmed from the Celtic for "high or great . . . song" (Rowland 97).[44] In the end, "To a Skylark" is a poem to a signifier of overdetermined mistranslation.

In the poem, the mistranslation transcends linguistics. Without the title, and a few namings of the bird, the bald statement "What thou art we know not" (31) rings truer than the poet probably desired, unsure as he is whether his topic is "Sprite or Bird" (61). The lines "Thou of death must deem / Things more true and deep / Than we mortals dream" (82–84) also make one wonder whether mortals dream way too much, worry *way* too much about death, and place too much value in an individual *Homo sapiens* because, in part, he or she does dream way too much. The "Sprite or Bird" soon absents itself from the poem via the multitudinous comparisons to, as usual, vehicles even less tangible, such as "a cloud of fire" (8), "an unembodied joy" (15), and "a star of heaven" (18). But, as with Coleridge's nightingale, what is not in doubt is the positive tenor of the lark's song, a "happy strain" presumably of "love" (72, 75). And so the coda is an entreaty to impart to the narrator a similar (and quite human) manic bliss:

> Teach me half the gladness
>   That thy brain must know,
> Such harmonious madness
>   From my lips would flow
> The world should listen then—as I am listening now. (101–5)

One is reminded of a similar entreaty of nature at the end of "Ode to the West Wind"; both are ultimately a homocentric wish to be a seer of millennialist prophecy.

Scholars have even praised the poem for its great symbolism. The bird is not really a "physical creature," but "an essence or idea of a feeling"; the "flight of the bird" is "a symbolic flight like its singing" (Doggett 552). Rowland is just as earnest in her symbol hunting, claiming that, in this poem, Shelley denied "that the skylark was a bird: it was a soul, fully winged, in its totality and perfection as described in Plato's Phaedrus; it was also the symbol of the poet and an apostrophe to the power of poetry itself"—in contrast to "the unhappiness of the earthly poet" himself (100–101). The expected appeal to Plato is symptomatic of an idealism central to both the poet and many of his commentators, to the detriment of any real bird. One must agree with Harold Bloom's analysis, in which Shelley's lark "becomes an inescapable motive for metaphor" ("Unpastured Sea" 388). Indeed, "the precisionist or concretist is probably Shelley's most effective enemy, since everything vital in Shelley's poetry deliberately strains away from the minute particulars of experience" (401). How far we are from Wordsworth's titmouse rifling a flower or, as we shall see, much of the descriptive poetry of John Clare.[45]

The skylark as analogue to the Romantic poet, to Shelley himself, has also been found to be a subject fit for praise.[46] The simile "Like a Poet hidden / In the light of thought" (36–37) certainly furnishes strong evidence for such a reading, and is, by the way, another example of the tenor-vehicle reversal that I've already noted, in which the vehicle ("Poet") is really the tenor, rendering the ostensible tenor (the skylark) tenuous and moot. Philip Jay Lewitt's reading is most ingenious: the reader knows that the poem's avian isn't real, for the bird is really the poet, so that, at last, "the poem *becomes* the skylark's song": "Can we hear the skylark's song? Yes, in the liquid syllables and flowing, irregular rhythms of Shelley's voice" (55, 56). This is no doubt attributing too much talent to Shelley, but the inevitable move from bird to human is clear.

In his *Defense of Poetry*, Shelley asserts, "A poet is a nightingale who sits in darkness and sings to cheer its own solitude with sweet sounds" (423). Yes, that's what the *poet* may well do, but, again, this tells us very little about real nightingales except that they are nocturnal and that many, often lonely humans find their vocalizations sweet. Gaull's critique is all too true, I'm afraid: "Shelley often conceived of nature . . . as . . . an expression of imagination but without any reality in itself" (305).

I end with one of Shelley's late Italian poems, "The Aziola." As with some interactions between Dorothy and William Wordsworth, the "better half" is really better with birds, here the Eurasian scops owl. "Do you not hear the Aziola cry?" (1.1), Mary asks. Her significant other initially thinks the bird to be "some tedious woman" (1.6), but Mary corrects him: "'Tis . . . a little downy owl" (1.12), and Percy's reply is symptomatic: "How elate / I felt to know that it was nothing human, / No mockery of myself to fear or hate!" (1.7–9). Shelley's apparent regard here for another species is, in fact, little different from Byron's: an escape from the inhumanity of his own species. And the poem's coda—"Sad Aziola! from that moment I / Loved thee and thy sad cry" (2.7–8)—is hardly love, but rather a momentary escape from his own oh so human "sadness."

Mary Shelley's own relationship to the avian bears mention. Like Dorothy Wordsworth, she was one of the exceptional women of her time and place in that she took habitual solitary rural walks (Hunt 52) and thus could tell an owl from a "tedious woman." *Frankenstein* is the central text here, and has received some ecocritical attention. However, this attention has often resulted in a resignification of the monster from its Romantic origins, Shelley's conception of the "wretch" as a melancholic, Byronic hero worthy of sympathy, and one, moreover, with obvious affinities to nature. Kroeber, for instance, views the monster as "a kind of anthropomorphized version of the atomic bomb" (*Ecocritical* 28); according to McKusick, "the inadvertent creation of a violent, uncontrollable 'new species' foreshadows the nightmare potentiality of genetic engineering in our own time" (30). The crucial idea that the creature is another species will be dealt with momentarily. But what such readings occlude is the monster's deep identification with the natural, including, as we shall see, birds and Native Americans.

But such ecocritical takes on the novel are correct in their critique of a Western technological (and imperialistic) science gone awry,[47] especially when divested of any emotional rapport with the rest of the ecosystem. Certainly this is Victor Frankenstein's lesson that he wishes to impart to Robert Walton, who would be just such an ambitious conqueror of nature as Victor had been. Frankenstein's "ardour" for "dominion" includes especially the natural realm, the secrets of which he would "divine" via "Natural philosophy" (38, 44, 46), the sad results of which make up this novel's plot. Furthermore, the imperial stance of this "dominant" voice of the book is so anthropocentric that the fate of the "wretch" becomes an emblem of the cold-hearted manipulation of other species, with little regard for their survival. Victor's refusal to make his creation a mate is, he admits, the conscious extinction of the monster's "race," of a "new species" (144, 58). Embittered by human cruelty, the monster at one point vows "everlasting war against the species" of humankind (122). That the monster is another species, then, is clear, and Victor's speciesist rationale for not creating a mate is worthy of the best utilitarian philosopher espousing qualitative hedonism: "My duties towards the beings of my own species had greater claims to my attention, because they included a greater proportion of happiness or misery" (184). The "wretch" knows the score regarding this species hierarchy, telling Frankenstein "You would not call it murder" if the good doctor had thrown his new creation off a cliff (128). Interestingly, "extinct" and "extinction" are repeated several times at tale's end (e.g., 189), allowing one to read this novel of rationalist ambition as an elegy to a species, new or not. Left with "no Eve," the monster speaks his own inevitable doom: "I shall die" (118, 188). He is found at book's end driving on toward that death and extinction.

Mary Shelley makes us feel all the more guilty, however, because there are live birds who sing their way through the novel. Even Victor, early on, is not "insensible to the charms of nature" (59); later, momentarily free of worry regarding the monster, "happy insensate nature" gives him "the most delightful sensations" (71). He can even vent in an uncharacteristic outburst: "Alas! why does man boast of sensibilities superior to those apparent in the brute . . . ?" (91–92). (Uncharacteristic, of course, because Frankenstein is, for much of the novel, the most vocal proponent of the opposite, speciesist, point of view.)

But it is above all the "wretch" who is made a bit less wretched by a sensitivity for nature—that "Happy, happy earth!" (106)—including his great appreciation for birdsong. Indeed, one of his first conscious delights is the sound "from the throats of the little winged animals," including the "blackbird and thrush" (96, 97). It is perhaps this appreciation that allows him to question Victor's speciesism and to acknowledge the possibility that the extinction of another species is murder indeed.

Such extinction extends to other human races, of course. Without the hubris of Victor Frankenstein and his ilk, "the empires of Mexico and Peru had not been destroyed" (59). The monster learns, from Safie's reading aloud in the cottage, of these Natives' fate: "I heard of the discovery of the American hemisphere, and wept . . . over the hapless fate of its original inhabitants" (108–9). It is no surprise, perhaps, that the monster's solicitation of a bride includes the promise to go to South America with her, to live like Rousseau's happy savages (129). Perhaps the winged and the "wretched" might fare better there.

A PLAIN BROWN BIRD: JOHN KEATS

> In the back fields,
> beyond the locked windows,
> a young man who couldn't live long and knew it
> was listening to a plain brown bird
> that kept singing in the deep leaves,
> that kept urging from him
> some wild and careful words.
> You know that
> important and eloquent defense
> of sanity.
>
> MARY OLIVER, "Members of the Tribe," in *Dream Work*

> Nothing startles me beyond the Moment. The setting sun will always set me to rights—or if a Sparrow come before my Window I take part in its existince and pick about the Gravel.
>
> JOHN KEATS, *Letters*

At first glance, the winged and the rest of nature seem to fare pretty well in the poetry of John Keats. Who could not praise "On the Grasshopper and Cricket," where he writes, "The poetry of earth is never dead" (1) and "The poetry of earth is ceasing never" (9)?[48] Trained as a physician and quite aware of the scientific theories of the day, Keats often conveys a naturalist's view of existence. "To Autumn" is the Keats opus most often praised as a paean of ecological soundness, in which the traditional season of decline and decay is given its rightful due in the annual cycle. Here autumn becomes a fertility god of "mellow fruitfulness" (1.1) and pregnancy ("maturing sun," "all fruit," "plump," "sweet kernel," "budding" [1.2, 6, 7, 8]). Never mind spring, since you, autumn, "hast thy music too" (3.2), including "the small gnats," "full-grown lambs," and "Hedge-crickets" (3.5, 8, 9). In this poem, Kroeber claims, "Keats enables the natural world with perfect ease to speak (even to sing) for and of itself. . . . There [is] no poem in our language," in fact, "that so faithfully . . . orchestrates the mutable tonalities of . . . ecological vision" (*Ecological* 77). But Kroeber offers this poem in contradistinction to much of Keats's (other) later poetry (78); the personification of the season as a Greek-like god and aesthetic "form" likewise points to a problem that underlies much of Keats's mature poetry: a preference, one might say, for Beauty over Truth.

Still, Keats's awareness of nature in the raw is, at times, stunning. More so than Wordsworth, he "saw / Too far into the sea; where every maw / The greater on the less feeds evermore." He looked "too distinct into the core / Of an eternal fierce destruction," for example, "The shark at savage prey—the hawk at pounce, / The gentle robin, like a pard or ounce, / Ravening a worm" ("Dear Reynolds, as last night I lay in bed" 93–95, 96–97, 103–5). How unlike the traditional, and Romantic, portrayal of the European robin as an icon of domesticity and daintiness! Such utterances that so contradict Keats's reputation as a myth-minded aesthete allow Gaull, for example, to emphasize the poet's background as "a student of medicine and an observer of nature," which led him "to see nature as an ecological rather than a moral or aesthetic system." But this is certainly overstating the case; to assert that "Keats' major poetry explores this [ecological] vision of nature" (224) is going too far. However much one would like to believe that Keats's vision was "an essentially scientific perception of human life as part of a natural as opposed to a human order" (226), the poetry itself belies such a faith, and a very human Beauty and Fancy and Art carry the day.

Having said all this, I must still attest to Keats's various moments of avian realism. Both beautiful and real is his description of a flock of goldfinches:

> Sometimes goldfinches one by one will drop
> From low hung branches; little space they stop;
> But sip, and twitter, and their feathers sleek;
> Then off at once, as in a wanton freak:
> Or perhaps, to show their black, and golden wings,
> Pausing upon their yellow flutterings.
> ("I stood tip-toe upon a little hill" 87–92)

That their "wanton freak" is to show off the striking coloration of their feathers may well be a fallacy of intent, but the gerund "flutterings" is wonderful. Elsewhere, the onomatopoeia of the "chuckling linnet" is noteworthy (*Endymion* 1.256), as is the coda of "To Autumn":

> . . . and now with treble soft
> The red-breast whistles from a garden-croft;
> And gathering swallows twitter in the skies. (3.9–11)

The verb "whistles" is simple, but, with the qualifications of high and "soft," so clear and right for the European robin. Despite the word's decay into triteness via overuse in the past few centuries, the onomatopoeic "twitter" (with the adjacent *sw* and *sk* sounds) is still a nearly perfect English transcription of the call of the barn swallow. The archetypal resonances of the avian account for a good deal of the power of the poem's finale, as the swallows' "gathering" for migration serves as a fitting avian moment of "fruition," in concluding accompaniment to the poem's abundant horticultural imagery.

Such naturalistic proclivities aside, this poet is also inordinately capable of aesthetic musings of great eco-insensitivity. The life-in-stasis paradoxes of "Ode on a Grecian Urn," for example, lead to some troubling representations of nature in the poem. Consider those famous "happy, happy boughs" that cannot "shed" their "leaves" (3.1, 2). How "happy" would a *real* tree be in such a situation? And the fourth stanza, describing those "coming to the sacrifice" in typical Romantic reverence for ancient ritual, is yet haunted, tainted by the object of that "sacrifice," the "heifer lowing at the skies" (4.1, 3). What kind of "pious morn" is this that allows another creature to be "for evermore" awaiting its own slaughter (4.7, 8)? "Cold Pastoral" (5.5), indeed, that can describe such tortures in "holy" awe. The Zen koan–like conclusion teasing us out of thought, dwelling on Platonic conundrums of time and timelessness, can be read, then, as really a linguistic obfuscation of such real matters as interspecies relationships; there is more that "ye need to know" than such fanciful equations as "Beauty is truth" (5.11, 10). Symptomatic, too, is an earlier utterance from the same poem: "Heard melodies are sweet, but those unheard / Are sweeter" (2.1–2). The clause's deeper psychological truth is all very well, but on another level, the words reveal much about Keats's naturalism. Ultimately, the "heard melodies" of real nature and real birds pale before a Romantic psyche that would translate the outer world into its own pleasing "internal noise."

If those inner melodies are a major- and minor-key medley of mania and depression, as we saw in Wordsworth, all the better, as more dramatically emotive. The subject of the "melancholy fit" of "Ode on Melancholy" is bid to project all troubles upon nature, to "glut thy sorrow on a morning rose" (2.1, 5). And the regenerated sage of *Endymion* objectifies his own bipolar psyche via the "birds from coverts innermost and drear," who are now "Warbling for very joy mellifluous sorrow— / To me new born delights!" (3.470–72). One would remind Keats (by way of Coleridge) that "there is nothing melancholy" in nature, but Keats (like Shelley) is more prone than the first British Romantic generation, through his exaggerated and stylized passages of pathos, to vent his psychic highs and lows upon the natural world. If true, this supports my suspicions that the later Romantics betrayed Wordsworth's and Coleridge's crucial (however intermittent) gestures toward interspeciality, as Nature as High Romantic Symbol came more and more to the foreground.

As a major instance of what I perceive to be a greater emphasis in second-generation British Romanticism on nature and the bird as symbol, Keats's synecdochic use of avian wings and flight—much like Shelley, and later Swinburne—as metaphors for the psyche or "spirit" or "fancy" is so rampant as to require note.[49] Admittedly, this is an age-old trope at least as venerable as mournful nightingales and boding owls, but the obsession in Keats and Shelley with the poetic creativity itself creates a comparable special infatuation with the motif of feathered flight. One of Keats's early sonnets, "As from the darkening gloom a silver dove," establishes a formula of *using* the ornithic vehicle as but a quick avenue to psyche and soul: just as the dove "Upsoars . . . So fled thy soul into the realms above" to "superior bliss" and to (who knows what) "pleasures higher" (2, 4, 11, 13). Here the primary meaning is that of "spirit," as in the Christian afterlife, and fittingly, the new arrival in heaven joins an "immortal quire" (9) that is also somewhat (if oddly) birdlike.

But this hackneyed equation of bird and immortal (and angelic) spirit becomes, later in Keats, an inveterate analogizing of wings in motion with the creative psyche at work in *this* world. Thus the winged effusion of the later "Fancy":[50]

> Then let winged Fancy wander
> Through the thought still spread beyond her:
> Open wide the mind's cage-door,
> She'll dart forth, and cloudward soar. (5–8)

This extended personification only implies the vehicle of the bird per se, but still presents the psyche's usual close-mindedness as the caging of a bird, and the mind's occasional effusions of imagination as a bird in high flight. A more subtle, indeed stunning, use of this generic trope is found in "Ode to Psyche." "The winged Psyche," in love with Cupid/Amor, is tritely figured, initially, as a "happy, happy dove" (6, 22), as the first part of the poem playfully circles around the time-worn myth. But Keats then steps back, as Wordsworth does in "The world is too much with us," and mourns the loss of the ancient gods who walked the earth, "When holy were the haunted forest boughs" (38). (And "holy" they still are, I would editorialize, without any aid from Greek deities.) And then the incredible final stanza, where Psyche lives on in the mind of Keats: "I will be thy priest, and build a fane / In some untrodden region of my mind / Where branched thoughts" will populate a psychic forest of trees and mountains and birds: "And there by zephyrs, streams, and birds, and bees, / The moss-lain Dryads shall be lull'd to sleep" (50–52, 56–57). "Dryads" jars the naturalist sensibility, but the metaphorical turn is striking; here a state of mind is peopled with images from nature, in contrast to the more usual Romantic method, in which outward nature is peopled by the poet's affects, and the poetic *effect* reminds one more of an 1890s symboliste poem than anything else.

The phrase "untrodden regions of the mind" also introduces a corollary to this general "wings as imagination" topic, the close connection of birds and other animals with the unconscious source of Romantic creativity. First of all, this equation is common in Shelley, too, as in *Adonais*, where "Dreams" are dubbed "The passion-wingèd ministers of thought" (9.1–2), and in sundry passages of the psychodrama that is *Prometheus Unbound*. Witness "The Earth" calling on the avenging "spirits" to rise against Jupiter:

> I bid ascend those subtle and fair spirits,
> Whose homes are the dim caves of human thought,
> And who inhabit, as birds wing the wind,
> Its world-surrounding ether. (1.658–61)

No longer angels of another world, these imagined avians are from the "dim caves" of the living psyche, just as Keats speaks of "some untrodden region of my mind" as the abode of birds. (Paul Shepherd's notion that the [collective] unconscious may actually "contain" other species, in an evolutionary sense, may be relevant here.) Again, though the cultural association of birds and heavenly spirits is certainly a palimpsest-template behind such images in Keats and Shelley, what is new is the introjection of these images into the mundane psyche itself, with the potential of more fruitfully eco-critical (that is, *naturalistic*) readings of such poems.

But the association of the animal with the unconscious—indeed, often with sheer *unconsciousness*—results in an untoward binary of the human poet cursed by ego consciousness contrasted with other species blessed by unconscious spontaneity. In lines anticipatory of Whitman's well-known passage in *Song of Myself*,[51] Shelley praises the "sweet unconscious tone / Of animals," and as we have already seen, praises the skylark's singing as an "unpremeditated art," replete with an "ignorance of pain" ("The Zucca" 5.2–3; "To a Skylark" 5, 75), however much Bewick, W. H. Hudson, and others have testified to this species' frequent, and assumedly painful, death by hunting. Oddest among Shelley's identifications of the bird with the unconscious are tropes of a sort of double unconsciousness attained by putting the animal itself, already constructed as "unconscious," *asleep;* thus Asia's soul in *Prometheus Unbound* is not only like the oft-discussed "enchanted boat," but is also "like a sleeping swan" (2.5.72–73), and the moon's serenity is elsewhere likened to "an albatross asleep" ("Lines written in the Bay of Lerici" 4). If the bird itself is, in general, a being of "unpremeditated" bliss, how much more so when in the thrall of Morpheus?[52]

Keats's frequent conflation of the animal and the (human) unconscious arises in part from his notion of creativity as instinctual; he explains his poetic attitude at one point as that "graceful, though instinctive attitude my mind [may] fall into" (*Letters* 2.80). Such an attitude is very much an animalistic (even avian) one, moreover, as he intimates in the same letter, while pretending to privilege reason over instinct and creativity, that poetry is "not so fine a thing as philosophy—For the same reason that an eagle is not so fine a thing as truth" (2.81). The poet is eagle-instinct, as it were, or wren-instinct, perhaps:

> Where's the Poet? Show him! show him!
>
> . . . .
>
>   'Tis the man who with a bird,
> Wren or eagle, finds his way to
>   All its instincts. ("Where's the Poet" 1, 8–10)

Keats's letters include several other instances in which he gives himself over to an avian unconscious, as when he imagines himself on the ground among the sparrows: "Nothing startles me beyond the Moment. . . . If a Sparrow come before my Window I take part in its existince and pick about the Gravel" (1.186); or when he tries to forget human intellectual travail via the example of the "idle" morning thrush: "I have not read any Books—the Morning said I was right—I had no Idea but of the Morning and the Thrush said I was right—seeming to say—[quotes own poem beginning 'O thou whose face hath felt the Winter's wind']" (1.61–62). In this poem (named by later editors as "What the Thrush Said"), the wintering thrush tells the human, too anxious for spring, to "fret not after knowledge—I have none, / And yet my song comes native with the warmth" of spring (9–10), without having to worry about its advent at all. The final line, "And he's awake who thinks himself asleep" (14), is a reversal of the Western privileging of consciousness or waking over the unconscious: he who can be conscious and yet still live instinctually and for-the-moment (as in Zen Buddhism's walking zazen, perhaps) is not only less miserable, but truly alive—like the thrush.

This general exploration of Keats's attitude toward the animal and unconscious leads directly to "Ode to a Nightingale," in which such a conflation is crucial to its understanding. Moreover, my longtime Jungian reading of the poem's basic tension between ego consciousness and the unconscious is fruitfully modified by an eventual closer attention to the "actual" avian in the poem.[53] But let me first present the poem from within the paradigm just laid out. The bird is initially noted as blithely unburdened by consciousness, "too happy" in singing "of summer in full-throated ease" (1.6, 10). In contrast, the narrator's consciousness, or "heart," "aches," despite futile verbal gestures regarding "drowsy numbness," "hemlock," "opiate," and "Lethe" (1.1–4); intoxication, be it figurative or literal, is no feasible passageway to the nightingale's native unreflective bliss. But the second stanza asks again for such a passage, "for a draught of vintage" (metaphorical once more) from the exotic South, so that he, too, can "leave the world unseen, / And with thee fade away into the forest dim" (2.1, 9–10). Stanza three is a translation of "What the Thrush Said" from the human point of view, in its contrast of human knowledge and animal instinct, in the narrator's drive to "forget / What thou among the leaves hast never known, / The weariness" of human culture and cogitation, "Where but to think is to be full of sorrow" (3.1–3, 7). The first three stanzas thus establish the ubiquitous circumstance of the

Romantic poet lamenting an alienation from a spontaneous natural world, here epitomized in the nightingale.

But the true poet, as we saw in "Where's the Poet?," is really one with the eagle and the wren, and poetry itself allows the human to find "his way to" the animal "instincts." And so the fourth stanza of the "Ode" marks a turning: "I will fly to thee," my feathered friend, "on the viewless wings of Poesy" (4.1, 3). The night setting receives its first emphasis here, too, and the overlaid signifieds of sleep, intoxication, bird, and darkness all work toward the poet's "forgetting." And *not* seeing: for "Poesy," significantly, is an avian flight on "viewless wings," as the night's darkness and the nightingale's sheer *sound* allow the poet some surcease from the domination of the most conscious sense of all, sight.[54] Indeed, this emphasis on hearing, vis-à-vis avian alterity in particular, is crucial. I may eventually argue that bird*song* is the most viable means to cross-species communion, including its incorporation into poesy. But what actual *sound* do we hear in this poem, besides the mellifluous fancies of Keats's own pen?

By stanza five, the poet has achieved a welcome trance-like state: "I cannot see what flowers are at my feet" (5.1). (And really, he has never seen the bird, either. As with the skylark, the bird's "invisibility" here is a bonus for Romantic poets.) This is the Romantic union with the Other, or immersion in the infinite, usually doomed to failure by poem's end, as it will be here. In "embalmed darkness," he can now rediscover the other, more "unconscious" senses of smell and hearing via the aromas of plants such as the "musk-rose," via the "murmurous haunt of flies" (5.3, 9, 10). Stanza six extends this "flight" to the realm of *thanatos,* the final unconscious(ness): "Darkling I listen . . . half in love with easeful Death" (6.1–2). But this lachrymose trip to a psychic Lethe and Hades has an unfortunate result, as this morbid chthonic stasis detaches him even from the sounds of his "ethereal" avian; he now fails to even *hear* the real bird: "I have ears in vain— / To thy high requiem become a sod" (6.9–10). As in many of the more pregnant lines of Keats and Shelley, this fanciful turn is truer than the poet seems aware of. By this point in the poem, it is clear that any real listening to a real bird is a mere epiphenomenon of the poet's gestures toward aesthetic melancholy and masochism.

The next stanza, as if one more frantic attempt to recuperate the trance, idealizes the bird even more, as a being "not born for death" and "immortal," as some Yeatsian universal who has sung for ancient "emperor[s]" and even in “faery lands forlorn” (7.1, 4, 10), in a willful confusion of individual and species. But the poet and narrator is a human individual, alone, writing a poem of words, not birds. “Forlorn!” the final stanza begins, and the word takes “me back from thee to my sole self!” (8.1, 2). Exactly. Has he ever really been gone, and hasn’t he always been stuck in that “sole self,” with notions of immortality, yearnings for death, and above all, the sheer misery of being a rational ego consciousness who must see and understand?[55] The small brown bird that may have occasioned an authentic effort toward transspecies empathy ends as but another of those “cloudy symbols of a high romance.”

Or perhaps the poem’s middle section is yet an epiphany, a momentary merger with a nightingale’s voicings? Gaull, for one, claims for Keats the ability “to overcome the limits of self and enter into the being of something else,” but her own example is the “pick[ing] about the Gravel” letter (223), and this ability seems more evident in Keats’s tossed-off prose and minor poems than in his high-flying odes.[56] More recently, the ecocritic Elizabeth A. Lawrence has championed Keats’s privileging of sensation over thought, roughly equivalent to my working division of unconscious and conscious, which allowed the poet “to feel at one with nature”; therefore, the poet’s merger, or “unity,” with the nightingale “came naturally” (26). But the tortured and torturous metaphorical peregrinations of the “Ode” hardly seem natural; what is much more natural is an ecoscholar finding good things to say about Romantic nature poetry.

The poet and narrator of this “Ode” certainly leaves open the question regarding the quality of the natural epiphany, ending the poem in a paradox or indeterminacy (much as he does with “Beauty is truth”) that seems to beg for the attention of the new critics and the Yale school: “Was it a vision, or a waking dream? / Fled is that music:—Do I wake or sleep?” (8.9–10). The inconclusiveness of the final questions thus makes moot, perhaps, any discussion of the relative merits of consciousness and unconscious, intellect and animal, sight and sound. But one might return to the “Thrush” poem—“he’s awake who thinks himself asleep”—for a clue to Keats’s ultimate feelings on the matter. The entrancement in “embalmèd darkness” is a (conscious) attempt to be asleep, as it were—like an animal, a nightingale—while remaining (humanly) awake and aware. But the poem is at last another “failure of the imagination,” like “Kubla Khan” and the “Intimations” ode.[57]

I conclude that the poem’s ultimate failure is that this bird is not a bird.

Armstrong states the obvious: "What it [the 'Ode'] describes is not the bird's song—which is indescribable—but the visions aroused by the song" (245).[58] Speaking of the stanza in which the same bird is said to have been heard in far-off times and lands, W. H. Hudson is perhaps as exasperatingly literal-minded as I have been in some of my own previous readings: Keats's "imagination carries him too far" because the real bird's song "could never be heard in more than one spot . . . he sings at home only" (232)! The poetic soul in all of us who have one would severely remonstrate against such an unfair ham-handedness. That the nightingale *species* has uttered its syllables in many eras and climes is the point of the hardly novel extended metaphor involved here.

But what of readings from the opposite extreme? Philip Jay Lewitt can blithely ask, "Why birds? . . . Why [for Shelley, Keats, and Whitman] . . . should a hidden bird be such a potent symbol of the power inside Nature, of separation and the longing for unity and oneness, of . . . our potential to transcend, to go beyond . . . [and] to go beyond the beyond?" (61). A seminal question. But Lewitt is in favor of such mystical flights, and I would ask the question from another angle. Why should birds *serve* ironically as emblems for another species to "go beyond the beyond," when they themselves have no need to do so? The irony here includes the possibility that, as I have suggested, so much of human spirituality may well be based on our coevolution with birds, from theological notions of winged angels to literary tropes for the soul. Doggett, too, perceives Keats's nightingale residing in "an imagined and idealized realm," a "true symbol" of only "apparent actuality" (556, 557). For Doggett, of course, this is a praiseworthy enterprise. But one can agree with Doggett's dictums and yet lament the result: this "symbolization" of other species is a detriment to interspecies relationships and to a healthy ecological consciousness, and ecosystem. To treat another species as a mere signifier is to render it fit for othering, abuse, and extinction.

Keats's usual naturalistic observations, from crickets to swallows, stem largely from his book learning, often replete with a fancy filled with Greek names, as if in compensation for his lower-class origins. Regarding real nature, John Clare even had the nerve to criticize Keats as an urban dweller who "often described nature as she appeared to his fancies" (qtd. in Armstrong 245). One must finally concur completely with Karl Kroeber on this point—though he barely deals with the nightingale itself at all—that the "Nightingale" ode reveals Keats's later and greater "ambivalence" regarding the Romantics' naturist agenda. In his championing the more naturalist or "democratic" implications of the "blank verse lyric," Kroeber suspects Keats's late choice of the "formalized, rhyming ode," in the first place, to be less eco-efficacious, as it were. Keats's grand odes are, above all, plaints of separateness, of "human self-consciousness" (*Ecological* 76), and the "Ode to a Nightingale" epitomizes "the theme of humanity's self-consciousness as separate from the world of nature, a decisive presupposition of most post-romantic poetry" (77). The "Ode to a Nightingale," specifically, "foretells anti-ecological tendencies in later poetry and criticism," including the art for art's sake movement (78). Kroeber's scientistic agenda is transparent, but fits well here with my observation that later British Romanticism is a falling off from the real bird.

But Keats does have his intermittently felicitous moments of crossing the borders of human and avian, most successfully, as I have argued, in his occasional prose and more impromptu verse. Elizabeth A. Lawrence is certain that even the "Nightingale" ode and "Where's the Poet?" are evidence that "Keats rejected the Western concept of Cartesianism that definitively separates humans from animals," instead "emphasizing the shared vulnerability of bird and poet in a hostile world" (27). Rare moments aside, I would claim instead that the poet, in expressing his own great vulnerability, found in the bird a facile outlet for pathos. Returning to "Ode to a Nightingale," one is impressed by Lawrence's ingenious argument that Keats and the nightingale are comparable beings (as Keats imagined he and the sparrow to be): both were "small of stature" and remained "concealed" and "inconspicuous" in their "singing," and Keats's period of "lyrical outpourings" was "brief," like the nightingale's song (24). But a similar implied equation of poet and bird by Lewitt seems less satisfactory: like Shelley's skylark, the real bird is absent yet present in the "Ode," as at last Keats himself "sings the song of the nightingale" (57–58). No. Maybe Whitman sings the song of the mockingbird, and Hopkins effectively imitates the rhythms of the woodlark and the cuckoo,[59] but that Keats's verbiage *is* the bird's actual syllabification is too tenuous a metaphor. Not only does the bird not care a whit for the wonders of iambic tetrameter and pentameter, but it would probably never wonder whether it were awake or asleep.

Still, as Mary Oliver's poem about Keats reminds us, the nightingale is, indeed, a "plain brown bird," and Keats's avian enthusiasms can be said to be closer to Wordsworth in their "humility" than to, say, the eagle-pinioned

Byron. As in Wordsworth, an even smaller brown bird, the wren, accounts for some of Keats's more impressive, and effectively subdued, avian passages. At one point in *Endymion*, Peona is so quiet, trying not to interrupt Endymion's sleep, that even "a wren light rustling / Among sere leaves and twigs" could "be heard" (1.451–2). In the same poem, the moon goddess's effect on the rest of nature includes a rather uncanny description of another species looking up at—I don't dare say enjoying—the lunar light:[60]

> . . . the nested wren
> Has thy fair face within its tranquil ken,
> And from beneath a sheltering ivy leaf
> Takes glimpses of thee. (3.63–66)

But Keats's characteristic move is to return from the high vision, to look back down to the ground, which metaphorically could be said to describe even the psychological progression of "Ode to the Nightingale." Book 3 of *Endymion* can thus conclude its fantastic sights and flights with the title character returning to the mundane home of the "forest green," which acts much like the comforting maternal nest we shall see so rampant in Clare's imagery: the place "Lull'd with its simple song his fluttering breast. / How happy once again in grassy nest!" (3.1029, 1031–32).

But I don't mean these last few examples of Keats's becoming a wren, as it were, to mislead. Keats's corpus is still, by and large, an even more "Romantic," that is, symbolizing use and abuse of the avian as signifier than is found in the first generation of British Romantics. Here, indeed, in Byron, Shelley, and Keats, may be the beginning of an othering of the avian that becomes more and more egregious, climaxing in the Victorian and Modern periods. This chapter will conclude with a passing look at significant bird poems of these later literary eras, in which, to exaggerate my point, the "sedge has wither'd from the lake" and the poets are all pale "knight[s] at arms, / Alone and palely loitering" in a cultural landscape and mindscape in which "no birds sing" ("La Belle Dame sans Merci" 1–4). Keats's poetry might itself be deemed a place where "no birds sing," where most references to birds are obviously metaphorical, often overt similes, to the point that one is little surprised that his famous "Nightingale" ends in distance and silence and doubt. Rachel Carson has already popularized this revisionary use of the "And no birds sing" refrain, of course, as epigraph to and chapter title in *Silent Spring*, in which these four words become metaphorically fraught with future (and dire) consequences in the environmental realm. I would reinscribe the metaphor to encompass the cultural-literary realm, too, as a literary history in which the bird becomes Symbol, and then becomes dead. I then must wonder how much the romanticization of the "Skylark" and "Nightingale" have been complicit in the Weltanschauung that has eventually led to our present ecological plight, and might well believe at last that this representational or linguistic evolution is intrinsically, *causally* related to the ecological decline that Carson traces and the ecological death that she forecasts.

CLOWN AND SHEPHERD: JOHN CLARE

> I love to see the nightingale in its hazel retreat and the cuckoo hiding in its solitudes of oaken foliage and not to examine their carcasses in glass cases yet naturalists and botanists . . . merely make collections of dryd specimens classing them after Leanius into tribes and familys.
>
> —JOHN CLARE, *John Clare*

My ambitious literary-evolution hypothesis falls before one major exception, John Clare's peculiar, almost *egoless* empathy for that actual environment that comes to permeate his very language and style. In *Biographia Literaria*, Coleridge condescendingly disparages Wordsworth's earlier attempts at a poetry of "rustic life" and language. Poetic language is "the product of philosophers, not clowns or shepherds," our poet-turned-philosopher concludes (335, 333). But in many ways, John Clare was just such a clown and shepherd, and not to the detriment, I will argue, to his poetry. Coleridge's intellectual and urban-cosmopolitan elitism also holds that true poetry involves the "ideal" and universal, not some localized theme or agenda (337–38). How different from John Clare, again, whose immediate spots of ground were his all-in-all, who could only see the world in a grain of sand—or in the eggs of a particular Eurasian wryneck's nest.

In one of the more interesting instances of synchronicity in British literature, Godwin's *Caleb Williams* includes the minor character Mr. Clare, a nature poet, one of those who would "fly to solitude and converse with woods and groves" and "see through nature at a glance" (27). Written in 1794, this rather good-natured poke at the Thomsons and Youngs of the Age of Sentiment anticipates the brook-sitting paeans of the *Lyrical Ballads*, published only a few years later, but the chance choice of the name Clare is also a wonderful link to a later poet whose main bent as well is to converse with his native habitat.

However, and as usual, I would look askance at ecocritics who recast a writer from almost two hundred years ago as the latest and greatest political spokesperson for the environment, but such recent critical moves must be noted. James McKusick convincingly argues that Clare possessed "a detailed knowledge of the local flora and fauna, an acute awareness of the interrelatedness of all life-forms, and a sense of outrage at the destruction of the natural environment" (78), though Clare would likely smile at the semiscientific jargon. In "affirming his solidarity with the plants, animals, insects, and waterways of his 'native place,'" in "attributing intrinsic value to all the flora and fauna that constitute the local ecosystem," John Clare should be deemed "the first 'deep' ecological writer in the English literary tradition" (79, 85, 78).[61] But while McKusick's conclusion here has a great measure of truth, blanket generalizations regarding the "interrelatedness" and "intrinsic value" of "all" other species go beyond any conscious eco-agenda on Clare's part. McKusick's application of this purported deep ecology stance to Clare's poetic style is, however, illuminating, especially coming on the heels of my discussion of Keats's aestheticism: as a nascent deep ecologist, Clare "does not primarily see it [nature] as existing for human purposes, and he resists its appropriation for economic use or even aesthetic contemplation" (81). (Note, however, that "resisting" does not guarantee success in entirely avoiding such appropriation.) Clare's poetry, then, might be envisioned as the first wholesale attempt in British poetry at an anti-anthropocentric art, if such a phrase is not a blatant contradiction of terms in itself.

But to return first to a few of Clare's main expressions of solidarity with the rest of nature. For one thing, as a rural poet, Clare unsurprisingly expresses a good deal of scorn for urbanization and, in what some think to be his very last poem, would still "long for scenes, where man hath never trod" ("I Am" 13).[62] His journals and letters, however, are loudest in voicing an anger against city life rarely heard before, as when he scoffs at "Londoners" who "fancy every bird they hear after sunset a Nightingale," for "such is the ignorance of nature in large Citys that are nothing less then over grown prisons that shut out the world and all its beautys" (*John Clare* 457).[63] The claustrophobic malaise of Blake's "London" is nothing new here, but the note of outrage at such woeful ignorance regarding other animals is rather a pleasant shock.

Clare continues a protest in verse we first witnessed in William Cowper (and that perhaps culminates in Hopkins's "Binsley Poplars"), against the felling of trees. For Clare, such a green being is a "Friend not inanimate" ("To a Fallen Elm" 29). His identification with the arboreal victim is sometimes amazing, as if he himself were feeling the offending ax's edge:

> Change cheats the landscape every day
> No tree no bough about it grows
> That from the hatchet can repose.
> ("Wandering by the rivers edge" [henceforth "The Fens"] 92–94)

Even more seminally, Clare perceives that any inimical change to the ecosystem at large is also inimical to our own species: "As are the changes of the green / So is the life of man" ("Helpston Green" 63–64). "The Fens" ends with the sterile result of all this ax wielding and wood clearing: "all is nakedness and fen," "all is level cold and dull" (98, 115), a place where, presumably, "no birds sing." Once again, environmental reality and the dominant metaphors of British literary history seem to infect each other. This environment of stubble and sterility infects many of the codas (and entire poems) of much Victorian poetry; one thinks of the "starved ignoble nature" of Browning's "Child Roland" (10.2) and "Love among the Ruins," Tennyson's "Locksley Hall," Swinburne's "Forsaken Garden," Hardy's "Neutral Tones" and "The Darkling Thrush," and even the "naked shingles" and receding "Sea" of Arnold's "Dover Beach"—fit reason, indeed, for an "eternal note of sadness" (28, 21, 14). (Victorian fiction, likewise, may be said to culminate in the fearsome and native wild that is Conrad's *Heart of Darkness*.) In such a poetic milieu, the real birds, too, sing less and less, fading into generic references and vacuous similes.[64] Many of these same poems are also usually read as symptoms of a psychic or cultural sterility and alienation, an interpretation readily available in Keats's "La Belle Dame sans Merci." But Keats's fanciful eco-blight is a real future for Clare, and the "dry terrain" that serves as the ground of much Victorian verse might well be viewed as more than imagined settings precursory to a Modernist *cultural* "Waste Land."[65]

In another of his "Letters on Natural History," Clare records his observation that many British birds, including "Martins and Swallows and other birds of passage they seem to diminish but for what cause I know not" (*John Clare* 457). The loss of wooded habitat may have had something to do with it; Clare may also have well remembered another of his heated defenses of other species, the gratuitous cruelty to birds by humans epitomized in the frequent raiding of birds' nests.[66] In one of these complaints regarding such a practice, "mischief boys" set up ladders:

> Sly they climb and softly tread
> To catch the sparrow on his bed
> And kill em O in cruel pride.
> ("The sinken sun is takin leave" 91, 93–95)

Here "bed" does not come across as some blithe anthropomorphism; rather, it is as if Clare's porous empathy for other species allows for a transparent equation of the sparrows' sleeping place as like his own: a "bed," then, that renders the "cruel pride" all the more cruel. But this empathy also allows for a significant ecological truth: such boys "Neer see the good which sparrows do" (120), in terms of insect control, as vital residents of an ecological niche.

But every would-be ecosaint must fall, it would appear. In his poem on the green woodpecker ("The green woodpecker flying up and down"), Clare recounts, with no guilt whatsoever, his own theft of the bird's eggs; he also admits in a letter to trying to "procure" nightingale eggs—for nature study purposes, of course (*John Clare* 455); and despite an expressed concern regarding caged goldfinches, he is not above capturing a passerine for a pet. The house sparrow "is well known but not so much so in a domestacated state as few people think it worth while bringing up a sparrow [but] when I was a boy I kept a tamed cock sparrow 3 years" (*John Clare's Birds* 35–36, 32). Granted, it is so like Clare, and much to his credit, to deem such a "low" species worthy of fellowship; but "kept," in this context, is not a word that the "first 'deep' ecological writer in the English literary tradition" should use so comfortably.[67]

I need to emphasize that, as in Gilbert White,[68] Clare's primary naturalist interest was the avian. In marked contrast to Coleridge, the birds in Clare's corpus actually increase in frequency as the years go by (with the possible exception of his final, most eccentric, or "mad," poems).[69] Although he may still be better known for a few widely anthologized poems about mammals, such as his poems on the badger and the hedgehog, his bird poems make up a far larger percentage of his corpus, and he wrote many of them with the explicit intent of publishing a book-length collection to be called *Birds Nesting* (*John Clare* 492). In "the bird poems of his mature years, he makes us follow him, on hands and knees" through his native countryside "till we almost touch the bird's nest with our noses" (Robinson and Fitter x).

Clare's ornithological credentials, and indeed, his real contributions to the science in his own region, are impressive: he "knew from personal observation about 145 wild birds, of which 119 can be identified with reasonable certainty as county [i.e., the Soke of Peterborough] records—65 of them 'first records'" (xii). Because of his "remarkably detailed and accurate knowledge of local wildlife," which he incorporated into his verse, "he was able to identify most local flora and fauna by sight," and "he made careful observations of each species' habitat, distribution, behavior, and seasonal variation or migration" (McKusick 81).[70] I must frequently remind myself that academic minds schooled in the belles-lettres may find all this peripheral to literary studies. Indeed, as Richard Lessa puts it, Clare's "accuracy of observation" is as "often noted by way of depreciating his poetic achievement as praising it" (26), as if naturalism in literature were a fault. But one subthesis throughout this work has been that such a naturist bent has positive ramifications in the actual world of birds and trees and streams. Clare's editors note a related audience concern: his "passion for exactitude [regarding bird description] must have seemed strange to Clare's contemporaries, though perfectly comprehensible to the modern ornithologist" (Robinson and Fitter xiii). This passion may still seem strange to the contemporary literary scholar, as I've said, but that this strangeness might become less so should be one of ecocriticism's, or zoöcriticism's, main goals.

The vast preponderance of Clare's bird poems center on, or at least include references to, birds' nests, nest building, and eggs. Robinson and Fitter identify this concentration in Clare as central to the poet's stature as a unique combination of Wordsworth and Gilbert White. Arguing against Raymond Williams's alignment of Clare with Wordsworth as both projectors of pathos, these scholars find in Clare a finer melding of observation and feeling: "Many of Clare's poems about birds have a poetic intensity which stems as much from his studious involvement with the details of their nesting habits and the characteristics of their nests as it does with any 'projection of personal feeling' [quoting Raymond Williams] into his observation" (xvii). In sum, Clare equals White plus Wordsworth, to coin a formula. "Indeed the combination of poet and field-naturalist has never been bettered in our literary and scientific history" (xviii).

Once again, such eco-hagiography may fall before an examination of the evidence. Robinson and Fitter even provide, in a telling aside, an entry into this critique: in some of Clare's bird poems, "the birds reflect Clare's sense of loneliness, his timidity or even his persecution by the barbaric unfeeling elements of his society" (xii). In partial rebuttal to these scholars' earlier equation, I would claim that Clare's bird nest poems especially serve as projective vehicles for the poet's own yearning for a nest, for ontological security in the safety of some ornithic womb, as it were. This explains, without explaining away, the great empathy that Clare reveals in many of these poems for the mother bird, often fearfully insecure and endangered, sometimes safe in her hidden nest, but always potentially vulnerable to the onslaughts of the "cruel boys" of the world. If Robinson and Fitter are correct in asserting that, despite his faith in "poetic feeling," Clare "never allows his poetic sense to produce slipshod observation" (xiv), that accuracy in naturalistic description may still have served a subtext of "poetic feeling" of which Clare himself was relatively unaware.

Clare's descriptions of birds' nests (their building and composition) and eggs (their number and color) are so abundant that only a small sampling must suffice.[71] But these very passages more often than not combine a yen for verisimilitude with a great affect of insecurity. Thus "The Yellowhammers Nest" describes so well "Five eggs pen-scribbled over lilac shells" (13), but ends with a snake invading the nest; the finch can only sing sadly then, when "such like woes hath rent its little breast" (30). Clare's incredible empathy is evident again, but the motif of nest- and mother-vulnerability becomes such an obsession in these poems that one is tempted to paraphrase Nietzsche in claiming that even the naturalistic impulse, like the metaphysical one, is ultimately "unconscious" autobiography (*Beyond Good and Evil* 13).

Likewise, "The Pettichaps Nest" describes the warbler's ground nest and eggs with telling details (13–26), but the emphasis is finally on the parents' "fears" of "dangers," the need for "safetys lap" (28–29, 35). The nidification of the "Hedge Sparrow," too, turns on the "danger" that a cat might catch "their young before they leave the nest" (12, 14). "The Wrynecks Nest" ends on a strong naturalist note, however; the invasion of its nest by "peeping [human] idlers" does occasion "terror," no doubt (4, 9), but she wins the day by "hissing," as wrynecks do, like a snake (11–14)![72] But Clare lays his cards plainly on the table in the poem that begins "In the hedge I pass a little nest": developing the fear motif throughout by way of parenting birds (who "Cheeped loud a danger warning" [4] at an approach to their nest), the poet transforms avian to self in the final strophe. Though not as experienced in the ways of the world as many, yet he is cautious enough, like the birds, to

> Yet chuse not haunts that many know
> Though many much pretend
> For ye are sure to find a foe
> Where many pass for friends (45–48)

The undertone of paranoia distinguishes this reluctance from a bird's natural fear of natural foes; Clare's own lifelong flight, as it were, seems to flutter between a painful site of maternal origin (the insecure nest) and a fear of leaving the nest, aware as he is of the fate of many a young bird who does venture forth into a world of foes (cf. the troubled biographies of Byron and P. B. Shelley), preferring instead "haunts" obscure and unknown.

Two more bird's nest poems end quite strangely. "The Nightingales Nest" is similar to the poems above in its overriding theme of nesting insecurity: the mother bird's "fear" for her young (3) is warranted when nest-robbing "rude boys," in search of "her secret nest," create in the bird a "choaking fear" (52, 53, 60). But the poem *ends* with a description of the mode of nest building and the number and color of the eggs (87–91), and the reader thinks, "Huh?" The usual standards of narrative development and even poetic taste beg for a reversal: describe first; emote second. Or might this awkward inversion of the expected sequence be a deconstructive reprivileging of our notions of mere naturalistic description and poetic emotion? "The Robins Nest," similarly, begins with an emotional defense of the nest as a "harbour" from "the ruder worlds inglorious din" (5–6). Ninety lines or so later, the poem concludes with an oh-by-the-way descriptive note of "five brun-coloured eggs snug sheltered there" (99), in a nest that began as homocentric shelter and ends as an odd, eccentric *realism*. As I will argue in my discussion of Clare's style, strange stylistic maneuvers such as this may ultimately allow Clare's poetry to rise above and revel over accusations (such as my own psychoanalytic critique above) of anthropocentrism.

Clare's attention to birdsong is another powerful avenue to such transcendence. McKusick's contention that the poet's "birds'-nest poems exemplify . . . Clare's struggle to create a language adequate to the expression of the bird's distinctive way of life" relies in the end on Clare's use of birdsong, or "language," especially onomatopoeia (90). Robinson and Fitter observe that "Clare was something of a pioneer in his interest in bird song" (xii); indeed, "he is probably one of the first naturalists to take such precise notice of bird calls, their form, the occasions when emitted and their different purposes" (xiv). I suggest that bird *sound* is a feasible communication with the Kristevan semiotic, as a rhythmic (and alter-species) language prior to the Lacanian ego prison of a Symbolic in which heard *parole* has become (book-read) *langue*. In contrast to, say, Keats's "Ode to a Nightingale," it is Clare's appreciation of the sheer *vocalization* of the avian that is my focus here.

For instance, it is hard to imagine Keats or Shelley describing the robin's song as a "joy that almost choaks his little throat" ("The Robins Nest" 73), the obvious empathy supported by the hard phonemics *j, ch, k,* and *thr,* until one *hears* the bird trying so hard to sing. One also hears, and feels, the heron's "crank and reedy cry" ("High overhead that silent throne" 4); the stark alliteration of the parent turkeys who "bring a brood of *ch*elping *ch*ickens home" ("The turkeys wade the close to catch the bees" 4; emphases added);[73] and the "skreeking" nuthatch ("In summer showers a skreeking noise is heard"). The common whitethroat's vocalizations in "The Happy Bird" seem a more generic, poetic presentation of a bird's song, as "she mutters inward melodys," then "Swells out in raptures gushing symphonies" (7, 10). But a more clearly audile element is evident in the poem, in the lines describing the bird "on the sweeing bough / Swayed by the impulse of the gadding wind," until "This way and that she swees . . . when off she flies" (1–2, 13–14). Lessa notes that the consonance of the "*s, sw* and *sh* sounds . . . suggest the rush of the wind" (31), but they might also intimate, after all, the sibilant voice of the warbler.

Clare's care for real bird sounds includes a consciousness of various species' lesser notes, as in the call of a blackbird on an unexpectedly warm winter day, when a city poet might assume that all avians would have burst again into spring aubades: "I thought he'd have whistled but he only said prink" ("Birds: Why are ye Silent?" 18). "The Autumn Robin," similarly, has but a "tiney whispering song" at that time of year (4). Even more "humble" than those of Wordsworth and Keats, some of Clare's birds are such "wee" singers that one is eventually surprised that they can be heard at all.

These gestures toward aural verisimilitude are hardly surprising for a poet whose naturalist prose includes many discerning passages similar to the following, on a mother nightingale's calls: "I always took the 'chur chur' as a food call and the tooting noise ['toot toot'] as a token of alarm" (*John Clare* 461). A long letter on the nightjar describes the bird's "odd noise" as "a trembling sort of crooing sound." More so than even Gilbert White and Charlotte Smith, Clare implies an egalitarian nonprivileging of birdsong, as if deeming the goatsucker's buzz comparable to a nightingale's ditties: "It [the nightjar's call] is a beautifull object in Poetic Nature (*nay all nature is poetic*) . . . one cannot pass over a wild heath in a summer evening without being stopt to listen and admire its novel and *pleasing* noise" (453; emphases added). "All nature is poetic" must be read as more than a Romantic truism unsupported by the praxis of most Romantics (who, after all, preferred butterflies to slugs), or even as some Naturphilosophie faith that outer nature is a perfect match for humankind's imaginative yearnings. If the dictum is reversed—all that is truly poetic is the *natural*—we have, I think, a tenet not too far from Clare's own view.

Another prose note concerns the song of the common quail: "It makes an odd noise in the grass as if it said 'wet my foot wet my foot'" (*John Clare* 468).[74] This knowledge is dutifully transformed in the sonnet "Summer Moods" (*The Rural Muse* 105), in which the quail's call combines with that of the corncrake in an eerie sestet:

> . . . the hidden quail
> Cries "wet my foot" & hid as thoughts unborn
> The fairy like & seldom seen land rail
> Utters "craik craik" like voices underground
> Right glad to meet the evenings dewy veil
> & see the light fade into glooms around. (9–14)

If Clare's corpus is notably bare of metaphor,[75] the tropes "hid as thoughts unborn," "fairy like," and "like voices underground" impart to the birds here a status less than real. In this poem, at least, the almost supernatural birds are not the point anyway, according to Lessa, for whom the sonnet's "images of seclusion" apply equally to birds and narrator; the "identification of the poem's speaker and the timid birds is reinforced by an ambiguity concerning the subject of" the last two lines (13–14). This grammatical ambiguity is a major factor in Clare's unique style, as we shall see. *Who* is happy that night is coming is unclear, allowing Lessa to conclude that it is the poet himself who is content with the "dewy veil, from beneath which he will utter his song as do the secret birds" (30).

A final bird call poem, "The Landrail," is another derealization of the corncrake's call, à la Wordsworth's cuckoo: "Tis like a fancy every where / A sort of living doubt," an "undiscovered song" (13–14, 34). The usually naturalist- and avian-minded Robinson and Fitter are less helpful here: "The corncrake" combines, for Clare, the "intimate" and the "remote" in "its mysterious disembodied call" (xii). But the critics seem to fall for the dominant Romantic tradition of privileging the "invisible bird" of "mystery"; I imagine instead Clare getting up the next morning to pursue a closer study of the corncrake.

Clare's descriptions of other avian behavior in his poetry are often outstanding. If Shelley imagined, against all ornithological evidence, kingfishers nibbling on berries, Clare knows that "King fishers watch the ripple stream / For little fish that nimble bye" ("The Fens" 14–15). If, like Keats, Clare can put himself in the place of "little birds in winters frost and snow," he also knows of the necessity of bill preening, as they "chirp and hope and wipe each glossy bill" ("Helpstone" 23, 29). "The Pettichaps Nest" includes a note on the warbler's plumage that sounds like a birder mentally narrowing down the species possibilities by color and size and reveling in his or her eventual success in doing so: "tis olive green / Well I declare it is the pettichaps / Not bigger then the wren and seldom seen" (38–40).

Birds also fly, waggle, and swim through Clare's corpus, including the expected kite "sailing in the sky . . . On stilly wing and forked tail" ("The Fens" 58, 60) and the more unexpected, almost lugubrious, herons, who "swee about the trees a flopping herd" ("The passer bye oft stops his horse to look" 5), as if they were (very thin) cows whose wings are barely keeping them aloft. Another semicomic bird is "Little Trotty Wagtail," whose wayward ground running Clare describes in doggerel lines just as awkwardly ambulatory: "tittering tottering sideways he near got straight again," and "He waddled in the water pudge and waggle went his tail" (2, 7). The playful tone is as if the poet were describing some young nephew getting dirty in the mud. Fittingly, the third-person description becomes a familiar second-person address by the third and final stanza: "So little Master Wagtail I'll bid you a 'Good bye'" (12). (In contrast, Blake's nursery-rhyme efforts in

Songs of Innocence sound almost too consciously literary.) And then there is Clare's description of dabbling ducks in "The Fens," "bobbing there" in the water with "Tails topsy turvy in the air" (39–40). There is indeed much in Clare's poetry that sounds like children's verse, but for the same reason, perhaps, that Charlotte Smith wrote about birds and for children. As Othered objects of the dominant Western *I*, children and women and animals—and unschooled lower-class rural poets—have long endured an enforced affinity as simultaneous victims. "Little Trotty Wagtail" is one semiludicrous, semicharming result of this cultural conflation.

But this is the same Clare who was a mature and close observer of nature, whose prose notes could testify that "wild ducks always rise against the wind" rather than take off with the wind at their backs (*John Clare* 452), that blackbirds and thrushes have a habit of breaking snail shells on rocks (460), and that the kestrel, Hopkins's "Windhover," is "the species that hangs in the air on trembling wings" (*John Clare's Birds* 6)—a naturalist who, in sum, made important ornithological contributions to his bioregion. But a closer look at Clare's prose reveals importance differences between Clare and the business-as-usual natural science of his time. Perhaps his poetic reluctance to wholeheartedly embrace that science stemmed from such personal experiences as the following, when his entomological interest in fireflies led to a great shock: "I have . . . taken them home to examine them by daylight but they was nothing then but a dead shriveld insect" (*John Clare* 455)! In the end, the Linnaean taxonomic system left him cold: "I dont know much of the new christning system of modern botany that has such a host of alphabetical arrangements as would fill a book to describe the Flora of a Village" (476). (One might guess this to be a dig at a certain Gilbert White if one weren't certain that there were scores of much drier examples of regional plant lists being published at the time.) Scientific curiosity is a fine thing, but the systematic desiccation of the living world is not, and needs the tempering of "poetic feeling": "I love to look on nature with a poetic feeling which magnifys the pleasure I love to see the nightingale in its hazel retreat and the cuckoo hiding in its solitudes of oaken foliage and not to examine their carcasses in glass cases yet naturalists and botanists . . . merely make collections of dryd specimens classing them after Leanius into tribes and familys . . . I have no desire further to dry the plant or torture the Butterflye by sticking it on a cork board with a pin" (458).[76]

Such "squeamishness," to nod in partial agreement to McKusick, is closer to contemporary ecological sentiments and the philosophy of deep ecology than to (traditional) mainstream natural science per se. Clare's deep ecology inclinations include a bio-egalitarianism that is a culmination of the thread that we have witnessed in the poems of Cowper, Burns, Wordsworth, and Keats. For Clare, this positive regard for all life extends even to weeds:

> I feel at times a love and joy
> For every weed and every thing
> A feeling kindred from a boy
> A feeling brought with every spring ("The Flitting" 189–92)

Just as the weeds overtake Wordsworth's "Ruined Cottage" as an act of eco-retribution, "So," in "The Flitting," "where old marble cities stood / Poor persecuted weeds remain / She [Time] feels a love for little things" (211–13). For John Lucas, this privileging of the common and "rank" is Clare's reaction against eighteenth-century rationalist order, a "refusal to keep to bounds," both aesthetically and politically (113). The new historicist must emphasize human politics here and Clare's class origins; for Lucas, the weeds are mere tropes for social insurrection. But the comment on Clare's "aesthetic" insurrection is more intriguing; moreover, it has an ecological implication that new historicism would scarce consider.

Clare also held dear the various "weeds" of the avian order. We have already seen his defense of the all-too-common house sparrow's worthiness as a pet. In "The Wren," he asks why the cuckoo and nightingale are "so fondly praised" in poetry (2), when his own preferences lie elsewhere, with "the wood Robin singing in the dell / And little Wren that many a time hath sought / Shelter from showers in huts where I did dwell" (9–11). That the wren has been a fellow housemate is no small reason for personal bias, of course; the wee creature's need for shelter is reminiscent of Clare's insecure nesting birds, and thus redolent of Clare's own projected insecurities. (The man *did* sleep in huts, after all.) But the abundance of smaller (not nightingale or skylark) passerines in Clare's corpus testifies that this particular privileging is in earnest.

The most remarkable of Clare's avian reinscriptions is his "Sonnet: The Crow," which ends as follows:

> I love the sooty crow nor would provoke
> Its march day exercises of croaking joy
> I love to see it sailing to and fro
> While feelds, and woods and waters spread below (11–14)

How the fields and bodies of water, the biosphere itself, finally "spread below," via such an unusually active verb, is simply stunning. One might even claim that the verb "spread" was suggested by (or suggests) a bird's spreading its wings, in line with Robinson and Fitter's claim that "much of the vigour of Clare's poetry is carried, or projected, in the verbs of movement associated with bird flight" (xiv). It is as if the crow's "sailing" wings have been imparted to the rest of the landscape. And as for the crow—my real point here—it is "sooty" and "croaking," as is its stereotypically corvid wont, but the "croaking" is a joy, and the bird is a subject of obvious high regard, even "love." The first two lines are in a similar positive vein, at first glance: "How peaceable it seems for lonely men / To see a crow fly in the thin blue sky" (1–2). However, the qualification "lonely" returns us, I think, to the "birds nest" problem: is the crow a natural magnificence in and for itself, or is the "poetic feeling" of loneliness a projective prerequisite for its appreciation? (Or both?) Are bird's nesting behaviors both wonderful in themselves *and* wonderfully pathetic when the human finds in them objective correlatives for his own need for sanctuary and security?

In this poem, there is another one of those idiosyncrasies of style that renders the poem even more problematic: while the introductory lines speak of "lonely" men in the third-person, line seven begins with Clare's favorite phrase, "I love . . ." Ultimately it is unclear whether the "I" is some sudden intrusion of one of those lonely men, or if the narrator or Clare is acknowledging that he is one of those lonely men, or whether the narrator or Clare is now speaking for himself, independent of any qualification of loneliness whatsoever. The clever ecocritic might argue (and McKusick does indeed make similar moves regarding other poems) that the undecidability of point of view renders moot my questions regarding what is natural and what is poetic feeling. Or rather, both are embraced as true.

On my way to a consideration of and as support for McKusick's novel insight into Clare's style, that the poet's very syntax connotes an ecocentric worldview, I would offer another contribution to this general theory. Yes, as Clare says in "The Flitting," he desires a very flat, nonemphatic style:

"Give me no high flown fangled things / No haughty pomp in marching chime"; rather, "I love . . . verse . . . mild and bland" (153–54, 161). Not only does Clare usually avoid any ornate phraseology that might attract attention, but he also usually avoids, apparently intentionally, any rhetorical development or buildup that one expects in a lyric by a nineteenth-century British poet.[77]

Indeed, the most notable result of this (non)aesthetic practice is the oh so "mild and bland" conclusions of many of his poems, including bird poems, to the point that the endings seem blatant non sequiturs. Considering such codas in Clare's avian-centered poems, one can point to the poem "The green woodpecker flying up and down," for instance, which, after describing the bird's nest drilling, actually gestures toward some drama and climax, as Clare recounts an act of his own nest robbing of the bird. But the poem then abruptly ends with the following couplet: "The eggs are small for such a bird they lay / Five eggs and like the sparrows spotted grey" (13–14). The incorrigible naturalist might applaud here, but aesthetically speaking, the couplet is an afterthought, a falling off (or worse, an obfuscation of Clare's guilt regarding his nest robbing). The poem on a heron's nest, after some fairly interesting observations on its nest building, also ends with an incredibly flat description of the eggs, with a final twist: "Their eggs are long and green and spotted brown / And winds will come and often throw them down" ("The passer bye oft stops his horse to look" 13–14). The final line may actually be the most exciting part of the poem, with the added interest of the mother-nest-insecurity theme. But after the eggs-description formula (yes, Clare does this a lot), the reader who has been reading many of these poems could probably care less about these particular eggs' fate. This is not Clare's specific intention, of course; his general intention instead is to create such an *un*weighted verse that nothing becomes privileged over anything else.[78]

Clare's most curiously anticlimactic formula-of-an-ending in this regard has to be what I call his "cow codas," in which a sonnet, often a bird sonnet, receives an amazingly non sequitur ending in the form of a bovine appendix, if you will. Thus "The schoolboys in the morning soon as drest" describes a nest robbing by boys and concludes with the parent birds sounding their alarms at the thievery, and then cows ambling away: "The old birds sat and hollowed pink pink pink / And cattle hurried to the pond to drink" (13–14). Like tourists witnessing a mugging, perhaps, the cows apparently want nothing to do with such nefarious goings-on. Likewise, "One day across the fields I chanced to pass" describes the rather pathetic scene of a "wounded partridge" and her chicks (4). But the last line, "And old cows snorted when they passed the place" (14), renders the whole ordeal an ultimately unimportant occurrence in the grand scheme of things. As a final example, here is "Birds Nests," entire, sometimes deemed Clare's final poem (1863):

> Tis Spring warm glows the South
> Chaffinchs carry the moss in his *[sic]* mouth
> To the filbert hedges all day long
> And charms the poet with his beautifull song
> The wind blows blea[k] oer the sedgey fen
> But warm the sunshines by the little wood
> Where the old Cow at her leisure chews her cud

If this is his last poem, the final line is certainly appropriate, a fittingly bovine coda of codas. Clare's corpus then becomes one long, flat poem of natural description (plus poetic feeling) that ends with another species doing what comes naturally.

Ecocritics' favorite phrase in Clare, often quoted as a Clarean manifesto of sorts, is his call for a "language that is ever green" ("Pastoral Poesy" 13 [*Selected Poems* 141]). According to McKusick, Clare consciously explored experimentations in form for explicit ecological reasons (86).[79] "By refusing to punctuate his poems or conform to 'refined' standards of diction, grammar, and spelling, he created an 'unenclosed' verse that provides a linguistic analogue to the free, unenclosed landscape that it seeks to conserve and perpetuate" (91).[80] Moreover, Clare's formulaic "I love to . . ." is actually another eco-contestation of sorts, an "aesthetic" disruption of the "Western cognitive categories of causality and chronology" (82). I would add that Clare's methodology includes a disruption of poetic rhetoric itself, the assumption that a lyric should end with an appropriately emotional climax or denouement—not a cow.

The greatest of Clare's stylistic mannerisms that create a radical eco-view, as I have suggested, is his (intentional?) confusion of subject and point of view. Thus "The Morning Wind" begins "Theres more than music in this early wind / Awaking like a bird refreshed from sleep" (1–2 [*Rural Muse* 143]). No matter the rest of the poem, for our purposes: immediately posed by the possibly dangling-modifier syntax is the question, who is awakened? the wind? the narrator? or the rest of nature entire? Following McKusick, I would reply that the answer is each, and all, and that the syntactic confusion asks the reader to seriously consider all such possibilities.

McKusick's most ambitious analysis in this line involves Clare's "Sand Martin" sonnet:

Thou hermit haunter of the lonely glen
And common wild and heath—the desolate face
Of rude waste landscapes far away from men
Where frequent quarrys give thee dwelling place
With strangest taste and labour undeterred
Drilling small holes along the quarrys side
More like the haunts of vermin than a bird
And seldom by the nesting boy descried
Ive seen thee far away from all thy tribe
Flirting about the unfrequented sky
And felt a feeling that I cant describe
Of lone seclusion and a hermit joy
To see thee circle round nor go beyond
That lone heath and its melancholly pond

McKusick notes that the apparently undue repetitions ("hermit": 1, 12; "haunter," "haunts": 1, 7; "lonely," "lone": 1, 12; "heath": 2, 14; "frequent," "unfrequented": 4, 10) seem amateurish, as if the poet were in need of a thesaurus. However, several of these duplicate words are applied to bird, then human, thus creating a double point of view, and so these words' reappearances are "aesthetically justified . . . by a doubling of poetic perspective" and thereby create a "deep sense of identity between the speaker . . . and the bird" (93, 92). Intriguing, too, is McKusick's reading of the bird's final, circular flight: "The bird's motion at the end of the poem is a 'circle,' thus contrasting the rectilinear forms of human industry with the sweeping and cyclical curves of the natural world" (93), a world in which the speaker, via the poem's dual perspective, is a part. Through his analysis, the critic is firm in his faith that this is no anthropocentric act (92): rather, "this poem mediates upon the very possibility of a meaningful relationship between humans and the world of living creatures that surrounds them. Clare acknowledges the otherness of the bird but does not dismiss it as unknowable" (94).

However, McKusick also acknowledges that in this poem, "Clare is pondering the affinity between his own situation, as a failed poet and social outcast, and the situation of the [isolated] bird" (93): it may be Clare, at last, who is most at home in his "lone heath and its melancholly pond." (We are returned to the birds nest poems and the question of *whose* insecurity they actually concern.) Whether Clare thought in terms of species otherness or alterity is also debatable, either because the discourse of his age disallowed it or because his own "poetic feeling" for the sand martin and other species was of such a porous nature that the question itself would have seemed absurd. But the question remains, for us, whether Clare indeed transcended anthropocentrism at times, in poems in which avian and human worldviews interpenetrated and merged, or whether a certain unlearnèd, dangling-modifier style of writing led to linguistic and tropic tricks that have allowed a few ecocritics to wax euphoric.

Certain uncharacteristic poems by Clare, indeed, question his own ability for such a transcendence, focusing instead on a Wordsworthian nostalgia for the lost "clouds of glory" of a (relationship to) nature that used to be, and even beckoning to a subsequent literary landscape where "no birds sing," where Clare's own songs made nary an echo or whisper. In these poems, Clare is the self-acknowledged alienated stranger, as in *Childhood*, a long lament on nature's fading into the "light of common day," as if a Clarean gloss on the "Intimations" ode. As a child, he wondered at and reveled in at the birds' instinctual nesting abilities, among other natural glories, but no longer:

> I seek no more the buntings nest
> Nor stoop for daisey flowers
> *I grow a stranger to myself*
> In these delightful hours (129–32; emphasis added)

"The Flitting," despite the various naturist passages quoted earlier, is yet another poem whose tone is, in general, elegiac regarding the environment, where "summer like a stranger comes" and even birdsongs seem "strange and new" (3, 21). But Clare is the "stranger," after all, "alone and in a stranger scene" (49): "Here every tree is strange to me," as is every "weed and blossom" that *used* to give him a "welcome 'how do ye do'" (97, 126, 128). Both these poems were written early enough (by 1832) that they must be considered but temporary dark nights of the soul, not some marked change in Clare's character and poetic development. Indeed, if these are some of Clare's most melancholic fits, they seem remarkably muted, for a Romantic, and may provide a final piece of evidence that his general approach to nature was in much less measure psychic projection, with its symptomatic highs and lows, than in the other poets I have discussed. On the manic-melancholic continuum proposed in my treatment of Wordsworth, both extremes are notable for their relative absence in Clare's bird poems; his most manic moments are more of a muted enthusiasm, his darkest moods rather a quiet stoicism.

BRITISH ROMANTICISM: A CODA

> Everywhere animals disappear.
>
> JOHN BERGER, "Why Look at Animals?"

To be "alone and in a stranger scene" would become a more common motif in the British literature to follow, as if Clare intuited a stance toward the environment that would become the norm. The main question underlying this work is: *can* one really know the bird—and ultimately, any other species—without the self-serving projections of human ego consciousness, of the "stranger"? The preliminary answer here has been *no*, not through this worldview, this general psychocultural orientation, at least. But among the Western writers of the past half millennium, the Romantics must be said to have made the best effort, however much the magnificent efforts of Wordsworth and Coleridge were magnificent failures, however much one might suggest anthropocentric motives for perhaps the most successful of them all, John Clare. "At no time before or since have domestic and wild animals been so conspicuous within, and arguably central to, Western conceptions of human social interconnection and subjectivity," Fosso claims for this period (15).[81] And this centrality, as I have argued, includes the deep consideration of human-animal interconnection itself and humankind's own role as one animal in the ecosphere.

I must also reconsider my longtime prejudice against the merits of poetic anthropomorphism. Though I have often been as harsh as possible on even the most innocuous homocentric projection on the part of Wordsworth et al., it is clear that many of these examples are miles from the blithe appropriations of animal imagery in Western cultural productions in general, be they neoclassical poetry or contemporary advertisements. Indeed, we have seen that the rise of biological science lent a new (if temporary) validity to "analogy and personification" (Gaull 356), and certainly the notion that other living things are "just like us" and thus fit objects for our projections is better than the alternative: a later, harder science that would fulfill Clare's worst nightmares and a later cultural criticism that would condemn the pathetic fallacy as a watered-down substitute for religion. I would claim instead, and Shepard would agree, that this reprivileging of the animal was an attempt at a pagan and animistic religious revival of sorts, in the wake of a Christianity that had cast other species out of the pantheon of deities.

Unfortunately, the Romantic concern for nature has been so politicized in recent years by new historicism that the animal-human relationship has been almost completely occluded by human social concerns (until the welcome combative voices of Bate, McKusick, and others). But one can even return to Jerome McGann's new historicist reading that British Romanticism changed from an initial optimistic "ideology" to self-critical despair (107–9), and reread that interpretation as something other than a testament to the intrinsic bankruptcy of a naturist ideology. McGann argues that these writers' belief in Nature and Imagination as "touchstones of stability and order" was actually a displaced faith in an illusion "of last resort," as opposed to the real political issues of the age (67). To translate this evolution from optimism to despair more *ecologically*: yes, it was a veritable optimism, as the human poet very nearly approached the swallow and sparrow and wren on their own terms; and yes, it was a veritable despair and bankruptcy when the skylark and cuckoo became etherealized emblems of intrapsychic hope and angst, when the avian and animal were turned into overwrought, overly conscious symbols of human strivings and of human inadequacies.

A crucial correlative factor in this fall from what might have been was the relationship between science and the belles-lettres in this era, a mixed-feelings medley of positive influence that gave the poets greater faith in the interconnection of species, and a negative influence, eventually victorious, that distanced the human from the animal via an increasing objectification of other species and a widening gulf and more earnest theoretical (that is, evolutionary) distinction between *Homo sapiens* and its ecosystemic confreres. Thus Gaull notes that "Keats, like Erasmus Darwin and Thomas Beddoes, two other poets trained as physicians and scientists, lived in two worlds . . . the world of art and the world of nature. While his poetry attempts to reconcile the two, it also demonstrates how fundamentally irreconcilable they had become . . . in a natural . . . landscape that had become alien, indifferent, and inhospitable" (225). One is reminded in this context of the poet-naturalist Clare's scorn for Linnaean taxonomy, for an overly left-brain science that would stick nature "on a cork board with a pin."

Thomas Hardy's poetic gloss on "Shelley's Skylark" is pertinent here, both as a laudable deconstruction of the Romantic symbolization of the avian and a lamentable, and thoroughly Victorian, vision of the avian as a dead thing: "Though it only lived like another bird, / And knew not its immortality" (7–8), the skylark did provide "immortal" subject matter for Shelley's "Ecstatic heights" (24). But at last that bird itself—if Shelley did have an individual bird in mind—is now but a "pinch of unseen, unguarded dust" or a "little ball of feather and bone" (4, 10). The evolutionist and materialist in Hardy refuses to see anything more than this.[82] It is then a small step, I would claim, to twentieth-century animal experimentation, animal factory farming, and even a belated and nostalgic concern for endangered species.

John Berger, in his well-known essay on zoos, expresses his certainty that "in the last two centuries, animals have gradually disappeared. Today we live without them. And in this new solitude, anthropomorphism makes us doubly uneasy" (9). My own uneasiness with the anthropomorphic has been obvious throughout. Does my cynicism arise, in part, from my own modern distance from the animal? Is my frequent obeisance to the dictates of poststructuralism symptomatic of an intellectual distancing from the body, from the Real? "Until the 19th century"—and including the early Romantics, I would add in qualification—"anthropomorphism was integral to the relation between man and animal and was an expression of their proximity" (9). But even the "treatment of animals in 19th century romantic painting was already an acknowledgement of their impending disappearance. The images are of animals *receding* into a wildness that exists only in the imagination" (15). Again, my argument has been that this recession occurred at a crucial juncture: when Wordsworth's individual wren and robin became "thoughts that lie too deep for tears," when Keats's sparrows picking about the gravel became a fanciful nightingale, when Shelley's *heard* lark became an emblematic "Skylark" in print—and then a "little ball of feather and bone."

"Everywhere animals disappear," Berger tells us (24). My main point has been that the literal disappearance of the avian, and the corresponding degradation of the ecosphere in general, was not only well chronicled *metaphorically* in the annals of nineteenth-century British poetry, but also was anticipated and perhaps even *occasioned* (in part) by a discourse that would eventually other the avian and animal even more, perhaps, than the previous Christian and Cartesian worldviews. The Romantic gesture toward the animal was valiant, even glorious. But the good fight was lost, and the result for our contemporary age is in the end but a guilty nostalgia: "As human numbers increase and the Others recede . . . we feel like calling, as the birds fly away, 'Come back! . . . Hear me! . . . Look!'" (Shepard 141). This work, then, is a look back at the bird, and, like the oh so pathetic call to Paul Shepard's fleeing flock, it says, "Hear me."

CHAPTER 4

The Eagle and the Crow

Avian Returns in Native American Literature

More interest is evidenced in the history of the Passenger Pigeon and its fate than in that of any other North American bird. Once the most abundant species, in its flights and on its nesting grounds, ever known in any country, ranging over the greater part of the continent of North America in innumerable *hordes*, the *race* seems to have disappeared during the nineteenth century, leaving no trace.

—EDWARD HOWE FORBUSH, "Passenger Pigeon," in *Birds of America* (emphases added)

Reconsider Indian history. Whites were advancing not only on the Indians but on the chickadees listening, the bird unconcerned, the deer scratching.

—WILLIAM BEVIS, "Native American Novels: Homing In"

This and the next chapter offer a fairly radical departure from my emphasis on British Romanticism and mainstream ecocriticism. But if many of the figures discussed to this point have often been designated major forebears of the concerns of contemporary ecology and animal rights, I think it is important to examine another body of literature that may be deemed perhaps even more ecocentric, that is, Native American literature(s). Indeed, the traditional Native American worldview, or rather, worldviews have been championed at least as often as the British and American Romantics by ecoscholars as a way of being closer to the animal, as less othering and more conducive to interspecies egalitarianism.[1] The Native scholar Paula Gunn Allen finds a prior claim to the eco-egalitarianism proposed by deep ecology in American Indian worldviews, which "see all things as being of equal value" and deny the "opposition" of human and nonhuman "that characterize[s] non-Indian thought" (*Sacred* 56). Given my conclusion in the preceding chapter—shared in good part by Karl Kroeber—that the Romantics generally ended up in ego alienation rather than veritable eco-empathy, it is significant that Kroeber, after his groundbreaking ecocritical studies of British Romanticism, turned his attention to Native American poetry, finding the aesthetics therein to be a transformation rather than a "creation" of "tensions," an ultimately eco-conducive "public activity" rather than a Romantic ego's turning in upon "itself" (qtd. in Bevis 617–18).

The Lakota writer Vine Deloria Jr. frames the distinction even more radically: "The single attribute that characterizes the Western approach to human knowledge, indeed to almost all human activities," is "isolation"; in contrast, "relatedness is a much better description of the Indian way of looking at the world" (137, 141).[2] More so than any other Native activist, Deloria has emphasized again and again the vast difference between the Western and Native worldviews in their approach to the environment and to other animals, a dichotomy expressed in terms of a Native wisdom largely independent of Western projections: "In the religious world of most tribes, birds, animals, and plants compose the 'other peoples' of creation and, depending on the ceremony, various of these peoples participate in human activities. . . . [In contrast,] non-Indians have engaged in senseless killings of wildlife and utter destruction of plant life and *it is unlikely that they would have understood any effort by other forms of life to communicate*" (208, 209; emphasis added).

Certainly, that most Native American worldviews themselves entail an ideology of familial alliance with birds is a consideration crucial to any discussion of the subject. For instance, the traditional Lakota faith in the close relation of the human tribe to such birds as the eagle and the meadowlark and the many claims of actual interspecies conversation, especially during a vision quest (*ha*^{n}*blecia*),[3] may be viewed, at first sight, as the same conflation of the avian and the Indian performed by Western colonial ideology. However, the originating worldviews and, just as important, the resulting cultural lifestyles are vastly different. The Euro-American attitude is one of belittlement, distance, and difference; the Native attitude, one of kinship and positive regard.

The centrality of birds to the Native vision that Deloria describes, of "the eagle and the crow," lends a good deal of support to the recent scholarly esteem for Native American ecology. But to arrive at the native New World bird and a Native worldview thereof requires quite a peregrination through centuries of Euro-American ideology and othering. Thus in the ornithologist's 1917 description of the Passenger Pigeon as a "race" of "innumerable hordes," the terms "hordes" and "race" might be said to encapsulate centuries of Euro-American pathological objectification of both the New World avian and the indigene.[4] Regarding such a dual denigration, M. L. Pratt has undertaken one of the most earnest applications of the Foucault-Said critical thread to the Americas. As a prime example of Pratt's "contact zone" of colonizer and colonized,[5] North America was the victim of a scientific "anti-conquest" in which the native environment was "written as uninhabited, unpossessed, unhistoricized, [and] unoccupied" (51), a tabula rasa for both socioeconomic and Linnaean imperialism. That is, along with guns and a racist political ideology, the Europeans brought their own nature with them, including a full-blown avian nomenclature, along with predictable attitudes toward the bird. Pratt finds it *not* coincidental that such a scientific "systematization of nature coincides with the height of the slave trade, the plantation system, [and] colonial genocide in North America and South Africa" (36). Indeed, colonialism's will to power and natural science's "anti-conquest" will to knowledge were two sides of the same coin (or, as Paula Gunn Allen so wonderfully phrases it, "two wings of one bird" [*Sacred* 169]).

That this "anti-conquest" would be accompanied by actual violence toward other species was evidenced early on by the burning of Mexican aviaries by Cortez and his men, "fires that burned the green hummingbirds and nesting blue herons, burned even the sound of wings and the white songs of egrets" (Hogan, *Dwellings* 43). In sum, the colonization of the New World was also "a relentless, ongoing war against" nature itself, a two-pronged attack against both Natives and land: "What happens to [indigenous] people and what happens to the land is the same thing" (44, 89).

What Pratt describes as a "Victorian discovery rhetoric" applies equally to the earlier colonization of North America: the rhetoric was an othering of nature that included a "sprinkling" of the native scene "with some little bits of England" (204).[6] Certainly contemporary American stereotypical understandings of the eagle, crow, and robin still bear in large measure the weight of their Old World counterparts.

AVIAN AND NATIVE EXTINCTION, AVIAN AND NATIVE RETURN

> I call birds few when I shoot less than 100 per day.
>
> JOHN JAMES AUDUBON (qtd. in Kastner, *A World of Watchers*)

Last of her species, died at 1 p.m.,
1 September 1914, age 29, in the
Cincinnati Zoological Garden.
EXTINCT

Original display-case label for Martha, the last Passenger Pigeon (Smithsonian Institution)

Perhaps this is why the Smithsonian Institution keeps so many of our ancestors tucked away in boxes—someday they hope to mount and display the last Indian and give him a cute name like they did "Martha." And, no doubt, they will feel a certain pride in having the last one before we became extinct—just like they do with "Martha."

MIKE WICKS (qtd. in Camp, "Hiding Genocide")

Rather than the eagle and crow, I might have referred instead to the passenger pigeon and the house finch, for there is a story there, of avian and indigenous return, markedly analogous to the Native American experience of the past two centuries. Many native bird species have actually had their ranges and populations radically altered by the incursions of Western civilization; the European propensity to introduce Old World birds into North America is a sad emblem of Western colonization itself. But the negative effects of European expansionism are most tellingly manifest in the various instances of the murder of entire species, and it is the passenger pigeon that has become the epitome and template in the American psyche for abrupt and wholesale extinction. Indeed, at the same time that the Native American was making a forced retreat to near extinction, this pigeon, whose numbers just two centuries ago made it "perhaps the most numerous of all birds" (Forbush 2.39),[7] became the New World dodo in the span of a century. Even before the later acknowledged trauma of the near extinction of the buffalo and American indigenous peoples, this ending was an undeniable certainty for Euro-American culture, perhaps the first major wake-up call to an awareness that the colonizing enterprise was as much about death and injustice as it was about life and justice. Ultimately, this bird's extirpation stands as an Ur-reminder of the colonial ideology that would *imagine* a frontier and wilderness, that would then breach that frontier and destroy that wilderness, and that would ultimately create a recuperative sense of nostalgia about the whole happy enterprise.

A return to the nineteenth century is illuminating. Late in that century, even the bird-loving John Burroughs, noting the passenger pigeon's apparently sudden scarcity and mourning the "greed and cupidity of man" in the bird's "death and destruction," admits his own culpability: "The last time that my eyes beheld a passenger pigeon was in the fall of 1876 when I was out for grouse. . . . I killed it, little dreaming that, so far as I was concerned, I was killing the last pigeon" (94). Still earlier, the most famous American ornithologist of all, John James Audubon, reports circa 1813 that the "multitudes of Wild Pigeons in our woods are astonishing," leaving everyone "struck with amazement." "When the woods are filled with" them, "they are killed in immense numbers, although no apparent diminution ensues" (262, 265). As for the fear "that such dreadful havock [that is, hunting] would soon put an end to the species," Audubon has blithely reassured himself, "by long observation, that nothing but the gradual diminution of our forests can accomplish their decrease, as they not unfrequently quadruple their numbers yearly" (267). So much for the dramatic ironies of one great naturalist's foresight.

In his visit to the Missouri River basin, however, Audubon does have some cause to fear the extinction of the indigenous humans there, if for no other reason than the smallpox brought by the Europeans (641). But these same journals also evince such a scorn for the Native tribes that he likely would have not lamented *their* extinction overly much: "This morning the dirty Indians, who could have washed had they so minded, were beating the tambour and singing their miserable scalp song" (668).[8] It is symptomatic of the conflation of Indian and bird that the passenger pigeon was commonly known as the "Wild Pigeon" (French: *Pigeon Sauvage*) in the nineteenth century (Schorger 251, 253), and that the Native American ornithologist (and contemporary of Burroughs) Simon Pokagon could thus write pointedly, "They [the whites] naturally called it a wild pigeon, as they called us wild men" (48). To say that the gradual near disappearance of both Native tribes and avian species was the result of Euro-American greed, malice, and ignorance may be saying so much as to say nothing at all, but it is noteworthy that indigenous peoples whose cultures were so closely tied to the bird should be even more tied to them, eventually, through a similar dismal fate. The slaughter that was colonialism would transform a mythos of New World abundance and fertility to the reality of a retreating frontier, of vanishing tribes and species, and to a new mythos of guilt and anxiety, to a death culture more obsessed with endings, not beginnings. Thus can Linda Hogan refer to the tragedy of Ishi, "the last Yana Indian," living his last years alone and among an alien race, like a last, lone pigeon, as a "story" that "speaks of loss and of emptiness that will never again be filled, of whole cultures disappeared, of species made extinct" (*Dwellings* 110–11), a story that, I would argue, has its first page engraved with a photo of the last passenger pigeon.

However, Audubon did serve as a fairly outraged witness to the nineteenth-century massacre of the passenger pigeon: he "narrated their slaughter in uncounted numbers with all the horrifying particulars his practiced eye could gather," including a "communal butchering near the Green River in Kentucky that lasted a day and a night, when thousands and thousands of birds were knocked down with poles." Most stunningly, he "recorded that a man in Pennsylvania took more than 500 in a net one day" (Gibbons and Strom 72).[9] But we must remember that this is, after all, the same gun-toting fellow who writes in one of his journals, "I call birds few when I shoot less than 100 per day" (qtd. in Kastner 70).[10] Audubon apologists inevitably quote one passage about our pigeon as an example of the ornithologist's poetic soul: "When an individual [passenger pigeon] is seen gliding through the woods and close to the observer, it passes like a thought, and on trying to see it again, the eye searches in vain; the bird is gone" (262). Today, Audubon's finale, "the bird is gone," echoes as a haunting and ironic, or all too apropos, refrain.

The last passenger pigeon, Martha, actually died in the Cincinnati Zoo in 1914. She was named after Martha Washington, just as her last male companion, George, was named after the first president. (First lady, last bird? The irony is dripping.) But George died in July 1910, and so Martha survived over four years as the last of her species (Schorger 28–29). Christopher Cokinos writes, "Probably she could not have missed George in what we'd call memory[!], but who can say? Certainly she lived in the insistent aloneness of each moment after George's death." So how did she pass the time? "From time to time, Martha . . . stretched her wings, missing the flight she never really had. Mostly she sat. She ate at feeding time and stared beyond the metal mesh" (259, 261, 262–63).

The bird's belated postmortem inclusion in Pearson's imposing ornithological tome *Birds of America* (1917) is especially troublesome for a book on bird *life*. Accompanied by a pathetic zoo photo of an already defunct

Martha, the text reads like a surreal obituary. (The claim of the entry's author, Forbush, that this species' "story reads like a romance" [2.40] makes one wonder what tales of gothic cruelty made up *his* early reading.) The entry for the bird's geographical range is disturbing enough: "Now extinct" (2.39). After several pages describing the birds' incredible numbers before 1850, Forbush has the nerve to write, "It often is asked how it was possible for man to kill them all" (2.44), and his subsequent ruminations on potential vulnerabilities due to the species' nesting habits hardly serve as a satisfactory answer. Forbush's conclusion is an incredibly muted aside about the bird's diet, much like an anthropologist's report on a now defunct indigenous tribe, that renders the entire essay—or epigraph?—all the more ironically poignant: "They were fond of currants, cranberries, and poke berries"; however, "we know little of their food habits, for no scientific investigation of their food was ever made" (2.46).

Intermittent gestures of guilty nostalgia continue through the twentieth century, as in the Wisconsin monument to the passenger pigeon in 1947:

> Dedicated
> To The Last Wisconsin
> Passenger Pigeon
> Shot At Babcock, Sept. 1899
>
> This Species Became Extinct
> Through The Avarice And
> Thoughtlessness Of Man
> (qtd. in Schorger 230)

This monument (if not the bird) was itself memorialized in Aldo Leopold's words on the dedication of the monument: "We have erected a monument to commemorate the funeral of a species. It symbolizes our sorrow." Underlying the great naturalist's praise are reservations, however: "There will always be pigeons in books and in museums, but these are effigies and images, dead to all hardships and to all delights." And so this monument, too, is just such an ineffectual effigy. Certainly, it is a nice spectacle and gesture, Leopold says: "But no pigeons will pass, for there are no pigeons, save only this flightless one, graven in bronze on this rock. Tourists will read this inscription, but their thoughts will not take wing." As a scientist deeply concerned about the preservation of the wild, Leopold takes this opportunity to cut at the heart of the whole enterprise of Western colonization and industrialism: "Perhaps we now grieve because we are not sure, in our hearts, that we have gained from [our] exchange" of civilization for the wilderness (116, 118). And isn't that the crux of the matter, that whatever concern humankind has expressed for the various native species and habitats that have succumbed to our advancing colonialism is really our own self-doubt in this venture of civilization and our angst in the vague consciousness of feeling rootless in a land that we have never really known?

Leopold himself has enough faith in science and Darwinism to remain complacent in his own human superiority. "For one species to mourn the death of another," why, that's a behavior worthy of applause for our species, "a new thing under the sun." (But again, I would question whether we are even or ever veritably mourning this other species at all.) Leopold continues: "In this fact—[of altruistic mourning] lies objective evidence of our superiority over the beasts" (117). Oh, the hubris! Don't tell me, then, that Martha's fate has helped spur some great leap in environmental ethics or ecological consciousness. As long as even our most esteemed naturist writers continue to assume the Western ideology that *Homo sapiens* is evolution's gift to the planet, any authentic regard for the intrinsic worth of other species is still light-years away.

As the most blatant example of recuperative nostalgia, however, listen in on a 1949 radio skit in which "Buttons," the nickname of the last Passenger Pigeon slain in the wild (1900), is given a speaking role (Cokinos 228–29, 256). The bird—now stuffed!—is made to say, at the end of this pro-conservation morality play, "See? I told you I was important and that I could tell quite a story. I'm back on my shelf at the Museum now. And I like it very much. . . . I hope lots of children come here to the Museum to see me because I like children and I know that when they look at me they think about conservation and all it means to our country" (qtd. in Cokinos 257). One can only conclude, in retrospect, that "conservation" hasn't meant *much* if a bird can be *imagined* as saying that she prefers her taxidermic status in furtherance of an inane discourse claiming that, environmentally speaking, all is going swimmingly.

What have we really learned, then? When will we stop patting ourselves on the back about our newfound eco-sophistication, when the reality remains that we are still stuck in a mainstream anthropocentric worldview that overrides any little cutesy animal rights gestures that we make? Unlike the (apparent) amazing rediscovery of the ivory-billed woodpecker recently in Arkansas—another return of the Native?—no sighting of another individual passenger pigeon can be expected. We are left instead to ponder, with postmodern ironic smirks, Audubon's early nineteenth-century appeal:

> Oh Walter Scot where art thou? wilt thou not come to my Country? Wrestle with Mankind and Stop their Increasing ravages on Nature & describe her Now for the Sake of Future Ages—neither this Little Stream—this Swamp, this Grand Sheet of Flowing Watter nor these Mountains will be seen in a century hence, as I see them now.—Nature will have been rob[bed] of her brilliant Charms . . . the Hills will be levelled with the Swamp. . . . Fishes will no longer bask on this surface. the Eagle scarce ever alight, and these Millions of Songsters will be drove away by Man—Oh Walter Scot come, Come to America! (186–87)

Audubon's 1826 appeal to an icon of British Romanticism strikes one now as almost ludicrous, but the sentiment is certainly laudable. No, not merely laudable: it is *grand*. But the naturalist's ideology must finally appeal to those birds most esteemed by humans (and Euro-Americans): the eagle and songbirds. We have no similar laudatory discourse regarding those pleasingly plump birds designated "fowl," which includes pigeons. If we had, if somehow the passenger pigeon had been deemed our national bird, or had earned a level of domestic love on the level of the robin, or had not so pleased the human palate—well, then I might not have any subject to write about now, the subject of extinction and of genocide. Compare John Burroughs's merely nostalgic remarks on his shooting of his last passenger pigeon to his following words: "What would it profit me could I find and plunder my eagle's nest, or strip his skin from his dead carcass? Should I know him better? I do not want to know him that way" (142). No, not *our* noble raptor. But a good billion of Marthas were known that way, and have gone the way of history, into nostalgic shame and guilt and repression. We feel today (or should feel) a great guilt and shame in remembering the many indigenous tribes of *Homo sapiens* whose last bones are now in museums. We should feel at least as much for the murder of another, entire species of being.

The story continues—and has a slightly happier ending, I might claim—

with the native house finch and its relationship with the house (or English) sparrow, the latter brought to the New World and intentionally set free in the wild by a New York museum in the 1850s (Gibbons and Strom 214).[11] By 1884 Burroughs can already note their "rapidly increasing" numbers and even foresee the need to "wage serious war[!] upon" this species.[12] But Burroughs admires them nonetheless, above all for their "Old World hardiness and prolificness," much like his own European colonial forebears, of course. And the poor native birds being driven out by the house sparrow? They are "less shrewd," "less quick-witted," and "less sophisticated" (44–45), like their *human* Native cohabitants, no doubt. Homi Bhabha speaks of the "objective of colonial discourse" as the construction of "the colonized as a population of degenerate types on the basis of racial origin" (70). With apologies to postcolonial theorists who would apply such dictums exclusively to the human sociopolitical realm, such an othering, or Orientalization, of the avian has certainly long been at work, too, in the colonizing agenda via race (i.e., species, that biological difference from which the notion of race itself arose) and via degeneration (loosely speaking), in the sense that the "lower" animals have traditionally been seen as brute and instinctual beasts. Burroughs's distinction between English sparrows and native birds is complicated by the imposition of human racial divisions upon another biological order. The former are both praised as hardy European types and othered as pugnacious, quick-breeding *animals*; the latter birds are mere naïve also-rans in the battle of evolution through their status as *both* other-species animals and other-racial *natives*.

The immediate result of this Old World sparrow's rapid adaptation to U.S. urbanization was a drastic population reduction and range redistribution of native sparrows and finches, including the house finch, to the widespread laments of ornithologists.[13] (Of course, Native Americans suffered an even more severe reduction and forced redistribution of their population.) However, in the second half of the twentieth century, due to the vagaries of natural selection and changes in urbanization, the house sparrow actually declined in many urban areas and was largely replaced by the native house finch (Ehrlich, Dobkin, and Wheye 632, 646).[14] And just so—if I can be indulged a wayward fancy—has the dominance of the Euro-American worldview, in roughly this same time span, met with some new and firm contestation from human indigenous worldviews, both from Native writers themselves and from a strong network of non-Indian sympathizers, including many proponents of the more radical ecological views presented in my introduction. Indeed, it is as if the calls for and predictions of a return of the Native, most eloquently formulated in Leslie Silko and Joy Harjo, are now being realized in both the human and nonhuman spheres. Thus the Native poet Wendy Rose can write,

> One way or another
> we'll get somewhere soon
> for I have seen crows
> dance on Manhattan snow,
> a hawk on Henry Street,
> smoke plumes from the lips
> of street kids,
> mesas along the Hudson.
>
> I am getting ready. ("Leaving Port Authority for Akwesasne" 11–19 [67])

But all such spacious generalizations come with caveats and qualifications. First of all, the facts of both cultural and biological *hybridity* between the European-American and the Native, as we shall see, make any dichotomous assertions regarding "white" versus "Indian" deeply problematic. Second, better at seeing relationships than "isolations" myself (following Deloria), I still cannot get it out of my head that there is some fundamental affinity between the best of what we have seen in Wordsworth et al. and what I shall present as representative traditional and contemporary Native American attitudes toward nature and the avian. Norma Wilson, too, perceives "definite parallels between the poetry of the English Romantics . . . and Native American poetry," evident in the Romantics' "celebration of nature, their recognition of particular birds as symbols of freedom and spirit, and their emphasis on spirituality"; furthermore, beginning with the American Transcendentalists and Walt Whitman, Anglo-American writers themselves have long "sought the unity the Native peoples have always felt with the land" (*Nature* 3). Moreover, "Indian-inspired ideas" "were active in the minds of individuals like Thoreau, [John Wesley] Powell, and Muir" as they "helped to form the conservationist philosophy in America" (Hughes 139). In previous chapters, I have been more skeptical regarding the motives of the Romantics' celebration of nature and the bird, especially their use of the avian for symbolic purposes; I promise to be just as skeptical about recent critical elevations of a Native American "Nature," if there be such a thing. But I still hold to my initial instinct, that Romanticism was an attempt to revitalize the ecosphere and reaffirm the intrinsic being of other species, and I hope to finally argue that a native New World post-Romanticism offers the best current, or rather, future worldview through which to fulfill that original Romantic promise.

(REAL) INDIANS AND BIRDS

> See! the eagle comes,
> See! the eagle comes;
> Now at last we see him—look! look! the eagle comes,
> Now at last we see him—look! look! the eagle comes;
> Now we see him with the people,
> Now we see him with the people.
>
> CADDO GHOST DANCE SONG, in Mooney, *The Ghost-Dance Religion*

> Though they had great curiosity about nature and understood it well, the Indians satisfied their curiosity more by being descriptive than by being analytic. . . . For all their skill as observers, the Indians do not qualify, in modern terms, as birders. . . . The Indians, so far as anyone seems to know, did not keep [birding] lists. The white man, as soon as he came to America, did.
>
> JOSEPH KASTNER, *A World of Watchers*

Kastner's history of birding reveals a symptomatic blind spot regarding the Native relationship to nature, and a blithe preference for the colonizers' seemingly more civilized penchant for making lists, a Foucauldian will to power toward, and discursive ownership of, the nonhuman. Nor is it surprising that Mary Allen's 1983 study, *Animals in American Literature,* includes no Native authors and peremptorily dismisses Native views by claiming that "primitive man was mystified as to his relationship to animals" (8). Armed with examples from Melville through Hemingway, Allen sets out to establish (besides her love for italics) her thesis: "*An astonishing number of actual animals play impressive roles in American literature*" (10). Indeed, the "*abundance of our literary inheritance is in the free, willful, and often joy-inspiring animal*"; such a plethora of animals "give[s] American literature a cast like no other on earth, born as they [animals' roles] are of regard and love" (198, 199). I am left mystified myself, wondering if these are the same Melville and Hemingway that I have read, books of harpoons and rifles, of an ego fear and Other loathing forever eager to subdue not only other species but the "free, willful," and "joy-inspiring" aspects of the human psyche itself. Certainly I overstate my case as much as Allen does hers, but I do so in proposing once again that the Native American attitude toward the animal is radically different from the pathological objectification of the natural Other endemic to Western colonization:

Then they [the colonizers] grow away from the earth

. . . .

then they grow away from the plants and animals.
They see no life
When they look
they see only objects.
The world is a dead thing for them

. . . .

They will kill the things they fear
all the animals.

(Silko, "Long time ago" 90, 92–96, 112–13, in *Storyteller* 133–34)

In contrast, "close attention to the environment and particularly the animals that inhabit it," as Norma Wilson tells us, is a dominant feature of "Native American writing" (*Nature* 18). Happily granting this, one then treads upon the dangerous ground of offering this ecological vision as a "universal and cosmic truth" (13), an idealization that I see as an unwelcome surrender to, an unintentional co-optation by, the totalizing tendencies of Western metaphysics and monotheism—another form, ultimately, of Orientalism and Indianism. And as we have seen, all such positive assertions on behalf of indigenous naturism are problematized by their inextricable relationship to the West's already centuries-old romanticization of the Indian as Nature's Child. I would immediately offer my own alternative misreading of the Native American relationship to nature and "religion" by denying such compartmentalized categories as much as possible. The central problem in any critical reinscription of a Native way lies in the nearly inevitable imposition of a Western metaphysical dualism that has inveterately distinguished between "spirit" and "matter" and that posits the concept of religion as a specific experiential realm distinct from work and art. I find the characteristic traditional Native view to be, instead, a quite *naturalistic* one, in the sense that "spirit" and "matter" are one, with a preference (semantically speaking) for "matter," in its best, naturist sense. For one thing, the belief in an individual afterlife, those hallowed happy hunting grounds, seems more the exception than the rule in traditional Native American religion, until the syncretistic meldings with Christianity in the nineteenth century. And I would assert that even the vast majority of Native conceptions of so-called spiritualism are thoroughly immanent and materialist, even animistic, but without the connotations this last term has as some primitive, outdated way of seeing and with the implication that an emotional and intuitive—dare I now still say "spiritual"?—communion with other species is a positive thing. Admittedly, there is the common perception that even contemporary Native American poetry inevitably translates the natural world too glibly into the *ooh-ooh* of the Western metaphysical and spiritual, as in the (in)famous ending of Leslie Silko's "Indian Song: Survival":

> I am the wind
> touch me,
> I am the lean gray deer
> running on the edge of the rainbow. (47–50, in *Storyteller* 37)

And yet I would immediately retract the adjective "metaphysical" in my own comprehension of this poem as a marvelous intermedley of the human and nonhuman, both working their magic in this—and perhaps only *this*—world.

The desperate need by the West to posit a metaphysics separate from the physical realm is reflected in A. Grove Day's introduction to his classic compendium of traditional Native poems (or rather, *songs*), *The Sky Clears* (1951): "Even what seem at first to be poems descriptive of the beauties of nature are often found to be connected in the Indian mind with religion and worship" (7). Day can only conceive of nature description per se and religious worship as two very separate ontological realms in need of connection. And so, for Day, "*symbolism* is the key to Indian poetry" (19) because the apparently incredible privileging of other natural beings, such as eagles and coyotes, *must* be "symbolic" (of human "spiritual" strivings), not a mere celebration of these beings themselves and their essential roles in the biosphere. Day goes on to admit that "Chippewa songs," for instance, "reveal a knowledge of nature . . . derived from the Indian habit, born of necessity, of scanning his environment with eyes that missed nothing. . . . However . . . there are almost no poems to be found . . . which reflect in a lyrical manner the delight in nature for its own sake. The sort of white-man poetry exemplified by Wordsworthian passages . . . cannot be found among the North American Indians. . . . It was foreign to him [the Indian] to scan a landscape seeking literary raw material" (147). But such a culturally specific Euro-literary seeking is not necessarily a laudable thing, and in no way were the usual results of this "white-man poetry," as I have argued extensively in earlier chapters, some pure "delight in nature for its own sake." But Day must impose a Western division between aesthetics and religion, and he also cannot conceive of a vision in which nature and spirit are conjoined as one immanence. And maybe the term "immanence" itself is too Western a term for what I would posit as a naturist-materialist philosophy that yet allows for the magical synchronicity, numinosity, and even symbiosis that often characterizes the relationship between avian and Native. This is the sheer-wonder-of-physicality, or what might be called the "*natural* & super*natural* at once" (Rothenberg xv),[15] that the Westerner must translate as "spiritual."

This mistranslation via metaphysicality is nowhere more brazen than in the adaptations of traditional Native American songs by Gerald Hausman, who apparently channels the "spirit[s] of the past without the intermediary of interviewer, anthropologist, or scholar," so that his new version of a traditional lyric is "in harmony with its origin" (9). Quite a feat, indeed. Instrumental as they have been in the revival of appreciation for things Native American, the various New Age movements have themselves been often a folly of misreading, aided by many Native *poseurs* who make up what Vine Deloria calls the "New Age/Indian medicine man circuit" (261). The common conception of a central spiritual aspect in Native views is most certainly an Orientalist interposition, again, of a Euro-American metaphysics that turns such expressions of immanence such as the Lakota *Waka*^{n}*ta*^{n}*ka* (the "big holy"—and even that translation grossly misleads) into the Westernized and transcendental Great Spirit, with its cross-cultural resonation with the Holy Ghost.[16] It is an *immanent* spirituality, rather, that pays such close attention to the "environment and particularly the animals," for, in such a naturalist (anti)theology, that is all there is to pay attention to. To turn Keats's idealizing on its head, "That is all / Ye know on earth, and all ye need to know" ("Ode on a Grecian Urn" 5.9–10). As the Lakota medicine man Lame Deer puts it, "We Indians live in a world of symbols and images where the spiritual and the commonplace are one" (Fire and Erdoes 109). Better yet, in the words of the contemporary Chickasaw poet Linda Hogan, "What does god look like? These fish, this water, this land" (*Dwellings* 98). And Hogan again:

> They think heaven is so far away,
> beyond the farthest towns,
> not beneath the mortal sky,
> not the radiant fields of potatoes
> brown with dust,
> not the gold-eyed eagle perched
> in a tree,
> with perfect feathers and bones of air.
> ("Gate" 30–37, in *Book of Medicines* 77–78)

And again: "The Western belief that God lives apart from earth is one that has taken us toward collective [ecological] destruction" (*Dwellings* 85–86).

Besides the sameness imposed by Western modernizing appropriation, there is the converse (yet correlative) Orientalist gesture of "differencing," of othering Native American cultures as utterly alien in their primitiveness. Far from marveling at the poetic beauty of Native American songs, for instance, the early colonizers of the New World found such "hellish . . . yelling" to be a "satanic threat," just as early European "responses" to the New World landscape often included "horror and revulsion" (Swann, Introduction, *Wearing* xi; Sanders 184),[17] as the uncanny calls of the New World whip-poor-will and great horned owl, one might guess, likewise sent shivers up their spines. But this differencing also includes the positive Romantic idealization of the noble savage, evident intermittently through my preceding chapters. Indeed, early translations of Native American "poetry" were fostered by the British Ossian craze that had "stimulated an interest in apparently primitive poetry" (Clements 89).[18] This literary impetus was eventually epitomized in American literature by Longfellow's *Song of Hiawatha*, in which Gitche Manito becomes a mutant hybrid, if you will, between the Old Testament Yahweh and some transcendental Oversoul. (Or, as Gerald Vizenor expresses it, "Hiawatha became the sycophant of manifest manners in the literature of dominance" [*Manifest Manners* 39].)[19] This attraction to the primitive still invariably necessitates the appropriative reduction to the same, discussed earlier, for hand in hand with the attraction is a great deal of fear and loathing in need of such defense mechanisms,[20] consisting largely of rendering the New World animal and racial, mattered *body* as an Old World disembodied spirit. Thus Thomas Carlyle, the foremost purveyor of the British version of the Oversoul, could proclaim (admittedly through the slippery personae of *Sartor Resartus*), "Savage Animalism is nothing, inventive Spiritualism is all" (196).

This Orientalizing inventiveness is clearly evident in Western civilization's rationalizations regarding the relationship of the primitive to nature and the animal Other, like Wallace Stevens's imperial jar making all around it "no longer wild." And so the Emerson who would listen so earnestly to nature "was always a little too eager to hear the cultural mutterings of his own well-stocked mind" (Sanders 188). Here are the psychoanalysts Jelliffe and Brink, writing in 1917: "It seems" to be "the typical neurotic attitude, *like that of the savage*, to accord to animals a consideration and reverence, even a fondness" (qtd. in S. Baker 214; emphasis added).[21] Likewise Jung, in his condescending championing of the primordial and the primitive, explains what has later been dubbed eco-egalitarianism: "In primitive society one does in fact find that this assumption [of 'psychic uniformity'] extends not only to human beings, but to all the objects of nature, the animals, plants, rivers, mountains, and so on. . . . Even trees and stones can speak."[22] However, this human projection of "psychic uniformity," resulting in species equality, is "a vestige—but a very potent one—of a primitive frame of mind which is based essentially on an insufficiently differentiated consciousness" (*CW* 10: §280). It is painful to learn that the evolution of human consciousness has entailed a separation, indeed alienation from the rest of the biosphere. To revise Jung a bit, one might conclude that such a differentiation of consciousness may have been a survival strategy necessary for several aeons of human history. But if the human collective psyche still aims, above all, for species preservation (following Jung himself), it is high time that such a limited human egohood in blinders ends its hubris-ridden ways. Rather than continue to appropriate other cultures and other species into such a worldview of ego inflation and ego alienation, and the Orientalizing strategies that inevitably accompany such a view, one might better adopt an attitude of consideration and reverence for both the Native and animal Other.

To witness this general Western appropriation at work, one need only turn to anthologies of translated traditional Native poetry—and here, even the term "poetry" is alien, if deemed an art form independent of ceremony and dance and ritual.[23] Entire refrains of the original transliterations are often omitted, denying any power of incremental repetition that the original lyric possessed, and lines of what were taken to be nonsense syllables are also ignored at will. During the heyday of imagism, especially, the haiku-like suggestiveness and avoidance of an ostensible message in many of these lyrics were lauded and these features exaggerated in the very translation.[24] However much a literary accident, this Native-Imagist connection is revealing. After Ezra Pound's championing of a similarly imagistic Chinese poetry, the way was prepared for the highbrow embrace of Native American poems as precursors, too, to Imagism (H. Carr 224). Mary Austin, a nature writer and earnest student of Native Americans, was bold enough to claim that the imagists began "about where the last Medicine Man left off" (qtd. in Swann, introduction to *Coming* xxvi). This seeming close connection both appealed to the primitivist element of modernism and flattered American modernists, who might thus claim a more direct lineage to the continent's indigenous cultures, more talented in literature now than previously supposed, and so, finally, to the land itself. Such hyperbole from Austin and others led Carl Sandburg to quip, "Suspicion arises definitely that the Red Man and his children committed direct plagiarism on our modern imagists and vorticists" (qtd. in Nolan 95)!

But in fact, the *images* of birds in traditional Native lyrics do often partake in a haiku-like concision and a snapshot quality that presents their characteristic behaviors in their natural habitat as images outside of time; it is as if, as Native authors like Momaday and Silko claim, the sheer orality of the Native tradition itself is an ongoing (continually being spoken) re-creation of the universe, and of the bird, and of the human in the act of perceiving the magic of the bird.[25] But, to counter Day and others once again, to find some overriding symbolism or spirituality in these almost thoroughly naturalistic portraits is the height of cultural projection:

The great blue heron stands in the shallow water
near the shore.
The great blue heron spears clams and
skips them along the water
toward the beach.
("Great Blue Heron Children's Song," in Swann, *Wearing* 33)

The naughty wheat-ear
From its nest
Comes quickly out.
Wiutiu! it whistles. (in Day 37)

What is striking, above all, in such lyrics, coming as we are from two chapters on British Romantic bird poems, is the nearly total lack of homocentric projection and the relative absence of othering via a close naturalist description that is empathetic all the same. Through the quagmires of (mis) translation, then, one might yet discern a dominant gesture of alter-species privileging at last.

Another indication of such interspecies rapport involves point of view. We have already seen moments in the poetry of John Clare in which the confusion of pronoun references results in a confusion of bird and human, with the possible intent and effect of greater species interrelatedness. Such a playing with point of view also seems to be a characteristic of many traditional Native American lyrics, as in this Navajo "Owl's Song":

I am the owl.
I sit on the spruce tree.
My coat is gray.
I have big eyes.
My head has two points.
. . . .
Now it is dawn, now it is dawn.
The old man owl's head has two points.
(1–5, 12–13, in Levitas, Vivelo, and Vivelo 105)

Who is the speaker: the "I" that is the owl or the third-person human "I" who utters the matter-of-fact final line? Here it is almost as if the owl and human merge as one cross-species narrator and point of view. The Pima "Roadrunner Song" also employs a point-of-view switch in medias res:

"Here is the red-eyed Roadrunner. . . . This is the red-eyed Roadrunner" (1, 4). But then: "I run and hide! I run and hide! / Now I kill the Gray Lizard / And I eat his fat body" (5–7 [Day 89–90]). The interjection of the roadrunner's own exuberant voice is startling, and the shift in point of view suggests that the initial human speaker has been transformed into another species, in hot pursuit of reptilian flesh. (In fact, torn as this poem is from its probable ceremonial origins, the transformation may have been an actual fiat of a ritual that calls for a sudden, transformative identification with the bird.)

If the dominant mode of personification in the British Romantics' interaction with the avian was the usually quite anthropomorphic apostrophe, the characteristic Native way may well be that of prosopopoeia: that is, rather than "speaking to" the bird, the bird "speaks."[26] More important, the avian's very act of speaking is, in the Native view, beyond the figurative, the metaphorical; that birds *do* literally talk to humans is a dominant theme of both traditional and contemporary Native American literature, as we shall see. But to conceive of such an untoward cross-species interaction requires a radical shift of cultural paradigms. It is to put oneself in a worldview in which the holy bards of one's culture might well derive some of their more apocalyptic intuitions from speaking birds. Such a shift is from the hubris of homocentrism to a "shamanistic" view (as James Nolan terms it), wherein "neither the identity of the 'I' nor of the 'you' is fixed, nor are the boundaries between subject and object . . . or between the human, animal, plant, and mineral worlds" (158). My particular erasure-of-boundaries theme involves, of course, the Native human and native bird: "I *is* an eagle," to transform Rimbaud's famous utterance. Or, in the words of the contemporary Cherokee poet Norman H. Russell:

the bird the tree and you and i
are only here because your eye
and your mind has put us here
we are as wind that may not be held.
("Appearance" 15–18, in Bruchac, *Songs* 216)

ATE HEYE LO: ELK, BEAR, AND DEER SPEAK OF EAGLE

"He will appear, may you behold him!
An eagle for the eagle nation will appear.
May you behold!"
—NICHOLAS BLACK ELK, in Neihardt, *Black Elk Speaks*

Pretty bird, you saw me and took pity on me;
You wished me to survive among the people.
O Bird People, from this day always you shall be my relatives!
SITTING BULL, in Day, *The Sky Clears*

Let me turn to my own tribal heritage and discuss two birds, the eagle and (in the next section) the meadowlark, in the words and writings of three Lakota figures: Nicholas Black Elk (1863–1950), Luther Standing Bear (1868–1939), and John Lame Deer (1903–1976), three men who stood, in varying degrees, on the borders of a traditional Lakota worldview and the ideological pressures of twentieth-century Euro-American acculturation. Of the three, the *wicas*^{h}*a waka*^{n} (holy man) Black Elk was the most thoroughly imbued in the traditional ways.[27] *Black Elk Speaks*, as told to John Neihardt, might be thematized as "the story of all life that is holy," with "us two-leggeds sharing in it with the four-leggeds and the wings of the air and all green things" (1).[28] It is the "wings of the air" who are Black Elk's closest relatives. His first and subsequent visions are primarily mediated by the Spotted Eagle, and his attitude toward birds from his first vision on is one of reverence. He describes his response after his "Great Vision": "There was a bush and a little bird sitting in it; but just as I was going to shoot, I felt queer again [in memory of his vision], and remembered that I was to be like a relative with the birds" (39). He is also inordinately aware of the Lakota people's long-perceived close kinship with the avian: "Birds make their nests in circles, for theirs is the same religion as ours"; thus Lakota "tepees were round like the nests of birds, and these were always set in a circle, the nation's hoop, a nest of many nests." When his people were finally jammed into "square boxes," Black Elk became a lost bird, out of his native element (150–51).[29] Other of Black Elk's stories and ceremonies focus on the horse and the buffalo, but his immediate natural relationship with other species centers just as much on eagles and hawks and swallows, the "wings of the air" of western South Dakota.

Luther Standing Bear, educated at the Carlisle Indian School and later a performer in Buffalo Bill's "Wild West" extravaganzas, was much more accepting of the benefits of assimilation to white culture. And yet among his various laments and protests, too, was the stark contrast he perceived between white and Lakota attitudes toward nature and other species. Thus Standing Bear could only quote with a great deal of incomprehension a contemporary white doctor: "The association of men with animals is unpleasant and dangerous for both." He concluded that "the white race has come to fear nearly everything on earth—even his fellow [animal] being[s]" (*Land* 56). Of the three Lakota figures discussed here, Standing Bear was the only one not to claim medicine man status, and he was less knowledgeable, it would appear, regarding the more esoteric features of Lakota ceremonialism. But his contributions to our knowledge of the relationship between birds and Lakota folkways are just as crucial, above all, via his various references to the "bird who speaks Lakota," the western meadowlark. To believe that this bird could talk was no doubt one of the primitive fancies that the white editor of Standing Bear's *My People the Sioux* had in mind when he refers, apologetically, to a "certain naiveté" on the author's part (xix).

In *Land of the Spotted Eagle*, Standing Bear is bold enough to proclaim that the "Lakota was a true naturist—a lover of Nature. He loved the earth and all things of the earth, the attachment growing with age" (192). Standing Bear's self-praise is an at least implicit contrast with what he perceived to be the Western colonialist rapine of the land even in his day,[30] but it issued from an indigenous faith, I think, that preceded, in the main, the Western notion of the "Eco-Indian." There were Native points of view out there even in the early twentieth century that were not entirely co-opted by a Euro-American conception of what Indian naturism was supposed to be, that could be critical of Western attitudes toward nature from a specific—dare I say, authentic?—tribal view.

Standing Bear's attitude stands in stark contrast to those expressed in Shepard Krech III's recent book, *The Ecological Indian* (1999), in which the author's main blind spot is his very *Western* scientific definition of "ecology." Yes, one blurb on the back of his book even asserts that Krech's point is that to consider the Indian as an ecologist is "entirely anachronistic," but many of Krech's critiques are just that. His definition of "ecology," in fact, smacks very much of what the deep ecologist Arne Naess would consider a "shallow" one, with such positively valued notions as "rational goals" and resource management (22–24). One is reminded of the ecocritic Karl Kroeber's assertion that precolonial Native Americans *couldn't* have been ecological because ecology requires a knowledge of Darwinian evolution (*Ecological* 27). (I would remind the reader of Native critiques by Vine Deloria and Gerald Vizenor of evolution as but another incarnation of Western anthropocentrism.[31] Even a Western naturalist philosopher like John Gray can conclude, "We do not need Darwin to see that we belong with other animals" [3].) I'm especially irked that Krech can condescendingly ask, "Were these Indians ecologists or conservationists?" and blithely answer in the negative because, for one thing, he can't seem to get beyond his own Western perceptions in condescendingly describing the Lakotas' view of the buffalo as "animated other-than-human persons" (149, 147). (But what a wonderful phrase, really!) For they are, like the eagle and the meadowlark, after all, just another *oyate,* that is, different people, different "tribes," and different "persons." But in Krech's view, such an animistic attitude precludes the Native American worldview from any rightful inclusion in a feasible contemporary theory of environmentalism or animal rights.

John Lame Deer comes a generation or so later than Black Elk and Standing Bear, and his book *Lame Deer: Seeker of Visions* (1972) comes in the immediate wake of a revival of and appreciation for things Native American.[32] If the collaboration between Black Elk and John Neihardt can be deconstructed as an act of cultural hybridity and acculturation that overlaid Black Elk's original visions with layers of romanticization and monotheism, the influence of Lame Deer's white coauthor, Richard Erdoes, seems all the more co-optative. Both Lame Deer's trickster humor and sincere faith in the Lakota worldview are manifest, and yet the tone and diction of many passages, especially the ecological ones, are obviously aimed at a specific sympathetic white audience all too ready to idealize this simple medicine man's back-to-nature ways and to canonize Lame Deer (or Erdoes?) in the nascent New Age pantheon.

Lame Deer was probably fully aware of the persona that he was being asked to put forward, and this is an appropriate point at which to broach Gerald Vizenor's conception of the postmodern Native trickster, his "postindian warriors of simulations" (*Manifest* 3). "Native American Indians have endured . . . the puritanical destinies of monotheism, manifest manners, and the simulated realities of dominance, with silence, traces of natural reason, [and] trickster hermeneutics" (16–17). It is this last strategy that is most important in Native literatures. Simply put (which is necessarily a violation of Vizenor's poststructuralist theorizations), because the identity of "Indian" is a simulation or pose enforced by a white culture of dominance, all manifestations of identity by Natives themselves are necessarily simulations. However, the very act of *consciously* (and often ironically) adopting such a pose as a "postmodern simulation" may allow one, through literature as a political act, to "counter the manifest manners of domination" via "an aesthetic restoration of trickster hermeneutics," through "stories of liberation and survivance without the dominance of closure" (17, 4, 14). Are, then, Lame Deer's slippery narratives in *Seeker of Visions* examples of "postmodern simulation" that disrupt even Richard Erdoes's editorial attempts to privilege (and essentialize) the eco-Indian, just as previous cultural intermediaries had posited the Hellish-Heathen, the Noble Savage, and even the Haiku-Imagist Indian?

Vizenor's own brief allusion to Lame Deer in *Manifest Manners* is (like much in Vizenor, a great trickster himself) a bit equivocal,[33] centering on a quotation by Robert Bly: "Lame Deer mentions over and over in his autobiography that the Indian experiences the divine in a bit of animal hide, in mist or steam, and in ordinary events of the day." In the cultural context of enforced simulation, this statement, this experience, is apparently a grand thing. However, the reference occurs during Vizenor's less than equivocal lambasting of Bly himself, that "wild man of manifest manners" whose literary pose is, for Vizenor, nothing but an inauthentic simulation of the "native" and the "wild" (36), thus indirectly calling Lame Deer's utterance, too, into question. But if I could extrapolate a fuller Vizenorian reading of texts such as Lame Deer's and Black Elk's: the *re-visions* of Erdoes and Neihardt are of course Western appropriations, gross "simulations." But, in palimpsest fashion, some authentic inklings of the Lakota in Black Elk and Lame Deer peep through; above all, even Erdoes's and Neihardt's conscious and unconscious intents have been refashioned by a Native liberatory "survivance" that accepts the pose, plays the ironic *poseur* as trickster, and disruptively reinscribes the very text that would be purely appropriative—a difference, at last, erupting within a textual gesture toward the same. I am anticipating here the even more fruitful use of Vizenor's "postindian" and poststructuralist ideas vis-à-vis contemporary Native American poets who will tease and haunt their readers with visions of totemic animals and an apocalyptic future. But I offer Vizenor's twist at this point to counter any facile criticisms of the works at hand as either pure authenticity and naïveté or pure cultural appropriation.

Through this intercultural haze of misreadings and tricksteresque misspeakings, an unmistakable high regard for the animal and bird remains clear. As Standing Bear tells us, the Lakota dancer was such a "close observer of animal life" that "his imitations of walk, manner and behavior of animals were most artful" (*Land* 81). As "close observer[s]" of other species, Native Americans in general "had names for virtually every visible species of animal and plant that would be recognized by a modern taxonomist" (Hughes 79). For instance, in his earnest application of ornithology to Southwest Native culture, Hamilton Tyler has demonstrated that "perhaps 100 kinds [of birds] have an essential place in Pueblo ritual, ceremony, myth, or folklore" (xiii). A glance at a Lakota dictionary reveals a similar regard for and species distinction of the various avians that grace the air, trees, and ground of western South Dakota.

Primary is the eagle, of course, and a few general notes of this bird's importance to Native American cultures are in order. Perhaps Donald J. Hughes's statement that "All tribes venerated the eagle as a spirit being of great power" (n.p., plate after 48) is an overgeneralization, but its importance among the Native Americans of the Great Plains, at least, cannot be denied.[34] Because the Sun Dance ceremony is also of central importance to these tribes,[35] Jung's interpretation of the soaring, sun-soaked eagle as representative of the sun deity is illuminating, especially his ingenious reading of eagle-feather headdresses as solar rays (*CW* 5: §235n, §633, §268; for the eagle as spirit, generally, see 9ii: §118; 14: §453n). But therein lies the problem: the propensity to use "winged flight" for spirituality and the soul and to see the bird as a *symbol* of some transcendental essence.[36] In contrast, the eagles and other birds of Black Elk and Lame Deer are also *actual* birds, and, whatever spiritual quality they are imbued with by Black Elk and Neihardt or Lame Deer and Erdoes, their status as one of the veritable "wings of the air" remains paramount.

According to Lame Deer, "We Indians believe that the eagle is the wisest of all living creatures," especially "*Wanbli galeshka*, the spotted eagle" (Fire and Erdoes 190). For Black Elk, the spotted eagle was the central intermediary of his initial Great Vision and subsequent visions (Neihardt 22–30, 35–36, 154, 186); the bird's message very much includes a theme of species interrelationship. For instance, when the "fifth Grandfather" of Black Elk's initiatory vision turns into a "spotted eagle hovering," the eagle says, "All the wings of the air shall come to you, and they and the winds and the stars shall be like relatives" (23). Later in the vision, Black Elk himself becomes a spotted eagle flying over the people and animals (and people-become-animals) of his vision: "And as I looked ahead, the people changed into elks and bison and all four-footed beings and even into fowls, all walking in a sacred manner on the good red road together. And I myself was a spotted eagle soaring over them" (28–29). Most crucially, this vision, as we have already seen, fosters a lifelong interspecies ethics for this man, which includes an understandable reticence in the slaying of these "wings of the air." The actual bird in the actual air frequently reminds him of his ethical commitment: "When I heard a spotted eagle whistle," Black Elk says, "for a little while it seemed that I was in the world of my vision again" (49). One point regarding Black Elk's relationship with the spotted eagle deserves emphasis here: he not only sees the bird, he *becomes* the bird. This identification is a far different gesture from that of Byron and his Romantic ilk, issuing as it does from a worldview whose rapport with the avian is not based on poetic use value but on a familial relationship.

Before his transformation into the eagle, the most uncanny interaction between Black Elk and the spotted eagle occurs early in the Great Vision, when the third Grandfather hands Black Elk a peace pipe with "a spotted eagle outstretched upon the stem; and this eagle seemed alive, for it was poised there, fluttering, and its eyes were looking at" him (Neihardt 22)—a return of the gaze, as it were, a mirror recognition of two independent consciousnesses. Indeed, what strikes one most throughout Black Elk's various interactions with the avian in *Black Elk Speaks* is how often the birds are as much agents of consciousness and volition as the Lakota *wicas*^{h}*a waka*^{n} himself. It is Black Elk's cultural attitude of openness and let-it-be-ness toward the sheer alterity of other species that is considerably different, I think, from that of Byron and Shelley, or even Wordsworth and Clare. Black Elk evidences a much more thorough and continuous *dialogic* relationship; the Romantic poets, for all of, say, Wordsworth's finer moments, forever return to a monologic reassertion and reintegration of the individual ego. My discussion in the first chapter of Vizenor's distinction between animal similes and metaphors might also be illuminating here. In contrast to the Native animal metaphor, which entails a veritable interspecies interrelationship, the animals of Western literature are much more usually simile animals—(e.g., Byron's eagle and his feathered Romantic confreres), that is, straightforward anthropomorphic projections, mere "caricatures in literature," symptomatic of "speciesism and . . . the monotheistic separation of animals and humans" (Vizenor, "Literary Animals" 133, 136).

Victim as I am of Western ornithology, I must pause here for a moment to examine what bird the Lakota spotted eagle, *wa*^{n}*bli gles*^{h}*ka,* actually is.

There are only two eagle species in North America, the bald and the golden. But, as if true disciples of Carl Jung, the Lakota followed the magic number four, conceiving of many groups of entities (e.g., the winds) as quaternities. And so there are also four eagles, as Standing Bear explains: "the golden eagle of the east, symbol of the sun from whence comes life; the spotted eagle of the south . . . the black eagle of the west, denoting sunset or darkness; and the bald eagle of the north" (*Land* 122).[37] The key to the mystery of the spotted eagle is that both the golden and the bald eagle take several years before their characteristic adult plumage is attained, and the immature of both have a predominantly dark feathering, mottled with white; thus the spotted eagle has been identified as either the immature bald, or golden, or both.[38] (As the child or youth of the species, the spotted eagle may thus carry connotations of rebirth and rejuvenation, whether or not the Lakota were conscious of its juvenile status.) However, one might safely conclude that the immature golden eagle is more commonly the species envisioned as spotted: it is much more the high-soaring raptor of the high plains than the fish- and water-loving bald eagle. Black Elk comments on the spotted eagle's high flight, its whistling call, and its presence in a pine tree (Neihardt 140), all more characteristic of the golden than the bald.[39]

The soaring nature of the Spotted Eagle makes the bird ideal as primary "messenger of *Wakantanka*" (Powers 88, 165); however, this creates a problem for Western commentators, who would reduce the bird to pure transcendence. Joseph Epes Brown's notes to Black Elk's commentary on *wa*^{n}*bli gles*^{h}*ka* are revealing: "Since *Wanbli Galeshka* . . . flies the highest of all created creatures and sees everything, he is regarded as *Wakan-Tanka* under certain aspects. He is a solar bird." But Brown must then transform the bird into a transcultural archetype, concluding that the "Spotted Eagle corresponds exactly[?], in the Hindu tradition, to the *Buddhi*, which is . . . the formless and transcendant *[sic]* principle of all manifestation" (6n). This "exact" (but "formless") correspondence erases completely a specific avian body of bone and mottled feathers: the eagle has been completely denaturized.

How unfaithful to the quite natural, even visceral relationship that Black Elk and Lame Deer have with actual eagles. Most of Black Elk's later mystical ventures are accompanied by real birds. His Dog Vision, for instance, is initiated by a spotted eagle that "whistled shrill," a "chicken hawk," and a "black swallow"; then "the spotted eagle on the pine tree spoke," exhorting him to help his "people" in a time of potential cultural annihilation (Neihardt 140–

41). Later, in need of a certain medicinal herb, Black Elk sings a song from his original Great Vision; soon the plant's location is indicated by "crows and magpies, chicken hawks and spotted eagles circling" the spot (152). Lame Deer, like Black Elk, is a medicine man whose main power, spurred by an early vision, is derived from birds: "As for myself, the birds have something to tell me," especially the eagle (Fire and Erdoes 136). When preparing for a "big ceremony," an observer need only "look up at the sky and watch. Most of the time you'll see an eagle circling up there, just a tiny black spot going round and round. The eagle power is always there" (166–67).

The ubiquity of the eagle feather and the eagle bone whistle in Lakota ceremonies has been well documented, including their importance in the Sun Dance ceremony.[40] To perform a medicine man healing, Black Elk asks for "an eagle-bone whistle, which was for the spotted eagle of my great vision" (Neihardt 154). Standing Bear recounts his father's dream in which he heard an eagle "descending," "whistling" as it came; he awoke to a medicine man circling him "with one of the whistles made from the bone of an eagle's wing" (*My People* 5). Lame Deer's allegiance to the eagle as his medicine animal, essential to his ritual practices, has already been noted. There is no time or need here to wallow in distinctions between a feather-and-bone raptor and a bone whistle avian mysticism; one would no doubt end in dichotomous Western readings thereof, an ideological spectrum ranging from sheer superstition to pure embodiment of the One. My main point is that a bird itself can play an equal, even superior role in the habitus of a human culture; here we are very far from the eagle of Byronic alienation or the flag-waving iconography of the eagle as the totem animal of the United States.[41]

Nor is the relationship of Native human with the eagle of the Great Plains a static, ahistorical already-been. The eagle song of the Caddo tribe that I've already employed twice as epigraph—"See! the eagle comes . . . . Now we see him with the people"—is much more than some timeless aboriginal entreaty for the eagle's power, and indeed, has specific historical, and ecological, ramifications. As a song of the Plains Indian Ghost Dance of the 1880s and 1890s, it is representative of a yearning for an ecological apocalypse, including the return of the buffalo and, above all, a rejuvenated, unpolluted nature.[42] Thus similarly inspired Shoshone ghost dance lyrics include such images as ducklings swimming in "good water" and eagles in flight surveying green "Grass and shining water . . . flowing" and the hope for a time when "On new earth all the birds [will be] singing together at the same time"

(Vander 366, 369). The Caddo lyric is not only connotative of a traditional avian spiritualism, for "among the Caddo, the eagle was considered a sacred bird," but also asks for the "return" of the "power" of the eagle's feathers as an immanent and natural reality (Levitas, Vivelo, and Vivelo 196).

Black Elk's various songs regarding the return of the animal "nations" are no doubt proffered with a full consciousness of the historical backdrop of the Ghost Dance religion, although his closet Catholicism renders his enthusiasm for the movement per se rather ambiguous.[43] (Furthermore, the Ghost Dance religion itself, like the later Native American Church, was a mixture of traditional Native beliefs and a belated Christian eschatology and messianism.)[44] But Black Elk's lyrical gestures toward the return of the Lakota Sacred Hoop are in the full spirit of the Ghost Dance's gesture toward an eco-return. In preparation for his Horse Dance, for instance, though the horse is the focus of this ceremony, Black Elk still finds it fortuitous to sing, "He will appear . . . ! An eagle for the eagle nation will appear. / May you behold!" (Neihardt 128). "Nation" is the rather untoward standard translation of the Lakota word *oyate*, which is better rendered as "tribe" or "people"; not only does "nation" connote an inappropriate political body, but more to the point, Anglo translators of Lakota have been less willing to consider horses, eagles, and other animals as "people" than have the Lakota themselves.[45]

The most commonly anthologized Lakota Ghost Dance song goes as follows, both a human call to arms and a naturist call for ecological rebirth:[46]

The whole world is coming.
A nation is coming, a nation is coming,
The Eagle has brought the message to the tribe.
The father says so, the father says so.
Over the whole earth they are coming.
The buffalo are coming, the buffalo are coming,
The Crow has brought the message to the tribe,
The father says so, the father says so. (Mooney 1072)

"The fathers have told us this" or "The fathers have said this to be true" is closer to the original refrain, *Ate heye lo,* in its more polytheistic intent.[47] For it is no monotheistic Father saying this; the ancestral (and plural) fathers who have spoken are not only human Lakota ancestors, but those eco-confreres and kindred tribes, the animals and birds (including the Eagle and Crow), who have accompanied *oyate kin* (the Lakota tribe per se) from creation itself to their late nineteenth-century plight on the Dakota plains. The buffalo people will return, as prophesied and aided by the eagle people and the crow people. Was this mere superstition and wishful thinking? (If so, then woe to the planet.) Or was the Ghost Dance but premature in its hope for this eco- (and Native) return, a miscalculation of time that still allows for hope?

Leslie Silko, among other contemporary Native writers, believes that the hope was premature. I have dwelt at length on "old-fashioned" Natives and avians here because many of these traditional views of the eagle and other birds are rehearsed and reinscribed in much contemporary Native American literature. Silko, for instance, has a fictional Lakota medicine man recite a version of the Lakota Ghost Dance song quoted above as part of the climactic final pages of *Almanac of the Dead*, as apt accompaniment to her own prophesied indigenous insurrection and return (724–25). Silko's *Almanac* also provides a fruitful segue to another central traditional Native avian theme, the "marriage" of the bird and the reptile, epitomized in the union of the eagle and the snake.

In preceding chapters I broached the archetypal conjunction of the feathered and the scaled, in contrast to the one-sided preoccupation of Western creative writers with birds as ethereal souls-on-wings. (There is certainly much of the latter in, say, the Lakota view, too, with its central privileging of the eagle as guide to the spirit world.) Rowland characterizes the typical Western opposition of eagle and snake as "the most powerful of birds fighting the most dangerous of reptiles," as the heavens versus the earth, as, at last, the struggle "of light and darkness, good and evil" (56). In less value-laden psychological terms, "the bird is spirit and the snake is the earth of our most elemental self" (Shepard 10).[48] But after noticing that Momaday's *House Made of Dawn* and Silko's *Almanac* both perform mergers of birds and snakes, it occurred to me that there might be a fuller (and ecohealthier) recognition in Native literatures of the relationship of the avian and reptilian as correlative emblems of what has been called the reptilian brain, and thus less eagerness in Native literatures to split the two as dichotomous elemental forces. This "marriage" of bird and snake actually supports my reading of a Native American worldview that is ultimately antithetical to a metaphysical dualism, a vision instead of "spirit" and "matter" as cohabiting manifestations of the same realm of existence. The deep ecologist Delores

LaChapelle, in her synthesis of New Age ecology and Native American beliefs, speculates about MacLean's theory of the triune brain (the reptilian, the limbic or old mammalian, and the neocortex) in an intriguing fashion: "Perhaps by facilitating the expression of consciousness of these two older brains through rituals, the human being may be able to communicate with the consciousness of other beings, such as animals and plants"—and eagles and snakes—"perhaps even back to the rocks themselves" (72). (Black Elk, as did all Lakotas on vision quests, went through long preparatory rituals involving chanting and fasting before a great vision occurred; relatively devoid, let us say, of frontal-lobe functioning, his psyche entered a state, perhaps, in which the eagle and meadowlark and crow could now speak.)[49] As *coniunctio* emblems of an older brain both chthonic- and spirit-receptive, the eagle and the snake combined must have had an even greater archetypal power. Perhaps this is why the plumed-serpent deity Quetzalcoatl appealed so much to D. H. Lawrence, as a hybrid being supremely evocative of a time (and place, perhaps: in the brain) when "the power of man was in his blood and his backbone, and there was the strange, dark intercommunication between . . . man and beast" (qtd. in Lutwack 139).

In Silko's *Almanac*, the eagle is replaced by the macaw (in Spanish, *wacah*), a close Central American analogue via its association with the sun and its role as visionary interlocutor.[50] Silko's chef-d'oeuvre is a novel of near-future prophecy and insurrection, in which the Native and mixed-blood peoples of the Americas march north from Latin America in fulfillment of ancient Native prophecy. "Nature" is a key player in the book, both mythically and environmentally;[51] indeed, the novel's eco- and social revolution is largely initiated by two talking Spirit Macaws in Mexico, who adopt as their human go-between the chauffeur Tacho (hence "nicknamed Wacah"), who seems forever followed by these two "macaw spirit beings." They are "big blue-and-yellow birds" with "cruel beaks and claws," who say "Wacah! Wacah! Wacah! Wacah! Big changes are coming!" and who keep "reading off lists of orders" for Tacho (468, 339).[52] Tacho eventually becomes the spiritual leader of the Native Mexican insurgency (allied with his more politically minded twin brother) that finally marches north, a major political faction in the novel's brink-of-apocalypse climax.

But the novel is also framed by a serpent, a "giant stone snake," that, unearthed ironically by uranium mining on a reservation, has also come back as prophetic promise of the Natives' own return to their homeland (92–93, 702–3, 761–63).[53] And though much of the novel entails the sordid stories of individual whites whose alienation from the soil leads in good part to their just as sordid ends, the novel's coda returns us to the Indian character Sterling, on his own return to the earth, to his reservation, to see once more the Giant Stone Snake: he "knew why the giant snake had returned now; he knew what the snake's message was to the people. The snake was looking south, in the direction from which the twin brothers and the people"—and the two macaws—"would come" (763).[54]

Much of the novel's power issues from its incredible medley of nearly parallel myths from many Native tribes and even African oral traditions. Through the African American character Clinton, Silko is able to envision the union of animal spirits of "Africa and the Americas," as "Damballah, great [African] serpent . . . joins the giant plumed serpent, Quetzalcoatl" (429).[55] Indeed, the figure of Quetzalcoatl seems to lurk behind the entire novel, rarely explicitly mentioned but, I would suggest, nearly omnipresent in its splitting into the Spirit Macaws and the Great Stone Snake.[56] Significantly, Quetzalcoatl also signals a backdoor return of the eagle, for the mythic figure was traditionally pictured as "combining the features of a bird—a trogon [specifically, the resplendent quetzal] and sometimes an eagle—with a snake" (Lutwack 198). Whatever the specific iconography, the anticipated apocalypse signaled by the *Almanac* is a return as much of the "plumed" and the "serpent" as of the human Native; like its ideological ancestor, the Ghost Dance, Silko's novel is also a ritual entreaty for ecological renewal. The eagle—or here, the macaw—is still bringing "the message to the tribe."

Before leaving Silko for a while, I must note an early poem of hers entitled "Hawk and Snake." After noticing both creatures in the poem's initial perambulation, the narrator suddenly becomes a cross-species merger of both, and *speaks as both,* in the marvelous final stanza:

> I am back again
> I sweep high above the hills
> on brown spotted wings
> I peer out from my rocks
> coiled in noontime shade. (21–25, in *Laguna Woman* 30)

Such an intimate union of bird and reptile, of spirit and earth, if one must, and of human narrator seems nearly unimaginable in the canon of Western literature.

Early in Momaday's *House Made of Dawn*, Abel encounters his own *coniunctio* of eagle and serpent: "He had seen a strange thing, an eagle overhead with its talons closed upon a snake. It was an awful, holy sight, full of magic and meaning" (14). Given Momaday's frequent play with Christian symbolism (e.g., Abel), one might easily succumb to a typically Western reading of such numinous signifiers, bringing in dichotomies like good/evil. But I read the "awfulness" of the pairing as rather the spinal reaction discussed earlier, wherein both eagle and snake evoke a lower brain response that is augmented by the animals' sheer similarity-in-contrast. This union is recast a few pages later, where a pair of "golden eagles" perform a Whitmanesque "dalliance," a courtship in the air: the female is carrying "a rattlesnake," and the pair play catch with it as part of their courtship ritual (16–17). And ritual is again the order of the day, as the birds perform both natural act and mythic marriage of the feathered and the scaled, and any attempt to impose some Manichaean schism upon the sight seems ridiculous. Paula Gunn Allen's reading of this novel's "interplay," or interconnection, of good and evil may be too dualistic: "The idea is perhaps strange to the Westerner," who has "presumed that the forces of good are separate from the forces of evil, and the universe is conceived as a dualistic structure forever at war with itself" ("Bringing" 575). As commonly happens with Allen, there is still a lot of Jung's European mysticism speaking here,[57] fresh from the Gnostics and the alchemists, for whom the good carries the seeds of the bad, and vice versa. However preferable and enlightened it is to a naïve good/evil dualism, good and evil remain, nonetheless, false, human-imposed valuations, in which an actual eagle can neither fight nor play with an actual snake, in which an actual human, upon seeing such a sight, cannot feel a warm tightening of gut and a shivering of the spine without the neocortex sorting the parts of this primordial *coniunctio* into categories.

As with Tacho and his macaws, Black Elk's more apocalyptic intuitions were often imparted by speaking birds. For example, when he felt a sense of impending trouble, the need to prepare for war with the *was^{h}icu* (whites), he "could understand the birds when they sang, and they were always saying, 'It is time! It is time!'" (Neihardt 121; surely Silko has read this). Sitting Bull, too, as a lifelong interlocutor with flicker and meadowlark, was thus an "interspecies *wicasa wakán*" (Lincoln 404), a happy phrase that applies just as well to Black Elk and Lame Deer. The more secular Standing Bear would still proclaim that "so close did some of the Lakotas come to their feathered and furred friends that in true brotherhood they spoke a common tongue" (*Land* 193). Lame Deer's first vision has been delayed to this point, to reemphasize that his calling as medicine man was also a calling by birds, whom, as the vision develops, he could understand: "Down there with me in my cramped hole was a big bird" whose feathers were "touching my back and head." Then there came "a voice . . . trying to tell me something. It was a bird cry, but I tell you, I began to understand some of it. . . . All at once I was way up there with the birds." At this point the voice says to him, "We are the fowl people, the winged ones, the eagles and the owls. We are a nation and you shall be our brother. You will never kill or harm any one of us" (Fire and Erdoes 15–16).[58] This climactic epiphany of Lame Deer's vision quest offers a Lakota worldview that today's ecologically minded might quote fondly and yet still consider quaintly antiquated. Yes, the contemporary animal rights advocate might easily embrace Lame Deer's vision as a *metaphorical* truth, but to imagine the avian-human relationship as a speaking kinship, to envision other species as *oyate,* or peoples, on a level equal to humankind—so far, in Anglo ecological and ecocritical writing, this has been but a cognitive truth, not an intuitive one. Perhaps it is time for a new worldview, then, that synthesizes the theoretical utterances of deep ecology with the practical and emotional attitude that might conceive of an "eagle nation" as a veritable race and people worthy of negotiation.

OF MEADOWLARK AND CROW

> Unlike the animals of Romantic and much twentieth-century British and American poetry, the meadowlark is neither more nor less blessed than man; rather, he exists in the Lakota consciousness as both model and messenger.
>
> JULIAN RICE, "How the Bird That Speaks Lakota Earned a Name"

If the speaking avian intermediary of Lakota medicine men was characteristically a raptor, the prototypical bird talk for the Lakota *oyate* in general involved a more common, humbler bird, the western meadowlark, high prairie vocalist par excellence. In the words of the modern Dakota poet Elizabeth Cook-Lynn, "The little meadowlark, *tasiyakapopa* [in Lakota, *tas*^{h}*i-yagnu*^{n}*pa*], is the most beautiful of all birds and the most durable. . . . To the Sioux, her song speaks of all things in man's consciousness" (*Then Badger* 14). Another Dakota, Ella Deloria, explains, "We think we understand the speech of these birds, so we listen for their songs" (qtd. in Rice 427).[59] For the Lakota, too, a little further west, "meadowlarks spoke so often and so helpfully that they were recognized as 'the birds that spoke Lakota'" (Rice 425). This close relationship even expresses itself in the very *melodies* of the Lakota songs, which are usually quoted out of their musical context. Examining Densmore's transcription of one of Sitting Bull's songs, Kenneth Lincoln notes that, with its "descending fourth and two cascading thirds," it is "something like a prophetic meadowlark's song, a recurring pattern in plains chants" (35).[60]

Julian Rice's essay on this species' centrality to Lakota culture not only illuminates its subject, but provides a welcome Native antidote to the general Western tendencies to romanticize and archetypalize the birds of literature. Yes, the meadowlark is "a bird with strong, specific significance in Lakota stories, ceremonies, and everyday life." But "noting 'meadowlark,' the archetypal critic might simply list the bird in the 'animal guardian' column and move on," thus rendering both the specific human culture and specific avian species moot. Rice will have nothing of this, and his contrast of the Lakota relationship to the meadowlark and that of British Romantics to their poeticized avians is revelatory:

> Their [Wordsworth's and Shelley's] responses to the skylark . . . are radically different from the traditional Lakota perception of the meadowlark. While both the English Skylark and the American Western Meadowlark nest on the ground, and though both have notably clear and musical voices, Wordsworth and Shelley are moved to emphasize the skylark's soaring flight while the Lakota meadowlark is most often shown defending her nest or perched on a tipi pole speaking humorously and helpfully to human beings.[61] The two British poets derive no such warmth from their ethereal bird, which serves only to remind them of the burden of their humanity. (424)

Furthermore, in contrast with the Romantics, "envy and scorn" are rarely components of the Lakota view of other species (425). Rather, these beings are "our older relatives and should therefore be addressed as *Tunkasila* (Grandfather)" (441–42). *Tu*^{n}*kas*^{h}*ila* is closely related to the Lakota *ate*, "the father(s)," as in the ubiquitous ceremonial refrain *ate heye lo;* in both cases, the invocation of ancestral reverence is to more than one's human relatives. This general relationship of familial warmth between birds and Natives that

Rice notes is certainly rare in the British poetry we have looked at—Clare and his wagtail may be the rare exception—but it remains much more common, as I will argue, in contemporary poetry written by Native Americans and mixed bloods. The Abenaki poet and scholar Joseph Bruchac even contends that, in Native cultures, the "forces of nature are personified in ways that" are "essentially *nonromantic* and usefully realistic" ("Thanking" 195; emphasis added), that is, ecological and pragmatic. The hard-minded Western realist might balk at Bruchac's second adjective after reading of talking spirit birds and avian grandfathers; conversely, the term "personification" in regard to other species may not be appropriate at all, in the Lakota view: they are persons already. But the general point I derive from Rice and Bruchac is this: the appropriative othering that I have perceived to be the dominant Romantic mode of dealing with birds is *not* the dominant Native mode; indeed, such an appropriation, including poetic personification itself, which assumes that other species are in imaginative need of such humanization, is very nearly obviated by what the Lakota call *tios*^{h}*paye*, the extended family that extends to other peoples, that is, nonhuman species, and the related concept of *mitakuye oyasin,* "we are all related."[62] I will more fully address Walt Whitman's complex relationship to things Native American in the next chapter, but I note here Paula Gunn Allen's opposition of this very concept of *mitakuye oyasin* to "Walt Whitman's Kosmic myself-at-the-center stuff, the unauthorized and natural given world up against the copyrighted *logos*. . . . It's the old egocentric final word of a patriarchal Power, compared with a bunch of women gossiping" (qtd. in Lincoln 122). Thus Black Elk's own magnum opus is not only the "Song of My People" rather than a typically Western "Song of Myself" (*pace* Whitman), but it is also a song for and of the "eagle nation," in stark contrast to the Western "final word" of homocentrism.

Besides eagles and meadowlarks, there were other species deemed mysterious and close to the primordial Thunder Beings, including other diurnal raptors, nighthawks, and swallows, especially the "forked-tail" swallow (J. R. Walker 102; Fast Wolf 436; yes, the same barn swallow loved by Gilbert White and Dorothy Wordsworth). The swallow's remarkable Lakota name, *icaps*^{h}*i*^{n}*ps*^{h}*i*^{n}*cala,* is likely (and if so, wonderfully) onomatopoeic, but it is the bird's remarkable flight that makes it worthy of the Thunder Beings. As with the spotted eagle, when Black Elk sees "split-tail swallows" at one point, they serve as a flashback to his Great Vision: "The swallows seemed holy" (Neihardt 59). Densmore's Lakota song to the swallow, "Before the Gathering of the Clouds," is rendered in Soens's anthology of traditional Native "poetry" as follows:

In darting flight
I have sent a Swallow Nation!
The erratic flight I caused!
Ahead of the gathering clouds
The darting flight I caused!
  My horse, like a swallow,
  Was flying, running!
  My horse, like a swallow,
  Was flying, running! (222)

The singer for Densmore, Lone Man, says that the song is to make his horse "as swift [and evasive] as the swallow" (*Teton* 161), and it is easy to read such an identification with the avian as simply an example of Frazerian "sympathetic magic." But again, "Nation" is better translated as "people," and this close empathy between human and bird, indeed the sheer surprise and power of the image evoked by the first two lines above, speaks of an interrelationship that escapes such anthropological labels.

The crow is not as widespread in Lakota oral tradition as one might expect, in part because Coyote and Iktomi (the Spider) amply fulfill the role of Trickster in Lakota folklore. One immediately notes here that the oft-discussed "archetype" of the Native American Trickster reflects a worldview quite different from that portrayed by Western metaphysics and psychology, as a privileged god seemingly both incredibly mindless and ultimately cunning, both canny and uncanny, blessed by a fateful luck based on its status as sheer instinctual *animal*. To follow Jung's usual definition of the trickster as some special instance of the Shadow archetype—or more limiting yet, as Freud's id—is somewhat helpful, but its positive privileging in Native folklore transcends both the Shadow's status as compensatory foil to ego consciousness and the id's connotations of a primordial psychic force in need of suppression and sublimation.[63] Of course, this excursion into depth psychology points, again, to a great cultural chasm, between the privileging of individualism and rationalism (or rather, ego rationalizations, for the most part) and a view that acknowledges the arational in human behavior and cosmic events, a view that allows the contemporary Native poet Joy Harjo to envision crows forever laughing at humankind through poem after poem.

The best-known Native avian Trickster is the crow's close kin, the raven, the main Trickster figure of tribes of the Pacific Northwest.[64] But the crow's role in Plains Indian oral literature is actually closer to the eagle as spiritual intermediary than as Trickster per se. I have already quoted the Lakota Ghost Dance song in which the eagle bears a "message to the tribe," and then "The Crow has brought the message to the tribe, / The father says so, the father says so." Its messenger status here may arise not only from its obvious vocal abilities, but from its sheer size: that it is really as large as many hawk species never ceases to amaze me (and truly stuns those who grew up calling a grackle a "crow"). If one compares the following Cheyenne Ghost Dance lyric with the various eagle Ghost Dance songs already quoted, the crow's comparable mythic magnificence becomes manifest:

> The crow—*Ehe'eye'!*
> The crow—*Ehe'eye'!*
> I saw him when he flew down,
> I saw him when he flew down.
> To the earth, to the earth.
> He has renewed our life,
> He has renewed our life.
> He has taken pity on us,
> He has taken pity on us. (Mooney 1035)

The foremost translator and cultural interpreter of the Ghost Dance songs, James Mooney, glosses the crow as "the lord of the new spirit world" (1035), key to the revitalization of Native culture(s).[65]

Aside from these perhaps tenuous associations with the noble raptors, it might be difficult to understand such an ennobling of this bird in terms of Western symbology, if it weren't for the crow's ecological role as a vulpine carnivore, which, as we have seen in previous chapters, associates the species with death and evil. But in the Native view the bird's very niche in the ecosystem is really its saving grace. Hausman's interpretation of this view doesn't stray far from Western stereotypes,[66] at first: the crow is still "the embodiment of the spirit presence of death in all things." But it is, significantly, a "carrion-eater, like the raven," and therefore ultimately "a cleaner, in a sense, of the 'negative image' of death" (23). We can see this positive privileging of the crow's ecoduty of recycling, as it were, in Silko's poem "Preparations," in which a dead sheep on the roadside is "carefully attended[!]" to by these avian agents of cleansing and completion:

> Look at the long black wings
> the shining eyes
> Solemn and fat the crows gather
> to make preparations.
>
> . . . .
>
> Only a few more days
> they say to each other
> A few more days and this will be finished.
>
> (5, 6–9, 13–15, in *Laguna Woman* 33)

What better emblem for the ecological cleansing that the Ghost Dance beckons toward, one that requires a rejuvenation of the environment via an ending, the death of a Euro-American imposition of smoke and rails, of an Old World ideology for which nature is an alien ground on which to impose civilization and order—and ecological death? The trickster crows in the poetry of Harjo, too, are still laughing at all this hubris, perhaps (and hopefully) to signal its end. But if the Ghost Dance of the twenty-first century fails, they will be laughing at humankind in toto, with a tragic, indeed sinister and death-rattling laughter.

I must apologize for putting much of my discussion of Lakota beliefs in the past tense, but the reality is that the "bird who speaks Lakota" has been speaking less and less. One of Julian Rice's Lakota interviewees tellingly complains of a latter-day "alienation from nature which *wasicu* polarities have brought about"; now the meadowlarks can no longer be understood (439). Standing Bear's similar account of this fall from animal grace is even more poignant in its "naiveté" (to quote his editor again): "The larks in our State, at that time, talked the Sioux language—at least, we inferred that they did; but in California, where I now live, it is impossible to understand them. Perhaps they are getting too civilized" (*My People* 39)! This perceived distancing from the voices of eagle and meadowlark is symptomatic of a general degeneration of transspecies connectedness entailed by Western acculturation. Thus Standing Bear's elegiac coda to *Land of the Spotted Eagle*:

"We cannot have back the days of the buffalo and beaver . . . and we can never again expect that beautiful *rapport* we once had with Nature" (257). Black Elk, too, his tribe defeated and now living among the whites, feels "like a man who had never had a vision"; worse yet, his people, with their newfound ways of getting and spending, have "forgotten that the earth was their mother" (Neihardt 167).

There is nothing more tragic than such a loss, a winged relative's voice rendered inarticulate. One thinks immediately of a contemporary Native novel, James Welch's *Death of Jim Loney;* here the mysterious "large bird and dark" that is the dominant hallucinatory image of doom in the half-breed protagonist's descent into madness can be read as a negative, ironic version of the eagle as divine intermediary, of the spotted eagle as the being closest to Wakantanka. The bird is intentionally unidentifiable but seems very much a raptor,[67] with connotations, no doubt, of the death-boding owl but also of the diurnal raptors of the sky, of, ultimately, a (failed) connection to the realm of Native visions. "Sometimes I think it is a vision sent by my mother's people," Loney says, but the vision is never consummated. As noble and necessary as his final suicidal quest may seem, Loney remains ultimately detached from his Native heritage, like the lone bird itself, whose flight is often "out of tune" and who has thus been rendered an emblem of ontological insecurity. The novel's finale is an ironic avian ascent of failure and darkness: "The last thing he saw were the beating wings of a dark bird as it climbed to a distant place" (20–21, 104–5, 179). The bird's literal flight is upward, yes, and yet the novel's tone and theme have me hearing Wallace Stevens's coda to "Sunday Morning" behind this flight, of birds sinking "Downward to darkness, on extended wings" (8.15 [*Collected Poems* 70]).

But Welch's ironic bird is much more the exception than the rule in contemporary Native American literature. Indeed, the many speaking animals of contemporary Native poetry are no doubt concerted attempts to reinstate the previous state of animal grace, as in Harjo's "promise" of a vision in which "We once again understood the talk of animals" ("Grace" 3 [*In Mad Love* 1]).[68] This promise reflects an ongoing faith that such talk still greatly matters.

CHAPTER 5

A Beatitude of Birds

Contemporary Native Poetry

Contemporary Native poetry abounds with wild animals and is sensitive to them and their habitat, characteristic of the traditional lives of indigenous peoples for whom these animals were not alien creatures but clan relatives.

NORMA C. WILSON, *The Nature of Native American Poetry*

Let my words
be bright with animals,
images the flash of a gull's wing.
If we pretend
that we are at the center,
that moles and kingfishers,
eels and coyotes
are at the edge of grace,
then we circle, dead moons
about a cold sun.
This morning I ask only
the blessing of the crayfish,
the beatitude of the birds.

JOSEPH BRUCHAC, "Prayer," in *Near the Mountains*

When Paula Gunn Allen identifies a "sense of the connectedness of all things, of the spiritness of all things," as the central "identifying characteristic of American Indian tribal poetry" (*Sacred* 167), her examples thereof are largely *contemporary* Native poems, the poets of which have usually consciously embraced the "spiritness of all things," in part, as a means of identity, or even, in Vizenor's terms, as a "postindian warrior" act of trickster "simulation." In the Native American literary canon of Momaday and Silko, Harjo and Hogan, there is a general embracing of animals as "clan relatives," as Wilson notes. Momaday *is* a bear, or so he claims;[1] Harjo seems simultaneously a mute deer, a powerful horse, and a laughing crow; and Linda Hogan's writing seems indelibly marked by the great vision and sharp talons of the raptors about whom she writes so lovingly and often. But Vizenor's revisionist positing of a "postindian" identity, of the seeming necessity of simulation as either false poseur or postmodern trickster, problematizes the whole notion of the contemporary Native poet persona. And yet I would still most concertedly present in the following sections (as Vizenor would still believe in Momaday's bear identity) the possibility of a cross-species transcendence, beyond the human Symbolic—and finally, the possibility of an *interspeciality* that would allow for greater, more authentic ecological and animal rights concerns.

But I am aware how much of Native American writing, especially since the 1970s and the American Indian Movement, is a conscious political gesture fraught with cultural hybridity and the defensiveness of the colonized that all such "contact zones" of colonization entail. Worse yet, since Euro-Americans first put pen to paper to *write* the identity of the Indian, an ideology in which the Native's own supposed taciturnity became quite *convenient,* the actual relationship of Native Americans to the land and other species has been interminably clouded by Anglo projections, misrepresentations, and simulations, to the point that today even Native Americans with ecological sentiments based on real tribal traditions must still play within the game, must express their eco-love and eco-outrage through cultural filters that have become that game's very rules. Thus for me to speak of an "authentic" return to some aboriginal appreciation of other species in any but a reinscribed or metaphorical fashion would be disingenuous. The new reimagining of the bird and animal that I see to be in progress is really a cross-cultural pollination that includes the contributions of white authors such as Robert Francis, Wendell Berry, Gary Snyder, Robert Bly, James Wright, W. S. Merwin, and Mary Oliver in a revival meeting, as it were, at Joy Harjo's "center of the world," or "next world." Edward A. Armstrong may be forgiven the following assertion of ignorance because he was writing in 1975, but the inverse of his description was occurring well before then: "Nowadays poets, perhaps fearful of being charged with sentimentality, or too timid to tread where science reigns, are wary of writing verse in which birds are mentioned more than incidentally" (248). This may have described the literary environment occasioned by modernism and the new criticism (and even then, Stevens and Jeffers, and later, Francis, were notable exceptions), but the American poetry of at least the past forty years, both Anglo and Native, is so replete with ornithic imagery that my ability to confine myself to a very small representative sampling thereof has been severely challenged indeed.

HALF-BREEDS AND HALF-WHITMANIC "BARBARIC YAWPS"

> The spotted hawk swoops by and accuses me, he complains of my gab and
> my loitering.
>
> I too am not a bit tamed, I too am untranslatable,
>
> I sound my barbaric yawp over the roofs of the world.
>
> WALT WHITMAN, "Song of Myself," in *Poetry and Prose*

> Whitman is a born Hopi.
>
> ANGUS FLETCHER, *A New Theory for American Poetry*

Returning to the central importance of "hybridity," one must first point out that the hybrid status of current Native writing begins with *biological* hybridity, the undeniable fact that nearly all Native writers of any renown are mixed bloods, not only of "white" and "Indian," but of different Native tribes themselves.[2] Thus N. Scott Momaday is Kiowa, "Cherokee, Scottish, and French"; Lance Henson is "Cheyenne, Oglala, and French"; and the list goes on (N. Wilson, *Nature* 32, 66).[3] The poet Wendy Rose claims not only Native American blood (Hopi and Miwok), but also "English, German, Scottish, and Irish." Author of a collection of poems aptly titled *The Halfbreed Chronicles*, Rose contends that there are definite artistic advantages, and responsibilities, to being a "half-breed":[4] such an individual has the "important" job of "writing poems that cause us to reexamine and end our mistreatment of those who do not easily fit into any one narrow category of human beings" (N. Wilson, *Nature* 99, 107). The obvious extension here is that of species; no doubt the "mixed blood" on the borders of humankind is more likely to perceive, and to speak for, the borders, too, of human and animal. Thus can Tess Gallagher, in her essay "Venison Pie: From the Journal of a Contemporary Hybrid," identify so passionately with hummingbirds, because the "great variety of [hummingbird] hybrids is impressive" (417). As a human hybrid, Gallagher must admire such alter-species hybridity, and the relative ease with which this transspecies identification is made is also due in no small part, I think, to the writer's transethnic identity, or lack thereof.

In sum, the "hybrid poet," above all, "proves animal-human," and his or her ability to appreciate such "radical and mutual alterity" is what may finally "join and save us" (Lincoln 352–53).

But the realities of a mixed-blood identity entail mixed emotions, too, the result of long searches for "who I am" and sudden self-realizations that are often derealizations. Vizenor's several accounts of his hunting experiences are exemplary in this regard, as in the squirrel-hunting episode of "Death Song to a Red Rodent," after which he vows never to hunt again (*Interior* 167–70). His encounter with other animals in this text becomes a spur to *self*-analysis. Quoting one of his own purple-prose passages of empathy with other species in an earlier essay, he writes, "I pretend in the last sentence to be an arboreal animal, a romantic weakness [i.e., really, I am not another species]. I was neither hunter nor a tribal witness to the survival hunt. [Really, I am not even an Indian, at least in the traditional sense]." Instead, he is now "a crossblood writer and hunter in" his "imaginative autobiographies" (264–265).[5] The transitive interplay of cross-blood and cross-species is even more accentuated in an earlier version of "Death Song," which begins with an explicit reference to his multiple points of view (though here both are human): "The first and third person personas are me," he begins, and then immediately proceeds to discuss the compositional theories of one "Gerald Vizenor" ("Crows" 101)! This is simply the postmodernist deconstructing identity, one might say, but I would argue that such a chameleon sense of identity is more conducive to becoming an "arboreal animal," despite Vizenor's Trickster denial, and to make the existential choice (in the face of the lack of any essential humanist identity) to no longer raise guns to other (arboreal) species.

Closely allied to this biological hybridity is a cultural, including literary, hybridity that permeates recent American literature, or indeed can be said to be an intrinsic part of American literature from at least Walt Whitman on, as recent books by Kenneth Lincoln and Michael Castro have made clear. However, *Sing with the Heart of a Bear*, Lincoln's study of the two-century literary hybridity, or "fusion," of Native and Euro-American, is too glib and comfortable in finding a New World "barbaric yawp" from Thoreau and Whitman to Snyder and Merwin, as if the battle of appropriation and contestation between literary colonizers and colonized in this "hybrid new land" (xiii, 232) had been a smoothly inevitable evolution—as if the calls of Stevens's blackbirds and Harjo's crows were one long poetic glissando.[6] Lincoln moves, as I am doing, from oral traditions (including Sitting Bull and Black Elk) to the contemporary "Native/American poetics" of Momaday and Harjo (53); at the same time, his book just as thoroughly traces a uniquely "American [and Native] rhythm" arising in poetry from Whitman and Dickinson to Stevens and Roethke, to the point that his hybrid term "Native/American" is, by his own admission, "all mixed up, all mixed together" (401–2), in fact, an almost too feel-good story of American cultural hybridity and homo-heterogeneity.

In *Interpreting the Indian*, Michael Castro similarly traces the influence of the Native on twentieth-century Anglo-American poetics, from Mary Austin to Gary Snyder, with the assumption that the result of this cultural-literary miscegenation is good and inevitable, leading to "an image of the New Man in the New World that American poets attracted to the Indian have sought to create" (xx). However, this process of literary hybridity is not always a smooth one. For instance, Castro discusses at length Gary Snyder's white-Indian "Native Americanism," but then must deal with the criticisms of Snyder by Leslie Silko and Geary Hobson for invading their literary "native ground," as it were (Castro 139–52, 159–65).[7] The "progress" toward a near monovocal Native/American poetics is fraught with more ideological and racial tension than Lincoln and Castro are generally willing to acknowledge.

This tension is nowhere more evident than in the scholarship surrounding the towering figure of Walt Whitman. James Nolan's *Poet-Chief* may be a gourd-rattling overstatement of Whitman's indigenous American influences and "roots," yet the literary relationship between Whitman—poet of a "barbaric yawp," of speaking mockingbirds and hermit thrushes—and Native literature is a venerable one.[8] Nolan is at times even more consolidating than Lincoln and Castro, finding, for instance, that the "influences of Whitman and of American Indian poetry seem to blend . . . as if they sprang from an almost identical poetics" (2); indeed, Whitman was "the first non-Indian American to practice" a "poetics" issuing from the "land" itself (59). Whether it be environment or culture or both, this "poetics" issues "perhaps [from] a common source or model shaped by the singular nature of the American experience itself" (3). Too facilely conflating, I think, but it is supported by the fact that twentieth-century Anglo poets have often themselves assumed a close connection between the "Redskin" and Whitman's literary precedent of a persona, his self-admitted manic penchant to "go Indian," to spend "half the time naked or half-naked" and to become "all tanned & red" (*Correspondence* 3.99).[9]

Then we have the undeniable testimony of contemporary Native American poets themselves, as in Joseph Bruchac's claim that Whitman's influence on Native writers like himself has much to do with nature and animal alterity. With the magnificent animal passage in *Song of Myself* firmly in mind, Bruchac asks,

> if the old grey poet
> felt he could turn and
> live with the animals
> why should I be too good
> to stay and die with them ("Canticle" 7–11, in *Near* 63)

He even finds a common ground for Whitman and a certain Lakota *wicas*^{h}*a waka*^{n}: what "Sitting Bull said long ago" about our relationship with "our Mother Earth," well, "Walt Whitman knew that, too" ("Walking" 4–6 [*No Borders* 88]). However, the Mohawk poet Maurice Kenny has sounded the greatest note of protest against the general (and often Native) idolization of Whitman as Native, in his essay "Whitman's Indifference to Indians": Whitman's scanty mention of Native Americans in his poetry, the "shockingly insensitive" nature of some of his prose descriptions of them, and his hagiographic treatments of Custer all lead Kenny to lament "that the American Indian did not prove a fit subject for Whitman's powerful poetics" (*Backward* 98, 101, 106–8, 109).[10]

But Kenny has another Anglo anxiety of influence to purge: the immense influence of Wordsworth. Indeed, Kenny concedes, "Wordsworth held a firm grip on me for years: I've always contended that my worst poetry was that influenced by him" (*Between* 1)! We are thus returned to the central figure of the middle pages of this work. However much contemporary Native poets have expressed a love-hate relationship with the foremost American Romantic poet, Wordsworth lurks nearly as large in their literary heritage background.[11] Momaday, with his focus on "early experience and landscape," according to Ruoff, "combines Wordsworthian literary tradition with American Indian oral traditions" (60), and Jim Barnes's poems are often paeans to "what Wordsworth calls 'spots of time'" (99). Indeed, Barnes's "Decades" poem begins with an epigraph of Wordsworth's "splendour in the grass" passage, and then proceeds with such avian Wordsworthian lines as the following, with a subsequent nostalgic attempt at recompense: "In my first decade the days bloomed wild with ravens / gamming brilliance, jays thieving, martins feeding quick / above our roof" (7–9 [*Season* 39]). The "rehearsal" of Bewick and company's British stereotype regarding the jay's "thieving" ways is countered elsewhere in contemporary Native poetry, part of a general reprivileging of the corvid. But the other "rehearsal" is also clear, that of an early connection with the natural Other that is subsequently questioned via the reflection of (over-)self-consciousness.

As a final example of the problematics of literary hybridity versus cultural difference, I would point to a personal favorite of mine, Peter Blue Cloud's "Hawk Nailed to a Barn Door" (Rosen 141–42), a poem that I have taught forthrightly as a fine example of Native ecosensibility, but that the well-read cynic in me cannot read without hearing Robinson Jeffers's "Hurt Hawk" lurking in the backwaters of literary influence. The rough-legged hawk in this poem is already dead, and both poems are moving (and in varying degrees, misanthropic) meditations on another animal's mortality. Addressing the hawk now nailed, Christ-like, to the barn (by some unknown human killer), the narrator examines

> . . . your hollow eaten eyes and tight closed
> talons in last grasping, nailed through wing muscles,
> head down to side, crucified,
> curved beak slightly open to my own questions
> who has lost another particle of faith. (14–18)

As he removes the feathers for ceremonial use (for "sky lovers" [22]), he is overcome by the bird's very corporeality, especially when he grasps a "handful of breast down, / so warm looking" (25–26). Then he sits "down in anger for your senseless murder, / all set to write a bitter song" (30–31), and the reader of Jeffers's poem is prepared for the expected misanthropic harangue. However, "your feathers so close send me no messages of hate. / I look at your beautiful wings / and sense your flight" (33–35). Blue Cloud's attitude here is quite different from Jeffers's. Though he has "lost another particle of faith"—in humankind, apparently—the Native poet finds acceptance in the attitude of the natural world itself, and rather than succumbing to a naturalistic philosophy of blind fatalism, as is Jeffers's wont, he still has faith in the continuation of "flight," of hawks, of life itself.

CONTEMPORARY NATIVE POETS: AN AVIARY

> . . . we the people,
> as Aunt Jewell and Sun Dancers say,
> are an EAGLE NATION, now.
>
> CARTER REVARD, "An Eagle Nation, in *An Eagle Nation*

> i make this small sound
>
> LANCE HENSON, "woodpecker song," in *Another Song for America*

If there were a canon of Native American poems, it would have to include the Osage and Ponca poet Carter Revard's "Homework at Oxford" (*An Eagle Nation* 75–83), a meditative poem of more than two hundred lines very reminiscent of Wordsworth in tone and subject, as the narrator, stuck in the Old World hallowed halls of learning, like Wordsworth at Cambridge, thinks back to the nature and native birds of his home and youth. These include a red-winged blackbird "strutting, high on a dead top twig— / Tailspreading and flaunting his epaulettes and honey-creaking" (51–52). Revard then describes how the bird's "darkbrown mate and their friends would parley there" among the cattails (57), well aware that the female redwing's appearance is a quite different sparrowish brown. In another fine passage of poetic observation, "ducks flap[ped] skittering / Across the pond till webs hit waves and they bounced / Into the air with a silken shriek of wings beating in time" (84–86). The climactic avian image is the heron:

> —He moved on wings wide and slow-beating over the meadow,
> Rowing soft in the hush, in the rising sounds of twilight. . . .
> . . . .
> And now the bird comes down, the great blue heron,
> His long legs that had trailed like rope behind a rowboat
> Reach forward and down stiffly, his long neck straightens
> As the sailing wings cup and slow and he flaps drifting down
> Almost straight down, beside the water; he lands, folds his wings,
> Stands quiet watching; then stalks, breaking the pond's glimmer,
> And stabs—at what? minnow or frog? I move,
> And now his eyes look straight into mine, the wings
> Go up and his thin legs bend, he leaps, whooshes upward,
> He soars climbing the sky on his dusky wings. (102–3, 133–42)

After this uncanny Black Elk moment of an interspecies meeting of eyes (accentuated by the agency of the heron as the looker), the narrator reminds us in the very next line that this is no one-time chance encounter with the avian Other, that all the native birds have been (in Wordsworth's words) "chosen" for his "regard": "That time in May the birds would just be beginning at five" (143). Indeed, back home on the prairie, his avian experience is incredibly intimate, even tactile: "I know the very nests of its sparrows, / How warm, soft, scratchy-tickling[!] their linings when I worm my hand / Wristdeep to finger thinshelled eggs" and "the naked pulsing bodies / Of young birds hot and tender and blind" (161–64). As if conjuring the "one Tree" of Wordsworth's great ode: "I know where the scissortails' feathered cup-nest is set in a solid fork / Of one catalpa tree" (167–68).

Such fond avian flashbacks are intermittently countered by jarring returns to an Oxford present, especially the chilling image of "great wings nailed to the bookcase" (95), as if to contrast a New World attitude "wristdeep" in the affairs of birds to an Old World modus operandi that would reify and crucify their very flight. The poem's coda returns us to Oxford once more and now, appropriately, to English birds, to the "sweet gurgle of thrush" and "singing blackbirds" (242, 244). But he is stuck within Oxford's walls, finally, his own wings nailed to the wall, as it were, to "puzzle out fifty lines of *Beowulf*" (250)![12]

As for the multitude of other Anglo poetic influences on a multitude of Native poets, the long lists cited by critics and the Native poets themselves reflect in part a cultural insecurity, no doubt, a Bloomian anxiety of influence too consciously in need of claiming legitimacy through the adoption of a Western literary legacy. However, I offer these copious examples of hybridity *not* to destroy my argument that the avian in contemporary Native literature is somehow markedly different from the birds of Western literature, including Romanticism; as Norma Wilson reminds us, Revard's poetry is still very much a rebellion against the aestheticism and intellectual "arrogance" of, say, Stein and Stevens, who "esteemed art above the natural creation" (*Nature* 27). The birds in Revard, and in contemporary Native poetry in general, are more "natural creation" than othered artifact, for at least two reasons, or influences: the Native American oral tradition and naturist worldview itself and the twentieth-century (indeed, post-Columbus) Native consciousness of how that naturist way has been lost, the land ruined, and biodiversity rendered vulnerable to irreversible damage. So, while the third prong of influence, Western culture and literature per se, has resulted in a good many Native poems that similarly other the bird as generic recuperative icon (and do it, often, in well-turned iambics besides)[13], the former two prongs allow me to still speak of a new view of the avian reflected in much of the body of writing in question. In fact, the birder's obsession evident in the poetry of many contemporary Native poets, especially Joseph Bruchac, Carter Revard, Maurice Kenny, Duane Niatum, Lance Henson, and Linda Hogan, is rivaled in Western literature only by the poetry of John Clare and Mary Oliver.

The Cheyenne poet Lance Henson provides another instructive study of cross-cultural hybridity. Besides Whitman, Henson "acknowledges European, American, Spanish, Latin American, and Oriental literary influences," from Tu Fu and the haiku form to Allen Ginsberg (N. Wilson, *Nature* 69, 73–74). An earlier list of influences cites "Jung, Hawthorne, Melville, and Twain" (Velie 263). The best that one might conclude from such a compendium of influences, at the start, is that this poet is very well-read. Then one might easily point to the haiku as a seminal influence,[14] for Henson is a poet of precision, of a few well-chosen images and words, as in his "woodpecker song," quoted entire:

> i am making this sound upon the earth
>
> the curled leaf filled with water
> holds a looking glass of sky
>
> in a quiet place
>
> i make this small sound (*Another Song* 24)

Most impressively, the bird is doing the speaking here.[15] But the poet's corpus, too, can be said to be "this small sound," a "quiet" and "humble" deep imagist style that reminds one very much of James Wright and W. S. Merwin. When I asked him about the possibility of such an influence, Henson became quite effusive, acknowledging Wright and calling Merwin the most "mythic" poet writing today.[16] From a Native poet presumably imbued with the Native mythic writings of Momaday and company, this is high praise and indicates how far Anglo and Native American literary hybridity has come.

Indeed, the deep imagist school of the 1960s seems to have had an especially great influence on many Native poets writing in the 1970s and 1980s, including Linda Hogan. Paging through the Native American poetry anthologies of this time, one can even come away with a formula, if one is cynical enough. First, adopt two mannerisms from the oral tradition: (1) address birds and animals in the capitalized singular mythic present (e.g., "Crow," "Coyote"); (2) liberally employ oral refrains, preferably sprinkled with choice incantatory words from one's Native tribal language. Now add cryptic, semisurrealist, apparently non sequitur imagery à la Bly, Wright, Simic, and Merwin. Shake well.

However much my semi-tongue-in-cheek generalization borders on the truth in describing a certain body of second-rate Native poetry, I would be accepting too wholeheartedly the melting pot conclusions of Castro and company if I went no further. But, believing that the Native American political situation is still very much a colonial one, I would appeal once again to colonial discourse theory. Jonathan Bate, speaking of the development of Caribbean literature and identity, writes that such a "language . . . cannot help but be parasitic upon the colonizing language . . . as Caliban is upon Prospero"—thus the great literary hybridity that I have indicated. However, "as they develop they take on their own identity, their own freedom" ("Caliban" 157). More to the point, this identity through literature can be insurrectionary, even through the largely Foucauldian determinism of Homi Bhabha: "How easily the boundary that secures the cohesive limits of the Western nation may imperceptibly turn into a contentious *internal* liminality providing a place from which to speak both of, and as, the minority, the exilic, the marginal and the emergent" (149). The evolution toward a modern Native American identity has also had, in general, the advantage of the consciousness of Native cultural traditions and oral literature, so that writing in the language of the enemy need not be solely a mimicry of Western ideologies.[17] Rather than a thorough literary melting pot, I believe that there is yet a distinctive Native voice and vision at work today, and that it is in large part quite eco- and avian-centered, a mouthpiece for the "marginal and the emergent" of both race and species.

As the first significant voice in contemporary Native American literature, Momaday cannot be expected to fly freely above the Anglo literary heritage he has so willingly adopted, but one of his best-known poems, "Crows in a Winter Composition" (*In the Presence* 33), begs for commentary as a momentary eruption of the avian Real. The first stanza here is a mental and aesthetic composition of "snow" and "nothing" and silence (1, 4, 6), in which the poet artist is both "composing" and self-"composed" in his creation of a bare canvas from a palette of pure projection. But in the second stanza he is suddenly made quite uncomfortable by the arrival of stark, alien reality in the form of crows: "Whirling down and calling," they are "Altogether definite, composed[!], / In the bright enmity of my regard / In the hard nature of crows" (11, 15–17). The artist's "enmity" is a "regard" issued with a wink, certainly, an awareness of the irony of a nature poet's nature scene being interrupted by *real* nature. Norma Wilson compares this poem to Stevens's "The Snow Man," in its similar concern with reality and "nothingness." But Momaday emphasizes the real scene and landscape, and "life, not art," in contrast to Stevens, Wilson concludes; in fact, "the crows are the poem's reason for being" (*Nature* 40–41). However, one could as easily argue that Momaday's crows also work very much in the vein of Stevens's strutting and squawking grackles, which are life, not art, too, I think, gross reminders of reality in the raw and in the black. Likewise, in Momaday's poem is no idealized, softly feathered nature or bird; this is a hard nature, strange and disruptive in its otherness, and hard it is also, ultimately, to envision such a nature free from the desire to compose a landscape and an animal alterity more amenable to human needs and desires.

Returning to another Native Renaissance author whose other languages have included talking macaws, I would address a few more of Leslie Silko's utterances regarding avians. I have anticipated in earlier chapters one main critique of ecocriticism and ecoliterature in general: the thought that all this verbiage about the land and animals is a retreat from human politics, from human, especially minority and Third World, suffering. But I have also read Silko's *Almanac* as a two-pronged literary insurgency in favor of both (minority) human and ecological concerns; if any book is free of the "apolitical" label, it is the *Almanac*. Indeed, the backlash against the novel from various quarters led Silko to consider the possibility of quitting writing, that is, at least writing of a political nature. "I want to write about macaws and parrots and things," she claims. "So I'll probably write about animals and rocks and rain" and avoid the political altogether ("Poetics" 65). But then Silko reconsiders her previous words, for "how can you write about macaws and not be political since where they live is being destroyed" (66)? And as we have seen, "where they live" is often the same environment as the human indigenous, who suffer from the same ecological devastation.

Silko also speculates, in a quite ecocritical vein, on the causes of such destruction; as a writer, she knows that part of the blame resides in a culture's very language, in the dominant tropes that would reify and other the nonhuman, the discussion of which has made up a large part of this present work. Silko's particular complaint is the notion of the pathetic fallacy; taught in school that "the mountain cried" was just such a fallacy—"because mountains don't cry . . . and trees don't sing"—the future chronicler of uranium mining and aviary burning must vehemently object, inordinately aware that this "whole attitude," at last, "goes hand-in-hand with destroying the earth" (46).

This is not to say that the use of "personification"—by this point, I must put it in quotation marks—whether by British Romantics or contemporary Native poets, does not turn often into cliché or maudlin overstatement, with an equally inimically reifying and deadening result. But this is hardly the case in the poetry of, for instance, Joseph Bruchac, who would make his poetry "bright with animals" and filled with the "beatitude of the birds." He does this often figuratively, including via the simile, yet the dominant impression is not one of an othering or use of the bird as pure ornamental vehicle. The simile may be as unassumedly yet effectively imagistic as the "creosote [that] shines / like a grackle's wing" ("Cleaning the Chimney" 28–29 [*Near the Mountains* 39]; or it may furnish a poem's main emotive power, as in "For a Winnebago Brave," in which the title character is portrayed as a pathetic braggart, until the reason is revealed:

> it seems that a bird of light
> hides beneath his dark blemished skin
> and must beat its wings
> or die of a broken heart. (24–27, in Niatum, *Carriers* 43])

The "bird of light," reminiscent of the frustrated intrapsychic bird in Welch's *Jim Loney*, must still "beat its wings," must tell "warrior" tales in a nonwarrior culture, to express an "animal-within" of biology and heredity in a conflation, once again—though here, quite positive—of bird and Native. Most effective of all is the simile in "Memories of My Grandfather Sleeping" (*Near the Mountains* 37): "Each morning I would / pull back that blanket" that covered Grandfather "the way one parts tall grass / to see if a meadowlark's eggs / have finally hatched" (5–9). His concern for his grandfather is as careful as his approach to the bird's nest; neither side of the equation seems slighted in the least.

In college, Bruchac acquired the nickname "Owl" because he "went without sleep night after night / in that autumn of my twentieth year / as I walked the halls of a college fraternity" ("The Owl" 2–4 [*No Borders* 12–13]).[18] But the appellation reminds him of the bird's call, "*Ko-ko-has Ko-ko-has Ko-ko-has,*" both an "ancient song" and his "brother's name" (9, 13, 14), and he is painfully aware how little regard his fraternity fellows have for the bird, that he is alone "among young men who did not speak, / who could not sing the language of birds" (27–28). The fraternity is at last a place inimical to a bird of such fearsome repute, an ironic "brotherhood," and likewise a prison to a Native "soul" who views the bird quite differently:

They could hold my soul in that place
as surely as they did not hear
that call from a spirit world others still fear
Ko-ko-has, the protector of our dreams. (33–36)

The language of birds is ubiquitous in Bruchac's poetry, especially water birds. (Indeed, waterfowl as border creatures of water, air, and land are apt exemplars for poets in general who are navigating between two cultures.) "Geese Flying over a Prison Sweat Lodge" (*No Borders* 25), for example, contrasts the imprisoned Natives engaged in ceremony, "waiting to be born again," with "flock after flock" of those other, free *natives* overhead, whose "ancient calls" are "of welcome and question, / seeking relatives / after a winter's exile" (10, 12–16). To the "Hiss of water on stone" from the sweat lodge, "the cries of the geese / bark an answer," "speaking words never written / that always mean home" (17–19, 21–22). The poet is not simply projecting some anthropomorphic wish to hear the actual word "home" in the geese's calls; he is acknowledging a prelingual ("words never written"), perhaps reptilian brain connection between two species who both know of exile and home, of freedom and the lack thereof.[19]

Another border water bird is portrayed in "Great Blue Herons" (*No Borders* 73–76), as a Wordsworthian "small boy" is captivated "by the slow dream motion" and "the measured sweep / of the blue heron's flight"; the bird flies "so close [that] one wingtip / touched his shoulder" (1.1, 6–8, 9–10).

The heron is subsequently explicitly identified as a creature of ecological edges, just as the poet is a denizen of cultural borders:

Blue Heron
is one who has been given
the gift to seek
both land and water
for its life.
One day I see it,
its sword of a beak
spearing fish in the stream
the next day it stalks
the nearby field for mice.
It lives within
both worlds at once. (4.19–30)

In the poem's coda, the narrator still watches "the flight / of the great blue heron," and "accept[s] it / as a messenger" (4.37–38, 41–42). Previously, the heron's close clan association with Bruchac's Abenaki heritage has been made clear; now its continuing role as a *spokesperson* (messenger) for some crucial tribal truth is acknowledged, with the implication, too, of a new message, perhaps: how to survive in "both worlds at once."

But just surviving in the present world is not easy, with the threat of global ecological disaster, and Bruchac voices this concern on many occasions. In "Coming Down from Hurricane Mountain" (*No Borders* 24), he sees a pair of hawks, one flying overhead, its "wing feathers spread to hold the sky." But the other? It is "in a spruce tree dead / and dry from the acid in the rain" (12–13). Further complementing the scene are "backhoes and dozers" and a "black dead river" (17, 20), mute cause-and-effect witnesses to murder. In "Dog Song" (*No Borders* 29–32), a "Raven's call" brings back "a vision of an older balance" (31, 34), of

a bay clean of motors
ice bare of tread marks,
earth bearing no human weights
greater than those of wood, bone, and stone
the humans and animals
still joined together

in that ancient dialogue of survival
and prayer, unbroken by the
high prows of whalers' ships,
the easy thunder
of high-powered rifles. (35–45)

What is absent from a modern culture so out of balance, so capable of such outrage?[20] An ancient dialogue between species, the ability to hear geese and herons as messengers. The current mainstream culture relationship with birds in particular is incredibly ironized in Bruchac's "Corners" (*No Borders* 52), which plays on the culturally significant shapes of the circular and linear and the pun on "Thunderbird" as both traditional Native deity and modern brand of cheap wine. "On the corners / in front of package stores," he sees people who have "forgotten a world / once round" (1–2, 8–9); they are stuck in a sharp, angular world now, a world "sharper . . . than the jagged splinters / of the bottle which falls / and shatters the Thunderbird's wings" (12–15). Once the bearer of spiritual intoxication and awakening, the mythic raptor of the Pacific Northwest is now the agent of a physical intoxication, and forgetting.

Not surprisingly, Bruchac returns often to his Native heritage for alternative visions, including the ability to perceive hawk and snake as a magical dyad. "On Lenape Land" (*No Borders* 44–45) finds Bruchac telling another of his tribal customs and beliefs. He notes the "serpent" entwined around a "mottled pole" and then "speak[s] of the hawk carved" at the top of the pole, "strong gaze seeing further, better than humans, / wings spread to the beat in its chest" (13, 25–27). As he continues his instruction, a live raptor shows up in synchronistic fashion, as if straight from the annals of Lame Deer:

Sometimes, I say, just trust your heart
and if it's right, a sign may come.

As I say this, hand on the pole,
I see the gliding brown and white
of outspread wings as the osprey
swoops from across the lake.
It tries to perch on the branch above,
misses, grasps from below with one foot,
rights to land on the basswood beside us.

Then, as it lifts its feathered crest,
looks back at us with mild fierce eyes
John [the auditor] says, I think I understand.
And we walk quiet, away from there,
placing feet with care on Lenape land. (35–48)

Having begun my treatment of Bruchac with his sometimes amazing avian figures of speech, I should now return to another Native poet and chronicler of birds whose tropes are likewise noteworthy. I have already commented on Lance Henson's quiet style, and the tropes I have in mind are just as quiet. Again, the bird often serves as the vehicle of the simile or metaphor but functions organically and appreciatively, rather than as use-value ornamentation.[21] Moreover, this quietude often involves feathers or flight. Thus "evening comes on," in Henson, "like a plover feather" ("the fryslan poems 1" 6–7 [*Another Distance* 16]); as "dawn rises / things appear from a horizon of crows"; "dusk is an arc of drifting heron"; and a specific moment in time "is an hour standing apart" that is "open as a door or a hawk whose shadow / is a circling night" ("dream of birds" 1.1–2, 1.6, 2.3–5 [*Strong* 36]). At other times, as I noted in Henson's "woodpecker song," the quietness involves the birds' very voices, as in some of John Clare's lyrics in which the bird is barely audible. Bruchac's loud honkers become in Henson a mere "murmur of geese . . . their wings sore with dusk"; then we barely hear "a birds *[sic]* hushed song caught in a droplet in a tree branch" ("two fragments" 1, 4, 6 [Bruchac, *Returning* 152]). Elsewhere, there is the figurative quiet of color, the quiet of the sky, as Henson paints a "sky the color of a wrens *[sic]* breath" ("at chadwicks bar and grill" 1 [*Cheyenne* 25]) and "sky the color of a splash of quail" ("autumn birds" 2 [33]). In sum, besides the actual birds in Henson's poetry, his very tropes impart an avian tinge to his poetic canvas.

Besides the copious realistic (or at least stunningly impressionistic) avian images in Henson, the poet also has a few birds appear in his poems in fascinating intrapsychic (or expressionist) fashion, in which, as in Wallace Stevens and the deep imagists, psyche and bird blend together. The young girl in a "poem in july" (*Cheyenne* 26) is a living part of nature, as Wordsworth's Lucy could become only through death and in retrospect; when "a bird flies into her sleep," there can be little doubt of her nature-ness, the fact that "she is sky" (10, 13). Stranger yet are brief ventures into the psyches of birds themselves: "what remains of summer / is hidden in the memories / of crows" ("The Cold" 1–3 [Niatum, *Carriers* 63]). The poetic fusion of real birds and mental states, and the imagining of the mental states of other species, all this works to contest the dualism of human and animal and of subject and object.

Although Henson's birds are characteristically of the smaller, humbler ilk, raptors also commonly make their appearance in his work, but a reference to one poem will have to do, a lament that the tradition of privileging the raptor is no longer common. Today

> there is no applause
> for the hawk
> flying into the sun ("cheyenne winter" 3–5, in Velie 264)

If the hawk receives no applause, no wonder the "small songs" of woodpeckers and others are ignored. Henson's own "small songs" are often laments for the oppressed and forgotten, including both bird and Native. If Velie is right that Henson's poem "extinction," with its "bleak / sun" and "nothingness" (1–2, 7), is ultimately about the extinction of the Cheyennes (263–64)—*I* thought it was about a bird—that extinction is figured most effectively in the climactic death of a (once again, small) bird:

> in my hands i hold
>
> the last
>   aching
>   sparrow
>
> who
> remembers
> me (8–14 [264–65])

Like Bruchac and Henson, Carter Revard is as much bird poet as Native poet in the incredible number of avian references in his poems. These often reveal a fine combination of observation and impressionism, as in the kingfisher and waterfall in "Wazhazhe Grandmother":

the dark water turning into
a spilling of light,
was a curtain clear and flowing, under
the blue flash of a kingfisher's diving
into the pool above the falls
and his flying up
again to the dead white branch of his willow. (21–27, in *Ponca* 46)

Maybe this fails to match Shelley's description of kingfishers in *Prometheus Unbound,* but at least these birds are diving for fish, not plucking berries against all ornithological common sense. And the "dead white branch" is a perfect final touch of realism.

The most common roadside bird of many a midwestern car trip, the meadowlark, receives it due in Revard's "Driving in Oklahoma":

—a meadowlark
comes sailing across my windshield
with breast shining yellow
and five notes pierce
the windshield like a flash

. . . .

and wanting
to move again through country that a bird
has defined wholly with song
and maybe next time see how
he flies so easy, when he sings. (14–18, 24–28, in *Ponca* 25)

The "five notes" are accurate enough, though I would say five "phrases" instead, as there are really many individual notes in at least the last two slurred phrases. More important, this is a bird who defines the habitat with its call, defines the home to which the poet is returning. The bird's ease in both flight and song may also be a model and inspiration for the poet in his own continuing survival.

Revard's "Dancing with Dinosaurs," as if a reincarnation of the Ghost Dance, is one of many contemporary Native poems that ends with humans singing or dancing with the (often returning) birds. This is no invocation of the eagle, the narrator is careful to tell us, but a call for the "small birds only"; he has "called them here / to set them into song," these creatures

> who made their rainbow bodies long before
> we came to earth,
> who learning song and flight became
> beings for whom the infinite sky
> and trackless ocean are a path to spring;
> now they will sing and we
> are dancing with them, here. (2.23, 26–34, in *Ponca* 62)

The specific occasion of the healing ceremony aside, it seems most important to me that the birds are a "path to spring," of regeneration and renewal, like the birds and buffalo of the Ghost Dance: "Now we see *them* with the people." And both birds and humans are dancing.

But the eagle is also important in Revard's work, especially because it is the central avian of his own Osage Nation, who not only came "down from the stars" in their myth of origin, but "As eagles, we came down . . . ." ("Close Encounters" 1, 3, 25 [*Eagle* 25]). Revard's most impassioned eagle poem is "An Eagle Nation" (*Eagle* 31–34),[22] in which the narrator and family come upon "this cage set off to itself with a bald eagle sitting, / eyes closed and statue-still" (47–48). An older aunt speaks "Ponca to him, / so quietly that I could hardly hear / the sentences she spoke" (65–67), but the narrator catches "the word / *Kahgay: / Brother*" (70–72). Soon the eagle begins to take part in the conversation: "He partly opened his beak / and crouched and looked head-on toward her, / and made a low shrill sound" (74–76), to the amazement of the narrator and other onlookers. Though the narrator has a limited knowledge of Ponca, he is aware of Ponca tradition and "knew she [his aunt] was saying good things for us," and even "apologizing / for all of us, I think"; moreover, the eagle would "pass . . . along" the old woman's words (78–81). The narrator's lack of fluency in Ponca gives the poem a quality of estrangement; the old woman's language is almost as incomprehensible as the eagle's, making their relationship all the closer. But the nature of her apology is clear: we are sorry that this present mainstream culture sees fit to imprison a being who is our brother, and indeed, part of our own tribal origin. The encounter serves as a reminder to the narrator of this connection, and he ends the poem with a fervent reaffirmation of that truth:

the voices still
are singing, the drum-heart
still beating here, so whatever the placards on
their iron cages may have to say, we the people,
as Aunt Jewell and Sun Dancers say,
are an EAGLE NATION, now. (142–47)

Maurice Kenny is another prolific poet of the avian. A New York Mohawk, he has a special affinity for the water birds of his region, especially the loon. In "Dug-Out," among the "coots and grebes, mallards and loons / the loon sang the loveliest" (6.16–17 [*On Second* 159]).[23] But Kenny can turn just as quickly into a semiscientific observational naturalist, as in his marvelous essay, "Tremolo," a tribute to the loon as the crowning glory of the poet's rediscovered place and home. Back in the country, "watching for cardinals or simply listening for crows," he is "making friends of old acquaintances" (*Backward* 164), like Wordsworth at Grasmere, as birds serve once again as primary emblem of a Native poet's return to his native place. Then he hears "a wail, the sound scientists say loons use to announce their location. It penetrates to the soul, the very essence of being" (166). Comfortably moving from ornithic ethology to the "essence of being," Kenny concludes the essay with a proclamation of natural rights, the faith that he is as native to this region as the very birds: "I've come home before it is too late to see the herons, cranes, mallards and kingfisher, hear the cry or song of the loon not as a visitor but as someone who has a natural identity, a natural need to be a part of the north. . . . I have a [tribal] right to the north, home; to hear the song of the crow, growl of the bear, wind in the white pine, the loon" (170).

But Kenny is also a poet of the raptor, identifying with eagle and hawk so closely that he describes himself at one point by way of a "shadow on shoulder / wing on cheek / feather hanging in my hair" ("Eagle" 3–5 [*Is Summer* 14]). In "The Hawk" (*Between* 17), he clearly states his disdain for the killing of such birds: "I never frighten off the hawk / With a gun or with a cry"; instead, "I have sometimes held / It bread and bits of meat / To coax it from the sky" (3–7). "Coax" is such a gentle verb, and the hawk's eye "Shines with a strange kindness" (11). The syntax of the final stanza has echoes of Dylan Thomas's "The force that through the green fuse drives the flower," and yet ends with very much a Native gesture, an embrace of the bird as a vital Native tradition: "What drives the babe to suck / And kneads the blood with passion" also "Drives my hands to clutch" the hawk's "feathers and wear / Them in an ancient fashion" (13–14, 17–19).

Kenny's identification with the avian extends to the crow and to corvid laughter: "My eyes are crows / who laugh," he claims ("Essence" 13–14 [*In the Time* 28]). But just as quickly the poet's persona can turn into the butt of the crow's laughter, as in "Hawk," in which he imagines himself as the small prey of the pursuing raptor. The poem begins with the crow's "laughter shaking great oaks," gleeful "to see me prey" (2, 4 [*Is Summer* 12]). In vain, the rodent-poet protests: "crow has lied in his smile, his joke" (19), but there is an undertone, too, of acceptance that the crow's laughter is a fit and natural accompaniment to the inevitable workings of the food chain. "October 26, 1981" begins with someone misidentifying crows as "black hawks" (1 [*Mama* 29]), but Kenny knows better, for "there are different tricks in your flight / as your wings flap over rusty corn fields," and "your caw scratches the sky" (2–3, 5). More important is the crow's character itself, its unflappability (if you will): "You are impervious to our conversation / and of my journey which begins / when you clean the air" (13–15) with wings and sound. There is a suggestion that even the crow's "death-laughter" of the previous poem is an ecological cleansing. Finally, the poet would take that laughter with him:

> You hunt and laugh
> at prints we leave on the fields,
> laughter I will carry
> across these old hills. (18–21)

A final crow poem is yet another version of the common theme already seen, of birds serving as a return to one's homeland. Here it is a titular "Brooklyn Pigeon" whose "Wings flash black" in a momentary "trick" of the sun (1–2 [*Is Summer* 33]), and the image takes him back to "home, winter, snow / crow on white fields" (3–4). He is grateful: "may sun and pigeon fool my eyes / again tomorrow" so that he can again mentally "sight the mountains" of home (8–10).

When back home on Native ground, Kenny is an earnest feeder of the birds, resulting in both full avian bellies and some very charming poems. "Late Summer in the Adirondacks" (*In the Time* 93), for instance, turns a subject that has been rendered trite in the hands of lesser poets into a lyric of ceremonial majesty, via the use of repetition taken from the oral tradition:

They have come
they have come in numbers
they have come for my
wild and red berries
they have come for my
ripe rich raspberries
the blue jays
have come.

The birds' return "in numbers" suggests the Ghost Dance lyrics and their call for the return of the buffalo and eagle. The blue jays here are not announced until the penultimate line, making their arrival all the more triumphant.

A poet whose eyes gleam with crows' laughter must be indulged in a few overt attempts at humor. One of the more hilarious is "Wild Turkey in Massena, N.Y." (*In the Time* 70), a "heard poem," one could call it, as it is apparently a fairly verbatim transcript from a radio news report. The turkey involved has been "Found staggering" in the city streets (1), perhaps having "consumed / too much beverage / in the form of wild cranberries" (4–6). And then the dry journalistic coda: "The turkey was jailed. / Presently is drying out. / Will be released later" (11–13). Finally, "Corn-Planter" (*Smell* n.p.) is a satire on the fake medicine man with the expected avian paraphernalia (with a twist). After several stanzas in which the narrator recounts his eight-year failure at agriculture, he finally "succeeds," in the worst way possible: "I make chicken-feather headdresses[!], plastic tom-toms and beaded belts," and "grow rich" (18–20), yet another member of Deloria's "New Age/ Indian medicine man circuit."

As a member of the Klallam tribe of the Pacific Northwest, Duane Niatum is drawn to the avians who are integral parts of his tribal heritage, the "Thunderbird" ("Round Dance" 12 [*Drawings* 143]) and the Trickster "Raven stealing light" (20).[24] Both play vital roles in the "Klallam path" toward which Niatum beckons us in his bird-laced collection, *Drawings of the Song Animals* (1991):

Brother to chickadee and wolf,
raven and kingfisher, deer and cougar,
rain soaked and restless,
I hold to the ground of these cedarmen,

the earth shifting and sliding beneath my feet,
continue digging for the dream wheel
of my great-uncle, Joseph, elder to Thunderbird,
hawk, and sparrow.
("After the Death of an Elder Klallam" 4.1–8, in *Drawings* 35)

The Thunderbird, a huge paleo-condorlike bird,[25] is roughly analogous to the Lakota Spotted Eagle, as the central close-to-the-gods bird of tribal lore. Even today, its image serves as an icon for tribal survival and resistance to assimilation; thus "Hadlock elders resisted the invasion / by living behind the totem crest of Thunderbird" ("On Hearing a Marsh Bird Speak of Old Patsy's Clan" 3.1–2 [*Drawings* 30]). The poet, too, has been taught to believe still in such avian articulation, "to nourish my one syllable of faith / like the loon's cry" (3.12–13). "Never knife the animals in your soul" (4.2), he tells his Klallam readers (a dictum that, of course, transcends tribe); instead, "stand like your grandfathers on this Salish ground / where shamans gave our darkness to the stars" (4.4–5).

The title bird of "Raven" (*Drawings* 21–22) speaks his Native name: "I am Kwatee, the Changer, your friend" (34), that is, the Trickster. However, just as Standing Bear's speaking meadowlarks became less and less articulate articles of faith, so Niatum's poetry commonly complains of this decline and loss of avian numinosity. To the words spoken by Kwatee, an elder replies, "You're too late, our children have fled," and the man "spit[s] on the creature's black toes" (37–38). And so the Raven, now "alone, beat[s] huge wings to stars" (40), drained of its power by the narrator's elegiac lament: "if the Great Spirit ever spoke, it / must have been" to previous generations (12–13). Another poem, "The Man from Hadlock" (*Drawings* 23), concerns a medicine man both feared and doubted: "a storyteller to forget, not believe," even though he "spoke to beaver, wolf, and bear" and wore the "raven's birth mask" (2–3, 9).[26] In the end, the people grew to despise "his stories of the Changer: / eagle, fox, and blue jay" (17–18). Yet the narration includes a key question that begs for a positive answer: "Who but he lived / in Thunderbird's ashes" (23–24)? Niatum's answer is made more explicitly in his praise of another elder, in "Elegy for Chief Sealth" (*Drawings* 31). Here colonization has won the day, to the detriment of tribal culture and nature: "The waves of ships, covered wagons, / broke your arrows, pierced your shield, / shot the eagle from your sky" (16–18). The coda is a call to the ancestral spirits (including Chief Sealth himself), and an express hope that something of a Native "return" is occurring, as "the remaining / tribes regain a part of the soil": "leave your children a small joy, / the glimpse of a heron, shifting in the reeds" (24–27).

This is no triumphant eco-return as prophesied by the Ghost Dance, but the limited recompense of "a part of the soil" and a remaining "heron," to retain the Native connection with the ornithic. As in several other Native poets we have seen, water birds, in particular, loons and herons, seem particularly magical as recuperative avian reconnections with one's Native roots. Niatum's "Heron at Low Tide" (*Drawings* 100) is a tribute to both the heron and his great-grandfather's relationship to the bird and a final epiphany in which that relationship is momentarily felt by the great-grandson himself. His ancestor, Young Patsy, "saw this bird as the sun's / first born. It stands . . . salty and as steady as a reed" (3–4, 9). Now the poet watches the heron himself:

> So when it jumps upward
> in a great blue break
> to drift sideways down Oak Bay
> I can almost feel it snap
> once for Young Patsy. (10–14)

The bird's "snap"—made more emphatic by the line break, the delay of "once"—strikes me as so visceral that I imagine a similar "snap" of sympathy in the poet's brain or spinal synapses, a kinesthetic conjunction for one instant of bird and elder and poet.

Niatum's tribal use of birds makes him no doubt one of the most traditional and mythic of the Native poets we have examined. One of his most powerful avian poems, however, has a thoroughly modern and mechanized setting: behind the mundane wheel of an automobile, when an apparently mundane bird appears. And yet the first noun of the unrhymed sonnet, "The Owl in the Rearview Mirror," is *miracle:* "It was a miracle he glimpsed an owl sway / sideways through his eye" (1–2 *[Drawings* 73]). The poem's conclusion is yet another reminder—or wistful hope?—of avian power even today, as the owl

> pulls him into the back seat and out the window
> by the power of its agile, silent wing.

He is the mouse paralyzed by its shadow dance.
So he goes further, lets it drive him home,
leave his soul soaring for the yellow sky. (10–14)

My selections from Niatum might give the impression that there are not many humans in his poetry, but this is hardly the case. Not surprisingly, though, I find the most interesting of his human-interaction poems to involve an almost avian retreat from the human, as if trying to continually reinforce a primordial connection with the bird. Certainly there are husbands who may have wanted to say something like the following to their wives: "He told her there were days he felt / snared in a nightmare like a sparrow / in the eye of an owl." But the later self-immersion of this bird-possessed fellow seems particularly Native: "He stares into the teacup out of awe, / rarely vanity. The eyes grow raven, / and the flight of wings are his" ("Pieces" 5.1–3, 14.1–3 [*Harper's* 106–7]). Indeed, as the very title of his collection *Drawings of the Song Animals* suggests, Niatum's embrace is more of the animal than the human: "The animals that circle the nightmare / do not lead me to fear, but myself" ("Album of the Labyrinth" 6.1–2 [*Drawings* 109]); his avian "flights" are not *from* the human, but toward a deeper rediscovery thereof. But in this same poem, he acknowledges that he might be deemed an "odd duck" (pun intended), or even a misanthrope:

There are friends who call me a hermit.
The last woman who entered
and exited my house agreed with them.
Why didn't they see the crow
outside their window was my heart
turning to cedar in their names? (17.1–6 [111])

Or that he was too busy (thinking about) feeding the birds? In "First Spring" (*Drawings* 112–13), an old lover calls, and the poet answers: "I say,—*sorry, sorry, I'm too / busy with the friends still left. / I'll call you.*" But there is the "lie of copper on my tongue. / Why tell her they're the birds at the feeder . . . ?" (14–17)!

If Bruchac, Revard, Henson, Kenny, and Niatum might be dubbed the Big Five among male Native poets presently reimagining the bird in positive naturist or environmentalist fashion, the avian references in the work of the

Acoma poet Simon Ortiz are just as impressive, if only from the sheer bulk of his published poetry. Although his birds do not usually have the observational specificity of these other poets, he has received more praise, perhaps, from mainstream ecocritics for his ecological consciousness than any other male Native writer.[27] What ecocritic, for instance, would not adore a poet who "says that he learns to build his poems by watching the animals" (N. Wilson, *Nature* 50)? Or whose dominant refrain is that everything is a part of the (environmental) whole?

Fittingly, many of Ortiz's most eco-conscious utterances occur in poems about hawks or eagles. Back in the time of "Those Directions and Mountains," that is, the four directions of tribal tradition, "The Navajo mind must have been / an eagle" itself ("Spreading Wings on Wind" 26, 29–30 [*Going* 86]), and the eagle certainly inhabits the mind of this particular Acoma poet.[28] However, for Ortiz, the eagle is no Byronic ego über alles, but a being who knows its place in the ecosystem: "Everything that is around you / is part of you," his "Four Poems for a Child Son" (4.17–18 [*Going* 7–9]) concludes, and it is an ethic derived from the eagle:[29]

> You see, son, the eagle is a whole person
> the way it lives; it means it has to do
> with paying attention to where it is
> not the center of the earth especially
> but part of it, one part among all parts. (1.17–21)

"Many Farms Notes" (*Going* 26–30) begins with a hawk circling: "only he knows / how to follow / to the center" (1.3–5). A much later section of the poem turns to poetics, an imaginary dialogue in which the poet intimates that his poetry is like the circling hawk, a center among many centers, a part of the whole. "What would you say that the main theme / of your poetry is?," the poet is asked. He replies that it is "simply . . . to recognize / the relationships I share with everything" (11.1–5). The raptor of "Hawk" (*Going* 102) is another such exemplar of true living, with his "immense knowledge / of wind" and "his perception / of circling slow wind": "This man, he knows / what he is doing" (9–12, 19–20). Just as the Lakota refer to various bird species as "people(s)," this hawk is another "man," and a man, moreover, who knows his place.

"Vision Shadows," however, is an eagle poem with a radical shift in tone, as Ortiz hears of "strange news from Wyoming / of thallium sulfate" (23–24 [*Woven* 246]). The reality of environmental pollution is not only an affront to the tribal landscape—"Poisonous fumes cross our sacred paths" (34)—but an end of efficacy for the raptor's age-old circling. Now

> Jackrabbit is lonely and alone
> with Eagle gone.
>
> It is painful, aiiee, without visions
> to soothe dry whimpers
> or repair the flight of Eagle, our own brother. (41–45)

"Everything around you is a part of you." Even "Jackrabbit," presumably, perceives and mourns the absence, and the poet, by heritage "eagle-minded," is reduced to visionless impotence.

Because of this painful knowledge, perhaps, Ortiz is all the more fervent in his affirmation of an ongoing communication between human and avian. In the human-avian interaction of "Hearts and Hearts," there are "Blue jays and pheasants outdoors, / and we are indoors" (1–2 [*After* 11]). All partake in the knowledge of a bond of "place," co-suffering plaintiffs in the harsh South Dakota winter:

> They see us peering
> out of the window.
> We see them in the yard.
> Each of our lives a distance,
> yet together in this season.
> . . . .
> Feathers, skins,
> hearts and hearts,
> eyes that meet
> for seconds, instances holding
> to the fragile margin, the season
> we come to know as our bond. (5–9, 16–21)

Here there is an instant of bridging the gap of "feathers" and "skins"; particularly in the "eyes that meet," the "fragile margin" of species is transcended.[30]

Other avian communications in Ortiz are audile and verbal, as in "Brothers and Friends" (*Woven* 164), one of his most concerted tributes to the animal Other. The poem's three conversations involve a magpie, a skunk, and an owl—the avians, the very vocal Trickster corvid and the bird of proverbial darkness and death. The magpie is "telling stories / all morning at the top / of his lungs, sitting on a nearby pine" (2–4). The poet's rejoinder is casual and good-natured, almost jovial:

Magpie, you clown. Longtail,
you surely act goofy.
Get a job, be a good American.
Hey, it's good to laugh with you,
to enjoy the life. (5–9)

The native bird here is cleverly aligned with stereotypes of the Native American, via the inside joke about getting a job and being an upright citizen for a change, rather than playing the trickster-fool.[31] The final image of the owl is far different in tone, the serious portrayal of a psychic evolution, from viewing the bird through foreboding human projections to accepting the bird's call as an utterance as "welcome" as the language of all avians. Now, all are welcome: "Magpie. / Skunk. / Owl"—"All are my brothers and friends" (25, 28–31).

The relationship to death of another corvid, the crow, cannot be ignored; in Ortiz, it is realistically acknowledged, even embraced, its very carrion nature reinforcing the ecocycle of life and death. In "Returned from California" (*Going* 77), Ortiz turns the tables on the typical image of the crow scavenging among dead carcasses: here the carcass *is* a crow. "Death is a bundle of black feathers" (5–6), the poet opines, as if preparing for some grandiloquent avian elegy. But no. "Other crows," rummaging about the garbage, "They forget easy enough" (10, 14). The black humor is devoid of any suggestion, however, that the dead "bundle" is just a lowly crow and that other crows are mindlessly uncaring creatures. Rather, here is another model, I think, for human behavior, the animal knowledge of being only a part of many parts.

In other poetic communiqués between human and avian, it is the bird who does much of the verbalizing, another instance of the avian speaking back in, or at least speaking through, Native literature. At times it is an extended first-person avian voice, as in the incredible poem "Baby Bird Prayers for My Children, Raho and Rainy" (*Woven* 203–204). Ortiz attaches a matter-of-fact epigraph to the poem to explain that it is based on "watching little birds learning to fly." The speaker of the second section comes as a shock: "Be kind, sun, gentle. / I am yet small, my heart beats / with the fragile cycle of the universe" (2.1–3). Just as "the rush / of my mother's wings / startles" (3.1–3), the reader is startled that this is a newborn bird speaking: "She leaves and I shriek / and I shriek again with love / and hunger and growing" (3.12–14). The point of view later shifts to a poet's persona of protective empathy: "Protect these little things," the human says (who would, however, never call his own offspring "things"!); "They are mere blood, bone, / muscle, and they are filled yet / with delicate dreams" (4.1–4). The coda is yet another switch in point of view, or actually a melding of points of view. On one level it is the mother bird, promising a literal flight, but it is also Ortiz, learning again from the birds, promising his own sons an upbringing of equal love and care:

> Put your thoughts in mine,
> your small hands, your dreams
> with mine and walk with me.
> . . . .
> I will teach you
> for a while.
> And then you will fly.
> You will fly. (6.1–3, 8–11)

I began my discussion of Ortiz by noting that a purely naturist description of the avian is not as central to his corpus as it is for the birdwatcher poets previously discussed. References to the generic bird seem more common, often used as bare images in a poem or passage that really involves a general philosophy of poetics or even the nature of reality. Indeed, several Ortiz poems come close to Momaday's "Crows in a Winter Composition" in their Stevensesque refusal of human projections. Notably, "For the Bird to Be a Bird" (Smelcer and Birchfield 109–10) is an insistence on species separation, not anthropomorphic merger, so that at last, I would like to think, each species gets its due. "I want the bird to be a bird" and "me to be me" (13, 16), Ortiz says, and it is an ethical and ontological necessity: "We deserve to know the bird is a bird . . . and ourselves to be ourselves" (27, 29). Another passage reminiscent of Stevens's grackle musings concerns a gathering of a great many starlings, a phenomenon that commonly evokes human disgust and alarm. One might expect a minority poet to defend these alter-species as another race of despised *color,* or conversely, as I have done, wax metaphorical on the sad advent of Old World avian interlopers. But Ortiz will have nothing to do with any such homocentric response:

> This morning in the newspaper,
> I read about starlings at the Air Force base.
>
> I guess they were but all I knew yesterday
> was that they filled up the trees,
> the utility wires, the sky, the world.
>
> That's all I know. ("Four Poems for a Child Son" 3.4–9, in *Going* 8)

Subtexts of alterity and colonialism might be said to rest implicit in this avian onslaught, but Ortiz's main emphasis is the sheer *reality* of this avian Other making its impact evident in the world. In my way of thinking, there is no better poem than that, an onslaught of avian images, sans human projections and valuation. Ortiz privileges such an ornithic poetics in "What Is a Poem?":

> Four sparrows hop about in the backyard
> near the path to the trashbarrel.
> They pick scraps and bits off the ice.
> Two blue jays come upon them,
> and the sparrows don't hesitate to flee.
> What is a poem but that?
> What is a poem but that. (8–14, in *After* 66–67)

And yet the dominant strain in Ortiz remains the neo-Romantic pathos of a baby bird and the Native eco-ethics of greeting other species as brothers. I end this treatment of Ortiz, then, with his magnificent elegy "For Our Brothers: Blue Jay, Gold Finch, Flicker, Squirrel" (*Woven* 251–54), as one last reminder of the poet's deep emotional investment in the animal Other. "They all loved life," the poem begins, but "suddenly, / it just stopped for them," thanks to the "sudden sound of a speeding / machine" (1–5). First it was "Blue Jay. / Lying there, / his dry eyelids" now "tiny scabs" (7–8). Then "Gold Finch" died, and the poet

> took four tiny feathers
> from your broken body.
> I hope you were looking at me then
> out of that life, perhaps
> from the nearest hills,
> from that young cottonwood tree.
> I hope you blessed me. (32–38)

As in his familiar chatter with the magpie, Ortiz grows good-naturedly colloquial: "Well, I'm sorry for the mess." He promises to do his best "to prevent this sort of thing / because Gold Finch, goddammit, / the same thing is happening to us" all (65, 67–69)! This is no "humans first" self-concern, but a simple acknowledgment that mortality is the fate of all species. The flicker's fate is also graphically depicted, his body now "Askew," his "Head crushed. / Misshapen"; there are "Mere chips of rotting wood / for your dead eyes" (73–77). And then a final coda of interspecies collegiality: "Squirrel. Flicker. Gold Finch. Blue Jay. / Our brothers" (122–23). The critic Roger Dunsmore is similarly impressed "that the birds and animals of the poem are obviously literally real, and to take them only in their mythic, symbolic, or metaphoric meanings as a sort of poetic way of understanding them"—a major complaint of mine throughout this book—"is to reduce the reality of their living and dying to the conceptual categories of Euro-American literary consciousness" (58). Indeed, through life and death and poetry, this close fraternity of bird and poet goes far in elucidating the work of this particular Native poet.

Other Native poets have written noteworthy bird-speak poems, too many to give but a sample. To reiterate what I deem a crucial subtheme of this chapter, it is the first-person-bird who is often the most effective spokesperson for avian alterity. The "Owl" of the Mohawk poet Rokwaho (Daniel Thompson) is no distant feathered harbinger of foreboding, but the speaker of the entire poem, content in its owlness. "I hear them . . . the crickets / as relieved as I" that the sun has gone down (1–2 [Bruchac, *Songs* 203–4]), the owl begins and, after some dark commentary on the inability of diurnal creatures to understand the marvels of night, spends much of the poem talking to its prey (idiosyncratically spelled and named "Furr"). In the finale, the "I" becomes "WE," literally its mate and owlets, perhaps, but also, by extension, all creatures and all psyches who can imagine an alternate reality:

> I wasted not a drop
> of your blood, Furr.
> Now! WE will strike as One
> and pleasure in the fresh
> rending furr.
>
> It is a night passage
> for WE
> who know this. (85–92)

Such reality shifting on the part of the avian is more usually the role of the corvid Trickster. Noteworthy in this regard is the Tlingit poet Robert H. Davis's "Raven Is Two-Faced" (Niatum, *Harper's* 329–30), a playful, postmodern treatment in which, although not speaking in the first person, this "two-faced" bird seems to be actually writing the poem, as in some of Ortiz's efforts. For starters, the bird's very eyes are visual on-off binaries:

> Raven eyes blink
> day/night   day/night. (1–2)

The second half of the poem is itself a two-way "blinking" that is the Trickster still at work, although, to clarify my reference to its postmodern nature, the following also seems an apt description of Derridean deconstruction:

> definitely everything,
> He's made certain,
> is the opposite of something else.
>
> There's no way out
> of his two-sided setup;
> you can turn
> this poem inside
> out, trying to interpret
> its other meaning. (9–17)

The term "postmodern," however, might describe the characteristic avian images in the poems of a good number of (usually male) Native American poets in a different way, in the sense that a faith in the neo-Romantic privileging of the bird has been lost, however painful the consciousness of the poet who would still desire such a faith. Symptomatic among these poems, the bird no longer speaks, or is a blabbering miscreant, or is a bedraggled shell or effigy or parody of its former mythic or real magnificence. We have already seen that not all the birds in Native poetry involve "beatitude"; sometimes they are more a "blight," a reminder of a larger cultural context that used to be and no longer is. This descent of the avian is often accompanied by the consciousness that the Euro-American devastation of both Native cultures and the native environment has played no small role in such a decline. But in the end the poet is left to deal emotionally and aesthetically with a cultural and ecological fait accompli, as in the following by Jim Barnes:

> No one has the guts to say where's hope.
> Crow's a poor savior anymore. Croak
> and feathers made the night. But now
> what's left? The flayed god and the scowl
>
> on the face of Spirit Mountain.
> ("One for Grande Ronde, Oregon" 13–17, in *American* 65)

Part of this phenomenon that can be noted in the work of Vizenor, Welch, Barnes, Ray Young Bear, and Sherman Alexie may be in good measure a reaction against cultural-poetic expectations, the comfortable Anglo belief that Indians should be writing about hawks on the wing that remind them of days gone by. In the hands of hundreds of lesser poets, the circling hawks of Kenny and Ortiz have become, no doubt, poses and cottage industry clichés, much like mass-produced star quilts and turquoise jewelry. Thus Alexie's satirically titled "Nature Poem" (*Old Shirts* 24) begins with the epigraph question, "*If you're an Indian, why don't you write nature poetry?*" The poem itself rebuts the query by serving up nature in terms of the social reality of "Indian fire fighters" (4), who must fight fires in that nature and sometimes die as a result. Alexie's "Crow Testament" (*One Stick* 26–27) has more of the true Trickster voice, perhaps, than most of the hundreds of serious contemporary Native poems about (or "by") the singularized, capitalized Crow or Raven. But the final testament is the most significant, from a cultural point of view:

> Crow rides a pale horse
> into a crowded powwow
> but none of the Indians panic.
>
> Damn, says Crow, I guess
> they already live near the end of the world. (7.1–5)

Such contemporary Native poets are too conscious of living "near the end of the world" themselves to "panic" overly much before the loons, herons, eagles, and owls that poets in the vein of Revard and Kenny write of in reverence. By "panic," of course, I mean that visceral-tribal appreciation for the avian that might be taken as superstition, even fear. Thankfully, these formulations from "near the end of the world" are not the final word in the Native reimagining of the avian.

DANCES OF FEATHERS: CONTEMPORARY NATIVE ECOFEMINIST POETS

> Wake up, we are women.
> The shells are on our backs.
> We are amber,
> the small animals
> are gold inside us.
> LINDA HOGAN, "Turtle," in *Calling Myself Home*

> Let's dance the dance of feathers,
> the dance of birds.
> PAULA GUNN ALLEN, "Kopis'taya, A Gathering of Spirits," in Niatum, *Harper's Anthology of 20th Century Native American Poetry*

Kenneth Lincoln describes the recent advent of so many good women Native poets in grand terms: "Across the great divides of race and gender rise the darker sisters of Eve, daughters of Pocahontas . . . and Sacajawea, setting ancient tribal rhythms in verse" (xxiv).[32] Without contributing my own overgeneralizations regarding women and the body and the land, it is true that these Native daughters are usually even more eco-conscious than their brothers, and their various ventures into creative nonfiction, especially, often fit comfortably under the rubric of ecofeminism. Indeed, Linda Hogan, author of the ecoclassic, *Dwellings*, and coeditor of the ecofeminist collection *Intimate Nature* is as well-known as an eco- and animal spokesperson as she is as a Native poet. I have already noted at several points how women and Native Americans and other species make up a triumvirate of abjectness and therefore affinity. Hogan makes a similar point: "Women and Indians are often equated with animals, in ways that have negative connotations for all three" (qtd. in Alaimo 58).[33] Thus for these writers to protest the othering of all three is only natural. One might even argue that the Native woman ecofeminist is, in a fundamental way, *the* renascent Native voice today. As Joy Harjo claims, "There is a new language coming about" in, for example, the work of "Linda Hogan, Alice Walker—it's coming from the women" (*Spiral* 63–64). I offer the following examples of that language not primarily as some necessary antidote to or salvation from the decadence of Alexie and company, but as evidence of what may well be the most vital thread of contemporary Native American literature, both tribally and ecologically speaking.

The abundant ecological themes of Linda Hogan and Joy Harjo will be developed in later sections; here the breadth of this consciousness among other Native women writers can only be fleetingly indicated by a few examples. Paula Gunn Allen's "Los Angeles, 1980" (Velie 233–35), for instance, develops a line of thought already developed in Silko, that the contemporary West is a "death culture" (1), unaware of its plight. But the "trees know. / Look. / They are dying," and the "small birds . . . know" (10–13, 15). It is the "death people" (65) who do not know, cognitively, however much their genes know, however much "their silent hearts beat / slow with knowledge their bodies share / with the birds" (40–42). This knowledge of the "body" and the "animal" is what poets such as Allen would recover.

The rebirth via avians in Allen's "Kopis'taya, A Gathering of Spirits" (Niatum, *Harper's* 126–28) is of a more explicitly feminist nature. "We are the women of daylight" (22), Allen half-celebrates, half-laments, speaking for lives of hard work and troubled relationships. But at night, these women also have quite avian feelings of physical centering,

certain thoughts, a motion that is soft
imperceptible, a twilight rain,
soft feather's fall, a small body dropping
into its nest, rustling, murmuring, settling
in for the night. (7–11)

Lives disturbed by "daylight" here find a deep and comforting repose in a return to a "nest" of phylogenic memory. Allen's concluding call is for this avian connection to be returned to the light of day, to be made active and conscious rather than merely passive and unconscious: "Let's dance the dance of feathers, / the dance of birds" (47–48), both a powerful and specifically female (and avian) Ghost Dance of revivalism.

In such poets as Paula Gunn Allen and Louise Erdrich, a (re)turn to Native spiritualism sometimes may seem too hyperbolic to bear, and a similar complaint may be made against what has been called the "spiritual ecology" of Linda Hogan, although her even greater naturalistic tendencies serve as ample antidote. But the major reclamation project that many of these poets perceive as necessary may well be in need of such an infusion of hyperbole; I would argue that such a *pose* is as legitimate, in Vizenor's "postindian" sense, as the mocking personae of Alexie and his brothers.

Perhaps only a Native woman could satirize the still dominant Western patriarchal drive toward categorization and naming as well as the Yaqui poet Anita Endrezze does in "Birdwatching at Fan Lake" (Niatum, *Harper's* 307–9). Obviously, the poet narrator is only "along for the ride" in this poem, not an obsessive birder; this allows her an outsider's point of view that paints the whole list-making pastime as fairly (and rightfully) ridiculous. "In my lap: the red Book of Birds" (3), the poet announces early on, but the reader soon strongly suspects that the book belongs to her more earnest male companion. Certainly he would not make the serendipitous observation that "the mallard . . . floats / like bread on the water" (7–8). The narrator's need to poeticize the nature outing continues:

Waxwings sing to a chokecherry sun,

their throats shrill glass whistles.
We check our lists, compare.

Mine has notes like: the birds fly
into the white corridor of the sky.

Or: does the ruffed grouse's drumming
enter into the memories of trees? (20–26)

Having once written a poem that described the waxwing's voice in a quite similar metaphor, I can attest to Endrezze's fine observational veracity in this regard. But the whole occupation of list keeping becomes a joke to the poet, or rather an outlet for further imaginative leaps. Even her companion makes an attempt at metaphor: "You take my hand and call it *wing*" (41). Then Endrezze offers a cadenza flourish that lies completely, willfully outside the pale of the language of ornithology:

Look: the long-necked herons
in the green-billed water

are pewter. Their wet-ash wings wear
medallions of patience. We drift on,

buoyed by the tiny currents between us,
the light long-legged, the wind

full of hearts that beat quick
and strong. (45–52)

Here is another appreciation of herons, with a figurative twist. She has previously described these herons in terms of the adjacent flora: the birds are "tall reeds with eyes" (10); here, not the herons but the surrounding water itself is "green-billed." The great confusion of tenors and vehicles creates a rather symboliste merging of the scene, as bird, plant, and water, borrowing attributes from each other, blend into a marvelous watercolor that has been left out in the rain.

Endrezze's final lines regarding birds' "hearts" is, of course, another poetic turn encountered only rarely in only in the most effusive of naturist prose. But this is yet another particular strength, as I see it, of the poetry of Native women writing today, this very humanizing of the avian, without, relatively speaking, the Romantic gesture to thus render the bird completely *human*, and Same. To tentatively subscribe again to Buell's notion of good naturist literature as an imaginative act toward greater eco-consciousness, such poetic acts of humanization are welcome and necessary.

A DISCIPLE OF BIRDS: LINDA HOGAN

> Ours is a language of commerce and trade, of laws that can be bent in order that treaties might be broken, land wounded beyond healing. It is a language that is limited, emotionally and spiritually. . . . The ears of this language do not often hear the songs of the white egrets. . . . So we make our own songs . . . searching for a new way to speak . . . to say that wilderness and water, blue herons and orange newts are invaluable not just to us, but in themselves. . . . Now I am a disciple of birds.
>
> LINDA HOGAN, *Dwellings* 45–46, 148

Linda Hogan's relationship with other species is a quite personal, and communicative, one, in both her life and her writing. In her poetry, she "talks with and about plants and especially animals" (Lincoln 357). Lincoln stresses again and again Hogan's "interspecies insistence," her hope and need for "interspecies exchange," her overarching interest in "interspecies connections" (401, 350, 349). Furthermore, if Hogan's writing is as imbued with Native spirituality as the work of, say, Silko and Harjo, it is also, in the spirit of Rachel Carson and Annie Dillard, fully versed in Western ecology. And so Lincoln also dubs her a "spiritual zoologist, whose scientific empathy bridges ecology and *Takuskanskan*" (the Lakota "spirit," or *physics,* of energy in motion [345]). As earnest scribe of both Chickasaw culture and green politics, she combines "spiritual intuition with environmental activism" (357).

What Hogan hardly ever does is use her animals as traditional homocentric tropes. Ruoff's contention that "many of her poems focus on the power and beauty of nature, which Hogan often uses as a metaphor for [human] life" (98), is a gross misreading, a denial of her central theme of species egalitarianism and the integrity of nature itself. Indeed, Hogan's central tenet is that other species are integral beings *not* to be used, either imaginatively or physically, for the whims of humankind. This belief came to her at an early age. As she relates in an interview, "People used to think I was a very strange person, because when I was a child, I was speaking out for the animals, and I always will. I was in a workshop once, and they said, oh, is this another animal poem that you're bringing in today?" (qtd. in P. G. Allen, *Sacred* 168).

Hogan's liminal status as a mixed-blood woman "born between cultures" (N. Wilson, *Nature* 94), apparently irrationally enamored with bats and wolves and raptors, allows for a poetry and prose of great permeability, a porousness in which races and species interplay at will. Even her tribal heritage is a fusion of species: "The name Chickasaw is a bird sound. It whistles when you say it" (Hausman 36). Her stated literary influences include Neruda and Elizabeth Bishop, but significantly, she deems such influences only on a par with "trees, weather, dreams, insects, sun" (qtd. in N. Wilson, *Nature* 89). There is also a certain deep imagist, magicosurrealism in her style that reminds one of Bly or Simic, as in the "Landscape of Animals":

> The bodies of animals
> against earth.
> They are silent in the dark
> shadows of trees.
> . . . .
> The deer have gone over
> into birds
> and the birds
> fly through me
> a breath apart. (1–4, 19–23, in *Eclipse* 5)

Her poem "Magpie," moreover, is interesting both in granting its title bird the power of speech and in its quite Bly-like final strophe, in which the bird's black-and-white plumage undergoes a dreamlike transformation:

> Oyster white, a chest opens
> from black pilfered cloth,
> luminous
> pale breasts
> discovered on an old crone
> who buys herself
> out on bond. (23–29, in *Eclipse* 12)

Such stylistic mannerisms, however, never evolve into the full-blown retreat from the natural world that I perceive in the more surrealist poetry of James Welch and Ray Young Bear. Even here, the apparently out-of-the-blue image of the "old crone" is, after all, a woman, and a woman once in bondage, a conflated abject image of both bird and female well in accord with Hogan's ecofeminist beliefs.

It is difficult to distinguish the creative leaps of Hogan's poetry from the earnest ecological arguments of her nonfiction prose. The prose essays of *Dwellings*, for instance, are filled with pregnant paragraphs that might be deemed fine prose poems in another context. I pause here to note that this merger of the Western literary categories of "poetry" and "prose" has been a distinctive feature of the Native Renaissance from its beginnings, from the poetic prose of *The Way to Rainy Mountain* and the verse interludes of *Ceremony* to Harjo's recent long masterpiece, "Returning from the Enemy," which follows the example of Ortiz's *From Sand Creek* and *After and Before the Lightning* in interrupting the poetry with journalistic prose interludes.[34] On a more negative note, Kenneth Lincoln can ask in all seriousness, "Is Hogan's free verse prosaic, formalists might worry, her prose too lyric?" (358). Such a formalist distinction is, once again, too tied to Western categories; in fact, what better genre for a hybrid or mixed-blood writer than a hybrid or mixed genre, a transcending of the borders of genre, just as mixed-blood authors commonly attempt to transcend the borders of species?

Hogan's general call for a "bridging" or "crossing" of species "borders" issues from her belief that the "crisis of Western culture is ecological" (*Dwellings* 94) and that the cause of this crisis is Western culture's alienation from nature itself: "We have been wounded by a dominating culture that has feared and hated the natural world, has not listened to the voice of the land, has not believed in the inner worlds of human dreaming and intuition" (82). Now "there is a separation that has taken place between us and nature. Something has broken deep in the core of ourselves. . . . The result is a spiritual fragmentation that has accompanied our ecological destruction" (52). Hogan's remedy for this crisis of separation is a recovery of the repressed and abject, both in nature and in the human psyche, an acknowledgment of a long-denied "underside of our lives" that includes "the last, extinct song of a bird" (130). The bird is central here; indeed, the gist of many of the essays in *Dwellings* is the call for, even a prediction of, a new and imminent interspeciality, a rediscovery of humankind's "responsibilities . . . to the other species who share our journeys" (11). The book's very dedication is an affirmation of the relatedness of human ancestors and other species, and women: "For my Grandmothers, / and for Grandmother, / the Golden Eagle" (5).[35] Furthermore, this quest for "an ecology of mind" is, ultimately, a revolution in ethics, an "act of emergence, of liberation for not only the animals of earth, but for our own selves" (60, 54).

This turn to human psychology brings up a key, and potentially problematic, component of Hogan's work: like several other Native American writers who have turned to Western thinkers through which to defend a non-Western worldview, she has been influenced by Carl Jung and must therefore be ever wary of the danger of psychologizing away the animals and environment completely. For instance, aside from the many avians in *Dwellings*, one of Hogan's most notable crossings of the border is her encounter with timber wolves. In "Deify the Wolf," the wolf's cry becomes a Jungian evocation of a blood memory, "the language of an old song" that "stirs inside the body," recalling "a memory so ancient we have lost a name for it" (64). Also Jungian is her analysis of the wolf as shadow figure: "More than any other animal, they mirror back to us the predators we pretend not to be" (71). But nowhere does her use of Jungian concepts take her too far from the real wolf or the real eagle; in fact, it gives more validity to a belief system based on deep ecology that other proponents usually assume via intuition, begging the question by assuming the same of their audience.

Intuitive, emotional, and very poetic, Hogan's method of prose exposition is an inductive accumulation of powerful, humanizing observations leading to a spiritual or deep ecological conclusion, as she does in "The Bats." Here the creatures' "wing membranes" are described as being "etched like the open palm of a human hand" (*Dwellings* 23); they have "small handlike claws" (24); and even though ambiguous border creatures of air and sound, caves and darkness, they are yet "people of the threshold" (27). Their eerie, high-pitched communications are a "language" all their own, "a dusky world of songs a pitch above our own" (25–26). The tactic of showing how humanlike these animals are ends here, to the bats' advantage; in fact, better than we, bats "know the world is constantly singing" (27), a knowledge we have lost. The spiritual ecologist now invokes a living Gaia and asks, "How do we learn to trust ourselves enough to hear the chanting of the earth?" (28).[36]

As for the birds in *Dwellings*, the title essay itself includes an appreciation of a species already beloved by Gilbert White and Dorothy Wordsworth: the barn swallow, whose mud nest is "filled with the fire of living" (121). But the rhetorical climax of the essay is one of those occasions of happenstance or synchronicity that are common in Hogan's interspecies relationships. She finds a fallen nest that has a thread in it from one of her dresses: "I liked it, that a thread of my life was in an abandoned nest, one that had held eggs and new life" (124). There is also the implication that this is how it is, or should be, this close interspecies interchange, this common thread of near magical cooperation. A similar synchronicity occurs in "The Feathers." "For years," Hogan had "prayed for an eagle feather," but she wanted it from a live bird: "A bird killed in the name of human power is in truth a loss of power from the world" (15). Waking from a numinous dream, she saw her benefactor in the flesh: "A large golden eagle flew toward the window, so close that I could see its dark eyes looking at me" before it flew away and left a feather for her outside (16). The feather then becomes a participant in various other synchronistic events in her life, and she speculates, "Perhaps there are events and things that work as a doorway into the mythical world, the world of first people," as "a form of sacred reason" (19). This is in part a Native translation of Jung's notion of meaningful chance, or synchronicity, but it is also related to what Vizenor calls "natural reason," which includes an understanding of interspecies relationships (e.g., the "affinity" of the crane and Vizenor's own Anishinaabe tribe) that transcends the rationalism of a Western social science that would place all such goings-on under the rubrics of totemism and anthropomorphism ("Literary Animals" 120–22).[37]

The golden eagle is only one of a host of raptors who have made an impact on Hogan's prose and poetry. "Waking Up the Rake" includes an account of her work at a rehabilitation center for birds of prey. Like bats, these birds are, in many ways, more than the equal of humankind:

> This work is an apprenticeship, and the birds are the teachers. Sweet-eyed barn owls, such taskmasters, asking us to be still and slow and to move in time with their rhythms, not our own. . . . There is a silence needed here before a person enters the bordered world the birds inhabit . . . we listen to the musical calls of the eagles, the sound of wings in air . . . . The most difficult task the birds demand is that we learn to be equal to them, to feel our way into an intelligence that is different from our own. . . . And they know that we are apart from them, that as humans we have somehow fallen from our animal grace. (*Dwellings* 150)

Therefore Hogan has become a "disciple of birds" (148), not only because they possess something that once belonged to us, but because they also possess a radical difference, "an intelligence that is different from our own" that makes them special creatures in their own right. In the end, Hogan's drive toward interspeciality is not just a reductive assimilation to the Same via some ecological fiat of "we are all related." As Stacy Alaimo has noted, "While Hogan's poetry evokes profound connections with nature, it strives to affirm nature's differences, in part by refusing to engulf it within human projections" (56). However "sweet-eyed" and "grace"-filled Hogan's humanizing tendencies would make them, her raptors remain, in the best sense, "apart."

Dwellings is actually a fine introduction to Hogan's poems, which are often more imaginative and impassioned versions of the ideas presented in her already poetic prose. One of those threads, the ecofeminist tenet that the female and the animal and the body are intrinsically related, is very effectively realized in Hogan's several turtle poems, as she chooses another animal of the borders as appropriate emblem. "Turtle" is initially about said animal, but a strange terrapin it is, with "small yellow bones of animals inside / [that] are waking / to shine out from his eyes" (14–16 [*Calling* 3]). But this is not just a Bly-like surrealist fancy, as the human women later are not only turtles themselves—"Wake up, we are women. / The shells are on our backs" (25–26)—but they are empowered by this very animal inner nature: "We are amber, / the small animals / are gold inside us" (27–29). This may be evolution at work as Paul Shepard conceives it, in which one's genetics actually "contain" the other species encountered during evolution, or, as the spiritual ecologist might have it, no scientific explanation may be necessary: there are, in the deepest sense (call it metaphorical or "metaphysical"), other animals and voices within, centers of power in need of outlet. Speaking of the howls of endangered wolves and the songs of endangered whales, Hogan believes that "these are the songs of lives struggling against extinction"; "*even translated through human voices*, they are here inside the earth, *inside the human body*, the captive, contained animals" (*Dwellings* 35; emphases added). After a sweat lodge ceremony Hogan feels, "It is as if skin contains land and birds. The places within us have become filled. . . . The animals and ancestors move into the human body, into skin and blood" (41).

The skeptic may see this as too much Jung, that the animals have become *too* inner, too archetypal. But if we put the truth-value of such statements aside for a moment, something very interesting is happening here, in this porous intermingling of turtle, and woman, and wolf. Imaginatively, even pragmatically, the reader is confronted with a human body whose borders have been destroyed. Alaimo claims great things for such a move: Hogan "rewrite[s] the body as a liminal, indeterminable space that disrupts the opposition between nature and culture, object and subject" (51). Human subject and animal object are rendered suspect categories, as the wall of skin between inside and outside melts away.

In Hogan's "calling myself home," women are more immediately and explicitly related to turtles: they "are plodding creatures / like the turtle / born of an old people" (13–15 *[Calling* 6]). And like the nearly prehistoric reptile, they are practically a part of the land: "This land is the house" they "have always lived in," and "their bones are holding up the earth" (20–21, 23). But even turtle women, or perhaps especially turtle women, may be in need of a "ghost-dance" rejuvenation, perhaps in terms of a new appreciation by others of these women's very "faces":

The red tail of a hawk
cuts open the sky
and the sun
brings their faces back
with the new grass. (24–28)

This can be seen as another version of Paula Gunn Allen's feminist "dancing with the birds," a quieter but perhaps more realistic version, for these "slow" women cannot yet dance with the bird. They can only receive the hawk's good graces as a new beginning in their slow but sure emergence with the "new grass."

Light
Lumine
Our salvation
is a gold ring surrounding the eye
of a blackbird. ("The Women Are Grieving" 1–5, in *Eclipse* 25–26)

One is tempted to quote these lines out of context, as another rebirth through the avian, but they actually introduce one instance of Hogan using birds unflatteringly, in support of a feminist agenda. For these "red-winged birds" (men, really) have "returned from war / wearing bloody feathers," and so the "women are grieving" (6–9). The blackbirds' red wing patches thus become martial insignia, as the poem goes on to portray mothers' losses and sorrows in a time of war. Yet one incredible passage stands out as a moment in which woman and (female) bird may be said to merge:

In the night
a woman hears the blackbird on her roof.
Her dark neck,
her pale neck
her soft neck where the pulse moves
is mourning. (17–22)

This is a female bird, obviously, whose "dark neck" is "mourning," as a "pale neck" (the human) does the same. The two are joined, finally, in the image of the "soft neck," in a mourning of the loss of all children.[38]

Another theme of *Dwellings* is the loss of the animal, both by physical extermination and through psychological distance and repression. As we have already seen in Hogan, much of this animal loss is directly attributable to colonization and environmental rapine, and it is a loss that of course goes hand in hand with Native loss. In Silko, this loss is often countered by Native human spirits who walk the landscape as powers of memory and retribution. In Hogan, it is more usually the native animals themselves:

. . . the night animals,
their yellow eyes
give back the words
while you are sleeping
when all the old animals
come back
from their secret houses
of air. ("Left Hand Canyon" 26–33, in *Calling* 28)

Sometimes this is a veritable Ghost Dance of animal and eco-return, as in "Houses" (*Eclipse* 38–39). This "great expansion" of human houses is an environmental affront, resulting in a "tearing apart of land" (20–21). But then, in the rebirth of a conclusion, the "houses . . . disappear,"

and a tree fills
a house of birds

birds singing
birds
that remind us we are in this life,
we are this world. (44–51)

Whatever metaphysics a so-called spiritual ecologist supposedly subscribes to, Hogan's spirituality is an immanent one, one that never forgets that the eagle's gift of a feather and this poem's bird-filled Tree of Life are, above all, of "this world."

Many of Hogan's poems are an earnest closing of the gap between species, often, as we have seen, via a sudden awareness of the animals within. Sometimes, as in the finale of "Bright Wings, Daybreak" (*Eclipse* 62), the animal—here, the avian—tenor is only implied; with the sun's advent, her "own veins and nerves . . . want to open at the palms," want to "let wings rise, / weightless fire, above the body's ruins" (18, 20–22). This is very much in the deep imagist style of, say, Bly's "Waking from Sleep" (*Silence* 13); Bly-like, too, are the more startling animal passages in Hogan's "Small Animals at Night" (*Eclipse* 46):

Niño, the bridled raven
waiting for night
with dancing feet
and fingerbones about its neck
like the ones men fashioned
from the hands of slaves. (8–13)

But Hogan makes this style her own: the raven is the Native Trickster, the concluding leap of a simile intimates the worst sort of colonialism, and the combination of "bridled" and "fingerbones" not only describe (perhaps) the contrasting plumage around the raven's neck, but also connote a certain repression and enslavement of the bird, the animal, itself. In the conclusion (as in Bly's "Waking from Sleep"), the body and animals are both freed:[39]

But hear them.
They sing in their own heads
in the shivering blue bones of an ear
the voices here in grace
in the hollows of this body. (30–34)

The conjunction of these animals' "own heads" and "this body" of the human sleeper is a dizzying dissolution of the self-other boundary; to hear a pun in "here," as in "voices hear," makes the passage all the more confounding.

"The Ritual Life of Animals" includes the remarkable phrase, "In the sleeping bird / the dream is flying south" (21–22). In the wake of the various images of dreaming birds and birds as veritable entities in human dreams that we have encountered so far (e.g., in Henson), I am now prepared to conclude that these, too, are volleys against the fortress of selfhood, against the mistaken assumption that human consciousness is something inviolate and apart.[40] In "The Ritual Life" (*Book* 44–45) is also one of Hogan's most haunting passages regarding these dream or night animals:

> In the silence
> of night,
> in the warmth of human bodies,
> are the nocturnal wakings.
> Something inside gets down on its haunches.
> At the borders of our beds
> are the strange ways, voices,
> the slow shifting of eyes, turning of ears. (31–38)

Where (and who) these animals really are is once again confusing; they are creatures both beside "our beds" moving real heads *and* "in the warmth of human bodies." The phrase "Something inside" is the most concise expression of this bivalency: inside the house? or the psyche and the body?

The subject-object hierarchy is also upset in the tour-de-force of perspectivism, "Morning: The World in the Lake," in which the water's reflection creates two realities: "Beneath each black duck / another swims," a "shadow / joined to blood and flesh" (1–4 [*Seeing* 56]). Because of the reflection, "There's a world beneath this one. / The red-winged blackbird calls / its silent comrade down below" (5–7). Then a human element enters the picture (or rather, pictures), and the blackbird's reflection overlaps with those of poet and daughter:

> we are there, living
> in that revealed sliver of red
> living in the black

something of feathers,
daughters, all of us. (25–29)

For Hogan, such a reflection is the real truth, a canvas of interpenetrating figures in which bird and human, especially woman, are one.

As with blackbirds, crows are far from alien in Hogan. Her story "Crow" entails an actual speaking crow, filtered through the traditionalist views of the narrator's grandmother: "The crow listens when Grandma talks. . . . I swear that one night I heard it talking to Grandma." According to the old woman's traditions, the crows "were people and used to speak our tongues" (*Red Clay* 78), much like Standing Bear's meadowlarks. Not surprisingly, the crows in Hogan's poetry are often articulate linguists: they "speak like men / to one another," and their "gravel voices / are thunder breaking the sky" ("Crows" 1–3 [*Calling* 11]). But these are the sort of othered "people" that Hogan must defend against "men with blue guns" (8): against such a ballistic onslaught, "the feathers come apart, falling / specks of dust" (11–12). For the poet, the fallen feathers become synecdoches for the crows themselves, that would still speak, or at least "My ears want to hear them / begin to speak" (13–14):

They are quiet,
so still
I wait for a breath
to escape the warm feathers. (17–20)

The nonspeaking crows in Hogan are more eerie, even somewhat alien, as they carry on the business of their ecological niche, cleansing the environment in a manner commonly perceived by humans as disgusting. But in Hogan, this is fit fodder for her poetic instinct and spiritual ecology, as in "Crow Law" (*Book* 31):[41]

what remains of moose
is crow
walking out
the sacred temple of ribs. (8–11)

At poem's end, such a portrait of nature at work is spoken of as a primordial "war," in "the old forest / where crow is calling, / where we are still afraid"

(14, 17–19). One possible reading of this final fear is that we modern humans *shouldn't* be afraid, that this is the war unto which we are born as creatures of nature. But "afraid" could also be read in terms of Alexie's "panic" that his crow would like us to still feel: both the natural, genetic fear in the face of death's doings and the respect for the sheer numinosity of the bird that has been lost, for the most part, in our postlapsarian age.

Besides the crow, other favorite birds in Hogan's poetry are geese, those prototypical "Travelers" (*Book* 46) of high-flighted, long migration. Hogan's very personal relationship with birds, already evident in her work at the raptor center, comes to the fore again when she finds, one "brittle night," several "geese froze into water" who thus "couldn't fly" (17, 19–20). She breaks the ice to free them, empathetic auditor of the same "voice" that calls the geese:

South was their way that night.
They wanted to follow it.
Even my human ears heard its blue voice
in the outstretched and beating wings. (29–32)

The poet who can hear the language of bats and nameless bedside night animals could hardly be deaf to such a call.

The migratory instinct of this bird is, of course, crucial to Hogan's own poetic yearnings. "Water Rising" presents a close encounter of migrating geese, who fly "so close / their air brushed our shoulders" (5–6 [*Eclipse* 51]). As the geese ascend, to "once again fly past the old route" (40), the birds "hold our feet / and let us dance away / forever from the dark body" (44–46). The final image invokes a spiritual flight, of course, or it might be deemed laughable. Hogan's spiritual ecology gets the best of her here; the flight from the "dark body" is both uncharacteristic and even lamentable.

Hogan's most noteworthy geese poem may be "Changing Weather" (*Seeing* 18), which also involves a gaggle's ascent, but in a more impressively startling fashion. The poem also reminds one of Bruchac's several geese and prison poems in its subject and setting, with a comparable play on the theme of imprisonment and freedom. The geese are veritable insurgents, "trespassers," as they arrive, "huddled in the prison yard" (13):

By hundreds
they trespassed the barbed circles of wire

and guards on lookout in white suits.
The earth grew long necks
and spoke its own language. (14–18)

Hearing the call of migration—"There is something in the blood / and the geese have heard it" (19–20)—they take off in the final line: "The prison yard is flying" (30). In this natural rebellion against barbed wire and "white suits," even against the prison of human discourse—the earth itself has its "own language," after all—both birds and earth (merged in the image of "long necks") alight, in a marvelous final image that upsets all human bounds.

This language of the earth and, especially, the languages of other species are benefactors of the incredible emphasis the we have seen in poem after poem and, moreover, in the essays of *Dwellings*: "What we really are searching for," Hogan says, "is a language that heals" our broken "relationship" with other species, and the land (59). She speculates at one point in *Dwellings* on the implications for humankind of chimpanzees' ability to learn sign language, and the subsequent revelations, through this communication, of their rich emotional lives. Surely here is a "dialogue" bridging "the species barrier," a true "narrowing down of the difference between species" (111, 114). The bad news behind such a discovery, Hogan claims, is a human "identity crisis equal" to the Copernican revolution (112). But the good news regarding this rapprochement is far more important, the opportunity for "a healing of the betrayed trust between humans and earth" (115). It is the poetry of such Native women writers as Hogan and Joy Harjo that helps make such a healing, via a reimagining and rearticulation of other voices, possible.

A WHIR OF HUMMINGBIRDS: JOY HARJO

> I'm always aware of the spectrum of other languages and modes of expression, including, for instance, cloud language, cricket singing talk, and the melodic whir of hummingbirds.
>
> JOY HARJO, *The Spiral of Memory*

> For instance, that fool crow, picking through trash in the corral, understands the center of the world as greasy scraps of fat. Just ask him. He doesn't have to say that the earth has turned scarlet through fierce belief, after centuries of heartbreak and laughter—he perches on the blue bowl of the sky, and laughs.
>
> JOY HARJO, "My house is the red earth," in *Secrets*

It could easily be said that Joy Harjo's favorite animals, at least as poetic images, are not avians, but butterflies and deer, and especially horses.[42] Regarding one of her most well-known poems, "She Had Some Horses," Harjo says, "I have a kinship with horses that is beyond explanation. . . . You asked how I conceived of the horse. . . . Maybe, the horse conceived of me" (*Spiral* 109). Lincoln comments on the horse's centrality in Harjo's work as follows, though, as usual, he too readily conflates some very different American authors: "So the horse is Harjo's androgynous icon and imaginative catalyst, free to leap and gallop and graze where native instinct[!] takes her, no less than Stevens ringed by blackbirds, Momaday inspired by eagle and bear, Sitting Bull mentored by meadowlarks, Roethke solaced by snail, or Dickinson spirited by singing birds, flies, and butterflies" (364). (This may be the first and only time that Sitting Bull and Theodore Roethke have been mentioned in the same scholarly sentence.) Yet Harjo has also stated that she regards her "Eagle Poem" and "The Myth of Blackbirds" as two of her very "important" poems (*Spiral* 89). Not only do blackbirds (and hummingbirds) fly and "whir" throughout her corpus, but crows, too, permeate her pages with their trickster laughter.

Other species can move more comfortably, perhaps, through the pages of a mixed-blood poet descended from "other" peoples, including the Muskogee tribe.[43] Harjo's more general ecological statements, moreover, are often couched in terms of Native and natural alterity. Thus she complains at one point of the negative conflation of the animal, land, and human Native evident throughout this chapter; Native writers themselves have not received their rightful recognition because "most people" just "don't want to be reminded of the [American] holocaust, something they deny in their daily lives. It's the story the land, the animals, and the [Native] people will go on telling" (*Spiral* 110). As for species egalitarianism, Harjo is certain that the "human is not above the bear, nor is Adam [right in] naming the bear" (127). The current role of humankind in the biosphere is hardly a laudable one, in her view. Upon the birth of her son, she "wondered what would happen to us, where humans fit in the evolutionary scale. Were we truly necessary to the survival of the biosphere? . . . What do humans add besides stacks of trash and thoughtlessness?" ("when my son was born" 4 [*Map* 108].

Harjo's suggestions for the "healing" of this situation are similar to Hogan's in many ways: above all, an attentiveness to other voices. For Harjo, as we shall see, these voices not only are often nonhuman, but their very nonlinguistic nature is a redemptive quality fit for praise. As in Hogan, the reestablishment of a true rapport with the natural and the animal involves a holistic integration of nature and the psyche, of "both the inside and outside worlds" (*Spiral* 108). (By this point, I would prefer to not even speak in the divisive terms of "inside and outside," but it seems an inescapable metaphor.) In "Anniversary," one of Harjo's modern versions of a tribal creation myth, she celebrates a time when there was "no separation" between bird and human:

> And then a bird or two were added, the crow of course to
> joke about humanity, and then another kind so beautiful
> we had to hear them first, before our eyes could be imagined.
>
> And it was, we were then—and there was no separation.
> (4–7, in *Map* 106)

Harjo wonderfully expresses Shepard's notion of other species fashioning much of human consciousness in the process of evolution, as if humans had little need to truly *see* until they first noticed the beauty of colored feathers.

In combating the current chasm between species, Harjo's favorite avian other voices are those of crows and blackbirds. Although these two birds are not closely related, taxonomically speaking, they are both usually quite vocal and predominantly feathered in a color of traditional denigration. One might even claim that such birds are thus racially marked, as it were, just as the Native poets who champion them. Gretchen Legler has made much of Harjo's contestation of the "native body" in her poetry,[44] and I suggest that the cawing, feathered body may represent another aspect of such a Native insurgency. Harjo certainly enlists the crow in this "war" in the poem "Trickster," at the same time closely linking this laughing avian trickster with her own "fool" of a Native poet persona:

> Crow, in the new snow.
> You caw, caw
>   like crazy.
> Laugh.

> Because you know I'm a fool
> too, like you
> skimming over the thin ice
> to the war going on
> all over the world. (*In Mad* 13)

But this is an ecological and Native "war," of survival and identity, not the insane wars waged in the name of false political and religious ideologies that are mere covers for bloodlust and material gain. This "fool crow" has no such motives; it is a self-composed creature of this world who knows its own "center" and "doesn't have to say that the earth has turned scarlet through fierce belief, after centuries of heartbreak and laughter." And so Harjo's own politics, in this regard, are for the birds, as it were; in the former geopolitics of the cold war, for instance, she was "loyal to neither" the United States or the USSR, "only to the birds who fly over, laugh at the ridiculous / ways of humans, know wars destroy dreams" and "divide the country inside us" ("Nine Below" 2–5 [*In Mad* 60]).

Though Harjo's greatest strength is her appreciation of the sheer nonverbal nature of bird talk, she is also comfortable with the corvid interlocutors of Native tradition, an abiding belief that other species can actually communicate with humankind. Again, this is far different from and more ecologically sound than the converse imperial assumption that other species (and other races) are mere dumb animals. Such communication is evident in "the power of never," in which the speaking crows actually play a fairly independent role, as they help her adapt to her move: "I spoke with the crows before leaving for Los Angeles. They were the resident storytellers whose strident and insistent voices added the necessary dissonance for color. They had cousins in California, and gave me names and addresses, told me to look them up" (4 [*Map* 46]). Once there, she discovers that her feathered friends were speaking the truth: "The crows' cousins kept me company in that sometimes lonely and strange place as they paced the ledges of the crumbling buildings in my neighborhood" (5 [47]).[45]

But more commonly, the language of crows is less human, more suggestive and mysterious. In a prose note to "WHO INVENTED DEATH AND CROWS AND IS THERE ANYTHING WE CAN DO TO CALM THE NOISY CLATTER OF DESTRUCTION?" (*Woman* 26–27), Harjo claims, "*When I hear crows talking, death is a central topic.*" But the statement is more than the usual association of black carrion feeders with dark death; if death is the final mystery, crows are a mystery whose language is free of pat answers. "We're all dying," the poem begins, "even that crow talking loud and kicking up snow" (1). Perhaps the crow "thinks he can head it [death] off with a little noise, a fight," but he may just as well be bragging about his plumage (2). Harjo then momentarily considers the possibility that death is the bird's talking point. If so, "That's what I like about crows. . . . They aren't afraid to argue about the inarguable" (3). But then the crows are suddenly invested with a more mystical quality, acting on humans like Zen koans: "We fly into the body and we fly out, changed by the sun, by crows who manipulate the borders of reason" (4). (This flying may be just a trope for the imagination; however, in many other poems Harjo reveals a high regard for out-of-body experiences.) Yet, from another perspective, very much the perspective of Momaday's "Crows in a Winter Composition," crows are downright discursively exasperating, as she takes up the matter of "the talk of crows getting in the way of poetry," for indeed, there is something in her poetic "soul" that "has little patience for crows" (6), much as Momaday's poetic persona rankled at real crows spoiling his aesthetic "composition." We can witness how, elsewhere, Harjo steps back from her ruminations on a heron, realizing that she cannot know the "culture" of herons: "I did not see guilt in his posture, nor did I hear him admonish himself for some failure of the deep or near past, rather he absolutely enjoyed his heron-ness. . . . He had no doubt as to his right to be a heron. . . . But what do I know of herons? I do not know their language or their culture" ("Returning from the Enemy," prose interlude to section 11 [*Map* 90]).[46] In "WHO INVENTED DEATH" is a similar epistemological reticence, as the poem ends in "question" and "laughter" (8), and a final question for the reader: "What do you make of it?" (9). Like the crows in Momaday's poem, this is an acknowledgment of a radical alterity, as Harjo makes a graceful retreat from any blithe association of crows with death. As in Ortiz's desire "For the Bird to Be a Bird," Harjo insists on allowing crows to be crows: "If you look with the mind of the swirling earth near Shiprock you become the land, beautiful. And understand how three crows at the edge of the highway, laughing, become three crows at the edge of the world, laughing" (*Secrets* 4).

I have referred often to a common high regard among Native writers for crows and vultures as ecological cleansers of the physical environment; here one might say that they are capable of a human psychological cleansing, too, an avian shock wave through Blake's "doors of perception," a renewed psyche free of projections. Thus "Climbing the Streets of Worcester, Mass." can be read, on one level, as an attribution of the Native creation-via-the-word (so important in Momaday) to crows themselves:

> three crows laugh
> kick up the neighbor's trash.
> Telling jokes
> they re-create the world. (15–18, in *In Mad* 43)

But the re-creation can also be seen as occurring in the human realm, in the psyches of human auditor and poet and reader, so inveterately full of human "trash" in the form of false projections and ideologies.

Perhaps Harjo's most memorable images of crows do entail an association with death, but in a quite novel, even uncanny fashion. "In the Beautiful Perfume and Stink of the World" (*Map* 133–35) is one of Harjo's many accounts of an out-of-body experience, leading to a vision of her apocalyptic "fifth" world, her version of tribal and natural return, part Silko's "return of the Native" and part Ghost Dance renewal. But her manner of flight is rather startling: *"I had been traveling in the dark, through many worlds, / the four corners of my mat carried by guardians in the shape of crows"* (3–4). (Recall that, next to the eagle, the crow was deemed the most important spiritual intermediary in the Ghost Dance religion. Here we have four crows, as in the four directions and the four eagles of Lakota folklore.) In this poem, at least, the "fifth world" is not the utopian fruit of a sociopolitical revolution, but a new way of seeing, a cleansing of perception, a new awareness of the material here and now that includes the dirty, the "dark," and the "cawing, flapping" crow:[47]

> . . . And it is all here. Everything that ever was.
>
> *The cawing, flapping song of the beautiful dark*
>
> In the dark. In the beautiful perfume and stink of the world. (54–56)

Blackbirds serve as avian accompaniments to the crow in Harjo's work, with the great difference that the species she usually has in mind, the red-winged blackbird, possesses a distinctively colorful wing patch, so deliciously described in "The Myth of Blackbirds" as "the beauty of scarlet licked with yellow" (4 [*Woman* 28]).[48] Even more remarkable in this poem is her final thankfulness to "the blackbirds who are exactly blackbirds" (10), just as her "three crows" are above all just that, "three crows." Early in Harjo's corpus, she uses the blackbird to complain of the government's land-management practices, and even imparts to the blackbird an almost mystical (and native) means of survival: "The United States Army says / it knows how to kill / a million blackbirds." What is "doesn't know [is] / that every blackbird / has a thousand lives" ("Blackbirds" 1–3, 10–12 [*What Moon* 20]). Later the blackbird more characteristically becomes, like the crow, a bird of even greater suggestiveness. In the prose poem "Transformations" (*In Mad* 59), Harjo perhaps reveals the influence of Ortiz, in whose work a bird or animal sometimes makes or is the poem: "This poem could be a bear. . . . Or a blackbird, laughing," Harjo writes (and tellingly gives the blackbird corvid and trickster attributes). This is close to Ortiz's notion that writing a poem is something learned "by watching the animals." The title, too, is a tribute to other species: positive transformations are possible "if you have the right words, the right meanings, buried in that tender place in your heart where the most precious animals live." Now we are firmly in the spiritual ecology of Linda Hogan, an appreciation of the power of those "small animals" within. What sets Harjo apart, as we shall see, is her emphasis that the truly "right meanings" are usually beyond the realm of human words.

Harjo is one of the foremost contemporary Native purveyors of the trickster crow, yet one cannot ignore her several noteworthy raptor poems. In "Eagle Poem," language is once again at the poem's core and is said to transcend even sound; there are "languages / That aren't always sound but other / Circles of motion" (7–9 *[In Mad* 65]), epitomized in the semiotics of an eagle's flight:

> Like eagle that Sunday morning
> Over Salt River. Circled in blue sky
> In wind, swept our hearts clean
> With sacred wings. (10–13)

Another avian cleansing occurs here, via a living circular motion, yet another "sacred hoop," and as in Hogan, the *real*ization of the circle is ultimately an inner one, a conscious awareness of biological cycles, a knowledge that we live

> . . . and die soon within a
> True circle of motion,
> Like eagle rounding out the morning
> inside us. (20–23)

Harjo has stated elsewhere that the "Eagle Poem" is "most obviously a prayer. You could look at all poems as being a prayer for our continuance" (*Spiral* 123). The "continuance" in this poem is both an ecological one, emblematized in an eagle's flight, and a spiritual one, an ecotherapeutic internalization of all that the "circle" and "sacred wings" entail. For our current century of potential apocalypse, there may be no better *language*, this translation of the bird by the Native, for us to hear.

For Harjo, then, *language* can reside in silent life patterns and in inarticulate sounds. Plus, there is that faith throughout her corpus that human language is but one expression of nature's art, that other species' songs are "chants" for the cosmos, too, in the truest Native sense. In the end, to quote the title of another Harjo poem, "humans aren't the only makers of poetry" (*Map* 112). As for articulate human language, she would perform a radical critique and reinscription. The English language itself, for starters, is "a male language, not tribal, not spiritual enough" (*Spiral* 69). As with Silko, her great "frustration with the language . . . stems from anger with the colonization process in which the English language was a vicious tool" (99). Like Hogan, Harjo envisions a new, more eco-conducive language that will arise in good part through the efforts of Native poets, resulting in both a new "lyricism, [and] a land-based language" that acknowledges the "landscape, as something alive with personality, breathing" (70–71). In the title poem of *A Map to the Next World* (19–21), Harjo's "map" includes a rediscovery of "the language of the land" (5), including a reappreciation of the avian: "We no longer know the names of the birds here, how to speak to them by their personal names" (10). But our "relatives," the other species, are still here, waiting, in spite of ourselves: "They have never left us; we have abandoned them for science" (18). Furthermore, Harjo agrees (however ironically) with Jacques Derrida's notion of phonocentrism, in that the written word itself is really "a deevolution of the communication process. You lose human contact" and "a sense of relationship" (*Spiral* 99–100). To the obvious question, why write poetry, then?, Harjo's reply is both pragmatic and insurrectionist: it is the most effective means of speaking "in a language that was meant to destroy us" (118).

But at last Harjo's poetry is more an attempted articulation of the inarticulate, the raw caw of the crow rather than the learned, overly verbose squawk of a Gayatri Spivak. Besides, even the crow's purported "laughter," however much supported by trickster hermeneutics, is still a homocentric misreading and *use* of the bird's sound per se. One is more encouraged by statements elsewhere in her work that more decidedly privilege the superiority of nonlinguistic communication, a faith in the value of sound itself beyond human phonemic signification, as we saw in "Eagle Poem." Indeed, Harjo's is a poetic world in which the truth issues most from that place where "There are no words, only sounds" ("Bleed Through" 31 [*In Mad* 36]. This truth came to her at an early age, the poet claims; even when she was young, the sound of music led her to an understanding of "the failings of language, before I could speak" (*Spiral* 102). Now, as a poet writing words, she can write lines such as the following: "All poets / understand the final uselessness of words" ("Bird" 7–8 [*In Mad* 21].[49]

But what is an understanding, a consciousness "before I could speak," as Harjo says? In "Returning from the Enemy," she claims, "Before speech I took language into the soft parts of my body" (4.1 [*Map* 75]). This move to before and beyond human language immediately suggests the turn that Julie Kristeva has performed on Lacanian psychoanalysis, in redefining the pre-Symbolic as the *sémiotique* and reprivileging the rhythm and "hum" of prelingual "body" and "mother" over the Law of the Father. To anticipate a fuller discussion thereof in the epilogue, this semiotic is "rhythmic, unfettered," "musical, [and] anterior to judgment" (*Revolution* 29). Indeed, this maternal body is another vital aspect of Harjo's "Map to the Next World": "The place of entry is the sea of your mother's blood" (14), and "You will have to navigate by your mother's voice" (20)—in other words, via a recovery, a reinvigoration of the semiotic.

I might try to make much here of a point made in earlier chapters, that the bird as symbol has often been imbued with female and maternal associations, but even without doing so, I can still wonder whether the rhythms and melodies of birds, so often the obsessive subject matter of poets, might have a more crucial connection to the human realm than has usually been assumed—whether the crow's caw or cardinal's slurred whistle might entail some communicative, semiotic transcendence beyond traditional verbal signification. Harjo at least finds a rather semiotic and preconscious (dare I say transhuman?) "hum," a "very meditative sound," she calls it, in the hummingbird: "When I think of the sound of a hummingbird, I think of a bird who can fly in between worlds. They say the hummingbird makes the sound you make when you pass between sleeping and dreaming" (*Spiral* 91). Kristeva's theories seem inordinately helpful in speaking of Harjo's preference for "cloud language, cricket singing talk, and the melodic whir of hummingbirds" (99), and perhaps even why her ultimate vision of the "next world" in her recent work ends, not with a human or even Native American song, but with "*The cawing, flapping song of the beautiful dark.*"

SHERMAN ALEXIE: A STARLING POSTSCRIPT

Tell me: what is the difference between
Birds and us, between their pain and our pain?
We build monuments; they rebuild their nests.
They lay other eggs; we conceive again.
Dumb birds, dumb women, dumb starlings, dumb men.

SHERMAN ALEXIE, "Avian Nights"

I must belatedly admit, with some gratitude, that Sherman Alexie's more recent, twenty-first-century poetry seems, in general, less parodic and sardonic in its use of bird imagery. I point to his 2003 tour de force, "Avian Nights," an amazing deconstruction of human and avian difference. Not blackbirds or crows, but starlings are the ornithic subject matter, no doubt the most vilified "blackbirds" of contemporary urban society. (The European starling is an Old World mynah, really. I can already hear some of my students saying, "Ah, here is a Native American poet who's finally 'over it,' who is giving the Euro-colonizers their empathetic due." However, I'd greet any such reading with great suspicion.)

The poem itself is part narrative—he and his wife must get rid of the starlings who have "invaded" their attic—and part philosophical lament: aren't the starlings merely doing their natural job of setting up a household? How different is that from the endeavors of poet and wife in their own concurrent child rearing? In the 1990s, Alexie would have more likely ironized such a topic, distancing himself from any blithe conflation of "Indian" and "Nature." But here, a genuine pathos comes to the fore, more reminiscent of Simon Ortiz than of a hip postmodern cynic. Yes, these avian interlopers are mere "Rats with wings" (2), but it's a sad job that the exterminator does, pulling "three baby birds, / Blind and mewling, from the crawlspace above," only to "snap" their "necks—*crack, crack, / Crack*" (5–6, 9–10). When the starling "father and mother" return to find their offspring "gone, missing, absent, destroyed" (19, 21), sounding the "*screech-screech-screech* of parental instinct" (24), the poet clings, at first, to poor rationalizations: "We had to do this. . . . They woke up our son / With their strange songs and the beating of wings / Through the long, avian nights" (25–28).

But as a new father (and brilliant poet) himself, Alexie can't resist analogies: before they died, "The babies screamed to greet the morning light. / What could they've been so excited about?"

> What is starling joy? When a starling finds
> A shiny button, does it dance and shout?
>
> Do starlings celebrate their days of birth?
> Do they lust and take each other to bed?
> Are they birds of infinite jest, of mirth
> And merry? How do they bury their dead? (29–36)

One might initially be reminded of Wordsworth's imprisoned eagle and Clare's beleaguered mother birds and hear a quite similar tone of soul-searching outrage. But these are, above all, the questions—it should be clear by now—of such Native poets as Bruchac and Kenny, Harjo and Hogan, and to find them reiterated in the Young-Turk-with-a-'tude of Native literature is fairly invigorating.

The starlings' mourning, moreover, unlike that of civilized humankind, is a quite vocal one, as once again, bird *language* becomes a point of emphasis; in contrast to our own often stoic repression regarding death, the starling parents "Don't believe in silence. They scream and wail. / They attack the walls. We have never heard / Such pain from any human" (42–44). Alexie flashes back to the medical complications of his own son's birth, and now his human love and fear are invested with the language of the bird: "His mother and I sat / At his bedside eighteen hours a day. *Screech- / Screech-screech*. We cawed and cawed to bring him back" (62–64).[50]

The borders of avian and human having been blurred via the common bond of parentage, the finale is a marvelous return to the bird:

. . . Grief can take
The form of starlings, of birds who refuse
To leave the dead. How much love, hope, and faith

Do these birds possess? They lift their faces
And scream to the Bird-God while we grow numb.
The starlings are odd, filthy, and graceless,
But if God gave them opposable thumbs,

I'm positive they would open the doors
Of our house and come for us as we sleep.
We killed their children. We started this war.
Tell me: What is the difference between

Birds and us, between their pain and our pain?
We build monuments; they rebuild their nests.
They lay other eggs; we conceive again.
Dumb birds, dumb women, dumb starlings, dumb men. (66–80)

What *is* the difference, indeed?, to repeat a key subtextual question of this entire book. Besides the common Native theme regarding the "war" that humankind has waged against the other species of "brute creation," Alexie's coda is distinguished by its implicit call for an end to such a war, given the ultimately close connections between human and bird. Both are "dumb," finally. Though I could perform some deconstructive reading of "dumb" as inarticulateness or silence versus the incredible *vocalizations* that make up the rest of the poem, I prefer to read "dumb" in its vernacular sense: both humans and birds are just plain stupid, as earth-dwelling organisms irrationally attached to their own and inordinately prone to articulate that attachment in songs of love, in songs of mourning. Birds and humans are both inveterate users of *language*, finally. The theists' and scientists' and humanists' adamant claim for some special rational faculty in humankind has had one main result (besides pollution and global warming and reality television shows): the tragic distancing of our species from all others. As a teacher, I am sometimes asked, "Why read poetry?" My best answer is just this: to bridge the gap, to cross the borders of species. Contemporary Native poets offer us the best opportunity for such a crossing.

Epilogue
The Avian Speaks Back

It's not just humans who sing for rain, make poetry as commentary on the meaning of life.
We aren't the only creatures, or the most likely to succeed.

JOY HARJO, "humans aren't the only makers of poetry," in *A Map to the Next World*

The animals are speaking to us, through us, and with us.

LINDA HOGAN, Deena Metzger, and Brenda Peterson, introduction to *Intimate Nature*)

He who is chaste is a good prophet, natural as the birds, and the prophecies of birds are not contrary to nature but are of nature.

PARACELSUS, qtd. in Jung, *Collected Works*

John Berger's well-known essay on why humans are attracted to zoos is based almost exclusively on a philosophy of specularity, above all, the uncanniness of other species' regard. Whether one accepts Berger's theory of the development of consciousness, that "man becomes aware of himself [by] returning the look" of other animals (3), his complaint that contemporary humankind is now unhealthily distanced from that Other's regard is still most intriguing. "That look between animal and man, which may have played a crucial role in the development of human society . . . has been extinguished," and the zoo trip is an ever appealing yet always failed quest for the recuperation of a transspecies relationship: "Looking at each animal, the unaccompanied zoo visitor is alone" (26). With his emphasis on *seeing*,[1] however, Berger can only look at animals, not hear them, and the gap between species, he says, is due to the animal's "lack of common language, its silence," which "guarantees its distance . . . its exclusion, from and of man" (4). But Berger's sin (or oversight) is the Western privileging of sight itself, what Wordsworth calls the "most despotic of our senses" (*Prelude* 11.174): in just *seeing* the bird, you have essentially reduced it to a two-dimensional museum exhibit, a color plate in a bird guide; in your hearing the bird, not only is the process of time and becoming made more manifest, but communication and *language* enter the picture, whether cognitively comprehensible or not. Even if understanding fails, in linguistic terms communication is occurring. Whether via a connection with the reptilian brain or the Kristevan semiotic, the bird is *speaking*. Maybe the best thing we can do, following the example of the usually verbose-about-himself Walt Whitman, is shut up for a second or two:

> I think I will do nothing for a long time but listen,
> And accrue what I hear into myself . . . and
> let sounds contribute toward me.
>
> I hear the bravuras of birds. . . .
>
> . . . .
>
> I hear all sounds as they are tuned to their uses.
>
> ("Song of Myself," in *Poetry and Prose* 53)

That there are languages of many other species beyond the scientifically ascertainable semiotics of chimps and dolphins is another common refrain in ecoscholarship,[2] in case there were no Black Elk, Silko, Hogan, and Harjo to remind us of as much. Moreover, these are languages that need listening to. Christopher Manes calls our attention to "the language of birds, the wind, earthworms, wolves and waterfalls—a world of autonomous speakers whose intents . . . one ignores at one's peril" (15). (And if "attending to ecological knowledge means metaphorically relearning 'the language of birds,'" one viable recourse to such an "ontological humility," Manes claims, is "the ontological egalitarianism of native American or other primal[?] cultures" [25].) But how can such beings be understood, besides in some vague metaphorical sense, unless one appeals to old Lakotas or young poets, both of whose attitudes and perceptions are still deemed by most to be on the near lunatic fringe?

Here I would take recourse again to the ideas of Julia Kristeva, especially her neo-Lacanian notion of the pre-Symbolic *sémiotique* and its ability to intermittently disrupt the Symbolic realm (that is, human discourse). Intriguing for my purposes, first of all, is her discussion of "nonverbal" music as "exclusively" semiotic (*Revolution* 24), a pure, alingual rhythm and sound closely allied to her pre-Symbolic chora, which is itself "analogous only to vocal or kinetic rhythm" (26). In Kristeva's analysis of literature, it is the "music" of the text that creates an "irruption of the semiotic within the symbolic" (63). Then why not treat the world itself as "text" and find a similar "irruption" in other nonverbal tones and rhythms? Thus I have made various efforts throughout this work to reprivilege the audile and the phonic over the visual, the specular. To speak of a cardinal's song as capable of taking one outside the Symbolic, à la a Zen koan—my occasional appeals in this regard have been preliminaries in such a direction.

Kristeva's semiotic communicates, moreover, in a Bakhtinian, overdetermined fashion: "Music and dance," for instance, not only "defy the barrier of meaning," in a linguistic sense (104), but create their own plurality of "meanings"; in such a way, for example, the Dionysian rituals performed a "dissolution" of the "symbolic order" via "dancing, singing, and poetic animality[!]" (65, 79)—not too unlike, one might suggest, a Native American ceremony calling for the power of the eagle or a Native ecofeminist poet calling for a dancing with birds. Kristeva acknowledges the influence of Bakhtin's *carnival* (*Desire* 65), for the carnivalesque, in Bakhtin's own words, speaks a "sensuous" language untranslatable "into a verbal language" (*Problems* 122), like Kristeva's chora.

Carnival is also closely related, in Bakhtin, to his study of parody, which is itself, as a genre, "an intentional dialogized hybrid" (*Dialogic* 76). (One thinks immediately of the hybrid genres in contemporary Native literature.) Like carnival, parody is a "ritualistic" gesture of "the primordial[!] thinking of man," including the characteristic gesture of "ritual laughter" (*Problems* 122, 126). Having just proposed that birdsong might be a feasible part of the world's semiotic, I must make this "laughter" an avian one, too. Are not the alingual sounds of the crows in Harjo and others part of this "laughter," this "poetic animality" that would turn the Symbolic order on its head? The crow or raven's role as Native Trickster is, in fact, much in line with Bakhtin's musings on the carnivalesque, with its ambivalent joining of "blessing and curse . . . praise and abuse . . . face and backside, stupidity and wisdom" (126). It is a sharp-tongued voice of profane "blasphemies," of "obscenities linked with the reproductive power of the earth and the body" (123). Finally, like certain large and black birds, Bakhtin's concept entails an ambiguity that includes the "perspective of negation (death)" (125). Human laughter itself might well be said to be an "irruption" of the semiotic, a nonverbal embrace of the comic and tragic at once; how much more disruptive of the rational and the status quo, then, when this laughter is (at least perceived to be) coming from another species?

Momaday's grand theme of the power of spoken language is relevant here, too, for some of his remarks on the subject seem to define Kristeva's semiotic: "Much of the power and magic and beauty of words consist not in meaning but in sound," and "expression, rather than communication, is often first in importance" (*Man* 7, 16). When language is conceived of in such a way, interestingly enough, a meadowlark's whistle is just as much a verbal act as a presidential inauguration speech. Moreover, besides the frequent invocation of singing birds and laughing crows, Native American literature also seems aimed at speaking through the semiotic by way of several of its formal characteristics. Paula Gunn Allen notes that "ceremonial" refrains and "lengthy passages of 'meaningless' syllables" have an "entrancing effect," producing "a state of consciousness best described as 'oceanic'" (*Sacred* 63).[3] I have also been entranced by "lengthy passages of 'meaningless' syllables" in listening, on many a summer afternoon, to a red-eyed vireo.

The semiotic music that Kristeva has in mind is human, of course, be it the musical art itself or the musicality of words in a text. But bird*song* has traditionally been deemed music, too. In his discussion of animal music, Shepard praises birdsong in particular (156), to the surprise of no one who has read more than a few pages of British or American nature writing. Annie Dillard, speculating on why birds sing and why their songs are beautiful (107–108), is able to turn the avian's vocalizations into something strange and marvelous (in part, by merging bird and reptile): "This modified lizard's song" is a "wild, utterly foreign music" (108). And that is as should be, rather than allowing the sounds of the sunrise robins to become a trite background of white noise. Philip Jay Lewitt's brief study on specific bird poems by Shelley, Keats, and Whitman has already been alluded to in a previous chapter. In his concluding meditation, Lewitt, as I am doing, calls attention both to the importance of listening and to birdsong as a crucial object of that listening (61–62). With no bird in sight as specular distraction, "perhaps, then, where the eye fails, the ear opens" (61). Elizabeth A. Lawrence, in her essay on Keats's "Nightingale" ode, concludes with a similar call. Given today's ecological disasters, she argues, "the aesthetic significance of natural phenomena such as birdsong to the human psyche" becomes perhaps all the more important (21). The avian audile that the "ear opens" to is beyond or before the human verbal: it is rhythm, sound in motion, repetition, "poetic animality," and it requires attending to. And yes, following Joy Harjo, this entails a redefinition of *language* itself, as in the sheer phatic brilliance of a cardinal's song or the ever changing semiotic patterns of migrating geese in flight. Birdsong, especially, is as much poetry as the so-called nonsense syllables of Native American dance chants.

The current intellectual atmosphere of linguistic-centered constructivism, a monomania for human language and discourse, has, as many ecocritics have argued, militated against seriously listening to other species. In poststructuralism specifically, it is the Lacanian tenet that verbal language creates, is necessary for, consciousness that has fed this enforced isolation within human discourse itself, to the point that all is signifying and signified, and nature itself becomes a denaturized text.[4] In the first several chapters of this work, I have complained of feeling nearly paralyzed by the postmodern philosophy that human consciousness is so inextricably bound within language, within the Law of the Father, that to somehow reach a Real Other that is not some mere slippery-signifier-metonym-displacement for the Imaginary Other (at last, the Mother) seems an epistemological impossibility. If the Real, including the "real" bird, is beyond representation (and therefore knowledge), at least Slavoj Žižek's Lacanian take on the Real offers a ray a hope: the Real is a "non-symbolic kernel that makes a sudden appearance in the symbolic order, in the form of traumatic 'returns' and 'answers'" (qtd. in Kerridge, introduction 3). Maybe the great horned owl that surprised me when I was a boy, flying silently a few feet over my head, disappearing immediately into the next stand of pines, was once such "trauma" of the Real. And maybe that's how, or at least one way —that the nonhuman Other speaks. And asks humans to speak for it. (I realize that such an experiential response would be viewed by the poststructuralist as a red-herring attempt to emotionally elicit a truth that is ultimately fraught with gaps.)

Opposed to the Lacanian dictum that language equals consciousness, Antonio Damasio's recent studies in brain physiology support the age-old intuition that there is a preverbal consciousness, and that complexes of images and emotions form an ego-body prior to the acquisition of language (e.g., 107–8, 184–89). As a consequence, one might presume, the individual interacts with and learns about the world and reality before the prison of the Symbolic arises; sheer physicality (including the semiotic) and intuition, then, may well teach us much about such things as our connections with other species before the sad event of Self-isolation-in-the-Symbolic occurs. Even after the arrival of the Symbolic, a semiotic (re)connection is possible: "We have feelings that can't be spoken," as Linda Hogan says, and these feelings include "a deep-moving underground language in us," whose "currents pass between us and the rest of nature" (*Dwellings* 57). Such a pre- or nonverbal reconnection with natural alterity is central to many of the so-called mystical and visionary perceptions of humankind, from St. Francis to Black Elk.

In sum, the "idea that language constructs reality . . . reveals a disturbing human arrogance and one-sidedness" (Raglon and Scholtmeijer 251). In *Arctic Dreams*, Barry Lopez remonstrates against this severe textualization of the world: "Language is not something man imposes upon the land. It evolves in his conversation with the land. . . . The very order of language, the ecology of its sounds and thoughts, derives from the mind's intercourse with the landscape" (278). This interaction of nature and the evolution of language brings to mind Momaday on the importance of names: "The names at first are those of animals and of birds" (*Names* 3). Furthermore, these names are very often onomatopoeic, as in "chickadee" and "jay."[5] In one real sense, then, one could say that the birds have been *speaking*, through human language itself, all along.

In chapter 1, I embraced the positive contributions of poststructuralism toward an ecological ethic as much as possible, especially its decentering gesture that allows one to ask, along with the decentering of the hierarchal binaries of race, class, and gender, why not species? Indeed, it may well be a question, as Manes claims, of "learning a new ethics" via "a new language . . . that incorporates a decentered, postmodern, post-humanist perspective" (17). In terms of literature itself, the postmodern shifts in point of view that I have indicated in various places are certainly conducive to a crossing of the species barrier—although, as we saw in certain traditional Native lyrics, this is hardly exclusively a postmodern trait. Thus can Maurice Kenny begin a poem as follows, both postmodern and Native in its stylistic merging of points of view, of human and nonhuman:

I hawk the sky
wolf the mountain
bear the woods
("April 22, 1985" 1–3, in [*On Second* 98])

Harrington and Tallmadge claim as one of ecocriticism's and ecoliterature's goals the "transgression of boundaries that frame conventional thought and experience of a world shared with the Other" (x), including, presumably, Hogan's "bridging" of the species "gap." These authors go on to voice their appreciation for the "postmodern impulse to use language to erase the boundary that separates us from the rest of the universe" (xv). Apparently there is still a good measure of eco-conducive positives in the current postmodern climate, in both literary technique and critical theory.[6]

Of course, my employment of Kristeva and Bakhtin is such an acknowledgment. Bakhtin is of further use in his idea of polyphony or double-voicedness in literature,[7] which creates "an assumption of *equal rights* for simultaneously existing, experiencing persons" (*Problems* 37). Why cannot these "persons" be nonhuman? Thus I have spoken at times of an owl or other bird irrupting into the human discourse that is the poem, with this notion of polyphony in mind. Bakhtin's privileged genre is the modern novel, epitomized in Dostoevsky's human panoramas of eternally arguing characters-as-tyro-philosophers. But why cannot a nature poem, of both human and avian discourse, as it were, be just as dialogic and polyphonic, if not more so? Although Bakhtin's own notion of hybridity is also framed in terms of dialogism in the novel, it still seems quite open to such a possibility: "A hybrid construction is an utterance that belongs . . . to a single speaker, but that actually contains mixed within it two utterances, two speech manners, two styles, two 'languages,' two semantic and axiological belief systems" (*Dialogic* 304). Bakhtin's later terminological refinement of polyphony, heteroglossia, likewise "permits a multiplicity of social voices" (263); then why not a naturist poetry that allows for a "multiplicity" of other-species "voices"?[8] Such a reading is no great leap in a critical milieu in which Bakhtin's notions have already permeated the scholarship of critics speaking for the minority and postcolonial Other. Repressed female voices speak back as subtexts in a patriarchal novel; the Native speaks back in a work that is an ostensibly complete colonizing act. The literary act of othering is thus never completely monophonic.

The ecocritics Raglon and Scholtmeijer find such a polysemic discourse of disruption in nature writing itself, especially in fictional narratives. In such stories, nature can "resist" anthropocentric "imposition[s]" and rebel "against human dominance" in the very context of human discourse (251, 253). These scholars' continual use of the general term "nature," however, rather deflates their argument; to speak of "the power of nature to resist, or question, or evade the meanings we attempt to impose on the natural world" (252) is a statement both magnificent in its ambition and problematic in its apparent personification of an abstract nature as an embodied character. More to the point, it is the particular (imagined, textual) oriole or oak that might be said to resist. In terms of ecological discourse and praxis, indeed, appealing to the rest of humankind in general holistic terms, invoking Mother Earth or even global warming, is less efficacious, I would claim, than pointing to the wonders of that single bird in the backyard.

In the ongoing ecocritical squabble over the relative pragmatic value of naturist genres, Raglon and Scholtmeijer deem fiction to be even more eco-conducive than nonfiction prose because fiction can "allow nature to change the shape, direction, and outcome of the narrative" (254). I find this conclusion difficult to understand, however, finding the naturist nonfiction prose of, for instance, Hogan and Kenny more ecologically powerful than most of the animals in fiction per se. I am chastened by Steve Baker's similar praise for the disruptive power of animal narratives (120–21), although I would now claim this power for naturist writing in general and for poetry in particular. Following Le Guin, Baker proposes that the "talking-animal story has the potential to subvert" human anthropocentrism and rationalism, which includes the "denial of the animal" (125); animal characters' alter-status often involves, furthermore, a "slipperiness" that works against the "'rules' of orderly, rational narrative" (131). Baker's disruption does issue in part from the specific genre of the talking-animal tale, from the insecurity of identity arising from the reader knowing full well that these talking animals are actually humans. Or are they? I would argue that the disruption that occurs in encountering a speaking bird in a true narrative such as Black Elk's is even more subversive. The reader's ontological confusion is not just that of identity, but of culture: there are groups of people who actually believe that other species can communicate with them? But most contemporary readers are too careful of their own ideologies to let this disturb their consciousness as something more than superstition. It is then that contemporary Native poetry can exert its power, as it meets the reader halfway, via a genre that the reader is more comfortable with. That is, in poetry, the reader is more at home in imagining the uncanny, the talking bird, the language of clouds. Finally, to even *imagine* an alternative, less anthropocentric worldview is the first step toward questioning one's own.

Literature's ability to effect a positive change in eco-awareness is nowhere more evident, as I have argued, than in those works in which other species really *speak back*, not as obvious anthropomorphic characters in an allegory or children's story, but as that "strange personation" that puzzled Frances Densmore as she tried to understand the irruptions of nature and other beings in Anishinaabe dream songs (*Chippewa* 1.128). Having the animal Other speak was long a common gesture in traditional Native oral lyrics: "Animal songs were sung, worded as if spoken by the animals." For instance, the "Navajos had a song for practically almost every known creature" (Hughes 24). In more recent Native literature, we have looked at several instances of this special case of prosopopoeia, in which another species is the speaking lyricist of the poem, such as Ortiz's baby bird, Rokwaho's owl, and Henson's woodpecker. By the time Henson's "woodpecker song" concludes with "i make this small sound," we have been made as close to another species via human literary discourse as is perhaps possible. More commonly, in other Native poems, there is still a speaking human narrator, but one who is inordinately aware that other species *are* speaking. Harjo's crow is one of the more notable examples here, and the abundance of hawks, herons, owls, jays, hummingbirds, and sparrows in the writing we have examined attests to the centrality of an avian chorus in contemporary Native poetry. Many of these birds speak long and loud; others speak in the sheer process of being named and acknowledged as beings worthy of existence, in literature and in the world.

I have not been able to offer a translator's phrasebook of bird language that would allow one to literally understand the bird speaking back. I have offered only several tentative ways in which the literary bird can be said to speak and reasons why the real bird deserves an audience (with an emphasis on the *aud*ile). Arguably, all this speculation is wrong-headed in its emphasis on the possibility of interspecies communication; maybe it is the final, real chasm between the languages of human and bird that makes the possibility so attractive. But this continuing attraction is a positive in itself, I would think. If Standing Bear's meadowlark never really *spoke*, something within us still needs to believe that it could have and still can.

REIMAGINING THE POSTHUMAN

O thin men of Haddam,
Why do you imagine golden birds?

Do you not see how the blackbird
Walks around the feet
Of the women about you?

WALLACE STEVENS, "Thirteen Ways of Looking at a Blackbird," in *Collected Poems*

I think we are moving in a circle, or maybe a spiral, going a little higher every time, but still returning to the same point. We are moving closer to nature again. . . . I am trying to bring the ghost dance back, but interpret it in a new way. . . . I believe that more and more people are sensing what we meant when we prayed for a new earth and that now not only the Indians but everybody has become an "endangered species."

LAME DEER, in Fire and Erdoes, *Lame Deer: Seeker of Visions*

In the 2006 film *A Prairie Home Companion*, Garrison Keillor recounts the joke about "two penguins standing on an ice flow. The first penguin says, 'You look like you're wearing a tuxedo.' Then the second penguin says, 'What makes you think I'm not?'" Indeed, how does the contemporary couch potato *see* a penguin—in terms of representational epistemology—but as a tuxedoed Disney character, smiling like a hebephrenic buffoon, your child's most real image of another hemisphere, of another radically different water-and-ice habitat, of another species? *That is how we see, or misrecognize, the bird.*

And the crimes continue. Gary Snyder offers the great scene of a hawk or eagle soaring above the Capitol in Washington. The policeman and politicians have no idea of the true "power" in flight above: to them, that "center of power is nothing! / Nothing here." But the hawk and the real world of "Earth-sky-bird patterns" go on, "above" the realm of smug anthropocentrism (and to the vast impoverishment of that realm; "It Pleases" 10, 13–14, 17 [*Turtle Island* 44]). Just so did I watch in wonder a Bald Eagle above the University of Iowa's golden dome at the very time I was first deliberating upon Snyder's poem, and then regarded in greater wonder the scores of students and faculty aiming their empty eyes at the narrow strip of sidewalk in front of them as the bird flew overhead. Truly, the "center of power" is "nothing here," too, in a midwestern academic setting well aware of Ecology with a capital E, all too ready to read and laud Leopold and Eiseley and other nature writers as "one of our own" but still largely blithely unconscious of a natural world breathing and flapping outside the windows of their cloistered, bookish lives.

When the last dusky seaside sparrow sang its final song to its last spring a few years back, the aporia went unnoticed by academics writing learned poststructuralist treatises on "imaginary communities" and "strategic essentialism," still towing, really, the same Euro-homocentric line that they've condemned for years. When the last *Homo sapiens* dies because our own species' will to knowledge could never transcend such a limited worldview, could never transcend our own antagonistic, Manichaean approach to the ecosystem of the planet, all debates about, say, the "third stage of the subaltern's dialectical progression toward postnationalism" will be *over.*

Yes, the world of human geopolitics is falling apart as human social groups wrangle over socially constructed rights and wrongs, over sects and sex. (The characteristic Native attitude toward such sectarian strife has been, after an initial reaction of great puzzlement, a crow's trickster laughter.) This book, ultimately, has been an attempt to remind us that the *human* is not all, and that, in fact, various cultural notions that the human *is* all are a crucial part of the problem. Adherents of various human social factions, often of the best liberal ilk, are constantly asking me, What good is all this animal rights crap, when *our* world is going to hell in a handcart, due to man's inhumanity to man? Exactly. My argument has been that it's such a narrow homocentric view that has us in such straits, that anthropocentrism is indeed the fundamental, original sin that has led to human-versus-human inequities. As John Gray complains, "Removing the [human hubris] masks from our animal faces is a task that has hardly begun" (38).

Wallace Stevens's great coda to "Sunday Morning," the terminal flight of its last line, haunts me: "Downward to darkness, on extended wings." Stevens's intent here, I think, is to contrast this flight of a *real* "casual flock of pigeons" (8.13 [*Collected Poems* 70]) to such false symbolizations as the Holy Spirit as dove. But one could also read the line metaphorically, as a fine summation of the philosophical direction of the twentieth century, from modernism to postmodernism, to a truly self-imposed descent into a spiritual darkness of arbitrary signs and deconstruction and erasure. The recent protests against this linguistic solipsism by, for example, deep ecologists and Native American writers have been copiously presented in this work, but Duane Niatum's hopes may be too happily righteous to be attainable: beyond the stereotypes of "native" and "beast" is a "golden path between our [white and Native] worlds, how we may with effort and will and patience not see the other man, woman, child, fish, mountain, or river, as a stranger, a type, or a category" ("On Stereotypes" 561). My critique of the literary use of birds as types and categories has been the main endeavor of this text, as a contribution, my own "small sound," to what Linda Hogan perceives to be a new "collective vision" regarding our relationship to other species (*Dwellings* 134).[9]

"If It Flies, It Dies." So runs the mantra of a group of South Dakota good ol' boys, who boast of their motto to me in a Vermillion, South Dakota bar. They speak with pride of shooting red-tailed hawks on a regular basis because there are "too damned many of 'em." They also sheepishly recoil from their initial boast of shooting bald eagles, too, possibly from recalling the patriotic iconography of the aftermath of 9/11, but their attitude toward other species is clear. My point is that this attitude is much more common—no doubt *the* attitude of the vast majority of Americans—than we might want to acknowledge, *especially* if we have spent much of our life in the hallowed halls of cloistered academia. Perhaps our own eyes-on-the-sidewalk dissociation from actual birds is just as lamentable a symptom of a general loss of relationship to the wild, and to the earth, and to, ultimately, reality.

We academics, so much in love with words, have it especially hard if we are also so much in love with a subject outside our halls, outside our discipline. In fact, as I just drafted a passage on biophilia, the biologist E. O. Wilson's explanation for our attraction to other species, our "innate tendency to focus on life and lifelike processes" (1), I first mistyped the word as "*biblio*-philia." The truth is out, I thought to myself. I have spent many years, thousands of hours, *indoors*, writing a treatise (with copious references to other *books*) about outdoor beings and the need to be outdoors.

But at last I still yearn for a worldview in which "things were larger then and vaster," as Jim Barnes says, concisely summarizing my plight:

O, but we must wash the whole world
in explanational blather and swirl
all essence that is not pure or plain
right down the heady sewer main,
or else the dirt piles high again
and mountains grow and comes the wind

whipped by ravens' wings and magic
rules as once we knew it did. Tragic
that education makes us bigger,
moves finger from nose to hair trigger. ("Ubi Sunt" 1, 13–22, in *La Plata* 33)

But "explanational blather" is expected in a human world of humanism; if *Homo sapiens* is defined as the ne plus ultra of tool users, the species' main and vaunted tool has long been the frontal lobe. The progressive Darwinism of Steven Jay Gould and others seems a promising way out, a way toward the posthuman (and the prehuman?), a reaffirmation, in some ways at least, of Darwin's original tenet (obfuscated by the discourse of Darwinism itself) that humans have arrived at their self-deemed exalted status more by tenuous chance than by divine privilege. Indeed, the whole notion of the "more highly evolved" is a crock, especially if one views the biosphere holistically. Evolution really involves the total system, and it is a success only via biodiversity; in the end, evolution is less about an individual (human) species than about increasing "biological diversity and sophistication" (Snyder, *Turtle Island* 108), an evolution of the "total field," to employ Arne Naess's phrase once again.

This finale must also be, on behalf of the bird, a call for the end of all human monotheism and of an attitude that embraces the materialism and immanence of science but refuses to see other species and so-called inorganic forms as mere objects of study, that is, some synthesis of Edward Abbey and Black Elk that perceives the here and now of a hawk as invested with enough spirit and mythos and *waka^n* in itself, an attitude that finds it sufficient to live out one's own (primate) days as an organization of atoms, happy to give back one's dust, to invoke Whitman, for the support of others' boot soles, or wings. (At bottom, a Native polytheism or pantheism and a Stoic or postmodern atheism can be one and the same, if atheism includes the ideas just expressed.) Like Lawrence Buell, I also yearn for the "Emersonian dream of nature" to be finally "purged of its theistic residue," assuming the true "status of an ecological ethic," as Buell claims occurs in the work of Robinson Jeffers (*Environmental Imagination* 162). I am moved by Jeffers's definition of "inhumanism" as a "shifting of emphasis from man to not-man; the rejection of human solipsism and recognition of the transhuman magnificence" (qtd. in Branch 49). But the rejection of humanism is difficult, if not pragmatically impossible. We apparently need to believe in our role as agents in the universe; to think otherwise—is that not but self-spite and misanthropy? David Ehrenfeld, in *The Arrogance of Humanism*, thinks otherwise. Indeed, to move *beyond* humanism is a "new freedom": "To understand that we are not steering this planet in its orbit does not mean paralysis—it means new freedom and a great relief" from impotent striving and impotent guilt (261). As for the charge of misanthropy, Ehrenfeld is quite aware of all the (oh so human) "unconscious, personal motivations" that may lead to a "rejection of humanism"; however, not only is an unselfish antihumanism possible, Ehrenfeld argues, but even its occasion by some neurotic misanthropy or sociopathy does not make it any less true: finally, "the general rejection of humanism . . . is now long overdue" (222–23).

The great nature writer Loren Eiseley almost gleefully imagines birds retaking the environment in the absence of humans: "Sometimes of late years I find myself thinking the most beautiful sight in the world might be the birds taking over New York after the last man has run away to the hills" (*Immense* 187). I wonder: is this misanthropy? Or a wisdom arising from the consciousness of "what man has made of man"? For one thing, we are a species that thinks way too much, even flattering ourselves that our knowledge of our future death separates us from other animals. But is *this* superiority?[10] In the grand scheme of things, even in the species survival evolutionary scheme of things, maybe the whole notion of individual life itself is an illusion, or the privileging thereof at least misguided. Why isn't the communality of a hill of ants or a flight of cranes the truer unit of being, and its continuing survival the greater verity? (And of course, the extension of this unit to the earth, or Gaia itself, has already become an ecocritical commonplace.)

Western civilization's privileging of the individual has had one main result, evident in much of the literature examined in this work: we individual humans are incredibly *alone*. Above all, alienated from the wild and our own animal selves as we are, we are inordinately drawn toward other species beyond some mere genetic biophilia. One of the most powerful arguments in Linda Hogan's *Dwellings* is her explanation of why humans need to touch a fawn, or even a dead wolf: "What need we humans have, a species lonely and lacking in love" (72); our alienation thus drives us to contact with anything wild, and "we can't tear ourselves away from any part of wilderness without in some way touching it" (73). Paul Shepard, too, is adamant about our need for reconnection with animals, our "desire to hold the wild" (145). His explanation of our loss of connection with other species centers on Christian dogma: "The saddest thing about the barnlike ark, the sainthood with its doting lions, and the green tunnel of the Garden of Eden is that they are so boring," and symptoms, above all, of "estrangement" (239–40). A religion of one nonanimal, spiritual Father has rendered us even more alone. Worst of all, the faith in another world after and beyond this world has allowed us to more easily ruin this one.[11] When that faith ebbs, what is left? Perhaps we can save ourselves by escaping this ruined planet and colonizing the solar system: "We hope there is another place, another world to fly to when ours is running out" (Hogan, *Dwellings* 133). Some of us place our hopes in the benevolent commanders of UFOs; some of us want to believe in the Yeti or Sasquatch—all desires for a union of the human with other (imagined) species, when the other, real species that would suffice sits in a tree in our backyard. Following Walker Percy, Shepard suggests that the contemporary search for extraterrestrial intelligence arises from the sad fact that, now that we are so thoroughly alienated from other animals, well, we need someone else to *talk* to (145–46).[12]

The tempting (at least implicit) conclusion of many works similar to mine runs as follows: know other animals; know thyself better. The modern environmentalist version of this dictum calls us to save other species and the wilderness—for *us*, either for our own enjoyment or our own survival. But what an insult to other species that is, and what ultimately anthropocentric gall. For instance, extending the canary-in-the-coal-mine cliché, Lutwack writes, "Birds have long been the measure of our fate, their extinction portending disaster for mankind" (241). Though true, such reasoning immediately shifts any sorrow and guilt for the extinction of the passenger pigeon back to a sorrow and fear for ourselves, a self-regard much less likely to prevent the future extinctions of other species. I would contend instead that subject and object, self and nature, are false dualisms: when you can make the imaginative leap that "you" *is* also a bird, another species, whether this is only metaphorically or mystically true, in the Western scheme of things, the world will be a better ecological place.

A final riposte to poststructuralism is in order here. Yes, we can know that real crow poking outside in the garbage, shitting irreverently on our SUV. In fact, we *need* to know that bird, this animal, and know that we, too, are animals, however cursed we are by some tragic, speciesist, center-of-the-cosmos hubris. In the intellectual context of poststructuralism, ecocritics are of course wrong-headed in positing a holism based on rationalist arguments. But what can a *rationalist* poststructuralism say against an *intuitive* holism and an intuitive hearing of the languages of other species, except that these human abilities lie outside its scope? My own motives can be attacked and deconstructed, to be sure. I'm pretty certain, for example (warped neo-Freudian that I remain), that my own experiential affinity for birds may indeed have some metonymic connection to my yearning for the warmth of the nest and return to the womb. And my exaggerated sensitivity to the plight of one wronged minority, the animal Other, may be but a displacement of my sensitivity regarding the wrongs felt by my own racial minority status. But echoing Ehrenfeld's treatment of the accusation of misanthropy, such motive hunting does not make my arguments any less true. The ecocritic Dana Phillips also defensively acknowledges the critique of poststructuralism in the very title of his essay, "Is Nature Necessary?" His thesis, too, is an acknowledgment of how difficult it is to go against the grain of recent literary theory: "The imagination of the real as real, and treating it as such, would be an historically original act" (219).

Treating the "real as real" entails a veritable praxis, a speaking for the alter-species whose languages do not register clearly in the *New York Times* and the *Congressional Record*. (This is all the more true if I am wrong and sociolinguistic constructivism is right: if the nonhuman Other has no discursive recourse to resistant counternarratives, its plight is rendered all the more tragic to whatever ideas of conscience and justice are left to the postmodern psyche.) A strong subtext in recent eco-minded literature is the (at least metaphorical) enfranchisement of other species, an acknowledgment of their voices in the very formation of public policy. Thus the Native American poet Elizabeth Woody speaks of her desire "to give voice to those who are not often heard from, like the salmon," the "trees," and "all that may die from our neglect" (qtd. in N. Wilson, *Nature* 125). In a speech before the United Nations in 1977, Oren Lyons's pleas for human racial equality were extended to the "four-footed," the "winged," and the "fish": "Someone must speak for them. I do not see a delegation for the four-footed. I see no seat for the eagles" (114).[13] Gary Snyder has been most vociferous in this cross-species suffrage: "what more democracy means" is not only that the Lakota reservations of "Rosebud and Pine Ridge maybe should be a separate nation," but "that trees and rocks should be able to vote in Congress, that whales should be able to vote—that's democracy" (*Real Work* 74). Conscious poetic hyperbole, no doubt(?), but the very act of asking the reader to imagine such a possibility is a strike in the right direction.[14]

I spoke of Snyder's poetic hyperbole, letting the negative connotations stand, for the moment. But imaginative nature writing—Buell's naturist literature (under which rubric I would include naturist poetry, not just creative nonfiction), remains one of the most effective social means of giving voice to the animal and bird, and thereby effecting change. On one level, pedagogically and critically, it is a simple matter of genre choice, of championing the type of writing that I have dealt with in this work, in contrast to the still dominant literature of human manners and morality that permeates both the popular bookshelves and the academic reading lists. Scott Russell Sanders asks, "What has become of nature in recent American writing?" (191). In spite of what I have perceived as a revival of the animal and bird in recent poetry, Sanders argues that, in recent fiction, at least, the reader is still "trapped inside a room" (193): "Fiction that never looks beyond the human realm is profoundly false, and therefore pathological. No matter how urban our experience, no matter how oblivious we may be toward nature, we are nonetheless animals, two-legged sacks of meat and bone dependent on the whole living planet for our survival. . . . Of course, of course: we all nod our head in agreement. The gospel of ecology has become an *intellectual* commonplace. But it is not yet an *emotional* one" (194).

One might speculate as to why explicitly ecological themes seem much more common in recent, especially Native American poetry (and personal essays) than in fiction; it must be more than the fact that Native writers especially have found it easier to get published in the short-form genres.[15] It may be, in part, a genetic Native preference for a lyrical, and ultimately oral form, a form also remarkably suited for the speaking of the Other. Even Lutwack points especially to poetry (e.g., Coleridge's *Rime*) as a central genre of consciousness-changing nature writing. Lutwack claims that such writings "have special relevance now, not only because of their eloquent renewal of the primitive's[!] respect for the animal and appreciation of the interdependence of human and animal, but because of their forceful statement of the consequences of our turning our hand, whether purposefully or carelessly, against the animal, the prime symbol[?] of nature" (232). In terms of sheer praxis, and for reasons laid out in my introduction, most effective is that naturist "literature stimulated by that most animated and communicative animal, the bird"; such works are "especially suited to keep those feelings [of eco-respect] alive" (251). The coda to Lutwack's book is an affirmation of the power of imaginative nature writing to effect an advance in eco-consciousness: ultimately, it is literature that "may help to keep alive the sensitivity that is absolutely essential in the conservation of wildlife and natural beauty" (254).

Karl Kroeber believes that the British Romantic poets had their own real "faith" in poetry as a force in changing attitudes toward the environment, a "usefulness in teaching interdependency" (*Ecological* 17). This belief is just as evident in recent Native poetry, to the point that a certain heavy-handed ecodidacticism may be discerned. It may all return, finally, to Momaday's faith in the efficacy of the *word*, as wielded by poets who would ask us to (re)imagine talking birds, to imagine voting whales. And to imagine that one might pray to a heron as the Mohawk writer Beth Brant does, and to imagine, and to hope, that the heron will still be there to be prayed to by one's children: "You [the great blue heron] have brought me so much. What can I bring you? Assurances that your territories will not be polluted and blasphemed by the corruptness of man? Promises I cannot keep? I *will* bring you this: As each of our grandchildren come into the age of seeing with their hearts, I will point you out to them. I will say your name with reverence. I will draw in my breath as we watch you fly. They in turn will know what prayer is—the hushed moment of discovery" (36). And if one's children have no birds to pray to? In an essay appreciative of Black Elk, Alice Walker prospectively mourns the loss of the avian: "The animals of the planet are in desperate peril, and they are fully aware of this. No less than human beings are doing in all parts of the world, they are seeking sanctuary. . . . Without free animal life I believe we will lose the spiritual equivalent of oxygen. . . . One day it occurred to me that if all the birds died, as they might well do, eventually, from the poisoning of their air, water, and food, it would be next to impossible to describe to our children the wonder of their flight" (326).

The time has come for a revitalization and reimagining of Wordsworth's "rocks, and stones, and trees"—and wrens and eagles. This can be best accomplished by listening, both to real birds and to the amazing speaking back of the avian now occurring in literature. *Listen*, then, to the coda of Paul Shepard's letter from the animal Others:

> We are marginalized, trivialized. . . . Once we were the bridges, exemplars of change, mediators with the future and the unseen.

> Their own [human] numbers leave little room for us, and in this is their great misunderstanding. They are wrong about our departure, thinking it to be part of their progress instead of their emptying. When we are gone they will not know who they are. Supposing themselves to be the purpose of it all, purpose will elude them. Their world will fade into an endless dusk with no whippoorwill to call the owl in the evening and no thrush to make a dawn. (333)

As we saw in a previous chapter, Lame Deer speaks of his ceremonies often being accompanied by "an eagle circling. . . . The eagle power is always there" (Fire and Erdoes 166–67). But we know now that, in ecological terms, this "always" is no certitude, and that the eagle and thousands of other species of birds may go the way of the passenger pigeon. Then the "power" will be gone. I think again of the flight of Jim Loney's "dark bird" that flew up and became a speck, and then disappeared, leaving Loney dead, and us alone.

Sad, too, are Nicholas Black Elk's last words in *Black Elk Speaks*, as Neihardt renders him a broken spokesperson for an irrevocably broken culture, for a dying dream: "Hear me, not for myself, but for my people; I am old." But his final words yet include some hope, of Native, and avian, return. It is with this still *present* hope that I would end:

> It may be that some little root of the sacred tree still lives. Nourish it then, that it may leaf and bloom and fill with singing birds. (210)

Notes

1. BIRDS OF A FEATHER

1. My choice to begin with British Romanticism is to begin at the beginning, with a literary epoch in which eco-consciousness and animal rights awareness have been deemed to have received their first great impetus. See, for instance, Worster's *Nature's Economy: The Roots of Ecology* (1977), which claims that the "Romantic approach to nature was fundamentally ecological" (58); Bate's *Romantic Ecology* (1991); Kroeber's *Ecological Literary Criticism* (1994); and McKusick's *Green Writing* (2000).
2. Parenthetical references to Jung's *Collected Works* (CW) follow common practice in indicating specific volume and paragraph (§), not page, numbers.
3. Edward A. Armstrong's *The Life and Lore of the Bird* offers another simple explanation for humankind's positive regard for birds: they don't *eat* us! "Birds are remarkable, indeed unique, in that no member of this huge group of animals has ever been a direct menace to man" (6).
4. For example, Arthur Wormhoudt's "The Unconscious Bird Symbol in Literature" begins with the Freudian assertion (and "clinical evidence") that "the bird may in dreams be a symbol for the breast as well as the penis" (173).
5. Similar to its cousins, the crows and jays, the magpie is, according to Rowland, "regarded almost universally[?] as a symbol of ill-omen," in part due to its "kleptomania," its "incorrigible addiction to pilfering." This "saucy" bird has also long been abjectly associated with the female because it is both "gossipy" and "argumentative" (104, 103), thus its British folk nicknames, "Chatter Pie" and "Tell Pie" (Lockwood 41, 153).
6. In accord with my "flights of fancy" angle, the thoughts that birds most often represent are "fantasies and intuitive ideas" (CW 12: §305). I find Jung's idealist interpretation of the birds inimical, however, to my own eventual emphasis on birds as real, em*bodied* beings. Jung reads the animal image in general as symbolic of the unconscious, instinct, and the "bestial" body; the bird, in contrast, as "inhabitant of the bright realm of the air, is a symbol of conscious thought, of the (winged) ideal, and of the Holy Ghost (dove)" (6: §458).
7. One must qualify Lutwack's reference to the blackbird, however. He has most in mind American poets and the American "blackbird," usually the common grackle (and perhaps, the European starling, too, often dubbed "blackbird" by the ornithologically challenged). The European blackbird (*Turdus merula*), in contrast, is the beloved songster of Wordsworth and company, close relative of the European

and American robins. It is as if centuries of praising its song in British verse had effaced the "black" connotations of its name.

8. Elsewhere in Lutwack, "birds must have seemed[!] to primitive humans to be mysterious creatures commanding attention and worship" (81). Likewise Rowland: "Primitive tribes still see the human soul as a bird" (xiv). Jung's own frequent damning-with-condescending-praise references to the "primitive" and "atavistic" are legendary (e.g., CW 5: §653, 14: §602).
9. "The sea is the favourite symbol for the unconscious, the mother of all that lives" (Jung, CW 9i: §298).
10. Jung also notes the antinomic pairing of dove and raven: "The raven is the black soul-symbol, the dove is the bright one" (14: §731n). Even more universal is the union of bird (often an eagle) and snake, the aerial and the chthonic, a motif to be dealt with in much more detail later. (See, for example, CW 12: §404, 13: §415–17, 14: §81, §483n.)
11. A similar polarity is at work in the owl, associated with both death and wisdom (Rowland 115). (The raven, too, was alternatively a "divine bird" in antiquity, "symbol of wisdom and science" [145].)
12. Fanon sees Jung's collective unconscious as a projection of a specifically "European unconscious" whose "dark shadow" is, naturally, the black race (and Native American race, as I see it). For Fanon, the collective unconscious is not genetic but a cultural construct, "the sum of prejudices, myths, [and] collective attitudes of a given group." Jung "was an innovator," no doubt; however, seeking "to go back to the childhood of the world . . . he made a remarkable mistake: He went back to the childhood of Europe" (188–90).
13. In Pueblo tradition, for instance, the turkey vulture is a positive "medicine man" or "priest" of purification, birds who "literally cleanse and purify the natural world" (Tyler 265, 269).
14. Jung's debt, indeed, epigonic relationship to nineteenth-century German Idealism and Romantic Naturphilosophie, especially Schelling and Richter, is well documented; see, for instance, Abrams, *Mirror* 211–12; Applewhite 11.
15 Fittingly, the supreme Aztec deity Quetzalcoatl was both snake and bird. This Native American *hierosgamos* of reptile and avian is discussed at length in a later chapter.
16. The Papez-MacLean theory positions this reptilian brain "at and near the top of the brain stem"; this part of the brain "seems to contain the ancestral lore of the species" (Hampden-Turner 80).
17. At one point Jung also points out a specific reptilian component of the collective unconscious: humankind's evolutionary "animal nature" includes "a whole series of lower storeys" (a favorite metaphor of Jung's) "in which the spectres from humanity's past epochs still dwell," including "the animal souls from the age of

Pithecanthropus and the hominids, then the 'psyche' of the cold-blooded saurians" (CW 14: §279). Similarly, Paul Shepard invokes an evolutionary, phylogenetic basis for "our forgotten lives as fish and reptiles" (79–80).

18. Elsewhere in Shepard, animals are explicitly Jungian: they "are guides, gatekeepers, couriers, and exemplars, as they are epiphanies of aspects of ourselves," which "mediate between our conscious selves and the archetypal figures of our innermost being" (329, 282). In earlier times, at least, "wild animals had been the archetypes," "the medium of communication of the hidden aspects of [human] experience" (324).

19. See Jung, CW 5: §261, §398, §421, §503; 6: §457–58; 7: §133; 9i: §660; 11: §600; 12: §169, §186; 14: §277. In Paul Shepard's words, the animals that we most vilify or fear "are clearly our unconscious proxies for something else" (271).

20. Interestingly, black slaves were commonly referred to as "blackbirds" in the nineteenth century (Rowland 13).

21. Thus in Jung, the raven is not only an "allegory of evil" but a "synonym for the devil" (9i: §428n, 16: §533).

22. Elizabeth Cook-Lynn posits an "anti-Indianism," which she uses in a sense similar to anti-Semitism (*Anti-Indianism* x, 3–4). I offer here the term "Indianism" instead, as a term more parallel to "Orientalism."

23. See Peter Singer's *Animal Liberation* (e.g., 7, vii, x).

24. For example, William Cowper, whose barnyard fowl in *The Task* are transformed into the "feather'd tribes / domestic" (5.62); John James Audubon, who speaks of the wood thrush as his "greatest favourite of the feathered tribes of our woods" (275); and (the very title of) John Mudie's early bird guide, *The Feathered Tribes of the British Isles* (1834). In the eighteenth-century Linnaean classification scheme, "tribe" stood between order and genus, analogous to today's taxonomic "family"; its use in English in the sense of a group of related animal species or genera dates back to 1640 (OED). Following this familial thread, M. L. Pratt notes that "the Linnaean genus and species labels [still employed today by biologists] look remarkably like the given and family names required of [human, bourgeois] citizens" (35). In a related vein, "race," taxonomically speaking, has been a synonym for biological subspecies to this day.

25. Paul Shepard makes a similar point: "Enclaves [such as zoos] 'protect' the defeated [animals], as they did American Indians, by assigning them to reservations and then eliminating them outside the sanctuary" of environmental concern and protection (233–34).

26. This sentence occurs as a damning refrain in the first chapter of Vizenor's *Manifest Manners*, "Postindian Warriors" (18, 21, 42, 43, 44).

27. For one of many analyses of deep ecology as a critique of humanism's hierarchical homocentrism, see Manes's "Nature and Silence" 22–24. Steve Baker also lauds

the benefits of a poststructuralist "decentering" for the specific concerns of animal rights advocates (xvi–xvii); thus Foucault's "notion of the decentring of the human subject is of paramount importance. . . . The decentring of the human subject opens up a valuable conceptual space for shifting the animal out from the cultural margins" (26).

28. See also Ehrenfeld 178, 180 for a critique of gestures toward other-species preservation based on thoroughly humanistic values. Steve Baker also perceives "the essentially selfish [i.e., anthropocentric] project of conservation" (182).

29. See Snyder, *Practice of the Wild* 25–29, 37–44 for a discussion of bioregionalism by the poet laureate of deep ecology.

30. For more on this relation of feelings and ecological philosophy, see also Naess's "Deep Ecology and Ultimate Premises" 131.

31. Also dubbed the "minority tradition," this "eternally" alternative worldview is very close to what Snyder calls the "Great Subculture which goes back as far perhaps as the late Paleolithic" (*Earth House Hold* 104). Devall and Sessions's contrast of their "perennial philosophy" with the dominant hegemonic view is also similar, however, to Worster's distinction between the "arcadian" and "imperialist" approaches to nature, and deep ecology is fraught with many of both the positives and negatives that the arcadian worldview entails.

32. For these influences on the "perennial philosophy," see Devall and Sessions 18–19, 45–46, 66, 79–85, 88–92, 96–101, 232–42. Interestingly, the contrasting Western philosophical mainstream, according to the authors, is also responsible for the recent obsession with a "solipsistic" sociolinguisticism in academia (254–55), an initial slam at constructivism that ecocritics such as Howarth, Bate, and Buell will develop.

33. One might deconstruct even further such a privileging of the bio- in "biocentrism": is our limited human point of view so sure, after all, that life is more important than nonlife? In other words, "ecocentrism" would seem to be the preferable term, although one might ultimately wonder whether any-centrism or center will hold. Lawrence Buell, by the way, also employs an alternative term, "ecocentricity" (e.g., *Environmental* 144), but this must be regarded as a less happy coinage because it might readily tempt less sympathetic readers to omit the "o."

But then *eco*centrism has its own problems, along with "ecology" and "ecocriticism," because *eco-* is anthropocentric in origin, stemming as it does from "house" or "household"; indeed, the assumption of some sort of *human, domestic* economy, etymologically speaking, underlies the whole science.

Deep ecology's "Self" is problematic, apparently equaling an organic wholeness that supposedly issues from Spinoza and smacks of Jung. The notion originates in Naess's proffering his ecosophy as a means to greater self-realization, but this last term has been so multitudinously signified by various schools of psychology that I can only read it, in context, with a feeling of *deep* perplexity. Though Naess clarifies what he means by this term in other utterances (i.e., as in Jung, "Self" does not equal "ego" [qtd. in Devall and Sessions 76]), the reader of "The Shallow and the Deep" alone is left wondering whether "Self-realization" means anything more than that "deep pleasure and satisfaction we receive from close partnership with other forms of life" (96).

34. Brian Tokar's neo-Marxist social ecology critique of deep ecology includes a direct accusation of classism (and even racism). Not only is deep ecology downright misanthropic, especially in its Earth First! activist manifestation (134), but its privileging of the right of solitary individuals to enjoy nature ignores class hierarchy. Its call for a human population decline is really a call for fewer *poor* people, with an implicit understanding that most of the world's poor are nonwhite (135–37). Killingsworth and Palmer have likewise observed the dangers of deep ecology's denial of, even conscious refusal to acknowledge, concerns of human social inequity (197, 202).

35. Naess confesses, "More than 2,500 years of literature and poetry have expressed wonder and awe [regarding nature] in a direct way that eco-philosophy or a Deep Ecology platform cannot, and may be *[sic]* should not, try to imitate" ("Deep Ecology" 129).

36. Dominic Head, for instance, claims that deep ecology especially—witness the fanaticism of certain radical environmental groups—is rather "dark Green" in its "drive towards fundamentalism" (27). Richard Kerridge also warns that environmentalism might become another well-meaning but ultimately fascist colonialism (introduction 7), and David Mazel reads (U.S.) environmentalism as a potentially new form of imperialist Orientalism (142–44).

37. Thus can Joni Adamson Clarke, a major spokesperson for environmental justice, argue for the interconnection of ecocriticism and human class and racial matters, in that the "issues of [human] race and human rights must be brought into any satisfactory ecocritical discussion of 'nature.'" This interconnection includes the similar "oppression of certain races and classes and the appropriation and exploitation of indigenous lands" (10, 12).

38. Merchant's "spiritual ecologists" range from Native American traditionalists to New Age (or are they "Old Age"?) Wiccas, Gaians, and hunter-gatherer primitivists (*Radical Ecology* 110–29). A characteristic work of spiritual ecology is Dolores LaChapelle's *Earth Wisdom*, a mélange of New Age beliefs and practices, ranging from Native American rituals to Jungian psychology to Tai Chi. The founder of "social ecology," Murray Bookchin, defines ecology as the "harmonization of nature and man," with humankind at the top of the "biotic pyramid," elite among the "higher forms of life" (Herber 322, 327); social ecology's goals, in the end, are "man-oriented," "*humanistic*" (339). Bookchin claims, moreover,

that "the very domination of nature by man stems from the very real domination of human by human" (qtd. in Killingsworth and Palmer 196). But I would have to agree with David Ehrenfeld's reading of Bookchin's social ecology as another optimistic, "humanistic cult," and Marxism in general as a glaring exemplum of the ultimate failure of humanism itself (127, 249–50).

39. Earlier, in *The Comedy of Survival* (1972), Joseph Meeker posited a "literary ecology," defined as "the study of biological themes and relationships that appear in literary works" (7). "Biological," however, may be too limiting a term, just as "biocentrism" is a less happy phrase (for, say, the rights of rock formations) than "ecocentrism." Karl Kroeber also makes a claim for origin, asserting in his 1994 *Ecological Literary Criticism* that he "introduced the term *ecology* into romantic criticism twenty years ago" (53) in his 1974 essay "Home at Grasmere."

40. Eric Todd Smith agrees that Glotfelty's definition "reproduces the dyad" of human versus nature (30). Hubert Zapf represents more recent ecocritics who would reinscribe "the culture/nature relationship in such a way that their essentialist binary opposition . . . is overcome and is replaced by a relationship of mutual interaction and interdependence" (85).

41. Later in the same essay ("Some Principles of Ecocriticism"), Howarth offers a more concise gem of a definition and agenda: "Ecocriticism seeks to examine how metaphors of nature and land are used and abused" (81).

42. One might argue that a fourth stage is already in progress and is explicit in the very title of Armbruster and Wallace's *Beyond Nature Writing* (2001). The editors call for "expanding" the "boundaries" of the ecocritical agenda beyond nature writing per se. Assuming that the "natural environment" is a base for all human interaction and discourse, even its relative absence (e.g., in the novels of Henry James) is worthy of study (Wallace and Armbruster 2–4, 7–8).

43. Bate is quoting the new historicist Alan Liu as his immediate opponent. But Derrida has also-already written, "There is no nature, only the effects of nature: denaturalization or naturalization" (170). For other pointed pro-ecocritical but anti-poststructuralist views, see Gray 54–55; Zapf 86.

44. As we have seen, "ecosophy" was first used by Naess in "The Shallow and the Deep," as the philosophy of deep ecology (99), but Branch gives Naess nary a footnote.

45. Glen A. Love is even less conciliatory toward poststructuralist theory: perceiving a new (ecological) "critical shift" in literary studies, he calls for "a major reordering of the literary genres" that "values unity . . . over post-structuralist nihilism" (236). Kerridge likewise posits a totality beyond poststructuralist critique: "Environmental crisis confronts postmodernity with another sort of totality, the global ecosystem. . . . Nothing is outside this system; it has no [Derridean] supplement or [Kristevan] abject" ("Small Rooms and the Ecosystem" 190).

46. Worster agrees that "almost all the leading voices" of first-generation Romanticism "refused to accept traditional Christian theology or ethics" (86).
47. See, for instance, Howarth, "Some Principles" 87; McKusick 32.
48. Granted, "there are many courses in 'The Nature Poets' in American colleges, but nature is usually left out of them" (Joseph Wood Krutch, qtd. in Buell, *Environmental Imagination* 9). Buell continues: "Writing and reading are acts usually performed indoors, unachievable without long shifts of attention away from the natural environment"; moreover, poststructuralism especially is "characteristic" of a "metropolitan-based" critical theory. Thus "to investigate literature's capacity for articulating the nonhuman environment is not one of the things that modern professional readers of literature have been trained to do" (84, 36, 10).
49. Eric Todd Smith also finds Buell's entire privileging of the "subjecthood of nature" to be "problematic" for this very reason (32). Conversely, Dana Phillips has critiqued Buell's flirtation with the "objective" side of his dual approach, that is, mimetic realism. Acknowledging Buell's careful attention to the "limitations" of such representationalism, Phillips concludes that such efforts aren't as earnest as Buell's "desire to flout the warnings of literature and philosophy about the naïveté of realism" (*Truth* 183). For example, Buell's high regard for Peterson's *Bird Guide* is misplaced: the reader of such texts doesn't become closer to real birds and real nature, but rather and merely with their "stylized image[s]" (179).
50. Later in "On Truth and Falsity in Their Extramoral Sense" Nietzsche writes, "It costs him [man] some trouble to admit to himself that the insect and the bird perceive a world different from his own" (94); moreover, "if we ourselves were only able to perceive sometimes as a bird, sometimes as a worm, sometimes as a plant," the mendacity of human essentialism and metaphysics would be readily manifest (95).

    Lawrence Buell apparently paraphrases Nietzsche as follows: "Both [Whitman and Janovy] affirm that the caddis fly is just as real as we are, has just as much right as you and I do to be taken as the center of the universe around which everything else shall revolve" (*Environmental Imagination* 107). Buell's transspecies intersubjectivity (as I call it) is, in part, a reeducation of the reader (and critic), raising "the question of the validity of the self as the primary focalizing device for both reader and writer: to make one wonder . . . whether the self is as interesting an object of study as we supposed, whether the world would become more interesting if we could see it from the perspective of a wolf, a sparrow, a river, a stone" (179).
51. Steve Baker, although quite pro–animal rights himself, still presents the constructivist attitude toward other species, with its emphasis on representation and denial of the real: the animal can "*only* be considered, and understood, through its representations. There [is] no unmediated access to the 'real' animal" (xvi), for

"the animal is necessarily a construction, a representation, and not an accessible essence or reality" (5).

52. In Buell's myth of kinship between human and nonhuman, "the extinction of a large nonhuman population begins to feel like a holocaust" (*Environmental Imagination* 304). Indeed, to my thinking, the extinction of an entire (other) species is even more tragic than a human-specific holocaust. The animal rightist in Coetzee's *The Lives of Animals* also compares animal cruelty to the Holocaust, to her audience's deep chagrin.
53. Kerridge also has such broadcast fare in mind when he says that "the natural world is an example of the repressed Other in postmodernity, repressed most fully by its own commodification" via television ("Small Rooms" 187).
54. Factory farming is "the most extensive exploitation of other species that has ever existed" (Singer, *Animal Liberation* 96). Lame Deer makes a similar complaint from a Lakota perspective: "A partridge, a grouse, a quail, a pheasant, you have made them into chickens, creatures that can't fly," and put them on farms where "they wear a kind of sunglasses so that they won't peck each other's eyes out"; the result is an "unnatural, crazy no-good bird." This general drive toward denaturalization "makes unnatural, no-good human beings" (Fire and Erdoes 120).
55. Lynn White Jr. has perhaps been most vocal in lambasting Christianity as *the* cause of our current general ecological plight, in "The Historical Roots of Our Ecological Crisis" (1967): "Especially in its Western form, Christianity is the most anthropocentric religion the world has seen" (9). However, this attack on "orthodox Christian arrogance" includes the surprising claim that "the remedy [to our ecological plight] must also be religious": "I propose Francis as a patron saint for ecologists" (14). John Gray is more thoroughly scornful of "Christianity's cardinal error—the belief that humans are radically different from all other animals" (37).

    Regarding the Cartesian mechanization of birds in particular, see Shepard 278–79.
56. For the deep ecologists, this is all wrong-headed. In the interests of eco-equality, Devall and Sessions call to task animal rights philosophies as a "moral extensionism" that is not egalitarian enough, that still maintains the hierarchies of animals over plants and "higher" animals over "lower" (55). Buell also finds the philosophies of animal rights—but also deep ecology's own biocentrism—walking on very soft ground: "Should the outer circle of moral consideration be extended to include only 'higher' animals, all sentient beings, all forms of life, or somewhere beyond that?" (*Future* 107).
57. Carolyn Merchant agrees, placing both Singer and Regan under the "utilitarian" and "homocentric" umbrella (64, 74).
58. Not surprisingly, Peter Singer's supplemental "Reflection" in *Lives* includes the

objection that "there is more to human existence than there is to bat existence" (90), above all, the faculty of reason. Thus he is quick to call Elizabeth's approach a "more radical egalitarianism" than he "would be prepared to defend" (86).

59. Buell, *Environmental Imagination* 200–201. According to Lovelock himself, "The Gaia hypothesis . . . postulates the earth to be the largest living thing in the solar system" (351). Aware perhaps that his science is questionable, Lovelock emphasizes the pragmatism, even the emotional benefits, of the theory: "It is an affair of the heart as well as the head." In sum, "it would be a good idea to assume that the earth and Gaia are alive. Then you can enjoy being a part of things and feel the outrage over the destruction of some part which is part of yourself as something real and not as just a sentimentality" (359).
60. Lutwack agrees, quoting approvingly a "distinguished" ornithologist who hopes that poets "will do their best to 'combine both the naturalist's practical observation and the poet's illuminated imagination'" (19).
61. Glen A. Love, deeming this book "the first genuinely new reading of literature from an ecological viewpoint," also remarks on its "curious nonreception" in a discipline that didn't know what to do with it. For humanities academics, "Nature . . . is vexingly interdisciplinary" (228).
62. John Gray reproduces this Schilleresque philosophy: "Language begins in the play of animals and birds" (76). Moreover, "if you seek the origins of ethics, look to the lives of other animals. The roots of ethics are in the animal virtues" (110).
63. This is, of course, the same cultural hegemony that deep ecology rails against.
64. For instance, Meeker's list of the "playful" attributes of the (eco)paradise that is Dante's *Paradiso* is really an exercise in superlatives: "perfect(ly)" "genuine(ly)," "exactly," "unimpededly," "powerful," "great," "complete," "fully," "really," and "best" (101–02).
65. Such early play is even a "precursor to poetry and other metaphor" (Shepard 88). Later, in adulthood, even our slang language about sexuality is all animal: "cock," "cunt" (i.e., "cony" or rabbit), "pussy," and "ass" (66).
66. "As the planet becomes destitute, the triple doorways of triage will open first to the rich; secondly, partly, to the poor; but the third class, the non-humans, already drowning, will not be saved by our toy arks, the zoos" (Shepard 234). John Berger's condemnation of zoos is just as heated (19–26): they are mere "monument[s]," "epitaph[s]," and "last metaphor[s]" of our previous relationship to other species (19, 24); the enclaved animals themselves are, like pets, at a pale remove from life itself, having been "*rendered absolutely marginal*" (22).
67. Shepard's critique of Christianity and monotheism echoes throughout his book (e.g., 7, 222–25). Earlier religions embraced the natural and the animal as deific, and the subsequent decline in animal symbolism corresponds to a subsequent decline in the quality of human religion (192–94). In fact, older polytheism—(a

misnomer, according to Shepard) is actually more holistic, in an eco-organic-naturalist sense (134–35). (John Gray's similar preference for polytheism over monotheism is deliciously damning: "Polytheism is too delicate a way of thinking for modern minds" [126].) The lack of animal deities in the three great modern monotheistic religions is really "the emptying out of their souls," a loss of authentic ties to natural life (Shepard 241), and the (unnatural, retreatist, and isolationist) notion of Paradise or Eden actually "expresses the fear and hatred of . . . animals" (228).

Jung had already made a similar "heretical" lament: in the old days, "the gods are symbolized as animals—even the Holy Ghost is a bird; all the antique gods . . . are animals at the same time" (*Earth* 84). "Why have the animals disappeared from the Christian teaching? When animals are no longer included in the religious symbol or creed, it is the beginning of the dissociation between religion and nature. Then there is no mana in it": it is "the beginning of the end" (170). Phyllis Simpson's essay on "The Primeval Bird" is especially relevant to my argument: "Where we find only one god, we find man at variance with most birds"; indeed, "the bird is most degraded where there is monotheism," which "inevitably reflects man's anthropocentricity" (99–100).

68. Steve Baker also mentions the U.S. eagle as an iconic devolution: "The symbol of the [bald] eagle simply stands for the nation . . . and because of its familiarity, and the immediacy with which it is recognized, the symbol is effectively invisible—effectively drained of its animality" (109). Expressed most concisely: "Symbols don't get their own claws dirty" (61).

69. Shepard also looks askance at the "shallower" variety of band-jumping animal protectionists: "The whooping crane was furiously protected in North America by many who wouldn't know it from a duck" (327)!

70. Even today humans "are space-needing, wild-country, Pleistocene beings, trapped in overdense numbers in devastated, simplified ecosystems" (Shepard 317). Shepard's various complaints about human overpopulation (the "hideous overabundance of humans" [319]), our need for the wild, and his emphasis on the ecological big picture place him pretty firmly in the deep ecology camp.

Indeed, Shepard's version of deep ecology is satirized in Silko's *Almanac of the Dead*, via a group whose motto is "Back to the Pleistocene" and who want "to return to cave living with the bears as their European forefathers had once lived" (689).

71. Moreover, the tropes of Native literature are also usually "translated . . . with minimal comprehension of native intentions and meaning" in the pedagogy and criticism of the dominant Western view (Vizenor, "Literary Animals" 134)—like animal alterity itself, I might add.

72. Vizenor calls such animals "heroic and ironic" (i.e., ironic as "human" charac-

ters and narrators). They are also "distinct creations of mutant omniscience" and "the contrarious animal other of animism and the ultramundane" ("Literary" 128, 131).

73. The author biography in the back of Momaday's *In the Presence of the Sun*, after recounting his various awards, ends with the short shock of a sentence: "He is a bear."

74. In other words, Vizenor's distinction isn't based on the formal or grammatical difference between the two, because he reads some formal ("as" or "like") similes as more akin to Native metaphor than to the anthropocentric similes of dominance and othering (which, grammatically, may well be metaphors).

75. If this sounds like Paul Shepard, it's not surprising, because Vizenor also quotes him frequently elsewhere in the essay. "Manifest manners" is Vizenor's term (and book title) for the dominant Western imperialist worldview and the "literature of dominance" that serves as its prop (*Manifest* 3). As for monotheism, he abhors its impact as much as Shepard does: "Monotheistic creation is a separation of animals and humans in nature and literature" ("Literary" 142).

76. Buell, as we have seen, argues similarly against a blanket condemnation of Western nature writing as imperialist. Vis-à-vis the "quest for environmental literacy" in Wordsworth, Snyder, and others, yes, "one could deconstruct this interest" easily enough: "Nevertheless . . . we would be obtuse in lumping all environmental representations together as fabricated impositions" (*Environmental Imagination* 108, 77).

77. To Lawrence Buell's credit, he has more recently lamented that "ecocritics are still only starting to explore minority canons" and that "minority ecocritics are still very few in number" (*Future* 118).

78. Some scholars employ the term "posthuman" in reference to just such technological futures; Gray, for instance, has the potential evolution of artificial intelligence specifically in mind (185–89). My use of the term points instead to a future evolution of consciousness regarding humankind's relationship with other carbon-based terrestrial life forms.

79. Of course, the term "hu*man*ities" must go, eventually, as symptomatic of the worldview I'm arguing against. See Ehrenfeld's *The Arrogance of Humanism* for an analysis of humanism as a religion based on a "supreme faith in human reason" (5). Ehrenfeld's critique is echoed in Manes's "Nature and Silence" (e.g., 20–21, 24) and in Gray's *Straw Dogs* (4, 24–25, 31–32, 37–38, 41).

For Hogan's call for a reunion of species as a "crossing" of "boundaries," a "bridging" of the "species barrier," see *Dwellings* 48, 59, 76, 111, 116, 153.

80. To Buell's credit once again, he praises Fletcher's notion in his most recent work, as perhaps a more viable ecocritical tack than his own earlier privileging of naturist mimesis (*Future* 50–56).

2. WANDERING VOICES

1. All poem and line number references to Wordsworth's poetry are to the five-volume *Poetical Works* (PW), unless otherwise indicated. Likewise, parenthetical references to other canonical poets will be to line, not page, numbers.

   Stephen Hunt makes a similar point: even the *Prelude* of 1805 "clearly privileges constructions of the human mind over the physical world" (57). The rampant psychological readings of Wordsworth during the 1950s and 1960s will be discussed in more detail later, but the poet himself certainly provides fuel for such a fire in such passages as the Simplon Pass episode in *The Prelude*, where the specifics of the natural scene

   > Were all like workings of one mind, the features
   > Of the same face, blossoms upon one tree,
   > Characters of the great Apocalypse,
   > The types and symbols of Eternity,
   > Of first and last, and midst, and without end. (6.568–72)

2. Indeed, as Harold Bloom puts it in *The Anxiety of Influence*, "Wordsworth, whose art depends upon persuading the reader that relationship with external selves and landscapes is still possible, is an immense master at estranging other selves and every landscape *from himself*" (126). More generally speaking, "all Romanticisms . . . are quests to re-beget one's own self, to become one's own Great Original" (64). Lawrence Buell notes, too, that this disembodied "objective self" of Western philosophy "does not have anything to do with a world of objects" (*Environmental Imagination* 279).
3. Matthew Teorey's argument that Wordsworth's "messages" can be seen as proto-ecofeminist (e.g., 34) is very problematic, as is his claim that "in Wordsworth's poetry, nature, women, and the poor have a sovereign, dynamic presence and authoritative voices, often equal or superior to his own" (45). In this chapter, I usually argue the very opposite.
4. The connection between the mentally ill and my own emphasis, other species, is made by Paul Shepard: "For centuries animals have been seen as demented persons" (231). See also Steve Baker's discussion of the Foucauldian "connection" between animals and "madness" (95).
5. All quotations from *The Prelude* are from the 1805 version (revised Oxford edition), unless otherwise indicated.
6. That the British have had an age-old fondness for animals in general seems a truism (despite the centuries-long reality of cruelty toward other species, including birds). According to Gaull, the nineteenth-century British, at least, "were genuinely fond of animals, especially horses[!]" (339). Steve Baker's study of ani-

mal iconography in the British popular press is more circumspect in its references to a "nation of self-proclaimed animal lovers" for whom animals have also provided a ubiquitous iconography of abjectness and evil (116).

7. Without furnishing a full bibliography of such works, I would especially acknowledge W. B. Lockwood's *The Oxford Book of British Bird Names* and Thomas P. Harrison's *They Tell of Birds: Chaucer, Spenser, Milton, Drayton* for their great aid in the species identification of various vague and obsolete avian names in British poetry. Patrick Cheney's *Spenser's Famous Flight* (1993) deserves mention as the only text I've encountered (before my own) that employs the phrase "avian 'Other'" (13).
8. Citing John Berger and Keith Tester, Steve Baker concludes that the "shift to a broadly 'modern' attitude to animals" happened "around the start of the nineteenth century" (18).
9. "Thus Wordsworth's philanthropy," according to Meihuizen, "is actually an extension of his love for nature" (54). In Wordsworth, this theme receives its fullest didactic treatment in *Peter Bell*, the title character of which is reformed through his very cruelty to an ass. Yes, the ass's grotesque grinning and his turning on Peter "his shining hazel eye" are easily parodied (825, 435), and Peter's own transformation borders on the maudlin. But through nature's general rejuvenating powers (1071–75) and Peter's newfound desire that his heart were half as good as that of the "poor beast" whom he has abused (1099), his former sociopathic relationship with his own species is also reversed: "His heart . . . opening more and more," Peter now "feels what he for human-kind / Has never felt before" (1052, 1054–55).

   As a parallel between Wordsworth's perception and a Native American view, Luther Standing Bear asserts that the "old Lakota . . . . knew that man's heart, away from nature, becomes hard" (*Land* 197).
10. In the common practice of British poetry from its beginnings through Romanticism, "warbler" often denotes songbirds in general, not just the Old World Warbler family designated by modern ornithology. Thus Coleridge addresses the nightingale, "Farewell, O Warbler!" ("The Nightingale" 87), William Wordsworth's "daring warbler" is a skylark ("A Morning Exercise" 44), and Keats's poem "Stay, ruby breasted warbler, stay" is an appeal to a wintering robin. The generic use of the name also attests to humankind's usual willful ignorance in distinguishing difference among all those little, mostly brownish birds that twitter a lot.
11. But elsewhere in *The Task* Cowper reaffirms the dominant mode of perception, and the colonizing gaze, as analyzed in M. L. Pratt's *Imperial Eyes,* assumes its usual place, on high ground: "Now roves the eye; / And, posted on this *speculative* height, / Exults in its command" (1.288–90; emphasis added). Such an ego exultation exemplifies Pratt's comment that "promontory descriptions are . . . very

common in Romantic and Victorian writings of all kinds" (202). Moreover, in line with Pratt's concept of self-effacing, ostensibly innocent "anti-conquest" (7), Cowper's "guiltless eye / Commits no wrong, nor wastes what it enjoys" (1.333–34).

12. All people of sense in Cowper's day, apparently, "hate[d] the rank society of weeds," an "overbearing race" who only "Disturb [the] good order" of a gentrified, fine-garden society (*The Task* 3.670, 672, 674).
13. See, for example, "To a Mouse"; "To a Louse"; "On seeing a Wounded Hare limp by me which a Fellow had just shot at[!]" ("Inhuman man! curse on thy barb'rous art" [1]); "The Auld Farmer's New-Year Morning Salutation to His Auld Mare, Maggie"; "Elegy on Willie Nicol's Mare"; "Poor Mailie's Elegy"; "The Death and Dying Words of Poor Mailie" (Mailie was a ewe).
14. Even the humbler plants gain an advocate in Burns, as in his paean to the "modest," "unassuming," and "humble" daisy ("To a Mountain Daisy" 1.1, 5.3–4), which anticipates Wordsworth's similar lyrics to flowers of lesser repute.
15. Burns's "green-crested lapwing" is the Northern Lapwing, a plover-like wader commonly found inland.
16. Indeed, according to Rowland, "Few writers are likely to use this bird as a praiseworthy symbol" (28).
17. Thus, according to Hartman, Blake "rejects Nature categorically as a source of Inspiration" (*Wordsworth's Poetry* 219). If Wordsworth's poetry was based on the "outward eye," as Frederick A. Pottle has it, "Blake . . . wanted to relinquish the control of common perception altogether" (286). More recently, Marilyn Gaull has contended that "to idealists such as Blake and Shelley, to whom nature was itself lifeless and the source of much error," nature merely "provided symbols, correspondences, and analogies" (304–05).
18. For example, "Auguries of Innocence": "A Robin Red breast in a Cage / Puts all Heaven in a Rage"; "He who shall hurt the little Wren / Shall never be belovd by Men" (5–6, 29–30). Pointing to this same poem, Lutwack claims that Blake's outrage against bird caging and cruelty was "one of the earliest . . . outcries," his example providing a theme that would continue to echo through English poetry (153–54). Lutwack also discerns a new concern for caged birds among the Romantics in general: the same writers who "began to reemphasize the close relation of man to nature" were also instrumental in the "great turning point in attitudes about keeping wild pets" (152–53).
19. References to *The Marriage of Heaven and Hell* are to page numbers.
20. The ecoscholar Patrick D. Murphy expresses this view well: "In order to be fully human, we need to have a healthy *geopsyche*" (42).
21. Tennyson may have had Erasmus Darwin partly in mind in "Amphion" when he laments a nonpoetic, "brassy age" in which the "modern Muses . . . read Botanic Treatises" (9.1, 10.4–5) and translate them into verse.

22. Gaull, too, has noted the "titillating sexuality" of Darwin's poetry, and how it "sexualized the study of nature" (187, 186).

23. Thus in the first chapter of *Biographia Literaria*, Coleridge comments on the popularity of the *Botanic Garden*, "which, for some years, was greatly extolled . . . by the reading public" (165).

24. For more on the rage of specimen collecting as a thoroughly imperialist way of knowing, see Pratt 27. A comparable nineteenth-century rage in the United States is documented in the early chapters of Christoph Irmscher's *The Poetics of Natural History*.

25. "As ornaments or status symbols, birds had been bred, hunted, stuffed, and cooked; they had appeared caged in libraries and ornamental gardens, in poetry, heraldry, hats, porcelains, and textiles"; thus Gaull explains the popularity of White's *Natural History* and Bewick's *History of British Birds*, which, "along with inexpensive and widely distributed handbooks and periodicals, helped educate a reading public in the procedures and pleasures of observing birds in their natural setting" (369).

26. Some passages in the book are "about as pretty a wedding of art and science as one could envisage" (Baldwin 150). His scientific observations alone make White the "greatest field naturalist of the eighteenth century, so far as influence is concerned" (Armstrong 242). White's seminal influence on later naturist writing will be discussed in more detail later, but it can be noted now that he is also "acknowledged by devoted birders to be the father of them all [birdwatchers, that is], past and present" (Kastner 219).

27. Thus McKusick claims that White's emphasis on a "local habitat marks a significant step beyond the single-minded specimen collecting and cataloguing that typifies eighteenth-century natural history" (27). John Clare also asserts, regarding his own "letters on Natural History," "I will insert nothing but what comes or has come under my notice" (*John Clare* 502).

28. White's several-pages-long collage-description of the flight and walk of various bird species (213–15) is a tour de force of avian characterization; for example, "Rooks sometimes dive and tumble in a frolicsome manner; crows and daws swagger in their walk; wood-peckers fly *volatu undoso*, opening and closing their wings at every stroke, and so are always rising or falling in curves" (214).

    On White's attention to birdsong, witness his description of the song of the blackcap (though Richard Mabey's notes tell us that he may actually be describing the garden warbler [271]): "The black-cap has . . . a full, sweet, deep, loud and wild pipe; yet that strain is of short continuance, and his motions are desultory; but when that bird sits calmly and engages in song in earnest, he pours forth very sweet, but inward melody, and expresses great variety of soft and gentle modulations, superior perhaps to those of any of our warblers, the nightingale excepted" (95). White's great attention to birds' "notes and language" leads him to many such descriptions, though the corvids come off quite poorly: "The amorous sound of a crow is strange and ridiculous; rooks . . . attempt sometimes in the gaiety of their hearts to sing, but with no great success" (216–17)!

The importance of the ear in bird study and appreciation has a rather tragic personal consequence for White. In his early fifties he complained, "Frequent returns of deafness incommode me sadly, and half disqualify me as a naturalist" (174).

29. A bird's "air" seems close to what is now referred to as gestalt (or "jizz"), the total pattern of a species' appearance and behaviors that the experienced birder comes to recognize intuitively.
30. In the United States this species is most closely related to the nighthawk and whip-poor-will.
31. Frank Stewart finds in White's "unusual compassion for" this "lowly reptile" the crux of White's eco-consciousness: that "White seriously considered an alternative view of the natural world, at once scientific but also sympathetic to and moderately respectful of the rights and emotional lives of nonhuman entities, placed him at the beginning of a revolutionary movement in science and ethics" (19–20).
32. Ironically or not, Mabey's note tells us that Timothy's shell is still extant "in the British Museum" (278). More ironically, from this shell scientists later ascertained that Timothy was a *she* (Highfield and Martin; Klinkenborg 159).
33. According to Barry Baldwin, "Absurd as it may seem, many otherwise sensible and learned men from various northern countries maintained the submersion theory, despite the ridicule of" the great naturalist Buffon. White's own obsession with the matter led him to expend much time and energy "scrabbling round bodies of water and buildings in his quest for torpid sparrows" (148).
34. Yet, just previous to his callousness toward deer, White mourns the "red deer" as another lamentable "gap in the *Fauna Selborniensis,*" in the region's species diversity, "for another beautiful link in the chain of beings is wanting" (22).

    The "brute creation" was the unfortunate phrase of the era for other animals, which White readily adopted (e.g., 128, 137, 141, 177, 243).
35. For Leopold's various defenses (and glorifications) of hunting in *A Sand County Almanac*, see 58–62, 129, 138–39, 153–54, 159–60, 227–30, 269, 283, 294. Like Gilbert White, Leopold assumes that there is such a thing as an instinctual, "hereditary hunting fever" that justifies, in part, a rather elitist wilderness preserve mentality (228).
36. In this regard, Worster notes the amazing apolitical nature of the book, its lack of mention of the political and cultural events of a quite tumultuous era (10–12). Hoagland, more kindly, calls White the "mildest of revolutionaries" (xviii).

37. White sounds most like the forebear of twentieth-century ecologists in his letter "in favor of worms," in which he stresses the importance of earthworms to the ecohealth of the soil: "Earth-worms, though in appearance a small and despicable[!] link in the chain of nature, yet, if lost, would make a lamentable chasm." However, White can sound like Erasmus Darwin, too, telling us that worms "are hermaphrodites, and much addicted to venery, and consequently very prolific" (196–97). According to Mabey's note, Charles Darwin would later write the detailed monograph on worms that White calls for here (281).

Regarding White's groundbreaking contributions to ecology, McKusick finds the *Natural History* to be "a landmark in the development of ecological consciousness" (25); indeed, "some of the most essential insights of modern ecological thought were first developed in the writings of Gilbert White" (26).

38. In his recent introduction to the text, Edward Hoagland asserts that "not since paganism had a solid citizen employed such a term" as "conversation" (xv) in reference to nonhuman species.
39. At last, "the arcadian harmony with nature" that White "found in his rural life" eventually made Selborne "a focal point on the map of dream and reverie" (Worster 9, 14).
40. However, Worster is careful to argue that Darwinian theory is also fruitfully fraught with more positive (biocentric) ramifications (e.g., 187).
41. As I previously indicated, M. L. Pratt has most vigorously called to attention the imperialist nature of the Linnaean system, a taxonomy of order and will to knowledge and power that, by itself, "launched a European knowledge-building enterprise of unprecedented scale and appeal" (25).
42. And so White's conception of Selborne as an "ecological whole," replete with the amazing "economic" workings of nature's interrelationships, was, as I have argued, dependent on a Christian notion of Providence (Worster 7).
43. The first volume of *British Birds* was published in 1797, the second in 1804; I have consulted the sixth edition, of 1826.

On a recent reopening of Charlotte Brontë's *Jane Eyre*, I was not greatly surprised to find Bewick's *British Birds* to be the book on Jane's lap when the reader first meets her in her window-seat (3–5).

44. As in Gilbert White, nature and its creatures are graced by Providence, "that Infinite Wisdom which appointed and governs the unerring course of all things" (190).
45. As if rebutting Bewick's bigotry against the jay, the contemporary Choctaw poet Jim Barnes writes, "The jay does not call / *thief! thief!*" Rather, his is a call of territory: "this bright land is his: / *fief! fief!*" ("Three Songs from a Texas Oilfield" 2.1–2, 5–6, in *La Plata* 40).
46. The reader may be amazed to learn that this little robin redbreast "feeds on in-

sects and worms; but never eats them alive." Sometimes, as these birds beat their prey to death, the "entrails" are "shaken out, leaving only the body thus cleansed from all its impurities" (Bewick 130).

The robin as an image of domestic feminization is common among the British Romantics. Keats's "Stay, ruby breasted warbler, stay," for instance, presents this bird of "pretty head" (4), "patient plume" (7), and "soft note" (20) as a metaphor for the kinder and gentler love after the first throes of passion; like said bird, these later "words of love beguile . . . And draw a soft endearing smile" (21, 23).

47. John Clare, in fact, would later complain that the European goldfinch is too pretty for its own good because "it is [thus] among the most frequent and commonest of cage birds" (*John Clare* 464). Indeed, both the goldfinch and the nightingale "were almost exterminated in England because they were so popular as" pets (Lutwack 156).

48. Stuart Curran asserts that Smith's *Emigrants* "is the finest piece of extended blank verse between" *The Task* and the original *Prelude* (xxiv); its nature and bird passages make such a link all the more cogent.

49. See also Stephen Hunt regarding Smith's problems with "projecting herself in the public domain" (59). As Steve Baker puts it, "Those adult others who are still persuaded by the child's naive identifications will be at least implicitly stigmatized: they will be marked out from the 'norm,' typically by demeaning their race, their class or their gender" (124).

Paul Brooks's praise of early women naturalists slyly continues the sexist connection of women with nature and children. Although these women led the charge against the feather trade and for the establishment of bird sanctuaries (165–80), Brooks remarks that they had, above all, a "special talent for interesting young readers," thanks in part to "their emotional commitment" to their subject (165); such women "had a special talent for bringing the love of birds into the *home*" (174; emphasis added).

50. According to her editor's gloss in her collected *Poems*, Smith also "identifies her natural subjects with their scientific names at the end of each volume" of the two-volume *Conversations* (177).

51. One other avian note, this by Smith's editor, must be addressed. Smith's mention of a "Swift" ("To the insect of the gossamer" 8) is footnoted as "a kind of swallow that feeds on insects" (67). Not only is it hard to think of a swallow species that doesn't feed on insects, but swifts are in *no way* swallows, not even belonging to the same order of *Aves*.

52. William Cobbett, writing in 1830, can still express disbelief that nightingales have the ability to "*cross the sea*," that is, migrate (2.253). We now know that they winter in Africa.

53. The previous stanza asks whether other bird species have been to Africa (32–35), and Smith footnotes the stanza, matter-of-factly, "The Cuckoo, the Rail, and many species of Doves, are all emigrants" (275n). The relationship between such avian emigrants and Smith's (human) *Emigrants* is, of course, worthy of closer attention.
54. In a lengthy letter on the nightjar, John Clare heaps great praise on Smith's poetized observations thereof: "I have never read one [of the poets] that mentions it except Mrs Smith in her sonnets. . . . I felt much pleasd with them [her poems] because she wrote more from what she had seen of nature then from what she had read of it" (*John Clare* 453).
55. The birds of the order *Caprimulgiformes* have a particularly strange reputation. They are still generally termed "Goatsuckers," a direct translation of the Latin and a name derived from the European superstition that they sucked the milk from peasants' goats on the sly. (Actually, these birds are commonly found around livestock because the latter attract insects.) Nor is the common name for the European species, nightjar, a very happy description of the bird's nocturnal call. Finally, there is the American species, the whip-poor-will. I am not familiar with its etymological story, but it can't be a pretty one.
56. John Clare's journal description: "They [lapwings] have a way of decoying any thing from their young or nest by swooping and almost tumbling over before them as if wounded" (*John Clare's Birds* 82–84). The American reader may have seen the killdeer, an American plover, perform a similar feint. The lapwing itself has been traditionally deemed a bird of perfidy for such "dissimulation" (Rowland 96–97), for simply protecting its young.
57. Once again she must battle the "fathers" in a footnote. Noting Gilbert White's comments on the limited areas in which wheatear trapping was practiced, Smith concludes, "But this is certainly a mistake"; the geographical range is greater (237n). Smith also devotes an entire poem, "The wheat-ear," to this despicable practice; not surprisingly by now, White's *Natural History* is also referenced in a note to this poem, too (194n).
58. I refer especially to two critics whom I cut my teeth on: Geoffrey Hartman and M. H. Abrams. Easthope refers to this revivalist period of Wordsworth studies as "*Celebrative*" (129), though it's rather hard to imagine some of Hartman's more cynical readings of Wordsworth as fitting such a glowing adjective. For Hartman, the Romantics' nature is all Maya (and a woman, it would appear): it is an "enchanted ground" of "veils" and "seductions," and if the "poet's mind seeks . . . to reaffirm its autonomy vis-à-vis nature" ("Romanticism" 54), that autonomy is finally "the engulfing solipsism of Imagination" (*Wordsworth's Poetry* 242). Wellek's famous three-part definition of Romanticism—the "concern for the reconciliation of subject and object, man and nature, consciousness and uncon-

sciousness" (129–30)—also downplays nature by conflating it with and denigrating it as "object" and the unconscious. In this psychologization of Romantic studies, one must also mention the archetypal approach of Northrop Frye, for whom Romanticism's qualities included, apparently peripherally, "a sympathy with nature *or what not*" (1; emphasis added)!

59. From Edward A. Armstrong's nonliterary, naturalist point of view, "considering the number of interesting and beautiful birds" in the Lake District, Wordsworth's "bird poetry is rather meager and sometimes his observation is at fault" (245). While Frederick A. Pottle concedes that "there is little in the scientist's vision that Wordsworth misses," he echoes Bateson in concluding that "it is a great mistake to consider Wordsworth a descriptive poet," for if "his images are firm and precise ('literal') . . . they are [still] very spare" (280, 281).

60. My Lacanian use of *Other* in discussing Wordsworth here is different, of course, from its general application so far in this work, which has been to real, external groups of abjectness and alterity (whether human or other species). Like many Lacanian terms, his "Other" is quite a busy signifier: in general, "the internalization of this Other" is equivalent to "the unconscious subject itself. . . . Sometimes 'the Other' refers to the parents: to the mother as the 'real Other' (in the dual relationship of mother and child), to the father as the 'Symbolic Other,' yet it is never a *person*. Very often the term seems to refer simply to the unconscious itself" (Wilden 264). Thus Lacan's famous dictum, "The unconscious is the discourse of the Other" ["Agency" 754]. In sum, Lacan's "Other" (or so, at least, the neo-Jungian would argue) is ultimately intrapsychic, and thus quite problematic in dealing with the more commonly denoted Other—who is "out there"—of race, class, gender, and species.

61. The results of my monomaniacal naturalist obsession to identify, count, and categorize every bird species mentioned in Wordsworth's poetic corpus are tabulated on my *Wordsworth's Birds* web page.

    Lawrence Buell is "bemused" by a recent similar effort to count the species of flowers in William Cullen Bryant, and "chagrined" that he never considered this tack himself: "That kind of passion went out with new critical formalism in the 1940s and seems almost antediluvian today" (*Environmental Imagination* 11). (But Buell intends this as a compliment.)

62. Wordsworth is at least known to have appreciated Bewick's woodcuts, as evidenced in the first line of "The Two Thieves": "Oh now that the genius of Bewick were mine." But the poet was likely most attracted to Bewick's images of rural life (which could well have adorned the *Lyrical Ballads*) rather than to the artist's ornithological efforts. Given the date of "The Two Thieves," Wordsworth knew of Bewick's work by 1800, and so "W. might have seen Bewick's *Select Fables* (1784), *Quadrupeds* (1790) or *British Birds* (1797)." (Wu 22).

63. Included in Tutin's list of "The Birds of Wordsworth" is the "pike" (*Wordsworth Dictionary* 208). A quick glance at "An Evening Walk" reveals this "bird" to be a fish, of course. Apparently Tutin wasn't the most knowledgeable naturalist himself. The mistake is absent in Tutin's similar list published a year after, in *An Index to the Animal and Vegetable Kingdoms of Wordsworth* (1892). Other characteristic works of this era are William H. Wintringham's *The Birds of Wordsworth, Poetically, Mythologically, and Comparatively Examined* (London: Hutchinson, 1892) and Alexander Mackie's *Nature Knowledge in Modern Poetry, being Chapters on Tennyson, Wordsworth, Matthew Arnold, and Lowell as Exponents of Nature-study* (London: Longmans, 1906).
64. Likewise Drummond Bone, in his essay on naturalistic details in British Romanticism: "Wordsworth was *criticised* by Coleridge for 'clinging to the palpable,'" but "there is self-evidently a lot more palpability in *Guide to the Lakes* than in much of the verse" (7).
65. But for this exception, all other page references to the *Guide* are to the 1822 edition, *A description of the lakes.*
66. This monistic gesture is perhaps most evident in the eloquent passage of *The Prelude* in which the poet felt "the sentiment of Being spread / O'er all that moves, and all that seemeth still" (2.420–21). While this "all" includes the avian Other, as it "beats the gladsome air," the emphasis is on the unitary whole: he "saw one life, and felt that it was joy" (4.426, 430).
67. Wintringham's 1892 study, *The Birds of Wordsworth*, identifies fifty-one species, and, in so doing, "portrays Wordsworth's particularity and fidelity in dealing with natural objects" (Patton 141). But in his day, "species" often applied to several birds of the same genus, later distinguished as separate species in the twentieth century, which likely accounts for my greater count of bird species (sixty).
68. Easthope, too, calls the "Early died" break a "banal, formal, and awkwardly inverted statement" (67). In line with the argument to be immediately developed, he makes much of the "effacement of Wordsworth's father and mother from" *The Prelude* (66–67). According to J. P. Ward, this repression results in a foregrounding of nature: "Whatever else happened when the parents died they were at one level simply removed presences . . . so that the hills behind step forward into visual place" (29).
69. Easthope summarizes this Lacanian travail as "the impossible task of fantasizing ourselves as complete, desiring (and thinking we find) a plenitude which will make good that originary lack" via a "discourse of the Other" (46). The critic speaks as if Wordsworth is aware of this need for the Other and so "wishes to make the best of a necessarily bad job by reducing dependence on the Other to the least possible" (47). How? Via children, women, and "a whole army of solitary individuals," each a "stand-in for the Other" (48), as are "natural" figures (52), such as Wordsworth's birds.

70. *The Prelude*'s snare-filching and boat-stealing episodes also "imply a guilt which corresponds to the Oedipal transgression," according to Easthope (66).
71. Lutwack points out that the poet obfuscates this woodcock-trapping guilt, however, by later deleting the frank admission "I was a fell destroyer" (1.318) from the 1850 edition (168).
72. All references to *An Evening Walk* and *Descriptive Sketches* refer to the earlier Quarto versions of each, unless otherwise specified.
73. Rowland notes that the domestic cock-fowl is a binary conjunction of spiritualism and eros, bearing both the Christian connotations of "regeneration" and "resurrection," and the "salacious" and "phallic" connotations arising from its barnyard "conjugality" (21, 26).
74. All quotations from *Home at Grasmere* are from MS. D of the Cornell edition.
75. Similarly, in "The Waterfall and the Eglantine," "The linnet lodged, and *for us two* / Chanted his pretty songs" (38–39; emphasis added). One is relieved to learn that the linnet had a reason to sing. "A Farewell," too, contains the bald appropriation, "And in this bush *our* sparrow built her *nest*" (55; emphases added)—further evidence that, in Wordsworth, "lovers are [often] related as birds to their soft and warm nests" (McGhee 284).
76. According to my content analysis, the skylark is referred to in 150 lines of twenty-seven poems, the nightingale in 70 lines of seventeen poems.
77. Freud also claims that one of the characteristics of melancholy is "a delusional expectation of punishment" (165), evident indeed in various places in Wordsworth, most memorably in "Nutting" and in the several passages of *The Prelude* to which I've already referred.
78. Characteristically, Kroeber bristles at all this psychoanalytical talk of melancholy and alienation; instead, "the fundamental romantic political commitment" is "founded on the conviction that we are not alienated." The warning message, then, of the alienated melancholic in "Lines Left upon a Seat in a Yew-tree" is as follows: "Recognize oneself not as an isolated being but as one fully existent insofar as reciprocally interacting with one's environment" (*Ecological* 70). The poem's deep ecology sentiment of bio-egalitarianism is indeed explicit: "he who feels contempt / For any living thing, hath faculties / Which he has never used" (52–54).
79. But one recalls the "penetrating bliss" permeating *Home at Grasmere*—"Oh, *surely* these [birds] / Have felt it" (234–35; emphasis added)—as contradicting Kroeber's assertion that Wordsworth always hedges his bets about animal sentience (44–45).
80. McGhee reads the various images of "instinctual" nature in this poem as metaphors for the libido: Wordsworth yearns for "a [psychic] power without consciousness, without identity—as close to the instincts of rainbows, roses, birds, and lambs as human being can be"; they are thus closely related to "those first

affections" of the child, that is, to "Wordsworth's conception of what Freud called the id" (131). But this last equation seems tenuous at best.

81. In the United States, the closest common analogues might be the house (or purple) finch and the American robin.

82. The woodland linnet and the throstle are also closely paired in Ecclesiastical Sonnet III.xxxiii ("Regrets") 12, "Evening Voluntaries" V (1–2), and "Inscriptions" VII (18). All quotations from "The Ruined Cottage" are from MS. D of the Cornell edition, *The Ruined Cottage and the Pedlar*. Emphases in each excerpt are added.

83. Wordsworth's biographer Mary Moormann claims that "Wordsworth knew little about the names and species of birds," a statement made in the context of the "woodland linnet" of "The Tables Turned": "Linnets are not 'woodland' birds at all," she continues; "they are merely symbols[?!]" of songbirds in general (380n). Yet, according to modern British bird guides, the linnet's characteristic habitats at least include "woodland edges" and "orchards" (Heinzel, Fitter, and Parslow 290; Svensson et al. 348).

84. The best U.S. avian analogue is the black-capped chickadee, our most common tit.

85. Parrill concludes her essay by emphasizing again "the frequency and aptness with which the Romantic poet identifies the songbird with his own creativity. No other Romantic symbol . . . incorporates so fully the qualities of the poet and the creative imagination as the Romantics saw them" (56).

86. According to my count, the Eurasian skylark (again) is referred to in 150 lines of twenty-seven poems, the European robin in 202 lines of sixteen poems. Oddly enough, however, the lark occurs only once in the entire *Prelude*, toward the end of the last book. But this mention, a reference to "this Song, which like a lark / I have protracted, in the unwearied Heavens / Singing" (13.373–75), is crucial in the sense that the "Song" is *The Prelude* itself.

87. Thus Parrill: "Perhaps the most important meaning in the metaphoric use of the songbird" is "the essence of height or the act of soaring" (47). However, her celebrative terminology implies a bias toward Wordsworth's own transcendentalism: "Poetic flight involves and requires a transcendence of self—both the physical self and the ego" (50). The impoverished soul that I am perceives only an immanence of lack.

88. Wordsworth explains in a note to these lines that, for the Druids, the "Cormorant was a bird of bad omen" (PW 3.342n).

89. Once again, my main reading here is rather far from the ecocritical reading of Kroeber, who wants to see the boy-owl interaction as a more positive "reciprocality of encounter" (*Ecological* 81). McKusick, too, finds the Idiot Boy's misrecognition as a redemption of sorts, which "bears witness to the uncanny other-

ness of those wild creatures of the night"; "although these voices [the owls' calls] are not intelligible, they nevertheless serve to remind us that there is another world out there, outside the boundaries of civilization, human language, and normal perception" (65).

90. In feminizing the bird, Wordsworth was following tradition again. "Nightingale," Lockwood tells us, stems from the West Germanic word for "night songstress": "The word itself was traditionally feminine, our ancestors not realizing that only the male bird sings" (107).

91. Coleridge, as we shall see, had already attempted a similar resignification in "The Nightingale" of the *Lyrical Ballads*.

92. The common positive privileging of the cuckoo in British poetry, despite its alternative uses as symbols of cuckoldry and silliness, even lunacy, arises, at least in part, from its concurrent status as a "symbol of spring" (Rowland 38, 40).

93. One might speculate here about the possible biographical relationship of Wordsworth's failing eyesight to his audile acuity. And yet his failing *hearing,* as with Gilbert White, was a cause for "melancholy," too, according to the Fenwick note to "The Cuckoo of Laverna": "Among a thousand delightful feelings connected in my mind with the voice of the Cuckoo, there is a personal one which is rather melancholy. I was convinced that age had rather dulled my hearing, by not being able to catch the sound at the same distance as the younger companions of my walks; and of this failure I had a proof upon the occasion that suggested these verses" (*PW* 3.495).

94. "Like Shelley, both Keats and Wordsworth doubt that their inspired singers are real birds or inhabitants of this world" (Parrill 49). Parrill then brings the metaphysics of the "Intimations" ode into the equation by concluding that "the song of the cuckoo brings back to the poet the insight into the supernal which he had as a child" (50).

95. For Frank Doggett, "Wordsworth's birds are natural creatures . . . yet at times they evoke the idea of the soul"; in particular, the cuckoo's "invisibility" and "mystery . . . suggest the idea of spirit" (551).

96. Pater had already observed the poet's forte for presenting nature "in its modesty," his power "to open out the soul of apparently little or familiar things" ("Wordsworth" [1874] 192).

97. Thus Wordsworth's ideal mother is "True as the stock-dove to her shallow nest" (*Excursion* 5.707) and "as duteous as the Mother Dove" (*Prelude* 1.151).

98. In terms of patriotic appropriation, not only is the bird more than once the "English robin," but in the poem "Fort Fuentes," set in the Alps, Wordsworth refers to "Some bird (like our own honoured redbreast)" (11), although the range of this "English" bird extends throughout Europe.

Verlyn Klinkenborg's retelling of White's *Natural History* from the first-person point of view of Timothy the tortoise includes the following critique of a similar nationalistic blindness (and an explanation for the naturalist's refusal to believe in swallow migration): "He [White] cannot credit the thought of Selborne's hirundines chattering out of English earshot. No longer *swallow*, *swift*, or *martin*" (30) and finally, no longer *English*.

99. Apparently this scenario was not uncommon, because Clare also devotes a long prose passage to a robin making itself at home in his house (*John Clare* 469–70).

100. The robin will also apparently eat out of the hand, at least in cold weather: "The redbreast, ruffled up by winter's cold / Into a 'feathery bunch,' feeds at your hand" (*The Excursion* 4.386–87). Dorothy recounts an actual instance of a fledgling alighting on William: "William told me that that very morning a Bird had perched upon his leg. He had been lying very still and had watched this little creature, it had come under the Bench where he was sitting and then flew up to his leg; he thoughtlessly stirred himself to look further at it and it flew onto the apple tree above him" (136–37).

101. Ironically, given the robin's status here as familiar and friend, its very familiarity and *commonness* resulted in its longtime mistreatment: "For centuries in Europe the robin, a very easy bird to capture because of its curiosity and friendliness[!], was eaten as a common dish, tormented as a child's plaything . . . or caged as a songbird" (Rowland 153).

102. However, Paul Shepard's analysis of birds as analogues of human economic classes is relevant here: "In the bourgeois world birds [in general] were clean, refined in their sexuality, devoted as mates and parents," like Wordsworth's swans; they were likewise "homebodies, singing, industrious," like Wordsworth's robins. However, "the grubby sparrows in the streets were a lower class" (112).

103. As Harrison reminds us, "sparrow" is a name "universal, even today, for all little, undistinguished birds" (136).

104. Although it would be difficult to read Hartman as a precursor of ecocriticism, his contrast between Wordsworth and Blake depends on their relative degrees of anthropocentrism: "Thus, though the landscape [in 'Resolution and Independence'] reveals a human form [that is, the leech-gatherer] . . . there is no wish in Wordsworth, as there is in Blake, to see nature purely under the aspect of the human" (*Wordsworth's Poetry* 201–2).

105. Dorothy's influence includes her prose descriptions of daffodils, of the leech-gatherer, and of little Alice Fell, all resulting in poems by William (109, 42, 92). Her various descriptions of beggars and drunken soldiers, and even a Highland lass, were also no doubt influential in this regard (16, 17, 28, 71–72, 103, 129–30; 64; 91).

106. Robert Mellin claims for Dorothy an ecological consciousness vastly superior to

her brother's, her journals evidence of a proto-"bioregionalist" bent, a "protoecological decentering" of the human, and a more "materialist" reading of nature than Wordsworth's more abstract idealizations (72–74, 68). According to Mellin, not only does Bate's study of Wordsworth efface Dorothy's positive influence on William's art, but her brother himself consciously repressed the heavy influence of female nature writers on his own "revolution," including those of his sister and Charlotte Smith (67–68, 70).

Dorothy's original haiku-esque entry on this lone dancing leaf led to Coleridge's more ornate passage in *Christabel* on "The one red leaf, the last of its clan" (1.49).

107. For example, 11, 20, 33, 38, 43, 91, 33, 36, 37, 48, 50, 52, 53, 54, 56, 57, 64, 68, 83, 87, 100, 121, 83, 84, 88, 121, 127, 32, 80, 89, 92, 120, 123, 129.
108. For example, 20, 51, 65, 74, 96, 99. The copious page numbers in this and the previous endnote indicate the sheer omnipresence of such chores and hardships in the *Journals*.
109. The stock dove was another of Dorothy's avian favorites. Rowland gives Haydon's anecdote of Dorothy's hilarious encounter with an old woman, with whom Dorothy struck up a conversation regarding their mutual love for these doves. Then the truth comes out: "Some like them in a pie," the old woman finally says, but *she* likes them "stewed in onions" (48)!
110. But, as if to conflate Native and bird, Wordsworth also presents his youth as an impulsive avian flight: "I, bred up in Nature's lap, was even / As a spoil'd Child; and . . . ranging like a fowl of the air, / I was ill tutor'd for captivity" (*Prelude* 3.358–59, 362–63).
111. Also in *The Prelude* is an indigenous reference during the poet's walking trip in the Alps: there he comes across "A green recess, an *aboriginal vale / Quiet*," with "*naked huts . . . like tents / Or Indian cabins*" (6.448–51).

3. BLITHE SPIRIT AND IMMORTAL BIRD

1. Some recent critics have suggested that Wordsworth himself may have been one of the first to be aware of this impasse of language. According to J. P. Ward, his new use of language and, above all, his awareness of a psyche split in time and language anticipate the notions of Lacan and Derrida (181, 191–92, 196, 208). Thus he was "the poet first open to these things" (191), "the primal poet of our modern language" (196).
2. After such a wonderful sentence of eco-praise, the following qualification is dispiriting: "To the author of the *Lyrical Ballads*, nature is a kind of[?!] home" (Hazlitt, *Spirit* 273).
3. Gaull's recent study on Romanticism continues such praise: "A careful and reflective observer, Wordsworth gathered information about nature that he would later interpret with the eyes of a painter, and the insight of a scientist" (310).

4. Meihuizen, too, claims that, in contrast to the Platonized birds of Shelley and Yeats, "Wordsworth's birds are presented as actual" (60).
5. Wordsworth, one must assume, had also watched herons at rest, "Drying their feathers in the sun, at ease" ("Farewell Lines" 16).
6. But wouldn't a professional ornithologist describe the same sound in less metaphorical terms? Well, a recent British bird guide describes it as a "barking call" (Heinzel, Fitter, and Parslow 78). Natural science marches on.
7. Dorothy Wordsworth describes a flock of bullfinches similarly, and one might guess that her brother had read this: "The young Bullfinches in their party coloured Raiment bustle about among the Blossoms and poize themselves like Wire-dancers or tumblers, shaking the twigs and dashing off the Blossoms" (128).
8. Writing in the Bate-Kroeber tradition, James C. McKusick makes similar claims for the timeliness of Wordsworth and company: the Romantic poets' "Green Writing is a legacy to our own troubled moment in the history of the Earth" (227). Indeed, McKusick extends Bate's championing of Wordsworth and Clare to the British Romantics in general, as "the first full-fledged ecological writers in the Western literary tradition" (19). Finally, McKusick posits the poetry genre itself as central to greater eco-consciousness, for the Romantic poets' contributions to Anglo-American ecology were as crucial as those by naturalist essayists (e.g., White and Hudson), notably the *Lyrical Ballads* (32, 69).
9. If English socialism itself "is at root more 'green' than it is 'Marxist,'" a large claim in itself, it may have very much to do with Wordsworth, whose *Prelude* is only "fleetingly red but ever green" (Bate, *Romantic Ecology* 58, 33). That Wordsworth's poetry is not, in general, "red" enough, and in fact is above all a displacement or suppression of "red" concerns, is, of course, the new historicists' main charge against him and the British Romantics in general (e.g., McGann's *Romantic Ideology*). Bate's partner in the Romantics' defense, Kroeber, answers the charge vociferously, too, claiming that their nature poetry was itself an earnest expression of their "deepest political commitments" (*Ecological* 2). If the new historicist can lambast naturists and ecocritics for a naïvely apolitical retreatism, new historicism itself can certainly be accused of an anthropocentrism of the narrowest sort.
10. However, Bate's at least occasional implicit acceptance of such a nature reserve system as a sufficient eco-answer also seems short-sighted. Buell deems this general attitude (referring to John Burroughs specifically) as "the discourse of nature-as-elite-androcentric-preserve" (*Environmental Imagination* 39). Paul Frye, responding to Bate in particular, dubs the beneficiaries of such a system the "kayak elite" (qtd. in McKusick 75)!
11. Or, as the editor of the Cornell *Salisbury Plain Poems* flatly describes the bird:

"The great bustard (*Otis tarda*), formerly common in England" (23n). Last breeding in England in 1832 (Lockwood 37), the species is still found in parts of Spain, Eastern Europe, and Asia (Heinzel, Fitter, and Parslow 113; Svensson et al. 120). Tragically fitting, "bustard" derives from the Latin *Avis tarda,* or "slow bird" (Lockwood 37).

12. Thus McKusick's reading of *Home at Grasmere* portrays the possible shooting of the swan pair as "an inscrutable crime against nature" closely allied to the slaying of Coleridge's albatross (72).
13. For instance, "Lines written in early Spring" is really about "'What man has made' of animals," and the purported interpenetration of human and other species in this poem reveals Wordsworth's search for greater "community" and "social cohesion" (Fosso 6).
14. From an ecocritical point of view, Kroeber, for instance, claims that in his early association with Wordsworth, Coleridge "composed poems as ecologically oriented as his friend's" (*Ecological* 67), and McKusick goes so far as to dub Coleridge "perhaps the single most important figure in the development of a full-fledged ecological consciousness in Britain and America" (28).
15. Halpern also observes that all of Coleridge's native birds can be found in White's *Natural History*, which the poet had read at least by 1810, "filling its margins with notes" (11). But given Halpern's own finding that Coleridge's later poetry is almost devoid of bird imagery, one is relieved to learn that he could have seen White's book much "earlier" (21); in other words, 1810 is too late to have been of much value to Halpern's thesis.
16. Coleridge's theory of aesthetic organicism originated in his "early views on the integrity and interrelatedness of the natural world" (McKusick 42).
17. All Coleridge page references, including those for *Biographia Literaria,* are to *The Major Works*. That the later Coleridge was unfortunately more monistic and idealistic, and so less truly naturalistic, than other, more "characteristic," Romantics is one of the complaints of Kroeber's *Ecological Literary Criticism* (e.g., 92). In support of Halpern's argument is Fosso's contention that the animal-human link waned for both Wordsworth and Coleridge in their later years (15).
18. Byron's intermittent scorn for the Lake Poets, so hilariously expressed in *Don Juan*, likewise finds a "transcendental darkness" in Coleridge, who is pictured "Explaining metaphysics to the nation— / I wish he would explain his Explanation" ("Dedication" 2.7–8). Like Peacock, Byron had too deep an eighteenth-century neoclassical strain in him to stomach much Wordsworthian naturalism. But then one also reads with some amusement the various "Nature" stanzas in the later books of *Childe Harold* that sound much like the very Lake Poets whom Byron lambasted so mercilessly elsewhere (e.g., *Don Juan* 1.90.5–8).
19. In the conflation of the animal and the innocent at work in "The Nightingale,"

Coleridge brings in a maid, then his son, to bear more authentic witness, if you will, as beings who "can respond spontaneously . . . to the world around" (Mileur 51).

20. Lutwack finds Coleridge's blessing of the "croaking . . . crow" to be analogous to the Mariner's blessing of water snakes (179); both reveal Coleridge's faith in "the ecological principle that our survival depends on our recognition of the worth and interrelatedness of all living things" (180).
21. Coleridge's reprivileging of animal sound "dissonance" is most evident in his early poem "To a Young Ass," whose "dissonant harsh bray of joy" is "more musically sweet to" him "Than warbled melodies that sooth to rest / The aching of pale Fashion's vacant breast!" (33–36).
22. As one egregious instance of symbol hunting, Rowland reads the "great white bird" as "a mother or breast symbol. Coleridge's choice of symbol must have been determined by a deep conflict associated with his mother" (4)!
23. Indeed, the development of twentieth-century psychology in general can be read as symptomatic of humankind's alienation from the animal and from nature in the raw. In tracing Western culture's estrangement from the landscape since the Renaissance, J. H. Van den Berg concludes, "Modern psychology became possible because of an interiorization of all human realities" (63). Steve Baker puts much recent critical scholarship—of a psychoanalytic or new historicist bent, for instance—in its rightful perspective: for such scholars, the signifying animal "is the sign of something else (*anything* else): political subversion, self-centredness, repressed sexuality, madness, a hatred of humanity—take your pick" (215).
24. Armstrong perceives the contradiction here: although "Coleridge objected to poets' reading their own sad sentiments into the nightingale's song," he yet "answered a child's query" in as grossly a sentimental, though contrary, way (246).
25. John Clare's letters include a similar meditation on whether nightingales' songs are "grave or gay," and inclines toward the latter: "Let him ask himself wether nature is in the habit of making such happy seeming songs for sorrow as that of the Nightingales—the poets indulged in fancys but they did not wish that those matter of fact men the Naturalists shoud take them for facts upon their credit" (*John Clare* 458–59). But Clare himself doesn't escape anthropomorphic projections, even in his prose, claiming that nightingales sing with "their wings trembling as if in extacy" and describing the robin's song, in another journal entry, as a "mellancholy sweetness" (456, 469).
26. Steve Baker's analysis of iconic animals "looking back," of a "reversal of the empowered gaze," is relevant here. Here is "the animal slipping out of its stereotypical role as 'the represented,' the objectified other, fixed and distanced by the controlling look of the empowered human, and instead" turning "that look back upon the humans, rendering *them* 'other,' dismantling their secure sense of a superior identity" (158).

27. Kroeber even employs this poem to generalize as follows: such "ecological thinking encourages the view that this Wordsworthian [and early Coleridgean] reciprocity [of humankind and nature] need be no mere verbal trick" (*Ecological* 73); that is, the poem's naturalist rhetoric is a true engagement of the human and other species.
28. Paul de Man attributes a similar anticipatory poststructuralist bent to Romanticism in general. Whereas their writing is in part "a return to a greater concreteness, a proliferation of natural objects," their drive toward naturalism "is essentially paradoxical and condemned in advance to failure" (66, 70). In certain texts of Wordsworth, Goethe, and Baudelaire, "the vision almost[!] seems to become a real landscape." But above all, the Romantic agenda was a deconstructive one: the Romantics were "the first modern writers to have put into question, in the language of poetry, the ontological priority of the sensory object" (70, 77).
29. Thus the "owlet's cry" in "Frost at Midnight" is but a mirror for the narrator's "solitude" (2, 5). In "Fears in Solitude" is the fascinating othering of the owl as godlessness incarnate:

> Forth from his dark and lonely hiding-place,
> . . . the owlet Atheism,
> Sailing on obscene wings athwart the noon
> . . . .
> And hooting at the glorious sun in Heaven,
> Cries out, "Where is it [i.e., the sun—and God]?" (81–83, 85–86)

As the height of irony, real owls probably *are* "atheists"! Kroeber's notion that the best of British Romanticism was a non-, even anti-Christian naturalism makes little sense in this context, until he ostracizes the later Coleridge as prime exception to the rule (e.g., *Ecological* 92).
30. In his catalogue of British avian imagery from Chaucer through Milton, Harrison notes that literary references to the owl as ill "omen" are most likely to this tawny owl, of "too whit too whoo" fame (136). In Keats, the owl's call becomes the "gloom-bird's hated screech" (*Hyperion* 1.171).
31. I consciously use Jung's term "enantiodromic" here because an intrapsychic Jungian reading has long been my own preferred misreading of the poem. Thus, for Applewhite, Christabel is the naïve ego; the serpent/Geraldine is the Shadow, or "Jungian messenger from the unconscious," come to "expand the world of Christabel" (100–101). While Applewhite can still deem the opposites of snake and dove as a typical Coleridgean opposition, his Jungian reading allows him to escape the good-versus-evil moralizing of G. Wilson Knight.
32. My impressionist criticism here may have been suggested by Hazlitt's essay on

Byron, in which the poet stands alone, with "his own will" and ego, and even self-scorn, "like a solitary peak" (*Spirit* 253).

33. Hazlitt: "*Manfred* is merely [Byron] himself" (*Spirit* 258).
34. Thus Manfred rebuffs the abbot's call for repentance: "I could not tame my nature down," and so "I disdain'd to mingle with / A herd, though to be leader—and of wolves. / The lion is alone, and so am I" (3.1.116, 121–23). Later Manfred is described as walking "the rocks / And forests like a wolf" (3.3.23–24).
35. The ecocritic might point to Manfred's marvelous "solar-worship" soliloquy as a welcome, almost pagan worship of material nature itself. The sun here is the "Glorious Orb! the idol / Of early nature, and the vigorous race / Of undiseased mankind," and finally, "Thou material God!" (3.2.3–5, 14). But Byron/Manfred's egoism *is* a "disease," and the sun becomes at last a symbol of the narrator's ego inflation.
36. As opposed to human vanity, Harold prefers "Maternal Nature! for who teams like thee . . . ?" (3.46.3). But the "teeming" description that follows is noticeably generic.
37. This is not to say that Shelley wasn't susceptible to the traditional glorification of the eagle himself. The "Freedom" returning to Greece in *Hellas* is emblematized by an eagle (76–84); in the same drama, "eagle-wingèd Victory" (715; cf. "Victory's eagle-wings" [*Charles the First* 1.144]) is contrasted to "Victorious Wrong, with vulture scream" (940).
38. All poem and line number references to Shelley's poetry are to *The Poetical Works of Shelley*.
39. In spite of the ecoreadings of the poem that follow, *Prometheus Unbound* is still, I think, very much illuminated via a Jungian reading. Indeed, it may be the most archetypal of any major English Romantic work, with its plethora of underground, water, and rebirth imagery and the ease with which the major characters can be interpreted as intrapsychic. Thus Jupiter is "rational" ego consciousness, opposed by various figures from the collective unconscious: Prometheus (the hero archetype), Asia (the anima), and Demogorgon (the unconscious Self). Applewhite summarizes the ensuing psychomachia as one in which "an archetypal embodiment of the sterile, masculine . . . consciousness" (Jupiter) is "overthrown" (129).
40. Gaull has it both ways: "The autonomy Prometheus achieves is expressed in a state of social communion, a prelude to love that redeems both nature and society"; at the same time, she contrasts this vision with Byron's, since Prometheus's communality is so "unlike the self-isolating autonomy of Byron's Manfred" (203).
41. Unfortunately, kingfishers are fish eaters, not berry pickers! Quoting this passage as evidence, and remonstrating that such birds do not "cling downward" or "feed

on berries," Armstrong flatly concludes, "Like Keats, Shelley was not interested in birds from an ornithological point of view" (246).

42. However, even Kroeber admits that the poet was more concerned with humankind as a "social," not as a "natural," animal (*Ecological* 120–23, 138).
43. Northrop Frye finds the Romantic natural landscape to be "a veil dropped over the naked nature of screaming rabbits and gasping stags, the nature red in tooth and claw which haunted a later generation" (21). But I would conversely read this vision of a savage nature "red in tooth and claw" as, in part, also the consequence of a further estrangement from nature.
44. Alternatively, from a proto-Germanic word for "little song" (Lockwood 94). This disagreement among even contemporary sources is telling.
45. F. R. Leavis anticipated Bloom's critique: whatever else he thought about Wordsworth's poetry, he affirmed that Wordsworth at least "seems always to be presenting an object"; Shelley, in contrast—Leavis had "To a Skylark" in mind, among other poems—presents pure emotion, "unattached, in a void," evidence of "a mind . . . little able to hold an object in front of it" (275, 276).
46. Parrill, for instance, considers "the bird's invisibility and isolation" analogous to "the poet's [own] need for solitude and invisibility" (50–53).
47. Thus Frankenstein warns Walton of even "pure" scientific ambition, which is "only the *apparently innocent* one of distinguishing yourself in science and discoveries" (185; emphasis added), as if having read M. L. Pratt's studies of the close complicity of science and colonialist imperialism. Fittingly, even Victor's friend and foil, the sensitive aesthete Clerval, plans to do business in India to assist "the progress of European colonisation and trade" (139).
48. All poem and line number references to Keats's poetry are to *Complete Poems*, unless otherwise indicated.
49. Thus Parrill comments on Keats's common use of "winged flight" as symbolic of the imagination (48–49).
50. Despite Coleridge's famous distinction between "fancy" and "imagination" (313), the former word remains one of Keats's favorite terms for serendipitous creative *imagination.*
51. Section 32, beginning "I think I could turn and live with animals . . . ."
52. In *Endymion*, Keats gives feathers to sleep itself: "O magic sleep! O comfortable bird / That broodest o'er the troubled sea of the mind" (1.453–54). Morpheus, too, has "owlet pinions," and dreaming is a "flight," a "high soaring" in an "airy trance, / Spreading imaginary pinions wide" (1.560, 1.582, 584, 585–86).
53. Applewhite's reading is characteristic of the Jungian approach: this poem is about the "dichotomy . . . between the self-conscious poet and the unconscious ease of the nightingale," between "articulate individuality and mute identification with nature" (24). I call this reading Jungian as opposed to, say, Freudian, in that Jung's

theory entails a much more positive, indeed Romantic privileging of the unconscious in general.

54. "His other senses [still] function, however," especially his hearing of the nightingale (Parrill 51). Northrop Frye has remarked on the Romantics' privileging of the ear, whereas vision is associated, in general, with mere "fancy," in the Coleridgean sense (23).

55. Of course, for the Jungian, there must be a return to everyday ego consciousness, or the result is ego death and psychosis. Applewhite therefore puts a positive spin on the Romantic pattern of "consciousness' escape from itself and return": in Keats's "Ode," this "temptation of reunion" with the cosmos and (therefore) ego "extinction . . . is . . . overcome" (24, 25). Harold Bloom's neo-Freudian reading is less positive. Keats's modus operandi exemplifies Bloom's notion of *askesis*, "a way of purgation intending a state of solitude," in reaction to the influence of the literary "fathers" (*Anxiety* 116). That is certainly the eventual fate of the narrator of our "Ode."

56. My favorite example of such interspecies empathy among Keats's major poems is the owl who opens "The Eve of St. Agnes," as first signifier of the stanza's incredibly sensual chill: "The owl, for all his feathers, was a-cold" (1.2). Notable, too, is the appeal to a sense other than vision, that of sensation or feeling.

57. For the deconstructionist, of course, all poetic ventures are failures; the Romantic apostrophe especially, as in the "Nightingale" ode, "often end[s] in withdrawals and questions" (Culler 143) and is ultimately "an act of radical interiorization and solipsism" (146). But the ideological ground of Culler (and de Man et al.) is certainly anathema to the critic who would champion and redeem nature: "The apostrophizing poet identifies his universe as a world of sentient[!] forces" (139), Culler says, with the intimation that this is sheer foolishness, indeed, a rhetoric that is "embarrassing" (135).

58. Chris Foss also points out that the narrator's "illusions of communing with his nightingale are thoroughly debunked in the final stanza" (22). Regarding the nightingale's final "fading away," this is "far more in keeping with a supernatural bird than with a real nightingale" (Parrill 49).

59. See Whitman, "Out of the Cradle Endlessly Rocking" (388–94); Hopkins, "The Woodlark" (who speaks, syllabically, "*Teevo cheevo cheevio chee*" and sings of a "Sweet, of a sweet, of a sweet joy / Of a sweet—a sweet—sweet—joy" [1, 42–43]); and Hopkins, "Repeat that, repeat" (83–84, 85).

60. Keats's wonderful lines here may have been influenced by Wordsworth's memorable description of the "single wren" in book 2 of *The Prelude.*

61. Indeed, even today, "only the most radical views of the Deep Ecologists can rival the scope and intensity of Clare's environmental activism" (McKusick 85).

62. All references to Clare's verse are from *John Clare* (Oxford edition), unless otherwise specified.

63. Clare's insouciance regarding the Queen's English has an eco-significance of its own, as part of a style that would topple all hierarchies.

64. No doubt any champion of Victorian poetry could furnish a whole book of examples from Tennyson and company to combat this assertion, but it remains my general impression after perusing, in particular, the nature and avian poems of the era. Doggett expresses an idea similar to my perception: "The singing bird of the first half of the nineteenth century illustrates the view that poetry issues from the creative fountain of the living creature. In the latter half of the century, the singing bird became again the voice of Philomela and old lost bitterness" (557).

65. If "the poems of [T. S.] Eliot provide central Romantic symbols of the hope of resuscitation," including the "singing bird," the theme of his earlier poetry, at least, is one of "failed resuscitation" (Applewhite 140). In particular, *The Waste Land*'s concupiscently conceived nightingale, singing "'Jug, Jug' to dirty ears" (2.27), hardly qualifies as even remotely "resuscitative." In fact, Buell finds "an increasing separation of mind from nature" in the "Anglo-American lyric from Victorian to modern" (*Environmental Imagination* 199). René Wellek contrasts Romanticism with modernist literature as follows: "The modern writer . . . has lost faith in the role of nature" (131).

66. For example, "The Landrail," "In summer showers a skreeking noise is heard," and "The schoolboys in the morning soon as drest" all concern nest robbing. "The sailing puddock sweeps about for prey" portrays another grim cruelty, in which boys cut captured raptors' wings and tie the birds "in the garden with a string" (14).

67. Clare also kept a tame falcon at one point, and a magpie, who was apparently tragically stuck in Lacan's mirror stage: "I kept one for years till it got drowned in a well it usd to see its self in the water" (*John Clare's Birds* 6, 12).

68. White was perhaps influential for Clare, too, if only peripherally, for "Clare's extensive knowledge of birds was not won from books." However, he did own a copy of White's *Selborne* (1825 ed.), which was the only one of the naturalist texts he owned that "could have helped Clare to make more detailed observations of bird behavior" (Robinson and Fitter xv).

69. "Clare's earliest poems about birds tend to stem from proverbs . . . or from conventional information"; he "was not yet writing with his eye on the object" (Robinson and Fitter vii–viii). Later, avians "increasingly become, as Clare matures as a poet, a quality of his [immediate] environment" (ix).

70. This is evidence for McKusick's distinction between Clare and Wordsworth: the former is the more thoroughgoing naturalist in incorporating such details into his verse "rather than merely loving 'Nature' in the abstract, as Wordsworth is prone to do" (81).

71. A few more notable examples not discussed in the main text: "The sinken sun is takin leave" (martins' mud nest building [15–20]); "The Thrushes Nest" (moss nest building and eggs description); "The Landrail" (hole nest and eggs description [53–56]); "The turkeys wade the close to catch the bees" (eggs description [31]); "The Yellowhammer" (nest composition: "Dead grass, horse hair and downy headed bents / Tied to dead thistles" [7–8]).

Buell praises Clare for "letting his persona get lost in the minute details of a nightingale's nest ('Snug lie her curious eggs in number five / Of deadened green or rather olive-brown' ['The Nightingale's Nest' (88–89)]), as against the lament for one's human immortality that suffuses Keats' 'To a Nightingale'" (*Future* 99).

72. Clare also records this bird's "hissing noise" in a prose note (*John Clare's Birds* 15).

73. The *ch*'s are a favorite alliterative device of Clare's; elsewhere he describes chickens who "chelped and skuttled in the grass" ("One day across the fields I chanced to pass" 2).

74. Such anthropomorphic syllabifications of bird calls are worthy of an essay in themselves. *Birds of Europe* (1999) still renders this bird's call as "wet-my-lips" (Svensson et al. 110)!

75. Lutwack's study of birds and literature glosses Clare as both a "poet and amateur field naturalist . . . notable for having written an extensive body of nature poetry with the barest minimum of metaphor" (21).

76. In the face of such natural eloquence, I am almost ashamed to remind myself that Clare *did* take eggs from nests to further the knowledge of naturalists.

77. "Like Gilbert White, Clare tends to present . . . details in a rambling, anecdotal fashion that undercuts the expectation of narrative development" (McKusick 81).

78. Even the awkward slant rhymes of, say, "The Blackbird" may be viewed as an emphasis on nonemphasis, for example, "heard"/"cud," "mellow"/"weather" (3, 4, 14, 16).

79. McKusick goes so far as to consider Clare's style a unique "*ecolect* . . . a language that speaks for . . . the Earth considered as a home for all living things" (89).

80. Kroeber's earlier ventures into a Romantic ecoprosody, to coin a word, may have influenced McKusick's reading of Clare. Wordsworth's early characteristic use of blank verse, for instance, supposedly allows the poet and his landscape to "speak in dialogue 'more naturally'" (*Ecological* 68), as if the freer cadences of blank verse enhanced the ecodemocratic leveling that Wordsworth strove for in his subject matter. As for the Romantics' experimentation in stanzaic forms, "Wordsworth and Shelley . . . use literally hundreds of metrical structures and variations

upon them," as "poets not of disorder but of superabundant forms" (91), that is, of ecoliterary diversity.

81. One must acknowledge here two contrasting views on the Romantics' "new" relationship to nature and animals. M. H. Abrams deems all this nature-privileging stuff to be an "eternal" mythos already evident in St. Augustine, among others (*Natural* 88, 139–40, 384). More intriguing is Van den Berg's theory, which traces an estrangement of self "from the landscape" (60) back to the Renaissance. At this time, the landscape "became estranged, and consequently it became visible"; indeed, natural "things have moved [so much] further away from us . . . today" that "hardly anybody feels [that] the delight is so great, so overpowering, that he is moved to tears"; the emotional appreciation of the landscape evident in Petrarch and Rousseau, for instance, was actually "the discovery of a loss [that] only became apparent in the twentieth century" (62, 63). This last view is similar to Shepard's and Berger's assertions that the contemporary epoch is a time devoid of any real connection with other animals, and Jung's belief that, as part of "the remoteness of the modern mind from" the environment, "animals have lost their numinosity" (*Earth* 74).

82. Applewhite claims that Hardy's naturalistic view "denied" him Wordsworth's naturist remedy: "Hardy's thought, confronting nature, was guilty of the crime or sickness that Wordsworth had diagnosed" (that is, murdering "to dissect"), and was thus unable to "reject the overanalytical, too conscious component of thought, to escape the skeleton ship" of Coleridge's Mariner (138). However, in his defense, Hardy also wrote many empathetic bird poems that make him, with Hopkins, an almost Clare-like exception among the Victorians. Indeed, the ecocritic Scott Russell Sanders sees Wordsworth and Hardy as "pockets of wildness surrounded by" the "domesticated landscape" that was nineteenth-century British literature (183).

4. THE EAGLE AND THE CROW

1. The eagerness that ecologists "of all stripes including the self-appointed 'Deep Ecologists'" have displayed in "claim[ing] a kinship with traditional Indian beliefs" makes Vine Deloria Jr. "wonder whether" Native Americans may have actually *won* "the Indian wars" (261). The ecocritic Gretchen Legler also notes the irony here: "The programme of cultural genocide aimed at getting the simultaneously *savage* and *noble* native off the land in the early part of this century, has turned into a veneration for the primitive"; she then refers to Vizenor's assertion that "American Indian spirituality" has become "*the* fashionable solution to environmental crises" (79).

   In contrast to this bandwagon enthusiasm, Joni Adamson criticizes the first generation of ecocritics for their relative silence regarding both Native American literature and "multicultural" concerns in general (14–19, 76–84).

2. Framing this contrast in another (and no doubt more simplistic) way, Deloria offers the following aphorism: "The white man . . . has ideas; Indians have visions" (105). If Deloria's later critiques of Western culture and religion are miles beyond the incendiary diatribes of *Custer Died for Your Sins*, the preceding cultural distinction still serves him as support for such condemnations as the following: "The Christian environment is always a ruined and destroyed, a totally exploited, environment" (159).
3. Lakota spellings, unless in direct quotations, follow Buechel's Lakota-English dictionary. Unreplicable diacritical marks have been omitted, although I have indicated, via superscript, the *sh* sound as "s^{h}" and the nasal *n* as "^{n}" (e.g., *gles^{h}ka*; *waka^{n}*). It is also helpful to know that *c*'s are always pronounced "ch" in Lakota, as in *wic[h]as^{h}a*.
4. Thus Buell speaks of the "conflation of indigenes with the environment" as one of the "vatic sublimities of earlier [nineteenth-century] wilderness representation" (*Environmental Imagination* 79).
5. Pratt defines the "contact zone" as "the space of colonial encounters . . . usually involving conditions of coercion, radical inequality, and intractable conflict" (6).
6. For example, the "thrasher" was originally the British song thrush, but it is now (also) "an American word denoting New World species" (not even of the same family), the name having "been carried abroad by early settlers" (Lockwood 154). The transference of name from the European robin to the American species is probably the best-known example: "Whereever *[sic]* the English have settled . . . the prevailing attitude toward the robin appears to be similar to that in England." In sum, both the European robin and the American thrush of the same name are rendered familial and "regarded as a *person*" (Rowland 153).
7. Circa 1806, the famed ornithologist Alexander Wilson estimated that one huge flock of pigeons was 240 miles long and over a mile wide, numbering well over two *billion* birds (17). According to A. W. Schorger's definitive postmortem study (1955), "No other species of bird, to the best of our knowledge, ever approached the passenger pigeon in numbers." Schorger estimates the total population "at the time of the discovery of America" to be between three to five *billion*, that is, an amazing 25 to 40 percent of the entire U.S. bird population (199, 204–05).
8. Half-breeds are even more despicable, in Audubon's mind, and are better "at telling lies, than anything else" (705). See Robert Young's *Colonial Desire* for an analysis of the approach-avoidance psychopathology that characterized nineteenth-century views of mixed-blood "hybridity" (e.g., 6–18).
9. The gruesome particulars of another such slaughter can be found in Audubon 265–67.
10. For a discussion of the controversy surrounding Audubon's "gun-toting" natural-

ism, see Irmscher 214–16. In contrast to such superfluous slaughter are Luther Standing Bear's words: "Killing for sport was unknown to the Lakota. His attitude toward living creatures would not permit him to slaughter a species until it was exterminated" (*Land* 69).

11. This interloper was joined by the European starling by the 1890s, thanks to the efforts of an eccentric who was "determined to introduce into America all the birds mentioned by Shakespeare" (Gibbons and Strom 216). According to *The Birder's Handbook*, "North American birds and people have been suffering ever since" (Ehrlich, Dobkin, and Wheye 633)! See Dillard's *Pilgrim at Tinker Creek* for a semihumorous treatment of starlings' continuing status as great plagues on civilization (37–42). Dillard's own attitude includes, above all, an utter admiration for their hardiness.
12. See Kastner 39–47 for the particulars of the controversy that came to be known as the Great English Sparrow War.
13. Pearson et al. (in 1917) make frequent observations on the undesirability of such European imports as the starling and the house sparrow, the latter a "persistent enemy of many native birds" (3.18). Yet with all the moral objections raised by these authors, it is curious (or symptomatic) that no parallel between *human* colonizers and colonized is ever made.
14. I have witnessed this species displacement in my own lifetime, in the expansion of the house finch's range both from the western United States into Rapid City, SD, and from the eastern United States into Vermillion, SD, with a concurrent decline in the previously ubiquitous house sparrows.
15. Likewise Paula Gunn Allen: "American Indian thought makes no such dualistic division . . . between what is material and what is spiritual" (*Sacred* 60).
16. James R. Walker is less than reassuring for anyone who would conceive of *Waka*^{n}*ta*^{n}*ka* as akin to a Judeo-Christian monotheistic deity. This was "the Great Spirit," Walker tells us; however, "he did nothing. . . . Indians did not know much about him" (102). The problem with Western attempts to perceive *Waka*^{n}*ta*^{n}*ka* as a single being, as Raymond DeMallie tells us, is that such an identification "has no parallel in recorded Lakota religious tradition" (91). When Lame Deer asked an elder Lakota medicine man about the Great Spirit, he received a pointed reply: "The Great Spirit is no old man with a beard" (Fire and Erdoes 39–40); rather, that Spirit is very much *of this world*, a pan-*physical* "spirit splitting itself up into stones, trees, tiny insects even, making them all *wakan* by his ever-presence" (114). It does sound much like Wordsworth's earlier immanent "pantheism," no doubt. One is even tempted to wonder whether Standing Bear's (editor's?) definition of *Waka*^{n}*ta*^{n}*ka* as "a great unifying life force that flowed in and through all things" (*Land* 193) doesn't have "Tintern Abbey" lurking somewhere in the backwaters of influence.

17. Likewise Joy Harjo: "The Western viewpoint has always been one of the land as wilderness, something to be afraid of" (*Spiral* 71).
18. Helen Carr even suggests a two-way circuit of influence, in which "the very language of Ossian may also have [already] been influenced by (translated) Native American models" (61). Kenneth Lincoln traces an entire lineage of "cultural romantics" in love with the New World noble savage, from Rousseau, Schiller, and Coleridge, through Cooper and Whitman, to Snyder, Merwin, and Bly (39).
19. The European (Finnish) origins of *Hiawatha*'s rousing "tom-tom" trochaic tetrameter has often been noted. Worse yet, the first actual translation of a Native American lyric, in 1765, was rendered in heroic couplets (Swann, introduction to *Coming* xxi)!
20. See Bhabha's *Location of Culture* for a neo-Lacanian analysis of the approach-avoidance mechanisms of colonization's "frontier/border" mentality (e.g., 69, 72).
21. Years later, the psychologist Bruno Bettelheim claimed, "In animistic thinking, not only animals feel and think as we do, but even stones are alive" (qtd. in S. Baker 123). Similarly, Densmore presents one Chippewa lyric ("Sometimes / I go about pitying / Myself / While I am carried by the wind / Across the sky") as "an example of the strange personation[!] which characterizes many of the [Anishinaabe] dream songs," in that "the singer contemplates the storm mystery of the sky until he feels a part of it and sings its song" (*Chippewa* 1.127–28).
22. Regarding the consciousness of animals, at least, "the Indian does not regard awareness of being [i.e., consciousness] as an abnormality peculiar to one species" (P. G. Allen, *Sacred* 60).
23. For the lamentable history of the Western textualization of Native oral literature, see William M. Clements's *Native American Verbal Art: Texts and Contexts*. Clements's quotation from an anonymous 1831 source is both precious and telling: "The eloquence of the North American Indian has never appeared to full advantage, the interpreters generally employed being ignorant and illiterate persons" (16). Even to this day, a "rogues' gallery of anthologies" of Native American poetry present the reader with scant cultural context, each poem serving as "the anthology equivalent of a museum exhibit card" (195, 187).

The editors of one such anthology, *American Indian Prose and Poetry*, can remark as late as 1974, "Perhaps more surprising to non-Indians is the fact that much of what we consider poetry was created by the Indian to be chanted or sung" (Levitas, Vivelo, and Vivelo xxviii). This is due in good part, no doubt, to all those little imagist versions by Densmore and others that populate anthologies like *The Path on the Rainbow*, in which there is no indication, for instance, that

Densmore's renditions are usually "tiny extrapolation[s] from a large ceremony" (Swann, introduction to *Coming* xlii).

24. "Frances Densmore's translations . . . indeed look remarkably like imagist poems" (H. Carr 225). James Nolan's explanation of traditional Native lyrics' similarity to Imagism sounds like a definition of the haiku, with the added stereotype of Indian laconism: "American Indians, legendary for their silence[! —who was *listening*?], construct songs with exacting, ecological detail, employed to suggest large, unstated complexities" (95). For Native lyrics' similarity to the haiku, see Velie 74–75. For a summary of the important differences between Imagism and traditional Native poetry, see Castro 22–25.
25. "In American Indian poetry, the power of the word gives reality to language as a 'world in itself,' since words are used not to duplicate the world but to pronounce it into existence" (Nolan 93).
26. James Nolan's claim that the "apostrophe to supposedly inanimate objects is an inherent characteristic of American Indian poetry" (80) may still hold true, but when these "objects" are other beings, they just as characteristically "speak back," too.

    I use "prosopopoeia" in the very limited sense established by the Yale school, as in J. Hillis Miller's paraphrase of Paul de Man's definition: "the ascription of a name, a face or a *voice* to the absent, the inanimate, or the dead" (245; emphasis added), with my own emphasis on "voice" (thus distinguishing it from the apostrophe) and an extension of possible voices to nonhuman life forms. Obviously, by this point I cannot adhere to the Yale school's analysis of this trope as a mere rhetorical symptom of deconstructive self-referentiality.
27. *Wicas*^{h}*a waka*^{n} translates literally to "man of power." As usual, translations such as "holy man" and "medicine man" are suffused with misleading connotations, projections as they are from the ideological drives of Western religion and Western primitivism.
28. More commonly, according to Vine Deloria, the Lakota privileged the "winged" as among the "two-legged" beings: "Thus our species, birds, and bears are considered to be the 'two-leggeds,' and we behave in many respects as if we were a single species." Deloria defends this Native taxonomy in full knowledge of, and disagreement with, evolutionary theory, preferring a view that deems avians more closely related to humans, based on such criteria as behavior and even "personality" (142).
29. See also Fire and Erdoes 112–13 for Lame Deer's similar contrast between this Lakota "circle" and the white man's "square." Noting Black Elk's privileging of the circle in Lakota culture, Momaday makes the suggestive claim that "language, too, is circular" (*Man* 26); indeed, as a pattern of language development evident both in the fiction of Silko and the expository prose of Vizenor, such a "circular" style

seems characteristically Native, in contrast to Western linear plot and argument development. One also thinks of the many images of circling eagles and hawks, already quoted or to be quoted henceforth, as a further seminal ornithic analogue.

Deloria has more recently reinforced this idea of the circle, adding a dire prediction for the future: "The traditional Indian stood in the center of a circle and brought everything together in that circle. Today we stand at the end of a line, discarding or avoiding everything on either side of us" (257). This "line," for Deloria, is also and ultimately Western linear history, a line that has become *not* the ascending slant of modern progress, but the descending-into-darkness of postmodern angst, the "story of endings" (Hogan, *Dwellings* 94), of the ending of so-called Western civilization itself.

30. "There was a great difference in the attitude taken by the Indian and the Caucasian toward nature": the former was a "conservationist," the latter a "non-conservationist of life." The former was "kin to all living things and he gave to all creatures equal rights with himself. . . . The philosophy of the Caucasian was, 'Things of the earth, earthy'—to be belittled and despised. Bestowing himself the position and title of a superior creature, others in the scheme were . . . of inferior position and title. . . . The worth and right to live were his, thus he heartlessly destroyed." However, Standing Bear doesn't limit a good naturist attitude to only Native Americans: "Every true student, every lover of nature has 'the Indian point of view'" (Standing Bear, *Land* 165–66, 195).

31. See, for instance, Vizenor, "Literary Animals" 125–27, 132; Deloria 142 (and see my note 28). The ecocritic Christopher Manes has also expressed an attraction to such a point of view, contending that the Western, including Darwinian, distinction between "'lower' and 'higher' animals" needs rethinking, perhaps with the help of the "decentered and hence more accurate taxonomy of many American Indian tribes who use locutions such as 'four-legged,' 'two-legged,' and 'feathered'" (23).

32. Thus can Kenneth Lincoln speak of a "*Native American renaissance*" beginning at this time, with such major figures as "Momaday, Harjo, Hogan, and Welch" (68). Michael Castro also reminds us that *Black Elk Speaks* itself achieved a "mass-market" appeal only with its 1971 reissue (96, 155).

33. As Ruoff has it, the "mixed-blood trickster as liberator . . . is a dominant theme in Vizenor's work" (83), evident not only in theme, but in a "circular," open-ended style that seems particularly postmodern and Native at once.

34. No, the eagle is *not* the central ornithic spirit of *all* Native American tribal cultures, no matter Hughes's claim in *American Indian Ecology* (1983), a book that is marred by its tendency to conflate various Native American groups into a single essentialist entity. There are at least several well-known tribal groups whose bird

of "great power" is not the eagle but the Sandhill crane, for instance, or even the mythical "Thunderbird." And no doubt there were some tribes whose discrete geographical history allowed them little access and therefore even knowledge of the two, probably never very common, eagle species of North America.

With that qualification, however, "early civilizations were almost unanimous in regarding the eagle as a symbol of the divine," including many Native American tribes, for whom it played "a prominent role as a totemic animal" (Rowland 51). It is a sad thing, really, that this is apparently true only for "early civilizations."

35. Aside from the eagle's central metonymic role in the Sun Dance, Momaday points to the importance of the environment of the Great Plains themselves in the development of the ceremony: "The sun is at home on the plains. Precisely there does it have the certain character of a god" (*Way* 7). See *The Way to Rainy Mountain* 6–12 for Momaday's elegiac account of the Kiowa Sun Dance. For the eagle as sky deity, see Momaday's story of Tolo, in which an eagle "seemed a spirit of the wilderness sky" (*Names* 141).
36. Admittedly, Black Elk's Lakota spotted eagle certainly connotes the "heavens," too, as the being closest to *Waka*^{n}*ta*^{n}*ka*. And I must acknowledge that Black Elk also associated "lofty" thought with the eagle: the connection between the ceremonial eagle feather and *Waka*^{n}*ta*^{n}*ka* "means that our [Lakota] thoughts should rise high as the eagles do" (Neihardt xxvi). However, Black Elk's notion likely had already been infected by Western idealist and monotheistic conceptions, and one must also recall that this is all filtered through Neihardt's very neo-Romantic lens.
37. But Black Elk tends to reduce the quaternity to the One, ironically, via the eagle; thus he conceives of the "four [directional] spirits" of Lakota cosmology as "only one Spirit after all, and this eagle feather here is for that One" (Neihardt 2). I suggest that this monotheistic transformation of four winds and eagles to one emblematic feather stems from Black Elk's conversion to Christianity prior to *Black Elk Speaks*, the great "unspoken" fissure and aporia in the text. Both Neihardt's mystically inclined editing choices in *Black Elk Speaks* and Black Elk's own knowledge of Christianity likely rendered his *Waka*^{n}*ta*^{n}*ka* a syncretic concept more monotheistic and idealist than traditional Lakota culture warranted.
38. For the spotted eagle as the immature bald eagle, see Jones and Tallman; as the immature golden, see Norman and Norman; as the immature of both species, see SanTara. Tyler's note on the Pueblos' black eagle is also relevant here; it "probably refers to immature eagles of both [bald and golden] species" (47), as does "spotted eagle."
39. Tyler also remarks that the golden eagle's high flight is superior to that of the

bald eagle (48). Moreover, the golden eagle's call has been described as a "yelping" whistle (Farrand 1.254).

40. For their use during the Sun Dance, see Standing Bear, *My People* 114; Fire and Erdoes 198, 206, 210. Lame Deer also notes the eagle's centrality in the *yuwipi* ceremony (136, 190), and Momaday mentions the use of the eagle bone whistle in a Kiowa ceremony (*Way* 39).

    Crazy Horse, by the way, was less ceremonial regarding the preparation of raptor plumage, according to Standing Bear's testimony: for battle, he wore no "war-bonnet," just "the full body of a hawk on the left side of his head" (*My People* 88)!

41. Between patriotism and commercialism, the icon of the eagle has become a travesty in the United States. The Shoshone and Anishinaabe poet nila northSun's "moving camp too far" presents the poignant irony of the image of "an eagle / almost extinct / on slurpee plastic cups" (12–14, in Lincoln 104). While one of my themes throughout this work has been a lament regarding the continuing use of birds as human metaphors, I most lament the current commercialization of such metaphors, and of birds themselves. Once divine augurs and sun gods, they are now the mundane icons of advertising. Rowland's analysis of bird tropes includes a consideration of this "lapse": today the wren "fails to excite the imagination as it once did," and even nightingales, "like everything else . . . are not what they used to be" (185, 111). But they still should excite the imagination, without some blatant return to homocentric superstition.

42. See Fire and Erdoes 123–24, 226–28, 235; Vander 358; Hughes 122.

43. Clyde Holler's *Black Elk's Religion* is a close examination of what Black Elk really believed. For one thing, even the venerable Sun Dance, as "portrayed in *The Sacred Pipe*" (another "as told by Black Elk" book) is a latter-day synthesis of the traditional Lakota ceremony, the revivalism of the late nineteenth-century Ghost Dance, and Black Elk's Catholicism (150–51). In fact, and amazingly, it was Black Elk's insistence on the compatibility of Christianity and Lakota tradition that "helped create the context of official tolerance" that led to the end of the U.S. government's ban on the Sun Dance (182). Whatever Black Elk really believed, Vine Deloria insists that, especially for many "young Indians," *Black Elk Speaks* "has become a North American bible of all tribes" (233); with Black Elk's other works, it "now bid[s] fair to become the canon or at least the central core of a North American Indian theological canon which will someday challenge the Eastern and Western traditions as a way of looking at the world" (234).

44. See Lame Deer for the Native American Church as a syncretism of traditional Native and Christian beliefs. For this reason, Lame Deer ultimately rejects it (Fire and Erdoes 216). Momaday also complains of the Ghost Dance's Christian influ-

ences, which created a "mirage" of faith in "a messiah and immortality, both foreign, European imports," resulting in "frightful suffering and death" (*Man* 91).

45. Thus Densmore asserts that *oyate*, when referring to "the Sioux, is translated 'tribe'; when used with reference to birds or animals, it is translated 'nation'" (*Teton* 162n).

46. Not surprisingly, the Mooney version in Cronyn's hoary anthology (first published in 1918) omits the "father" refrains (67). A very similar song attributed to the Arapaho supposedly "summarizes the whole hope of the [Ghost Dance] movement" (Swann, *Wearing* 48, 146).

47. For tribal worldviews in which Crow, Spotted Eagle, Meadowlark, Blue Jay, and others are signifiers of both other species and spirits, the "polytheism" label is useful, at least strategically, as a healthy antidote to a dominant, denatured homocentric monotheism.

48. "The snake is the supreme animal of myth" (Shepard 97)—"ancient" myths, that is, in which the snake is often the symbol of primordial power. Significantly, the Hopi snake dance, according to Frank Waters, "is the oldest rite in all America" (320). With "civilization," however, the serpent god has been repressed into the depths of the psyche and consequently demonized (see Shepard 271–72).

49. Scientists at least acknowledge that birds and other animals do, of course, communicate among each other nonverbally, as witnessed in the flocking behavior of birds. Significantly, in noting such "spinal-electric" communication, Silko cites lizards and birds together at two different points in the *Almanac* (601–02, 605).

50. In Pueblo lore, the macaw's primary association, like the Lakota eagle's, is with the Sun (Tyler 16). In Pueblo cosmology, "Parrot is joined with Eagle to represent the Sky" (25). Moreover—and crucial for the *Almanac*—as "Sun birds the parrots were known to have the capacity for human speech" (211). Another analogous sun bird is Vizenor's favorite avian, and the dominant Anishinaabe totem, the sandhill crane ("Literary Animals" 119, 120, 142; *Interior Landscapes* 3–5): "To the ancients the ring dance [of these birds] associated the cranes with the sun" (Rowland 31).

51. Environmentally speaking, Silko even notes how nature and the landscape itself seem to erupt as major "characters" in her fiction (*Yellow Woman* 44). As for the close association in Silko of social and environmental concerns, Killingsworth and Palmer have remarked that her novel links the "brownness" of the Native people with the very color of their native ground, and the "whiteness" of the colonizers with death and sterility (203–06).

52. For more on these macaws as talking oracular spirits, see Silko, *Almanac* 472, 475–76, 511–12, 711. Finally, the associated epithets of "Fire-Eye Macaw" (303) and "Death Macaw" (480) reflect the traditional Native beliefs in these birds' roles as agents of revenge and retribution.

53. In the novel's intertextual mingling of many slightly different Native oral traditions, the great snake is also a "giant water snake" whose lake had been drained (Silko, *Almanac* 92, 135), further emphasizing its primordial but "submerged" nature.
54. Although the actual appearance of a "giant stone snake" near a uranium mine in 1979 served as an initial creative spark for the *Almanac*, the image remained a shadowy, relatively unconscious (reptilian brain?) motivation during the novel's composition; it wasn't until Silko had written the final sentence that she "realized that the giant snake had been a catalyst for the novel from the start" (*Yellow Woman* 138–39, 144).
55. The ancient Almanac itself within *Almanac* also mentions the "Death Dog" with "bird and snake earrings, which is a rebus for Quetzalcoatl" (572); "Chichan is a giant snake half human and half feathered" (573); and "Marsha-true'ee *[sic]*, the Giant Plumed Serpent," is close Pueblo kin to the Giant Stone Snake, its "beautiful lake" having been drained, too (577).
56. Silko discusses Quetzalcoatl in a later essay, noting that this "Divine Serpent of Feathers and Flowers" was deemed the equivalent of Satan by Christian colonizers. Then this fascinating hypothesis: "Maybe the Old Testament garden of Eden story is the first strike by northern tribes [i.e., Western Judeo-Christian cultures] against" not only Quetzalcoatl and related Native American deities but "the religion of the Africans to the south and their worship of the great snake, Damballah. Those who loathe snakes have been brainwashed by the Old Testament" (*Yellow Woman* 147).
57. Straightforwardly Jungian, too, is Paula Gunn Allen's assertion that Native American literature is above all a "psychic journey," its ceremonialism a movement toward "a position of unity within" the "larger Self" (*Sacred* 68). Indeed, Vizenor considers Allen's statement that "American Indian thought is essentially mystical and psychic in nature"—so Western, and Jungian, a statement—as a reactive "simulation" of that unreal Indian promulgated by dominant white culture (*Manifest* 21). Maybe this simulation is ultimately positive in a postmodern trickster sort of way, but it is a simulation nonetheless. In fact, in no way are the "postindian warriors" that Vizenor has in mind the "new shaman healers of the unreal" (23), and contemporary Native American writers must ever guard against a "nostalgia [that] is the absence of the real" (25).
58. The young Sitting Bull likewise "became a friend of the birds," owing "the saving of his life to a dream in which an encounter with a grizzly bear was foretold by a bird." Thus his song to that avian savior, a "yellow-hammer" (the northern flicker [Day 112; see epigraph to this section]). Indeed, Sitting Bull "always spoke of birds and was fond of stories about the Bird people." Fittingly, then, it was a

meadowlark who told Sitting Bull of his approaching murder (Lincoln 23, 17, 404).

59. The mockingbird plays a somewhat similar role in tribes of the desert Southwest, important in its "teaching of [ritual] songs and speech" (Tyler 212, 217).

60. However, the Lakotas' use of the pentatonic minor scale itself might also partly explain at least the ubiquity of the descending fourth in their melodies.

61. I would remonstrate here that Wordsworth's skylark ends up much more "grounded" than Shelley's, as I have argued previously in this work.

62. Vine Deloria uses a common alternative translation of the latter term, "all our relatives" (or "all my relatives"), in his discussion of "birds, animals, and plants" as the "other peoples" of the Native American "religious world" (208–09).

63. But the Jungian drive toward a transcultural archetype lives on. Lincoln approvingly cites Lewis Hyde regarding the "global Trickster," an "archetypal" figure "driven by appetite and exclusion to reinvent order through disorder." This "Trickster is our ancient . . . liminal artist of mixed blood, seductive song, and tales of guile" (45–46).

64. William Bright's study of Coyote as Trickster—including, in contemporary literature, Silko and Snyder (341, 345–46, 372–73, 376–78)—also acknowledges Raven and Blue Jay (another corvid) as Trickster figures (341). Indeed, Coyote and Raven are the ultimate tricksters: they are both "scavengers and omnivores, and thus—like humans!—can be seen as symbolizing an equivocal middle position between herbivores and carnivores" (349).

65. Elsewhere, the crow is deemed the "most important symbol of the ghost dance" (Levitas, Vivelo, and Vivelo 219).

66. Tyler's explication of the Pueblos' view isn't much more positive: the crow is "ambiguous" and, for better or worse, "represent[s] the dead in a general way" (199). For the Pueblo, crows are sometimes just plain "bad" or "evil" (207–08)!

67. Just as Jim Loney's own identity is unidentifiable, as Dexter Westrum points out. However, Westrum's reading of the bird's (and Loney's) final flight as "his movement into a transcendent reality, to a distant place where everything is all right," from a deathbed realization, as it were, of his Native heritage (144–45), is in stark opposition to the view I will offer on the matter.

68. For Harjo's prose poems, paragraph numbers are given instead of line numbers, when helpful.

5. A BEATITUDE OF BIRDS

1. Momaday's *In the Bear's House* (1999) confirms Vizenor's perception of Momaday's "bear-nature" ("Literary Animals" 137), which he reaffirms in his introduction: "Bear and I are one, in one and the same story" (9).

2. Fletcher's ostensible hyperbole in the epigraph actually derives from some ap-

parently close parallels in Whitman's syntax and Hopi grammatical constructions (159–60). More dangerous, however, is his broader claim that "one always has the sense with Whitman" that he "depend[s] upon oral cultures and old customs directing the right way to live" (122), *as if* he were a true Native, a thread that I will develop and critique.

3. The Mohawk poet Maurice Kenny can even claim descent from the British poetic purveyor of *carpe diem*, Robert Herrick (*Mama Poems* 1)!
4. As for recent Native plays on the term "half-breed," one must acknowledge the title of the Lakota poet Tiffany Midge's first collection of poetry, *Outlaws, Renegades and Saints: Diary of a Mixed-Up Halfbreed.*
5. A mixed blood imbued in poststructuralism, Gerald Vizenor plays with identity more than any, in part as a reaction to the incredibly negative stereotype of the half-breed, which he reinscribes via the term "crossblood" and closely associates with the postmodern trickster itself. Vizenor would no doubt agree with Spivak's anti-essentialist dictum "I'm a negotiation. We're all sites of negotiation," in contrast to some "impossible ahistorical quest for purist positions" (148, 150).
6. In apparent support of what I think is an unfortunate conflation, Joy Harjo has recently noted (2002) that her blackbird poem "Desire" is a "poem [that] could not have been written without Wallace Stevens's 'Thirteen Ways of Looking at a Blackbird'" (*How We* 221).
7. See Snyder's *The Real Work* (154–56) for his rather pointed rebuttal of their criticisms, including his assertion that shamanism, at least, "has at its very center a teaching from the nonhuman, not a teaching from an Indian medicine man" (156).

   Setting aside the quibble that shamanism per se is actually a specific northeast Asian phenomenon, one need only look back to Black Elk's "possession" *by* the eagle to perceive a great distance between Whitman's avian uses and prototypical Native American avian mergers and those of Black Elk. Again, it boils down to the degree (or quality) of identification and the notable fact that the latter identification, that is, Black Elk's "shamanism," is *not* initiated by the ego.
8. See Ed Folsom's "Whitman and American Indians" for a more circumspect view of Whitman's relationship with Native Americans and Indianness. Killingsworth also ultimately laments that, despite Whitman's attraction to the American indigenous, he still "follows the trend of Anglo-American literature in treating Native peoples as already departed" (*Walt Whitman* 86–87).

   Nolan's attempts to render Whitman Native includes the following ornithic reference: "Often Whitman's flights are accompanied by the 'spirit helper' of a bird" (200). Yet the roles of the notable avians in, say, "Out of the Cradle Endlessly Rocking" and "When Lilacs Last in the Dooryard Bloom'd" hardly seem that of "spirit helper." Nor does the relationship of "the ocean-mother and the bird-brother" of "Out of the Cradle" really resonate, in my mind, "with the Native American mythology . . . of filial animals" (Killingsworth, *Walt Whitman* 127; see 37–38, 129–31 for other Whitman-Native affinities).

9. Citing Rahv's classic dichotomy of "palefaces" and "redskins" in American literature (with Whitman as the first wild "Redskin"), Nolan is too earnest again in searching out Whitman's Native roots: "Like the shaman," Whitman was "a medium for the voices of tribe and nature," reflective of the "American Indian roots in Whitman's persona" (46, 154, 197). Other scholars of Native American literature have been just as enthusiastic about Whitman's nativeness. Norma Wilson, for instance, has claimed that "Whitman's *Leaves of Grass* was the first truly visionary written expression in American Literature. Never before had an Ameropean . . . approximated so closely the Native Americans' conception of the spiritual and commonplace as one" ("Heartbeat" 14).
10. Ironic here is Ruoff's reading of Kenny's own poems as "Whitmanesque in their appeal to the senses through the vigorous piling up of visual images" (105).
11. For the acknowledged influence of Wordsworth on Carter Revard, see Velie 221. On Roberta Hill Whiteman, see N. Wilson, *Nature* 78.
12. For another discussion of "Homework at Oxford," see N. Wilson, *Nature* 16–18. This critic also surmises that "his hearing loss has probably intensified Revard's emphasis on sound" (18), like Wordsworth and several other British Romantics. This may also have occasioned Revard's attentive use of tactile imagery, evident in several of my quoted lines from the poem.
13. Not to single out the grand old man of the Native American renaissance in this regard, but Momaday's love for metrical forms, including epigrammatic couplets, is manifest. For the influence of Yvor Winters and formalism in general, see N. Wilson, *Nature* 34. For the influence of Dickinson, see Lincoln xiii. Most fascinating, for the convoluted story of a white modernist poet with some Native influences and propensities (Winters) as mentor to a Native American with a great regard for Anglo formalism (Momaday), see Lincoln 76, 242–48.
14. In Native American literature, the haiku form has been most earnestly adopted and adapted by Gerald Vizenor; for a brief narrative of this influence, see Vizenor's own *Interior Landscapes* 171–75.
15. As with many of Henson's poems, this "woodpecker song" is accompanied by the same poem in the Cheyenne language.
16. Personal conversation, Nov. 7, 2001. See also Lincoln 60–61 for Merwin's influence on other Native American poets.

    According to Norma Wilson, "Henson imitates" the woodpecker's song in part because it "is held sacred in the sun dance ceremony, in which the dancers aspire to be like the birds in the spirit of a strong and humble caring. The 'small sound' of the woodpecker is concentrated, like Henson's poems" (*Nature* 70). In my conversation with Henson regarding this poem, he said it was the red-headed woodpecker; to my remonstrance that I had pictured a smaller bird, such as a downy woodpecker, he claimed that the Red-headed species was "much smaller in Oklahoma." He also spoke of his son's ritual hunting of one of these birds and of how the bird couldn't be killed: "It was its spirit," Henson concluded. Finally, sensing my animal rights stance, he was careful, almost apologetic, in emphasizing that the woodpeckers are killed only for ceremonial purposes.

17. Obviously my use of the terms "hybridity" and "mimicry" are usually more traditional than the special uses of the term devised by Homi Bhabha, but his formulations are relevant. He defines "hybridity" as "the repertoire of positions of power and resistance, domination and dependence that constructs [the] colonial identification subject (both colonizer and colonized)" (67), with the connotation, however, that no one is too much to bless or blame in such a negotiation of power. Bhabha's "mimicry" is more to the point, however, as it is "one of the most elusive and effective strategies of [and against?] colonial power and knowledge" (85). The discourse of even the colonizers becomes "*almost the same but not white*" (89)—thus Whitman's "barbaric yawp," perhaps. For the colonized, "the ambivalence of mimicry" allows "potentially and strategically an insurgent counter-appeal" that "mimes the forms of authority at the point at which it deauthorizes them" (91). In this light, even the ostensible mimicry (in the older sense) of iambic pentameter can become a cultural parody, "deauthorizing" the very form via a Native content.
18. Bruchac's self-portrait elsewhere is also quite avian: "What do I look like? . . . a beaked nose . . . and dark eyebrows that lift one at a time like the wings of a bird" ("Notes of a Translator's Son" 197). Even as a child he "was different—raised by old people . . . writing poetry in grade school, talking about animals as if they were people" (198). Later: "I always dreamed of flight. I still do fly in my dreams" (200).
19. Bruchac's visits with Native American inmates—often during geese migrations, it would appear—result in at least one other similar lyric, "At Teeheelay Correctional Center for Women." Here woman and Native and bird are all reprivileged, as the women recite their Native names in an act of recuperative healing: to the "beat" of "those names reclaiming / their hearts," the "throbbing wings / of a thousand geese / take back the sky" (23–28 [*No Borders* 27]).
20. Unfortunately, it is now difficult to read Native Americans lamenting pollution without conjuring an image of the famous public service commercial of the noble savage shedding a tear to the backdrop of a polluted river. But such poetic gestures are often powerful all the same, as in this Bruchac poem, and in Maurice Kenny's "Boyhood Country Creek," where, because of "light machinery" and

"parking lot[s]," (6, 19), "mallards" and "rainbow trout / speckle / only the memory" (12–15 [*Smell* n.p.]).

21. "Wild animals frequent Henson's poetry," Norma Wilson tells us, "carrying the traditional Cheyenne respect for coyote, owl, and badger into our modern time." But Wilson also accepts Robert L. Berner's contention that "the animals in Henson's poems are totemic, representative of their ancestors in Cheyenne tradition and legend" (*Nature* 69). An overgeneralization, to be sure; reducing all of Henson's animals to tribal totems is, to voice my recurring complaint, a denial of the integral worth of other species themselves.
22. For another discussion of the caged-eagle encounter in "An Eagle Nation," see N. Wilson, *Nature* 28–29.
23. On a more mythic level in Kenny's work is the loon's association with the maternal and nature deity of "Sky Woman," who is accompanied by "loon, / crane, mallard" (2.9–10) in her progress of bringing "delight" via "the greenness of things" (2.31–32 [Bruchac, *Returning* 179]).
24. The poem's initial beckoning partakes of a striking ornithic simile: "I welcome you on this Klallam path / as the flicker does whose tapping beak / is as moon-inlaid as the cedar bark" ("Round Dance" 3–5 [*Drawings* 143]).
25. As a fascinating sidelight, sightings of a huge thunderbird-like raptor were reported in Alaska in 2002, the latest in a recent line of large cryptozoic birds of mythic return, including the "Mothman" of the 1960s. Apparently, there is still a human need or attraction for this archetype, for which the UFO phenomenon might be interpreted as a modern displacement.
26. Niatum's "Crow's Way" portrays another "falling away" of the Trickster's numinosity. Here the crow has grown reluctant even to laugh, in part because a "smog-edge sky blurs his eyes / Like a cataract" (1–2 [*Carriers* 133]).
27. Patrick D. Murphy complains that, although Ortiz is "frequently cited by other environmental writers," he is "not yet widely recognized . . . for his ecological vision" (46). Yet Joni Adamson Clarke's perceived connection "between the oppression of certain races and classes and the appropriation and exploitation of indigenous lands" (11–12, already quoted in chapter 1) is actually her paraphrase of Ortiz's poem "That's the Place the Indians Talk About." Norma Wilson contrasts T. S. Eliot's "personae" of "individuals alienated from their culture and even the earth" with, specifically, the naturism of Ortiz (*Nature* 50).
28. Elsewhere in Ortiz: "Eagle clearly soars / into the craggy peaks / of the mind" ("Vision Shadows" 2–4 [*Woven* 245]).
29. In another section of the poem, it is Ortiz's son who points out a hawk, a pattern repeated in "Earth and Rain, The Plants & Sun" (*Woven* 196–97). One recalls Coleridge's son bidding his father to listen to the nightingale's song: the child is still father of the man.

30. See also Ortiz, "Thanking the Pheasant Hens" (*After* 19), for another instance of pheasants jarring the poet out of mundane consciousness.
31. See also "How to make a good chili stew," a poem in which magpies are portrayed as garrulous "native" in-laws (*Woven* 174–76).
32. Lincoln is more than willing to essentialize Native women authors as ancient tribal matriarchs: "The *native* in American verse may well be feminist-as-cultured-other, singing out of carefully wrapped medicine bundles and clan genealogies" (141).
33. Buell discusses nature in the New World colonialist context as "the sign under which women and nonwhites have been grouped in the process of themselves being exploited even while being relished as exotic" and "spontaneous" (*Environmental Imagination* 21).
34. Norma Wilson points likewise to the "blending of poetry and prose" in Ortiz's *Fight Back* as "a style that Native poets Joy Harjo, Sherman Alexie, and others would use in later books" (*Nature* 58).
35. Hogan's feminism aside, the gender switch of the usually culturally masculinized raptor may also stem from her knowledge that the female bird of prey is usually the physically larger of the mating pair.
36. Hogan's deep and spiritual ecology includes such utterances as "Something lives in everything" ("Man Calling Deer" 12 [*Eclipse* 60]) and "Everything is alive" ("Turning" 20 [*Seeing* 38]).
37. "The totem is a native metaphor" that has been "reduced" by Western social science to "false categorizations," to "perverse distinctions of savagism and civilization" (Vizenor, "Literary Animals" 123).
38. For a poem in which the birds are markedly pitted against human warfare, see Hogan's "Folksong" (*Seeing* 8–9). Here the language of human politics is contrasted with "the sweet songs of sparrows" (11); in the midst of such human "blood feuds," "the birds are safe [only] if they keep moving / in neutral sky" (12–14).
39. Note also Hogan's "On the Circumference" for a specifically human-avian erasure of boundaries: "If I spoke / all the birds would gather . . . in the ridge of my throat"; there are "clay birds flying out / warm feathers / smell of blood," and they are "singing / against earth's bounds" (21–22, 24–29 [*Eclipse* 61]).
40. In this regard, see also Hogan's "Arrowhead" (*Calling* 21), about an old man who has "birds / falling / down his mind" (19–21).
41. This image seems a favorite one for Hogan, likely culled from personal experience, as it is repeated in *Dwellings* (with a comparable spiritualization): sometimes "a person happens across a coal black raven standing inside the wide arch of those [moose's] ribs like a soul in a body" (65).
42. One sees echoed in the second epigraph Black Elk's belief that, though the Black

Hills were central to his Great Vision, "anywhere is the center of the world" (Neihardt 33n).

Harjo's deer are usually mythic reminders of an animal and Native knowledge, for example, "Deer Ghost," in which "The deer knows what it is doing wandering the streets of this / city; it has never forgotten the songs" (2.9–10 [*In Mad* 29]). In "Song for the Deer and Myself to Return On," she imaginatively calls the deer into her Denver apartment: "Now the deer and I are trying to figure out a song / to get them, to get all of us back [to our Native homeland and Native ways], / because if it works I'm going with them" (11–13 [30]). "Preparations" includes the following wonderful lines: "Humans are the strangest of animals because they make laws / from lies"; "We should be like the antelope / who gratefully drink the rain" and " love the earth for what it is—their book of law, their heart" (12–15 [*Map* 57]).

43. For Joy Harjo on her mixed-blood status, see *Spiral* 61, 66, 125. Her heritage includes Cherokee, Irish, French, and Creek (Muskogee) (Lincoln 359).
44. Both the "body of nature and the native body" are "being contested for in Harjo's poems" (Legler 80).
45. Obviously, crows are praiseworthy creatures, too, for their survivalist skills in a wide variety of apparently inimical habitats: "crows survive anywhere / even in Iowa" ("Crows/And I Know My Part In It, Too" 1–2 [*What Moon* 34])!
46. In terms of literary hybridity, here again are echoes of Whitman's "I think I could turn and live with animals" passage.
47. It may be a gross misreading to perceive in Harjo's great vision an anticipation of her own final out-of-body experience, but the vision does resonate well with an intriguing statement in her prose poem "sudden awareness": "There are images, songs and words that will appear at your death like familiar birds to accompany you on your journey to the sky" (1 [*Map* 129]).
48. Indeed, there seems to be competition among Native poets to see who can best describe a redwing's wing. We have already seen Revard's "epaulettes"; Jim Barnes describes their red "chevrons . . . patched / onto the general genetic black" ("Around the Cow Pond" 5–7 [*Sawdust* 27]). But Linda Hogan's description is one of the best, of a "red-winged blackbird" keeping "vigil on a cattail": "He opens his wounds, a sleeve of fire" ("Porcupine on the Road to the River" 20–23 [*Seeing* 6]).
49. The poem's title refers to Charlie Parker, not to the avian. As a musician herself, Harjo is quite comfortable privileging music over poetry, because the former "doesn't have the added boundary of words" (*Spiral* 101).
50. An ornithological quibble here: I have heard starlings imitate many birds, but the crow isn't one of them. The "cawing" rather jars the naturalist's ear. But more

to the poetic (and Native) point, *caw* does invoke the crow, with all the Trickster associations thereof.

EPILOGUE

1. Steve Baker has also commented on Berger's reliance "on the evidence of sight," on "evidence [that] comes from *looking*" (11, 15).
2. Ecoscholars' rejection of language includes McKusick's critique of the "unexamined premise that the social production of human behavior is entirely distinct from the means by which the 'lower animals' learn to hunt, hide, play, and fight"; in truth, "many animals . . . are already fully involved in semiotic exchange" (16, 17). John Gray is more succinct: "The calls of birds and the traces left by wolves to mark off their territories are no less forms of language than the songs of humans" (56).
3. This "oceanic" state is described in quite New Age terms: one becomes "literally one with the universe" and "one rhythmic whole" (P. G. Allen, *Sacred* 63). Castro notes that, in Native literature, "repetition creates holistic awareness" (35); indeed, the phrase "holistic awareness" becomes an important refrain in Castro, as a quality by which both Native culture and poetry can be defined (5).
4. This has been due, in good part, to "literacy and Christian exegesis" (Manes 18): "At one time nature spoke; now texts do." With nature thus denaturized, a textual "book," "the things in nature could thus be seen as mere *littera*—signs" (19).
5. Lockwood's etymological analysis of British bird names indicates, above all, how many are ultimately onomatopoeic, derived from the birds' calls (8–10), including many common names that no longer seem obviously so because of language mutations (e.g., buzzard, 38; chicken, 41; coot, 46; crane, 48; crow, 49; dove, 54; finch, 62; heron, 82; kestrel, 90; kite, 91; oriole, 111; pigeon, 118; quail, 124; raven, 125; rook, 131; throstle or thrush, 154; turtle [dove], 159).
6. In "Postmodern Nature/Poetry," George Hart argues against "the rejection of much postmodernist poetry, as well as poststructuralist theory, by ecological critics," insisting instead that "postmodernist poetry's emphasis on the materiality of language brings nature and language together on the page in a manner that neoromantic poetics [e.g., that of Bly and Snyder] cannot" (315).
7. Polyphony, a happy *musical* metaphor itself, is described as both "double-voiced" and "dialogic" (Bakhtin, *Problems* 40), fraught with "multi-leveledness and contradictoriness" (27), the product of "contending voices" (30).
8. Michael J. McDowell likewise extends the concept of heteroglossia to other species in literature. Although, "at least on a literal level, trees and stones and squirrels don't talk," Bakhtin's liberal notion of alterity allows for such "dialogical interplay" that, in certain works, "animal participants often have almost equal representation with the narrators" (372, 375, 385, 381).
9. Elsewhere Hogan says that "white people are waking up" and "are starting to

see the animals, insects, the trees, as equal to themselves" (qtd. in P. G. Allen, *Sacred* 169).

10. Thus can the antihumanist John Gray assert, "Where other animals differ from humans is in lacking the sensation of selfhood." (But then, how do *we* know this?!) "In this they are not altogether unfortunate" (61). Better yet: "Why do other animals not seek deliverance from suffering? Is it that no one has told them they must live again?[!] Or is it that, without needing to think about it, they know they will not?" (129).
11. Possibly Jung's most expressly ecological statement is his defense of the "living" earth as "depreciated and misunderstood"; indeed, "for quite long enough we have been taught that this life is not the real thing . . . and that we live only for heaven" (*Earth* 2).
12. Gray even foresees a probable future "revival of piety" and mysticism, as compensation for humankind's isolation: "Like prayerful astronauts, its [the future era's] inhabitants will look to the heavens for sustenance—and they will not be disappointed" (150). However, rather than succumbing to such vatic mysticism, "they will do better to seek the company of other animals" (151), and rather than searching for extraterrestrials, "they would be better occupied trying to communicate with the dwindling numbers of their animal kin" (188).
13. Lyons's speech has become justly well-known. Hogan's poem "Who Will Speak?" is a direct tribute to Lyons, as one who "speaks of tomorrow," giving "voice to the small animals" and "a seat to the eagles" (27–29 [*Eclipse* 42]).
14. Radically egalitarian, too, is Snyder's "Tomorrow's Song," which claims that the United States has "lost its mandate" because "it never gave the mountains and rivers, / trees and animals, / a vote" (1, 3–5 [*Turtle Island* 77]). In a prose piece from the same book, "The Wilderness," Snyder more generally calls for a redefinition of "democracy" that would embrace the "nonhuman" (106).
15. Even as recently as 1991, Velie wrote, "For some reason there are more good Indian poets than fiction writers today" (211).

Works Cited

Abrams, M. H. "English Romanticism: The Spirit of the Age." In *Romanticism Reconsidered: Selected Papers from the English Institute,* ed. Northrop Frye. New York: Columbia University Press, 1963. 26–72.

———. *The Mirror and the Lamp: Romantic Theory and the Critical Tradition.* Oxford: Oxford University Press, 1953.

———. *Natural Supernaturalism: Tradition and Revolution in Romantic Literature.* New York: Norton, 1971.

———. "Structure and Style in the Greater Romantic Lyric." In *Romanticism and Consciousness: Essays in Criticism,* ed. Harold Bloom. New York: Norton, 1970. 201–29.

Adams, Hazard, ed. *Critical Theory Since Plato.* Rev. ed. Fort Worth TX: Harcourt, 1992.

Adamson [Clarke], Joni. *American Indian Literature, Environmental Justice, and Ecocriticism: The Middle Place.* Tucson: University of Arizona Press, 2001.

Alaimo, Stacy. "Displacing Darwin and Descartes: The Bodily Transgressions of Fielding Burke, Octavia Butler, and Linda Hogan." *ISLE* 3.1 (1996): 47–66.

Alexie, Sherman. "Avian Nights." *New Letters* 69.4 (2003): 21–23.

———. *Old Shirts and New Skins.* Los Angeles: American Indian Studies Center, 1993.

———. *One Stick Song.* Brooklyn: Hanging Loose, 2000.

Allen, Mary. *Animals in American Literature.* Urbana: University of Illinois Press, 1983.

Allen, Paula Gunn. "Bringing Home the Fact: Tradition and Continuity in the Imagination." In *Recovering the Word: Essays on Native American Literature,* ed. Brian Swann and Arnold Krupat. Berkeley: University of California Press, 1987. 563–79.

———. *The Sacred Hoop: Recovering the Feminine in American Indian Traditions.* Boston: Beacon, 1986.

Applewhite, James. *Seas and Inland Journeys: Landscape and Consciousness from Wordsworth to Roethke.* Athens: University of Georgia Press, 1985.

Armbruster, Karla. "Creating the World We Must: The Paradox of Television Nature Documentaries." In *Writing the Environment: Ecocriticism and Literature,* ed. Richard Kerridge and Neil Sammells. London: Zed, 1998. 218–38.

Armbruster, Karla, and Kathleen R. Wallace, eds. *Beyond Nature Writing: Expanding the Boundaries of Ecocriticism.* Charlottesville: University Press of Virginia, 2001.

Armstrong, Edward A. *The Life and Lore of the Bird: In Nature, Art, Myth, and Literature*. New York: Crown, 1975.

Arnold, Matthew. "Dover Beach." In *Poetry of the Victorian Period*, ed. Jerome Hamilton Buckley and George Benjamin Woods. 3rd ed. Glenview IL: Scott Foresman, 1965. 499.

Audubon, John James. *John James Audubon: Writings and Drawings*. Ed. Christoph Irmscher. New York: Library of America, 1999.

Baker, Houston A., Jr. *Blues, Ideology, and Afro-American Literature: A Vernacular Theory*. Chicago: University of Chicago Press, 1984.

Baker, Steve. *Picturing the Beast: Animals, Identity, and Representation*. 2nd ed. Urbana: University of Illinois Press, 2001.

Bakhtin, Mikhail. *The Dialogic Imagination*. Ed. Michael Holquist. Trans. Caryl Emerson and Michael Holquist. Austin: University of Texas Press, 1981.

———. *Problems of Dostoevsky's Poetics* [1963]. Trans. Caryl Emerson. Minneapolis: University of Minnesota Press, 1984.

Baldwin, Barry. "The Bird Man of Hampshire." *Hellas* 5.1 (1994): 147–51.

Barnes, Jim. *The American Book of the Dead*. Urbana: University of Illinois Press, 1982.

———. *La Plata Cantata*. West Lafayette IN: Purdue University Press, 1989.

———. *The Sawdust War*. Urbana: University of Illinois Press, 1992.

———. *A Season of Loss*. West Lafayette IN: Purdue University Press, 1985.

Bate, Jonathan. "Caliban and Ariel Write Back." *Shakespeare Survey* 48 (1995): 155–62.

———. *Romantic Ecology: Wordsworth and the Environmental Tradition*. London: Routledge, 1991.

Bateson, F. W. *Wordsworth: A Re-Interpretation*. 2nd ed. London: Longmans, 1956.

Berger, John. "Why Look at Animals?" In *About Looking*. New York: Pantheon, 1980. 1–26.

Bevis, William. "Native American Novels: Homing In." In *Recovering the Word: Essays on Native American Literature*, ed. Brian Swann and Arnold Krupat. Berkeley: University of California Press, 1987. 580–620.

Bewick, Thomas. *Selections from* A History of British Birds [1797, 1804]. 6th ed. [1826]. New York: Paddington, 1976.

Bhabha, Homi. *The Location of Culture*. London: Routledge, 1994.

Blake, William. *The Poetry and Prose of William Blake*. Ed. David V. Erdman. Garden City NY: Doubleday, 1965.

Bloom, Harold. *The Anxiety of Influence: A Theory of Poetry*. New York: Oxford University Press, 1973.

———, ed. *Romanticism and Consciousness: Essays in Criticism*. New York: Norton, 1970.

———. "The Unpastured Sea: An Introduction to Shelley." In *Romanticism and Consciousness: Essays in Criticism,* ed. Harold Bloom. New York: Norton, 1970. 374–401.

Bly, Robert, ed. *News of the Universe: Poems of Twofold Consciousness.* San Francisco: Sierra Club Books, 1980.

———. *Silence in the Snowy Fields.* Middletown CT: Wesleyan University Press, 1962.

Bone, Drummond. "Shelley, Wordsworth, and Byron: The Detail of Nature." *The Wordsworth Circle* 23 (1992): 3–10.

Boswell, James. *The Works of James Boswell: The Life of Samuel Johnson, LL.D.* [1791]. Roslyn NY: Black's, 1952.

Branch, Michael. "Ecocriticism: The Nature of Nature in Literary Theory and Practice." *Weber Studies* 11.1 (1994): 41–55.

Branch, Michael P., Rochelle Johnson, Daniel Patterson, and Scott Slovic, eds. *Reading the Earth: New Directions to the Study of Literature and Environment.* Moscow: University of Idaho Press, 1998.

Brant, Beth. "Prayer." In *Intimate Nature: The Bond between Women and Animals,* ed. Linda Hogan, Deena Metzger, and Brenda Peterson. New York: Ballantine, 1998. 34–36.

Bright, William. "The Natural History of Old Man Coyote." In *Recovering the Word: Essays on Native American Literature,* ed. Brian Swann and Arnold Krupat. Berkeley: University of California Press, 1987. 339–87.

Brontë, Charlotte. *Jane Eyre* [1847]. Ware UK: Wordsworth, 1992.

Brooks, Paul. *Speaking for Nature: How Literary Naturalists from Henry Thoreau to Rachel Carson Have Shaped America.* Boston: Houghton, 1980.

Brown, Joseph Epes, ed. *The Sacred Pipe: Black Elk's Account of the Seven Rites of the Oglala Sioux.* Norman: University of Oklahoma Press, 1953.

Browning, Robert. *The Complete Poetical Works of Browning.* Cambridge MA: Riverside, 1895.

Bruchac, Joseph. *Near the Mountains.* Fredonia NY: White Pine Press, 1987.

———. *No Borders.* Duluth MN: Holy Cow! Press, 1999.

———. "Notes of a Translator's Son." In *I Tell You Now: Autobiographical Essays by Native American Writers,* ed. Brian Swann and Arnold Krupat. Lincoln: University of Nebraska Press, 1987. 195–205.

———, ed. *Returning the Gift: Poetry and Prose from the First North American Native Writers' Festival.* Tucson: University of Arizona Press, 1994.

———, ed. *Songs from This Earth on Turtle's Back.* Greenfield Center NY: Greenfield Review Press, 1983.

———. "Thanking the Birds: Native American Upbringing and the Natural World." In *Keepers of the Earth: Native American Stories and Environmental Activities for*

Children, ed. Michael J. Caduto and Joseph Bruchac. Golden CO: Fulcrum, 1988. 193–96.

Buechel, Eugene. *A Dictionary of the Teton Dakota Sioux Language; Lakota-English: English-Lakota*. Ed. Paul Manhart. Pine Ridge SD: Red Cloud Indian School, 1970.

Buell, Lawrence. *The Environmental Imagination: Thoreau, Nature Writing, and the Formation of American Culture*. Cambridge MA: Harvard University Press, 1995.

———. *The Future of Environmental Criticism: Environmental Crisis and Literary Imagination*. Malden MA: Blackwell, 2005.

Burns, Robert. *The Complete Poetical Works of Robert Burns*. Boston: Houghton, 1900.

Burroughs, John. *The Birds of John Burroughs: Keeping a Sharp Lookout*. Ed. Jack Kligerman. New York: Hawthorn, 1976.

Byron, George Gordon. *Poetical Works*. Ed. Frederick Page. Rev. ed. Oxford: Oxford University Press, 1970.

Camp, Carter. "Hiding Genocide: The National Museum of the American Indian." American Indian Cultural Support. 1999. Accessed August 17, 2005. http://www.aics.org/natlmuseum.html.

Campbell, SueEllen. "Magpie." In *Writing the Environment: Ecocriticism and Literature*, ed. Richard Kerridge and Neil Sammells. London: Zed, 1998. 13–26.

Carlyle, Thomas. *Sartor Resartus* [1832]. Chicago: Donohue, Henneberry, n.d.

Carr, Helen. *Inventing the American Primitive: Politics, Gender and the Representation of Native American Literary Traditions, 1789–1936*. New York: New York University Press, 1996.

Carr, Samuel. Introduction to *The Poetry of Birds*. Ed. Samuel Carr. New York: Taplinger, 1976. 11.

Carson, Rachel. *Silent Spring*. Boston: Houghton, 1962.

Castro, Michael. *Interpreting the Indian: Twentieth-Century Poets and the Native American*. Albuquerque: University of New Mexico Press, 1983.

Cheney, Patrick. *Spenser's Famous Flight: A Renaissance Idea of a Literary Career*. Toronto: University of Toronto Press, 1993.

Clare, John. *John Clare* [The Oxford Authors]. Ed. Eric Robinson and David Powell. Oxford: Oxford University Press, 1984.

———. *John Clare's Birds*. Ed. Eric Robinson and Richard Fitter. Oxford: Oxford University Press, 1982.

———. *The Rural Muse* [1835]. Ed. R. K. R. Thornton. Ashington UK: Mid-NAG and Carcanet, 1982.

———. *Selected Poems of John Clare*. Ed. Geoffrey Grigson. Cambridge MA: Harvard University Press, 1950.

Clarke, Joni Adamson. "Toward an Ecology of Justice: Transformative Ecological Theory and Practice." In *Reading the Earth: New Directions to the Study of Literature and Environment,* ed. Michael P. Branch et al. Moscow: University of Idaho Press, 1998. 9–17.

Clements, William M. *Native American Verbal Art: Texts and Contexts.* Tucson: University of Arizona Press, 1996.

Cobbett, William. *Rural Rides* [1830]. 2 vols. London: Dent, 1912.

Coetzee, J. M., Marjorie Garber, Peter Singer, Wendy Doniger, and Barbara Smuts. *The Lives of Animals.* Ed. Amy Gutmann. Princeton NJ: Princeton University Press, 1999.

Cokinos, Christopher. *Hope Is a Thing with Feathers: A Personal Chronicle of Vanished Birds.* New York: Tarcher/Putnam, 2000.

Coleridge, Samuel Taylor. *The Major Works.* Ed. H. J. Jackson. Oxford: Oxford University Press, 1985.

Cook-Lynn, Elizabeth. *Anti-Indianism in America: A Voice from Tatekeya's Earth.* Urbana: University of Illinois Press, 2001.

———. *Then Badger Said This.* 2nd ed. Fairfield WA: Ye Galleon, 1983.

Cooper, Lane, ed. *A Concordance to the Poems of William Wordsworth.* London: Smith, Elder, 1911.

Cowper, William. *The Task* [1785]. In *Poems of William Cowper.* New York: E. P. Dutton, 1931. 307–428.

Cronyn, George W. *The Path on the Rainbow: An Anthology of Songs and Chants from the Indians of North America.* 1918. Rpt. as *American Indian Poetry: An Anthology of Songs and Chants.* New York: Liveright, 1962.

Culler, Jonathan. "Apostrophe." In *The Pursuit of Signs: Semiotics, Literature, Deconstruction.* Ithaca NY: Cornell University Press, 1981. 135–54.

Curran, Stuart. Introduction to *The Poems of Charlotte Smith.* Ed. Stuart Curran. New York: Oxford University Press, 1993. xix–xxix.

Damasio, Antonio R. *The Feeling of What Happens: Body and Emotion in the Making of Consciousness.* New York: Harcourt, 1999.

Darwin, Charles. *The Voyage of the Beagle* [1839]. Amherst MA: Prometheus, 2000.

Darwin, Erasmus. *The Loves of Plants* [1789]. Vol. 2 of *The Botanic Garden.* 2 vols. New York: Garland, 1978.

Day, A. Grove, ed. *The Sky Clears: Poetry of the American Indians* [1951]. Lincoln: University of Nebraska Press, 1964.

D'Eaubonne, Françoise. "The Time for Ecofeminism." Trans. Ruth Hottell. In *Ecology,* ed. Carolyn Merchant. Atlantic Highlands NJ: Humanities, 1994. 174–97.

Deloria, Vine, Jr. *For This Land: Writings on Religion in America.* Ed. James Treat. New York: Routledge, 1999.

DeMallie, Raymond J., ed. *The Sixth Grandfather: Black Elk's Teachings Given to John G. Neihardt.* Lincoln: University of Nebraska Press, 1984.

de Man, Paul. "Intentional Structure of the Romantic Image." In *Romanticism and Consciousness: Essays in Criticism,* ed. Harold Bloom. New York: Norton, 1970. 65–77.

Densmore, Frances. *Chippewa Music.* 2 vols. [1910, 1913]. Minneapolis: Ross & Haines, 1973.

———. *Teton Sioux Music* [1918]. New York: Da Capo, 1972.

Derrida, Jacques. *Given Time: I. Counterfeit Money.* Trans. Peggy Kamuf. Chicago: University of Chicago Press, 1992.

Devall, Bill, and George Sessions. *Deep Ecology: Living As If Nature Mattered.* Salt Lake City UT: Peregrine Smith, 1985.

Dillard, Annie. *Pilgrim at Tinker Creek* [1974]. New York: Perennial, 1998.

Doggett, Frank. "Romanticism's Singing Bird." *Studies in English Literature: 1500–1900* 14 (1974): 547–61.

Dunsmore, Roger. "Black Sun—Pure Light." *Mickle Street Review* 7 (1985): 54–60.

Easthope, Anthony. *Wordsworth Now and Then: Romanticism and Contemporary Culture.* Buckingham UK: Open University Press, 1993.

Ehrenfeld, David. *The Arrogance of Humanism.* New York: Oxford University Press, 1978.

Ehrlich, Paul R., Davis S. Dobkin, and Darryl Wheye. *The Birder's Handbook: A Field Guide to the Natural History of North American Birds.* New York: Simon, 1988.

Eiseley, Loren. *The Firmament of Time.* New York: Atheneum, 1960.

———. *The Immense Journey.* New York: Random, 1957.

Eliot, T. S. *The Waste Land and Other Poems.* New York: Harcourt, 1934.

Fanon, Frantz. *Black Skin, White Masks* [1952]. Trans. Charles Lam Markmann. New York: Grove Weidenfeld, 1967.

Farrand, John, Jr., ed. *The Audubon Society Master Guide to Birding.* 3 vols. New York: Knopf, 1983.

Fast Wolf, Calvin W. "Wakinyan and Wakinyan Wicaktepi." In *Coming to Light: Contemporary Translations of the Native Literatures of North America,* ed. Brian Swann. New York: Random, 1994. 432–40.

Fire, John [Lame Deer], and Richard Erdoes. *Lame Deer: Seeker of Visions.* New York: Simon, 1972.

Fletcher, Angus. *A New Theory for American Poetry: Democracy, the Environment, and the Future of Imagination.* Cambridge MA: Harvard University Press, 2004.

Folsom, Ed. "Whitman and American Indians." In *Walt Whitman's Native Representations.* Cambridge UK: Cambridge University Press, 1994. 55–98.

Forbush, Edward Howe. "Passenger Pigeon." In *Birds of America* [1917], ed. T. Gilbert Pearson. Garden City NY: Doubleday, 1936. 2.39–46.

Foss, Chris. "'Birds of a Feather': On Swinburne's Nightingale and Shelley's Skylark." *Victorian Literature* 89 (1996): 18–23.

Fosso, Kurt. "'Sweet Influences': Animals and Social Cohesion in Wordsworth and Coleridge, 1794–1800." *ISLE* 6.2 (1999): 1–20.

Freud, Sigmund. *General Psychological Theory: Papers on Metapsychology*. Ed. Philip Rieff. New York: Simon, 1963.

Frye, Northrop. "The Drunken Boat: The Revolutionary Element in Romanticism." In *Romanticism Reconsidered: Selected Papers from the English Institute*, ed. Northrop Frye. New York: Columbia University Press, 1963. 1–25.

———, ed. *Romanticism Reconsidered: Selected Papers from the English Institute*. New York: Columbia University Press, 1963.

Gallagher, Tess. "Venison Pie: From the Journal of a Contemporary Hybrid." In *Intimate Nature: The Bond between Women and Animals*, ed. Linda Hogan, Deena Metzger, and Brenda Peterson. New York: Ballantine, 1998. 414–19.

Gannon, Thomas C. "Wordsworth's Birds." Dec. 31, 1999; revised Apr. 15, 2007. http://incolor.inetnebr.com/tgannon/wordbird.html.

Gare, Arran E. *Postmodernism and the Environmental Crisis*. London: Routledge, 1995.

Gates, Barbara T. *Kindred Nature: Victorian and Edwardian Women Embrace the Living World*. Chicago: University of Chicago Press, 1998.

Gaull, Marilyn. *English Romanticism: The Human Context*. New York: Norton, 1988.

Gibbons, Felton, and Deborah Strom. *Neighbors to the Birds: A History of Birdwatching in America*. New York: Norton, 1988.

Glotfelty, Cheryll. "Introduction: Literary Studies in an Age of Environmental Crisis." In *The Ecocriticism Reader: Landmarks in Literary Ecology*, ed. Cheryll Glotfelty and Harold Fromm. Athens: University of Georgia Press, 1996. xv–xxxvii.

Glotfelty, Cheryll, and Harold Fromm, eds. *The Ecocriticism Reader: Landmarks in Literary Ecology*. Athens: University of Georgia Press, 1996.

Godwin, William. *Caleb Williams* [1794]. London: Penguin, 1988.

Gray, John. *Straw Dogs: Thoughts on Humans and Other Animals*. London: Granta Books, 2002.

Griffin, Susan. "His Power: He Tames What Is Wild." In *Intimate Nature: The Bond between Women and Animals*, ed. Linda Hogan, Deena Metzger, and Brenda Peterson. New York: Ballantine, 1998. 209–12.

Halpern, Jeanne. "Coleridge's Aviary: A Field Guide to Bird Imagery in His Poems." *Rackham Literary Studies* 5 (1974): 9–21.

Hampden-Turner, Charles. *Maps of the Mind*. New York: Macmillan, 1981.

Hardy, Thomas. *Collected Poems of Thomas Hardy*. New York, Macmillan, 1925.

Harjo, Joy. *How We Became Human: New and Selected Poems: 1975–2001*. New York: Norton, 2002.

———. *In Mad Love and War*. Hanover NH: Wesleyan University Press, 1990.

———. *A Map to the Next World*. New York: Norton, 2000.

———. *Secrets from the Center of the World*. Tucson: University of Arizona Press, 1989.
———. *The Spiral of Memory: Interviews*. Ed. Laura Coltelli. Ann Arbor: University of Michigan Press, 1996.
———. *What Moon Drove Me to This?* New York: Reed, 1979.
———. *The Woman Who Fell from the Sky*. New York: Norton, 1994.
Harrington, Henry, and John Tallmadge. Introduction to *Reading under the Sign of Nature: New Essays in Ecocriticism,* ed. John Tallmadge and Henry Harrington. Salt Lake City: University of Utah Press, 2000. ix–xv.
Harrison, Thomas P. *They Tell of Birds: Chaucer, Spenser, Milton, Drayton*. Westport CT: Greenwood Press, 1956.
Hart, George. "Postmodern Nature/Poetry: The Example of Larry Eigner." In *Reading under the Sign of Nature: New Essays in Ecocriticism,* ed. John Tallmadge and Henry Harrington. Salt Lake City: University of Utah Press, 2000. 315–32.
Hartman, Geoffrey H. "Romanticism and 'Anti-Self-Consciousness.'" In *Romanticism and Consciousness: Essays in Criticism,* ed. Harold Bloom. New York: Norton, 1970. 46–56.
———. *Wordsworth's Poetry 1787–1814*. Rev. ed. New Haven CT: Yale University Press, 1971.
Hausman, Gerald. *Meditations with Animals: A Native American Bestiary*. Santa Fe NM: Bear, 1986.
Hazlitt, William. "My First Acquaintance with Poets." In *Uncollected Essays*. Vol. 17 of *The Complete Works of William Hazlitt*. Ed. P. P. Howe. 21 vols. London: Dent, 1933. 106–22.
———. *The Spirit of the Age. A Reply to Malthus; The Spirit of the Age; Etc.* Vol. 4 of *The Collected Works of William Hazlitt*. Ed. A. R. Waller and Arnold Glover. 12 vols. London: Dent, 1902. 185–368.
Head, Dominic. "The (Im)possibility of Ecocriticism." In *Writing the Environment: Ecocriticism and Literature,* ed. Richard Kerridge and Neil Sammells. London: Zed, 1998. 27–39.
Heinzel, Hermann, Richard Fitter, and John Parslow. *The Birds of Britain and Europe*. Philadelphia: Lippincott, 1972.
Henson, Lance. *Another Distance: New and Selected Poems*. Norman OK: Point Riders Press, 1991.
———. *Another Song for America*. Norman OK: Point Riders Press, 1987.
———. *A Cheyenne Sketchbook: Selected Poems 1970–1991*. Rev. ed. Greenfield Center NY: Greenfield Review Press, 1992.
———. *Strong Heart Song: Lines from a Revolutionary Text*. Albuquerque NM: West End Press, 1997.

Herber, Lewis [Murray Bookchin]. "Ecology and Revolutionary Thought" [1964]. *Anarchy* 6 (1966): 321–40.

Highfield, A. C., and J. Martin. "New Light on an Old Tortoise: Gilbert White's Selborne Tortoise Re-discovered." *Tortoise Trust*. Accessed July 29, 2006. http://www.tortoisetrust.org/articles/algeria.html.

Hoagland, Edward. Introduction to *The Natural History of Selborne*. By Gilbert White. Ed. Richard Mabey. New York: Penguin, 1997. ix–xxv.

Hogan, Linda. *The Book of Medicines*. Minneapolis: Coffee House, 1993.

———. *Calling Myself Home*. Greenfield Center NY: Greenfield Review Press, 1978.

———. *Dwellings: A Spiritual History of the Living World*. New York: Norton, 1995.

———. *Eclipse*. Los Angeles: American Indian Studies Center, 1983.

———. *Red Clay: Poems and Stories*. Greenfield Center NY: Greenfield Review Press, 1991.

———. *Seeing through the Sun*. Amherst: University of Massachusetts Press, 1985.

Hogan, Linda, Deena Metzger, and Brenda Peterson, eds. *Intimate Nature: The Bond between Women and Animals*. New York: Ballantine, 1998.

Hogan, Linda, Deena Metzger, and Brenda Peterson. Introduction to *Intimate Nature: The Bond between Women and Animals*, ed. Linda Hogan, Deena Metzger, and Brenda Peterson. New York: Ballantine, 1998. xi–xvi.

Holler, Clyde. *Black Elk's Religion: The Sun Dance and Lakota Catholicism*. Syracuse NY: Syracuse University Press, 1995.

Hopkins, Gerard Manley. *The Works of Gerard Manley Hopkins*. Ware UK: Wordsworth, 1994.

Howarth, William. "Some Principles of Ecocriticism." In *The Ecocriticism Reader: Landmarks in Literary Ecology*, ed. Cheryll Glotfelty and Harold Fromm. Athens: University of Georgia Press, 1996. 69–91.

Hudson, W. H. *Adventures among Birds* [1913]. Vol. 1 of *The Collected Works of W. H. Hudson*. 24 vols. New York: AMS, 1968.

Hughes, J. Donald. *American Indian Ecology*. El Paso: Texas Western Press, 1983.

Hunt, Stephen. "Wandering Lonely: Women's Access to the English Romantic Countryside." In *Reading under the Sign of Nature: New Essays in Ecocriticism*, ed. John Tallmadge and Henry Harrington. Salt Lake City: University of Utah Press, 2000. 51–63.

Irmscher, Christoph. *The Poetics of Natural History: From John Bartram to William James*. New Brunswick NJ: Rutgers University Press, 1999.

Jones, Stacey, and Erika Tallman. "Bald Eagle." *The Natural Source: An Educator's Guide to South Dakota's Natural Resources*. Northern State University. 1992. Accessed Nov. 9, 2002. http://www.northern.edu/natsource/ENDANG1/Baldeg1.htm.

Jung, C. G. *Collected Works*. Ed. Herbert Read, Michael Fordham, and Gerhard Adler. 20 vols. Princeton NJ: Princeton University Press, 1953–1978.

———. *The Earth Has a Soul: The Nature Writings of C. G. Jung*. Ed. Meredith Sabini. Berkeley: North Atlantic Books, 2002.

Kastner, Joseph. *A World of Watchers*. New York: Knopf, 1986.

Keats, John. *Complete Poems*. Ed. Jack Stillinger. Cambridge MA: Harvard University Press, 1982.

———. *The Letters of John Keats: 1814–1821*. Ed. Hyder Edward Rollins. 2 vols. Cambridge MA: Harvard University Press, 1958.

Kenny, Maurice. *Backward to Forward: Prose Pieces*. Fredonia NY: White Pine Press, 1997.

———. *Between Two Rivers: Selected Poems 1956–1984*. Fredonia NY: White Pine Press, 1987.

———. *In the Time of the Present: New Poems*. East Lansing: Michigan State University Press, 2000.

———. *Is Summer This Bear*. Saranac Lake NY: Chauncy Press, 1985.

———. *The Mama Poems*. Buffalo NY: White Pine Press, 1984.

———. *On Second Thought: A Compilation*. Norman: University of Oklahoma Press, 1995.

———. *The Smell of Slaughter*. Marvin SD: Blue Cloud Quarterly, 1982.

Kerridge, Richard. Introduction to *Writing the Environment: Ecocriticism and Literature*, ed. Richard Kerridge and Neil Sammells. London: Zed, 1998. 1–9.

———. "Small Rooms and the Ecosystem: Environmentalism and DeLillo's *White Noise*." In *Writing the Environment: Ecocriticism and Literature*, ed. Richard Kerridge and Neil Sammells. London: Zed, 1998. 182–95.

Kerridge, Richard, and Neil Sammells, eds. *Writing the Environment: Ecocriticism and Literature*. London: Zed, 1998.

Killingsworth, M. Jimmie. "The Voluptuous Earth and the Fall of the Redwood Tree: Whitman's Personifications of Nature." In *Whitman East and West: New Contexts for Reading Walt Whitman*, ed. Ed Folsom. Iowa City: University of Iowa Press, 2002. 14–25.

———. *Walt Whitman and the Earth: A Study in Ecopoetics*. Iowa City: University of Iowa Press, 2004.

Killingsworth, M. Jimmie, and Jacqueline S. Palmer. "Ecopolitics and the Literature of the Borderlands: The Frontiers of Environmental Justice in Latina and Native American Writing." In *Writing the Environment: Ecocriticism and Literature*, ed. Richard Kerridge and Neil Sammells. London: Zed, 1998. 196–207.

Klinkenborg, Verlyn. *Timothy; or, Notes of an Abject Reptile*. New York: Knopf, 2006.

Knight, G. W. "Coleridge's Divine Comedy." In *English Romantic Poets: Modern Essays in Criticism*, ed. M. H. Abrams. New York: Oxford University Press, 1960. 158–69.

Kolodny, Annette. "Unearthing Herstory: An Introduction." In *The Ecocriticism Reader: Landmarks in Literary Ecology*, ed. Cheryll Glotfelty and Harold Fromm. Athens: University of Georgia Press, 1996. 170–181.

Krech, Shepard, III. *The Ecological Indian: Myth and History*. New York: Norton, 1999.

Kristeva, Julia. *Black Sun: Depression and Melancholy*. Trans. Leon S. Roudiez. New York: Columbia University Press, 1989.

———. *Desire in Language: A Semiotic Approach to Literature and Art*. Ed. Leon S. Roudiez. Trans. Thomas Gora, Alice Jardine, and Leon S. Roudiez. New York: Columbia University Press, 1980.

———. *Revolution in Poetic Language* [1974]. Trans. Margaret Waller. New York: Columbia University Press, 1984.

Kroeber, Karl. *Ecological Literary Criticism: Romantic Imagining and the Biology of Mind*. New York: Columbia University Press, 1994.

———. "'Home at Grasmere': Ecological Holiness." PMLA 89 (1974): 132–41.

Lacan, Jacques. "The Agency of the Letter in the Unconscious, or Reason Since Freud" [1958]. Trans. Alan Sheridan. In *Critical Theory Since 1965*, ed. Hazard Adams and Leroy Searle. Tallahassee: Florida State University Press, 1986. 738–56.

———. *The Language of the Self: The Function of Language in Psychoanalysis* [1956]. Trans. Anthony Wilden. Baltimore: Johns Hopkins University Press, 1968.

LaChapelle, Dolores. *Earth Wisdom*. Los Angeles: Guild of Tutors Press, 1978.

Lawrence, Elizabeth A. "Melodious Truth: Keats, a Nightingale, and the Human/Nature Boundary." *ISLE* 6.2 (1999): 21–30.

Leavis, F. R. "Shelley." In *English Romantic Poets: Modern Essays in Criticism*, ed. M. H. Abrams. New York: Oxford University Press, 1960. 268–88.

Legler, Gretchen. "Body Politics in American Nature Writing: 'Who May Contest for What the Body of Nature Will Be?'" In *Writing the Environment: Ecocriticism and Literature*, ed. Richard Kerridge and Neil Sammells. London: Zed, 1998. 71–87.

Leopold, Aldo. *A Sand County Almanac* [1949]. New York: Ballantine, 1966.

Lessa, Richard. "John Clare's Voice, and Two Sonnets." *John Clare Society Journal* 3 (1984): 26–33.

Levitas, Gloria, Frank Robert Vivelo, and Jacqueline J. Vivelo, eds. *American Indian Prose and Poetry: We Wait in the Darkness*. New York: Putnam's, 1974.

Lewitt, Philip Jay. "Hidden Voices: Bird-Watching in Shelley, Keats, and Whitman." *Kyushu American Literature* 28 (1987): 55–63.

Lincoln, Kenneth. *Sing with the Heart of a Bear: Fusions of Native and American Poetry, 1890–1999*. Berkeley: University of California Press, 2000.

Lockwood, W. B. *The Oxford Book of British Bird Names*. Oxford: Oxford University Press, 1984.

Lopez, Barry. *Arctic Dreams: Imagination and Desire in a Northern Landscape*. New York: Scribner's, 1986.

Love, Glen A. "Revaluing Nature: Toward an Ecological Criticism." In *The Ecocriticism Reader: Landmarks in Literary Ecology*, ed. Cheryll Glotfelty and Harold Fromm. Athens: University of Georgia Press, 1996. 225–40.

Lovelock, James. "Gaia." In *Ecology*, ed. Carolyn Merchant. Atlantic Highlands NJ: Humanities, 1994. 351–59.

Lucas, John. "Crabbe's Disorderly Nature." In *Writing the Environment: Ecocriticism and Literature*, ed. Richard Kerridge and Neil Sammells. London: Zed, 1998. 110–23.

Lutwack, Leonard. *Birds in Literature*. Gainesville: University Press of Florida, 1994.

Lyons, Oren. "I See No Seat for the Eagles. We Forget and We Consider Ourselves Superior, but We Are After All a Mere Part of the Creation" [1977]. In *Native American Reader: Stories, Speeches and Poems*, ed. Jerry D. Blanche. Juneau AK: Denali, 1990. 112–14.

Manes, Christopher. "Nature and Silence." In *The Ecocriticism Reader: Landmarks in Literary Ecology*, ed. Cheryll Glotfelty and Harold Fromm. Athens: University of Georgia Press, 1996. 15–29.

Marqusee, Michael. Introduction to *Selections from* A History of British Birds. By Thomas Bewick. New York: Paddington, 1976. 5–14.

Mazel, David. "American Literary Environmentalism as Domestic Orientalism." In *The Ecocriticism Reader: Landmarks in Literary Ecology*, ed. Cheryll Glotfelty and Harold Fromm. Athens: University of Georgia Press, 1996. 137–46.

McDowell, Michael J. "The Bakhtinian Road to Ecological Insight." In *The Ecocriticism Reader: Landmarks in Literary Ecology*, ed. Cheryll Glotfelty and Harold Fromm. Athens: University of Georgia Press, 1996. 371–91.

McGann, Jerome. *The Romantic Ideology: A Critical Investigation*. Chicago: University of Chicago Press, 1983.

McGhee, Richard D. *Guilty Pleasures: William Wordsworth's Poetry of Psychoanalysis*. Troy NY: Whitson, 1993.

McKusick, James C. *Green Writing: Romanticism and Ecology*. New York: St. Martin's Press, 2000.

Meeker, Joseph W. *The Comedy of Survival: Literary Ecology and a Play Ethic* [1972]. 3rd ed. Tucson: University of Arizona Press, 1997.

Meihuizen, N. "Birds and Bird-Song in Wordsworth, Shelley and Yeats: The Study of a Relation between Three Poems." *English Studies in Africa* 31 (1988): 51–63.

Mellin, Robert. "Dorothy Wordsworth, Ecology, and the Picturesque." In *Reading the Earth: New Directions to the Study of Literature and Environment*, ed. Michael P. Branch et al. Moscow: University of Idaho Press, 1998. 67–77.

Merchant, Carolyn, ed. *Ecology*. Atlantic Highlands NJ: Humanities, 1994.

———. *Radical Ecology: The Search for a Livable World.* New York: Routledge, 1992.
Mershon, W. B., ed. *The Passenger Pigeon.* New York: Outing, 1907.
Mileur, Jean-Pierre. *Vision and Revision: Coleridge's Art of Immanence.* Berkeley: University of California Press, 1982.
Miller, J. Hillis. *Tropes, Parables, Performatives: Essays on Twentieth-Century Literature.* New York: Harvester, 1990.
Momaday, N. Scott. *House Made of Dawn* [1968]. New York: Perennial, 1999.
———. *In the Bear's House.* New York: St. Martin's Press, 1999.
———. *In the Presence of the Sun: Stories and Poems, 1961–1991.* New York: St. Martin's Press, 1992.
———. *The Man Made of Words: Essays, Stories, Passages.* New York: St. Martin's Press, 1997.
———. *The Names: A Memoir.* Tucson: University of Arizona Press, 1976.
———. *The Way to Rainy Mountain.* Albuquerque: University of New Mexico Press, 1969.
Mooney, James. *The Ghost-Dance Religion and the Sioux Outbreak of 1890* [1896]. Lincoln: University of Nebraska Press, 1991.
Moorman, Mary. *William Wordsworth: A Biography. The Early Years: 1770–1803.* Oxford: Clarendon, 1957.
Murphy, Patrick D. "Anotherness and Inhabitation in Recent Multicultural American Literature." In *Writing the Environment: Ecocriticism and Literature,* ed. Richard Kerridge and Neil Sammells. London: Zed, 1998. 40–52.
Naess, Arne. "Deep Ecology and Ultimate Premises." *The Ecologist* 18 (1988): 128–31.
———. "The Shallow and the Deep, Long-Range Ecology Movement: A Summary." *Inquiry* 16 (1973): 95–100.
Neihardt, John G. *Black Elk Speaks: Being the Life Story of a Holy Man of the Oglala Sioux* [1932]. Lincoln: University of Nebraska Press, 2004.
Niatum, Duane, ed. *Carriers of the Dream Wheel: Contemporary Native American Poetry.* New York: Harper, 1975.
———. *Drawings of the Song Animals: New and Selected Poems.* Duluth MN: Holy Cow! Press, 1991.
———, ed. *Harper's Anthology of 20th Century Native American Poetry.* San Francisco: HarperSanFrancisco, 1988.
———. "On Stereotypes." In *Recovering the Word: Essays on Native American Literature,* ed. Brian Swann and Arnold Krupat. Berkeley: University of California Press, 1987. 552–62.
Nietzsche, Friedrich. *Beyond Good and Evil: Prelude to a Philosophy of the Future* [1886]. Trans. Walter Kaufmann. New York: Vintage, 1966.
———. "On Truth and Falsity in Their Extramoral Sense" [1873]. Trans. Maximilian

A. Mügge. In *Philosophical Writings*. Ed. Reinhold Grimm and Caroline Molina y Vedia. New York: Continuum, 1995. 87–99.

Nolan, James. *Poet-Chief: The Native American Poetics of Walt Whitman and Pablo Neruda*. Albuquerque: University of New Mexico Press, 1994.

Norman, Honye, and John Norman. "Yellow Knives Language." Dec. 7, 2000. Accessed Nov. 9, 2002. http://www.angelfire.com/scifi/yellowknives/YKlang3.htm.

Norwood, Vera L. "Heroines of Nature: Four Women Respond to the American Landscape." In *The Ecocriticism Reader: Landmarks in Literary Ecology*, ed. Cheryll Glotfelty and Harold Fromm. Athens: University of Georgia Press, 1996. 323–50.

Oliver, Mary. *Dream Work*. New York: Atlantic Monthly Press, 1986.

———. "Singapore." In *House of Light*. Boston: Beacon, 1990. 8–9.

Ortiz, Simon. *After and Before the Lightning*. Tucson: University of Arizona Press, 1994.

———. *Going for the Rain*. New York: Harper, 1976.

———. *Woven Stone*. Tucson: University of Arizona Press, 1992.

Parrill, Anna Sue. "Romantic Songbirds." *Innisfree* (1978): 44–58.

Pater, Walter. "Wordsworth" [1874]. In *William Wordsworth: A Critical Anthology*, ed. Graham McMaster. Harmondsworth UK: Penguin, 1972. 187–99.

———. "Wordsworth" [1889]. In *Essays from "The Guardian."* London: Macmillan, 1914. 91–104.

Patton, Cornelius Howard. *The Amherst Wordsworth Collection: A Descriptive Bibliography*. Hartford CT: The Trustees of Amherst College, 1936.

Peacock, Thomas Love. *The Four Ages of Poetry* [1820]. In *Critical Theory Since Plato*, ed. Hazard Adams. Rev. ed. Fort Worth TX: Harcourt, 1992. 509–14.

———. *Nightmare Abbey* [1818]. Ed. A. R. Tomkins. London: Blackie, 1966.

Pearson, T. Gilbert, ed. *Birds of America* [1917]. Garden City NY: Doubleday, 1936.

———. Introduction to *Birds of America* [1917]. Ed. Gilbert T. Pearson. Garden City NY: Doubleday, 1936. 1:xiii–xx.

Phillips, Dana. "Is Nature Necessary?" In *The Ecocriticism Reader: Landmarks in Literary Ecology*, ed. Cheryll Glotfelty and Harold Fromm. Athens: University of Georgia Press, 1996. 204–22.

———. *The Truth of Ecology: Nature, Culture, and Literature in America*. Oxford: Oxford University Press, 2003.

Pokagon, Simon. "The Wild Pigeon of North America." In *The Passenger Pigeon*, ed. W. B. Mershon. New York: Outing, 1907. 48–59.

Pope, Alexander. "Windsor-Forest." In *Poetical Works*. Ed. Herbert Davis. Oxford: Oxford University Press, 1978. 37–50.

Pottle, Frederick A. "The Eye and the Object in the Poetry of Wordsworth." In *Romanticism and Consciousness: Essays in Criticism*, ed. Harold Bloom. New York: Norton, 1970. 273–87.

Powers, William K. *Oglala Religion*. Lincoln: University of Nebraska Press, 1977.

A Prairie Home Companion. Dir. Robert Altman. Picturehouse, 2006.

Pratt, Mary Louise. *Imperial Eyes: Travel Writing and Transculturation*. London: Routledge, 1992.

Raglon, Rebecca, and Marian Scholtmeijer. "Heading Off the Trail: Language, Literature, and Nature's Resistance to Narrative." In *Beyond Nature Writing: Expanding the Boundaries of Ecocriticism*, ed. Karla Armbruster and Kathleen R. Wallace. Charlottesville: University Press of Virginia, 2001. 248–62.

Regan, Tom. *The Case for Animal Rights*. Berkeley: University of California Press, 1983.

Revard, Carter. *An Eagle Nation*. Tucson: University of Arizona Press, 1993.

———. *Ponca War Dancers*. Norman OK: Point Riders Press, 1980.

Rice, Julian. "How the Bird That Speaks Lakota Earned a Name." In *Recovering the Word: Essays on Native American Literature*, ed. Brian Swann and Arnold Krupat. Berkeley: University of California Press, 1987. 422–45.

Robinson, Eric, and Richard Fitter. Introduction to *John Clare's Birds*. Ed. Eric Robinson and Richard Fitter. Oxford: Oxford University Press, 1982. vii–xx.

Rose, Wendy. *Bone Dance: New and Selected Poems 1965–1993*. Tucson: University of Arizona Press, 1994.

Rosen, Kenneth, ed. *Voices of the Rainbow: Contemporary Poetry by American Indians*. New York: Seaver Books, 1975.

Rothenberg, Jerome, ed. *Shaking the Pumpkin: Traditional Poetry of the Indian North Americas* [1971]. Rev. ed. Albuquerque: University of New Mexico Press, 1990.

Rowland, Beryl. *Birds with Human Souls: A Guide to Bird Symbolism*. Knoxville: University of Tennessee Press, 1978.

Rudy, John. "Wordsworth's St. Francis and the Baptized Imagination." *Renascence* 40 (1988): 268–78.

Rueckert, William. "Literature and Ecology: An Experiment in Ecocriticism." In *The Ecocriticism Reader: Landmarks in Literary Ecology*, ed. Cheryll Glotfelty and Harold Fromm. Athens: University of Georgia Press, 1996. 105–23.

Ruoff, A. LaVonne Brown. *American Indian Literatures: An Introduction, Bibliographic Review, and Selected Bibliography*. New York: MLA, 1990.

Sachs, Peter M. *The English Elegy: Studies in the Genre from Spenser to Yeats*. Baltimore: Johns Hopkins University Press, 1985.

Said, Edward W. *Orientalism*. New York: Pantheon, 1978.

———. "The World, the Text, and the Critic." In *Critical Theory Since Plato*, ed. Hazard Adams. Rev. ed. Fort Worth TX: Harcourt, 1992. 1211–22.

Sanders, Scott Russell. "Speaking a Word for Nature." In *The Ecocriticism Reader: Landmarks in Literary Ecology*, ed. Cheryll Glotfelty and Harold Fromm. Athens: University of Georgia Press, 1996. 182–95.

SanTara, Sandra. "Eagle Spirit Shield T-shirt." Windwolf Studio, Inc. 1999. Accessed Nov. 9, 2002. http://www.windwolf.com/TShirts/EagleShieldT.html.

Schorger, A. W. *The Passenger Pigeon: Its Natural History and Extinction*. Madison: University of Wisconsin Press, 1955.

Shaver, Chester L., and Alice C. Shaver. *Wordsworth's Library: A Catalogue*. New York: Garland, 1979.

Shelley, Mary. *Frankenstein: or The Modern Prometheus* [1831]. Ed. Johanna M. Smith. 2nd ed. Boston: Bedford, 2000.

Shelley, Percy Bysshe. *A Defense of Poetry* [1821]. In *The Selected Poetry and Prose of Shelley*. Ed. Harold Bloom. New York: NAL, 1966. 415–48.

———. *The Poetical Works of Shelley*. Ed. Newell F. Ford. Boston: Houghton, 1975.

Shepard, Paul. *The Others: How Animals Made Us Human*. Washington DC: Island Press, 1996.

Silko, Leslie Marmon. *Almanac of the Dead* [1991]. New York: Penguin, 1992.

———. *Laguna Woman*. Greenfield Center NY: Greenfield Review Press, 1974.

———. "Poetics and Politics: A Series of Readings by Native American Writers." Unpublished seminar transcript. Tucson AZ. Apr. 6, 1992.

———. *Storyteller*. New York: Arcade, 1981.

———. *Yellow Woman and a Beauty of the Spirit*. New York: Simon, 1996.

Simpson, Phyllis. "The Primeval Bird." *Fabula: Journal of Folktale Studies* 15 (1974): 95–102.

Singer, Peter. *Animal Liberation: A New Ethics for Our Treatment of Animals*. New York: Random, 1975.

———. "[Reflection]." In *The Lives of Animals*. By J. M. Coetzee, Marjorie Garber, Peter Singer, Wendy Doniger, and Barbara Smuts. Ed. Amy Gutmann. Princeton NJ: Princeton University Press, 1999. 85–91.

Smelcer, John E., and D. L. Birchfield, eds. *Durable Breath: Contemporary Native American Poetry*. Anchorage AK: Salmon Run Press, 1994.

Smith, Charlotte. *The Poems of Charlotte Smith*. Ed. Stuart Curran. New York: Oxford University Press, 1993.

Smith, Eric Todd. "Dropping the Subject: Reflections on the Motives for an Ecological Criticism." In *Reading the Earth: New Directions to the Study of Literature and Environment*, ed. Michael P. Branch, Rochelle Johnson, Daniel Patterson, and Scott Slovic. Moscow: University of Idaho Press, 1998. 29–39.

Smithsonian Institution. "The Passenger Pigeon." *Encyclopedia Smithsonian*. Mar. 2001. Accessed Aug. 11, 2005. http://www.si.edu/Encyclopedia_SI/nmnh/passpig.htm.

Snyder, Gary. *Earth House Hold: Technical Notes and Queries to Fellow Dharma Revolutionaries*. New York: New Directions, 1969.

———. *The Practice of the Wild*. San Francisco: North Point Press, 1990.

———. *The Real Work: Interviews and Talks 1964–1979*. New York: New Directions, 1980.

———. *Turtle Island*. New York: New Directions, 1974.

Soens, A. L., ed. *I, the Song: Classical Poetry of Native North America*. Salt Lake City: University of Utah Press, 1999.

Spivak, Gayatri. *The Post-Colonial Critic: Interviews, Strategies, Dialogues*. New York: Routledge, 1990.

Standing Bear, Luther. *Land of the Spotted Eagle* [1933]. Lincoln: University of Nebraska Press, 1978.

———. *My People, the Sioux* [1928]. Ed. E. A. Brininstool. Lincoln: University of Nebraska Press, 1975.

Stevens, Wallace. *The Collected Poems* [1954]. New York: Vintage, 1990.

Stewart, Frank. *A Natural History of Nature Writing*. Washington DC: Island Press, 1995.

Svensson, Lars, Peter J. Grant, Killian Mullarney, and Dan Zetterström. *Birds of Europe*. Trans. David Christie. Princeton NJ: Princeton University Press, 1999.

Swann, Brian, ed. *Coming to Light: Contemporary Translations of the Native Literatures of North America*. New York: Random, 1994.

———. Introduction to *Coming to Light: Contemporary Translations of the Native Literatures of North America,* ed. Brian Swann. New York: Random House, 1994. xiii–xlvi.

———. Introduction to *Wearing the Morning Star: Native American Song-Poems,* ed. Brian Swann. New York: Random House, 1996. xi–xxv.

———, ed. *Wearing the Morning Star: Native American Song-Poems*. New York: Random, 1996.

Swann, Brian, and Arnold Krupat, eds. *I Tell You Now: Autobiographical Essays by Native American Writers*. Lincoln: University of Nebraska Press, 1987.

Swann, Brian, and Arnold Krupat, eds. *Recovering the Word: Essays on Native American Literature*. Berkeley: University of California Press, 1987.

Symons, Arthur. *The Symbolist Movement in Literature* [1899]. London: Constable, 1911.

Tallmadge, John, and Henry Harrington, eds. *Reading under the Sign of Nature: New Essays in Ecocriticism*. Salt Lake City: University of Utah Press, 2000.

Teorey, Matthew. "William Wordsworth and Leslie Marmon Silko: Toward an Ecofeminist Future." *ISLE* 11.1 (2004): 31–56.

Tennyson, Lord Alfred. *The Poems of Tennyson*. Ed. Christopher Ricks. London: Longmans, 1969.

Tokar, Brian. "Social Ecology, Deep Ecology and the Future of Green Political Thought." *The Ecologist* 18 (1988): 132–41.

"Tribe." Def. 5a. *Oxford English Dictionary*. 2nd ed. 1989.

Tutin, J. R. *An Index to the Animal and Vegetable Kingdoms of Wordsworth*. Hull UK: J. R. Tutin, 1892.

———. *The Wordsworth Dictionary of Persons and Places*. Hull UK: J. R. Tutin, 1891.

Tyler, Hamilton A. *Pueblo Birds and Myths*. Norman: University of Oklahoma Press, 1979.

Van den Berg, J. H. "The Subject and His Landscape." In *Romanticism and Consciousness: Essays in Criticism*, ed. Harold Bloom. New York: Norton, 1970. 57–65.

Vander, Judith. "Poetry Songs of the Shoshone Ghost Dance." In *Coming to Light: Contemporary Translations of the Native Literatures of North America*, ed. Brian Swann. New York: Random House, 1994. 357–73.

Velie, Alan R., ed. *American Indian Literature: An Anthology* [1979]. Rev. ed. Norman: University of Oklahoma Press, 1991.

Vizenor, Gerald. "Crows Written on the Poplars: Autocritical Autobiographies." In *I Tell You Now: Autobiographical Essays by Native American Writers*, ed. Brian Swann and Arnold Krupat. Lincoln: University of Nebraska Press, 1987. 99–109.

———. *Interior Landscapes: Autobiographical Myths and Metaphors*. Minneapolis: University of Minnesota Press, 1990.

———. "Literary Animals." In *Fugitive Poses: Native American Indian Scenes of Absence and Presence*. Lincoln: University of Nebraska Press, 1998. 119–43.

———. *Manifest Manners: Narratives on Postindian Survivance*. Hanover NH: Wesleyan University Press, 1994.

Walker, Alice. "The Universe Responds: Or, How I Learned We Can Have Peace on Earth." In *Intimate Nature: The Bond between Women and Animals*, ed. Linda Hogan, Deena Metzger, and Brenda Peterson. New York: Ballantine, 1998. 323–27.

Walker, James R. *Lakota Belief and Ritual*. Ed. Raymond de Mallie and Elaine A. Jahner. Lincoln: University of Nebraska Press, 1980.

Wallace, Kathleen R., and Karla Armbruster. "Introduction: Why Go beyond Nature Writing, and Where To?" In *Beyond Nature Writing: Expanding the Boundaries of Ecocriticism*, ed. Karla Armbruster and Kathleen R. Wallace. Charlottesville: University Press of Virginia, 2001. 1–25.

Ward, J. P. *Wordsworth's Language of Men*. Sussex UK: Harvester Press, 1984.

Waters, Frank. *Masked Gods: Navajo and Pueblo Ceremonialism* [1950]. New York: Ballantine, 1970.

Welch, James. *The Death of Jim Loney*. New York: Harper, 1979.

Wellek, René. "Romanticism Re-Examined." In *Romanticism Reconsidered: Selected Papers from the English Institute*, ed. Northrop Frye. New York: Columbia University Press, 1963. 107–33.

Westrum, Dexter. "Transcendental Survival: The Way the Bird Works in *The Death of Jim Loney*." In *James Welch*, ed. Ron McFarland. Lewiston ME: Confluence Press, 1984. 139–46.

White, Gilbert. *The Natural History of Selborne* [1789]. Ed. Richard Mabey. New York: Penguin, 1997.

White, Lynn, Jr. "The Historical Roots of Our Ecologic Crisis." In *The Ecocriticism Reader: Landmarks in Literary Ecology,* ed. Cheryll Glotfelty and Harold Fromm. Athens: University of Georgia Press, 1996. 3–14.

Whitman, Walt. *The Correspondence: 1876–1885*. Ed. Edwin Haviland Miller. Vol. 3 of *The Collected Writings of Walt Whitman*. Gay Wilson Allen and Sculley Bradley, general eds. 5 vols. New York: New York University Press, 1964.

———. *Poetry and Prose*. New York: Library of America, 1996.

Wilden, Anthony. "Lacan and the Discourse of the Other." In *The Language of the Self: The Function of Language in Psychoanalysis*. By Jacques Lacan. Trans. Anthony Wilden. Baltimore: Johns Hopkins University Press, 1968. 159–311.

Wilson, Alexander. "The Passenger Pigeon." In *The Passenger Pigeon,* ed. W. B. Mershon. New York: Outing, 1907. 9–24.

Wilson, Edward O. *Biophilia*. Cambridge MA: Harvard University Press, 1984.

Wilson, Norma C. *The Nature of Native American Poetry*. Albuquerque: University of New Mexico Press, 2001.

———. "Heartbeat: Within the Visionary Tradition." *Mickle Street Review* 7 (1985): 14–23.

Wordsworth, Dorothy. *Journals of Dorothy Wordsworth*. Ed. Mary Moorman. London: Oxford University Press, 1971.

Wordsworth, Jonathan. Introduction to *A Description of the Lakes*. By William Wordsworth. Ed. Jonathan Wordsworth. Oxford: Woodstock, 1991. n.p.

Wordsworth, William. *A Description of the Lakes* [3rd ed., 1822]. Ed. Jonathan Wordsworth. Oxford: Woodstock, 1991.

———. *Guide to the Lakes* [5th ed., 1835]. Ed. Ernest de Selincourt. London: Humphrey Milford, 1926.

———. *Home at Grasmere* [1806]. Ed. Beth Darlington. Ithaca NY: Cornell University Press, 1977.

———. *The Poetical Works of William Wordsworth*. Ed. Ernest de Selincourt and Helen Darbishire. 5 vols. Oxford: Clarendon, 1940–49.

———. *The Prelude: Or Growth of a Poet's Mind* [1805]. Ed. Ernest de Selincourt. Rev. ed. Stephen Gill. Oxford: Oxford University Press, 1970.

———. *The Ruined Cottage and the Pedlar*. Ed. James Butler. Ithaca NY: Cornell University Press, 1979.

———. *The Salisbury Plain Poems of William Wordsworth*. Ed. Stephen Gill. Ithaca NY: Cornell University Press, 1975.

Wormhoudt, Arthur. "The Unconscious Bird Symbol in Literature." *American Imago* 7 (1950): 173–82.

Worster, Donald. *Nature's Economy: The Roots of Ecology*. San Francisco: Sierra Club, 1977.

Wu, Duncan. *Wordsworth's Reading: 1800–1815*. Cambridge UK: Cambridge University Press, 1995.

Young, Robert J. C. *Colonial Desire: Hybridity in Theory, Culture and Race*. London: Routledge, 1995.

Zapf, Hubert. "Literature as Cultural Ecology: Notes towards a Functional Theory of Imaginative Texts, with Examples from American Literature." REAL: *Yearbook of Research in English and American Literature* 17 (2001): 85–100.

Index